Adobe® Dreamweaver® CS5 with PHP
Training from the Source

David Powers

Adobe

Adobe® Dreamweaver® CS5 with PHP: Training from the Source

David Powers

Adobe Adobe Press books are published by:

Peachpit
1249 Eighth Street
Berkeley, CA 94710
510/524-2178
800/283-9444

For the latest on Adobe Press books, go to www.adobepress.com
To report errors, please send a note to errata@peachpit.com
Peachpit is a division of Pearson Education.
Copyright © 2011 David Powers

Acquisitions Editor: Victor Gavenda
Project Editor: Rebecca Freed
Development Editor and Copyeditor: Anne Marie Walker
Production Editor: Becky Winter
Technical Editor: Tom Muck
Compositor: Danielle Foster
Indexer: Rebecca Plunkett
Cover Design: Charlene Charles-Will

ISBN-13: 978-0-321-71984-3
ISBN-10: 0-321-71984-0
9 8 7 6 5 4 3 2 1
Printed and bound in the United States of America

Bio

David Powers has been writing about Dreamweaver, PHP, CSS, and web development since 2003. This is his twelfth book on the subject. David started developing websites in 1994, shortly after assuming the role of Editor, BBC Japanese TV. He needed a way of advertising the fledgling channel in Japan but had no budget. So, he begged the IT department for a corner of server space and singlehandedly developed an 80-page bilingual website, which he regularly maintained for the next five years.

After a career spanning three decades in radio and TV news, David left the BBC in 1999 to work independently. He's an Adobe Community Professional and Adobe Certified Instructor for Dreamweaver. You'll often find him giving help and advice in the Dreamweaver forums and Adobe Developer Center—to which he has contributed many popular tutorials and training videos. He greatly enjoys traveling and taking photos—all the photos used in this book were taken by him.

David has also translated a number of musical plays from Japanese into English, and he likes nothing better than sushi with a glass or two of cold sake.

Acknowledgments

For several years I've bent the ears of the long-suffering Dreamweaver engineering team to improve support for PHP. Wow! They certainly came up trumps. My thanks to Devin Fernandez, Scott Fegette, Don Booth, Randy Edmunds, Chris Bank, Virgil Palanciuc, Jon Michael Varese, and the many others who have helped me dig deeper into Dreamweaver over the past few versions to understand the program's strengths and weaknesses (yes, there are some—and I'm sure the team is already working on eliminating them).

I'm particularly grateful to Scott, one of the Dreamweaver product managers, whose idea it was to get me to write this book. I hope it's not too far removed from what he was hoping for. Scott passed my name to Victor Gavenda, the Executive Editor at Adobe Press, while attending Adobe MAX at Los Angeles in 2009. For those of you who don't know, MAX is an annual geekfest that's a mixture of presentations by leading web professionals, sneak peeks into Adobe's future technology, and wild parties (Scott plays a mean guitar).

Victor welcomed me into the Adobe Press/Peachpit family with grace and courtesy. My thanks go to him and to the two editors who worked directly with me on the book, Rebecca Freed and Anne Marie Walker. Thanks also to the production team for going the extra mile to make the code easier to read.

Finally, I mustn't forget Tom Muck, a true Dreamweaver and PHP expert who checked the text and code for technical accuracy. This is the third book we've worked on together. Tom always manages to keep me on the straight and narrow, spotting important details I've missed and suggesting ways to improve the text. Any mistakes that remain are my responsibility alone.

Contents

Introduction

My first encounter with PHP came about 10 years ago. By that time, I already had plenty of experience developing websites. I had started out writing HTML in a text editor before settling on Dreamweaver as my favorite authoring tool. A new project involved publishing more than 30 articles a day. It was a subscription service, so the site needed to be password-protected and searchable. An ordinary website wouldn't do. That's when PHP came to the rescue.

PHP makes communication with a database a breeze, so content can be stored in the database, making it searchable. Instead of creating a new page for every article, pages are populated dynamically with the requested items. You can also password-protect the administrative or members-only area of a site. PHP does a lot more: It can send email, upload files, and attach files to emails—all of which you'll learn how to do in this book. PHP is also the driving force behind the three most popular content management systems: Drupal, Joomla!, and WordPress.

So, where does Dreamweaver come into the picture? Dreamweaver has supported PHP to some degree since 2002, mainly through server behaviors, which automatically generate PHP code for some basic tasks. But the level of support has taken a quantum leap forward in Dreamweaver CS5. The server behaviors are still there (see Lesson 6), but they take a back seat.

The big changes lie in code hinting, embedded PHP documentation (including examples), autocompletion of variables, automatic discovery of dynamically related files, and—perhaps best of all—the ability to view and navigate through PHP pages without leaving the Document window. As a result, it's now possible to style WordPress, Joomla!, and Drupal in Dreamweaver CS5 without the need to generate static pages. These changes are described in detail in Lesson 1, but in a nutshell they should appeal to designers and developers alike.

PHP's popularity springs from being easy to learn. You can achieve practical results very quickly. Of course, like any skill, becoming an expert takes time and practice. The new PHP features in Dreamweaver CS5 not only help the learning process, but you'll find them even more useful as you gain experience. Dreamweaver is my preferred choice for designing the look of a website and organizing files, but I was beginning to use dedicated PHP authoring tools for the dynamic aspects of development. Dreamweaver CS5 has changed all that. I now have the best of both worlds in the same program.

Who This Book Is for

This is a "beyond the basics" book, so you should already have a solid understanding of how a website is built. You should also have a good understanding of HTML, because PHP code needs to be embedded in the underlying structure of a page to display the dynamic output. It's not necessary to know every tag and attribute, but if you don't know the difference between a <ul> and an <li> tag, you'll be lost. All the example files and exercises are styled with CSS, but design is not the focus of this book. You don't need to understand CSS to work through the lessons, but your web development skills would certainly be the better for it. You'll also find it makes it easier to follow Lesson 4, where you create a new WordPress theme.

You don't need prior knowledge of PHP. This book doesn't teach PHP in a formal manner, but Lesson 3 provides a crash course in how to write PHP, and Lesson 5 teaches the basics of database design using MySQL, the most popular open source database.

If you already know some PHP, all the better. This book moves at a fairly rapid pace. Lessons 7–12 make extensive use of the Zend Framework, a powerful library of PHP components that take a lot of hard work out of creating dynamic sites. Lesson 12 also uses the jQuery JavaScript framework. Again, you don't need prior knowledge of jQuery or JavaScript, but it will certainly help.

How to Use This Book

Time is precious, so you probably want to jump straight to the solution for your current problem. If you have considerable PHP experience, that approach might work. However, the majority of readers should start with Lesson 1 and work through each one in sequence because each lesson builds on the previous one. If you skip ahead, you're likely to miss a vital explanation and will need to backtrack anyway.

The "Approximate Time" at the beginning of each lesson is simply an estimate of the time it will take to work through the exercises. Don't regard it as a challenge, and don't feel downcast if you take much longer. Each lesson is packed with information. Take time to absorb it, and break the lesson into smaller chunks to match your own pace.

Most lessons contain reference sections followed by hands-on exercises. Each step explains not only what to do, but also why you're doing it. The idea is to help you think about how you could apply the same techniques to your own projects. This isn't a point-and-click book, but instead is one that aims to stimulate your problem-solving abilities. The more you think, the more you're likely to get out of it.

Accompanying files

The accompanying CD contains all the files necessary to complete the exercises in this book. The only exceptions are the PHP/MySQL development environments described in Lesson 2 and the LightBox Gallery Widget in Lesson 12. PHP and MySQL are updated frequently, so it makes more sense to get the most recent versions from the source. In the case of the LightBox Gallery Widget, one object of the exercise is to show you how to install the Adobe Widget Browser and download widgets from the Adobe Exchange.

Lesson 2 describes how to set up the Dreamweaver site to work through the exercises in this book. The files for each lesson are in folders named lesson01, lesson02, and so on. There are no files for Lesson 13. For each lesson that contains exercises, there are normally three subfolders: completed, start, and workfiles. The workfiles folder is deliberately left empty; it's where you should create and save the files for the lesson's exercises. If you follow this structure, the exercise files will use the common style sheets that are stored in the styles folder.

To save time, many exercises have partially completed pages, which you should copy from the start folder to the workfiles folder for that lesson. The completed folder contains copies of the exercise files shown at various stages of completion.

In Lessons 10 and 11, you should create a folder called cms in the site root. The cms_complete folder contains a full working copy of the completed project.

✱ **NOTE:** The files were created on a Windows computer but are fully compatible with Mac OS X. However, the path in library.php needs to be adjusted to match the location of the Zend Framework files. See Lesson 7 for details.

Windows/Mac differences

The few Dreamweaver CS5 and PHP differences between Windows and Mac OS X have been pointed out at relevant places in the book.

Keyboard shortcuts are given in the order Windows/Mac, but in the rare cases where there is no Mac equivalent, this has been pointed out. On some Mac keyboards, the Opt(ion) key is labeled Alt. On a UK Mac keyboard, use Alt+3 to type the hash symbol (#).

Using a multi-button mouse with a Mac is now so common that the instructions refer only to right-click. If you prefer a single-button mouse, use Ctrl-click.

Code portability

One of the pleasures of working with PHP is that it's platform-neutral. All the PHP code in this book works equally well on Windows, Mac OS X, and Linux. However, it's important to realize that different versions of PHP and MySQL have different functionality. Also, server administrators have the ability to turn off certain features. To use this book, your web server *must* be running PHP 5.2 and MySQL 4.1 or later. The code will not work with earlier versions.

Getting help

When you encounter a problem, the first person to look to for help is you. Did you skip a step or mistype the name of a variable or function? One of the quickest ways of finding an error is to use Dreamweaver's File Compare feature (choose Help > Using Dreamweaver CS5 > Creating and Managing Files > Comparing files for differences) to compare your file with the version in the completed folder.

File Compare requires a third-party file comparison utility. If you don't have one installed, WinMerge (http://winmerge.org) for Windows and TextWrangler (www.barebones.com/products/textwrangler/) for Mac OS X are both free.

If you can't solve the problem on your own and a quick search on the Internet doesn't produce the answer, post a question in the Adobe forums. The best one for PHP questions is the Dreamweaver Application Development forum at http://forums.adobe.com/community/dreamweaver/dreamweaver_development. I'm frequently there providing help, so you might even get an answer from me.

I also post updates and tutorials on my website at http://foundationphp.com/, and you can follow me on Twitter @foundationphp.

Every care has been taken to eliminate errors, but if you think you have found one, please email errata@peachpit.com with the details.

Layout conventions

The following text conventions are used throughout this book:

- **Boldface text.** Words in **bold text** indicate input that you should type in a field or the name of a file you should create.

- **Boldface code.** Code that is added or changes is displayed in boldface.

```
if ($_POST) {
  if (empty($_POST['username']) || empty($_POST['password'])) {
    $failed = TRUE;
  } else {
    require_once('library.php');
```

- **Long code.** Sometimes, code won't fit on a single line on the printed page. Where this happens, an arrow indicates the continuation of a broken line like this:

```
$result = $recaptcha->verify($_POST['recaptcha_challenge_field'],
➡ $_POST['recaptcha_response_field']);
```

- **Italics.** Text in *italics* is for emphasis or to introduce important concepts.

Let the Journey Begin

Above all, enjoy the experience that lies ahead. Even if you find working with code uncomfortable to begin with, PHP is not hard. Welcome to the ever-growing PHP community.

What You Will Learn

In this lesson, you will:

- See how PHP builds web pages dynamically and communicates with a database
- Explore the greatly improved PHP features in Dreamweaver CS5
- See how to change Dreamweaver's default settings
- See how Live View can display pages from a PHP content management system, such as WordPress
- Understand how to access and filter dynamically related pages

Approximate Time

This lesson should take approximately 1 hour to complete.

Lesson Files

Media Files:

None

Starting Files:

None

Completed Files:

lesson01/time.php

LESSON 1

Why PHP and Why Dreamweaver CS5?

"If you had one extra day in your week to learn a new technology, what would you choose?" That's one of the questions the Adobe Dreamweaver product team asked users before starting work on Dreamweaver CS5. An overwhelming majority answered, "PHP or a PHP framework." It's a message the team took on board, which resulted in a version of Dreamweaver that turns it into a powerful development environment for PHP without losing any of its visual development features. Dreamweaver CS5 is a program that gives programmers and designers plenty to smile about. For designers, probably the most welcome change is the ability to see a WordPress, Drupal, or Joomla! site in Live View.

Dreamweaver CS5 can now display WordPress and other popular CMSs directly in Live View.

A Rich Mix of PHP Features

For programmers, many new features can be put at the top of the list: vastly improved PHP code hinting, automatic detection of dynamically related files, autocompletion of variables, and so on. But the feature that will appeal to beginners and experienced programmers alike is automatic syntax checking. Dreamweaver CS5 constantly monitors your PHP code and highlights any line in which there is a mistake.

One thing that hasn't changed—and this will come as a disappointment to some existing users— is the range or functionality of PHP server behaviors. A *server behavior* is a Dreamweaver tool that automatically generates PHP code for such things as inserting, updating, and deleting records in a database. Many people like server behaviors because everything is done through dialog boxes without the need to touch a line of code. Server behaviors are great for rapid prototyping or taking your first steps with PHP, but they take you only so far. You soon discover that you need to customize them to do anything beyond the most basic tasks—and you can't do that unless you understand the code. This book covers the main server behaviors, but also takes you further to make full use of the new PHP features in Dreamweaver CS5. However, that doesn't mean you'll end up typing endless amounts of PHP code.

Dreamweaver CS5 allows you to take advantage of a much wider range of resources coded by some of the most experienced people in the business. You'll learn how to work with one of the most popular PHP-driven content management systems (CMS), WordPress. You'll also learn how to upload files, send emails with attachments, and interact with a database using a selection of components from the Zend Framework. The framework is designed in such a way that you can cherry pick, making it easy to add sophisticated functionality to a website without needing to become an expert programmer beforehand.

You don't need previous PHP experience to use this book—although you'll be able to progress more rapidly or jump to lessons that interest you if you do. Everything is explained along the way, along with details of where to get more information. The only prerequisite is that you be familiar with building websites using HTML and CSS. Preferably, you should also be familiar with the Dreamweaver user interface.

> ✳ **NOTE:** I use HTML to refer to both HTML (Hypertext Markup Language) and XHTML (Extensible Hypertext Markup Language). All the HTML code in this book conforms to XHTML 1.0 Transitional, the default setting in Dreamweaver CS5.

Before embarking on the journey ahead, let's take a quick look at PHP and what it's for, and then take a brief tour of the features in Dreamweaver CS5 that make it such a good development environment for PHP-driven websites.

What Is PHP? What Does It Do?

PHP is a server-side technology that builds web pages dynamically. Let's say you have a product catalog. Instead of updating your web pages each time a product is added or removed, you can store the details in a database and use PHP to query the database and build the page automatically. Nor do you need to create a separate page for each product. Just build one page, and PHP fills in the details. Other uses of PHP include creating login systems, uploading files, and sending emails. Just about every online store, news website, blog, or social networking site uses PHP or a similar server-side technology.

Depending on how it's being used, PHP code can be embedded in a web page or stored in external files. However, unlike CSS or JavaScript, PHP code always remains on the web server. Visitors to your website never see it. All they see is the output. For example, lesson01/time. php contains the following code:

```
<p>The time in London is <?php
$now = new DateTime();
$now->setTimezone(new DateTimeZone('Europe/London'));
echo $now->format('g.i a');
?></p>
<p>In Los Angeles, it's <?php
$now->setTimezone(new DateTimeZone('America/Los_Angeles'));
echo $now->format('g.i a');
?></p>
```

The PHP code is embedded in a couple of HTML paragraphs between <?php and ?> tags. Even if you don't understand how it works, you can probably guess that this code has something to do with dates and time zones. In fact, it displays the current time in London and Los Angeles. It doesn't matter where you are or when you load the page, as long as the server clock is set correctly, you will always get the correct time in those two cities. If you right-click to view the source code in a browser, you see only the HTML output. All the processing is done on the web server.

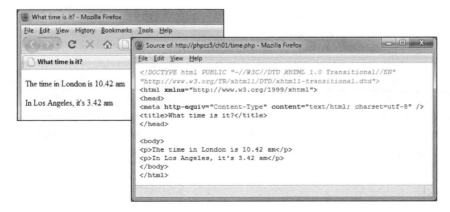

> ✱ **NOTE:** You won't be able to view this file on your computer until you have created a PHP testing environment, which you'll learn how to do in Lesson 2. Readers with eagle eyes will have noticed that the screen shot shows only a seven-hour difference, whereas there's normally an eight-hour difference between London and Los Angeles. The screen shot was taken in mid-March after the United States had switched to daylight saving time, but the UK had not. The PHP code is smart enough to adjust automatically for daylight saving time.

In this example, the PHP code does all the work itself. But in many cases, PHP acts as an intermediary to a database. The following diagram outlines the basic process.

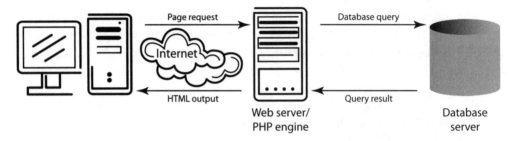

This is what happens when a browser requests a web page that uses PHP:

- The web server sends the page to the PHP engine—which resides on the server—for processing.

- If the PHP script doesn't need to communicate with the database, the PHP engine generates the HTML output, and the web server sends it back to the browser.

- If the script needs to interact with the database—getting the results of a search, or inserting or updating data—the PHP engine communicates with the database server. When the results come back, the PHP engine puts everything together, and the web server sends the resulting web page back to the browser.

A lot goes on, but most requests take only a few microseconds, and then the web page is on its way to the browser with no perceptible delay from the user's point of view.

PHP's role ends as soon as the output has been sent to the browser. The time shown by time.php is fixed; it won't update automatically a minute later. For that to happen, you need to refresh the page or create a JavaScript function to change the time within the user's browser. If you want PHP to do something in response to user action on a web page, it involves another round trip to the server. In the past, this meant reloading the page. However, as you'll see later in this book, you can refresh the page seamlessly by sending the request in the background and updating the content with Ajax.

What Is Ajax?

Normally, requests to a web server and the response are handled at the same time. Waiting for the page to reload is disruptive. As a workaround, you can use JavaScript to send requests directly to the server and update the content only when the result comes back. Multiple requests can be sent, updating the page as required. In technical terms, the process is asynchronous. In other words, the user doesn't have to wait for the response from the server to continue using the page. The update happens seamlessly when the response is received from the server.

Originally, the data was sent back formatted as XML (Extensible Markup Language), a tag-based language similar to HTML. That's where the name Ajax comes from, Asynchronous JavaScript and XML. However, data can be sent back in many formats, even plain text, so XML is not always part of the process.

Why choose PHP?

PHP isn't the only server-side technology available. In fact, Dreamweaver has varying degrees of support for seven. Most have similar capabilities, and choosing which is the most suitable for your circumstances isn't always easy. However, PHP has the following advantages:

- PHP runs on Windows, Mac OS X, and Linux. With only a few minor exceptions, code written on one operating system works on any of the others.

- It's open source and free.

- It's widely available.

- It's relatively easy to learn.

- There's a large community of active users, so help is rarely far away.

- It's simple enough to incorporate into a small website, yet powerful enough to drive some of the busiest websites, including Facebook, Wikipedia, and Yahoo!

- In a survey of media executives by the Society of Digital Agencies (SoDA), nearly 50 percent said they regarded PHP as an important tool for their company in 2010. The figure for ASP.NET was 32 percent. Fewer than 10 percent said they regarded Ruby on Rails as important for their company.

- In the same survey, more than 50 percent said they would be hiring people with PHP skills in 2010. The only web-related skills in greater demand were Flash and ActionScript.

So are there any disadvantages in choosing PHP?

Comparing server-side technologies is difficult, but the main disadvantage of PHP is, paradoxically, that it's easy to learn. Many people copy scripts from online tutorials without understanding the code, often leaving gaping security holes in their websites. PHP is as secure as any other server-side technology, and security-related bugs are usually dealt with very quickly. But just like the electricity in your house, it's safe only insofar as it's used and maintained correctly. Fortunately, it's not difficult to write secure code, and there is emphasis on security throughout this book.

What Does PHP Stand For?

If you really must know, PHP stands for PHP: Hypertext Preprocessor. Why such a convoluted mouthful? When PHP's original creator, Rasmus Lerdorf, released the first version in 1995, he called it Personal Home Page Tools (PHP Tools). It was a user-friendly set of tools to password protect pages, create forms, and process form data. A couple of years later, Andi Gutmans and Zeev Suraski—who later founded Zend, the PHP company—decided to cooperate with Rasmus, and turned PHP into a much more powerful language. The "personal home page" image no longer fit, but it was decided to keep the initials PHP. And that's how the rather clunky name came about. Although Zend is a commercial enterprise, PHP remains open source and free.

Many PHP developers offer an alternative explanation: PHP = Pretty Happy Programmers.

Which database should I choose?

More often than not, PHP is used in conjunction with MySQL, the most popular open-source database, which is fast, powerful, and well suited for use in websites. It's the database that runs WordPress, Drupal, and Joomla! and is also used by high-traffic websites like Flickr, Facebook, and YouTube.

MySQL is currently owned by Oracle Corporation, one of the leading database software companies, but the Community Edition of MySQL is free. The functionality of the Community Edition is identical to the for-purchase Enterprise version. The only difference is that no support is offered with the free version. But that's rarely a problem because of the active community willing to offer help online.

Like PHP, MySQL works on all the main operating systems, so you can develop on one system and later transfer your database to another. Also, most hosting companies offer PHP in combination with MySQL. For all these reasons, the combination of PHP and MySQL is used in this book.

PHP and MySQL have become so closely connected that many people think you can't have one without the other. Unlike love and marriage in Frank Sinatra's 1950s hit, you *can* have PHP without MySQL. PHP works with all the main database systems, including Microsoft SQL Server, Oracle, and PostgreSQL. You can easily adapt much of the code in later lessons to work with the database of your choice.

✳ NOTE: Dreamweaver's built-in PHP server behaviors (covered in Lesson 6) are tied exclusively to MySQL. Lessons 7–12 use the Zend Framework, which supports many databases in addition to MySQL, including Microsoft SQL Server, SQLite, and PostgreSQL.

A Tour of the Main PHP Features in Dreamweaver CS5

Let's take a closer look at why Dreamweaver CS5 has become such a good development environment for beginners and more experienced PHP developers. If you're completely new to PHP, it might be best for you to skim the rest of this lesson to get a flavor of what's in store. Come back later to read each section in more detail when you're more familiar with PHP to learn about particular features.

PHP features also in previous versions

For the benefit of newcomers to Dreamweaver, I'll describe briefly the basic features inherited from previous versions before moving on to the advanced PHP features that are new to Dreamweaver CS5. In addition, I'll explain how to set various options, so existing users will benefit from some of the information here as well.

Features discussed include:

- Line numbering
- Syntax coloring
- Balancing braces
- Code collapse
- Split Code view
- Applying and removing comment tags
- Live Code

Line numbering

When working with PHP scripts, it's essential to be able to find a specific line, because PHP error messages always refer to the line where a problem was identified. By default, Dreamweaver displays line numbers in a column on the left of Code view.

If line numbers are not visible or if you want to turn them off, click the Line Numbers icon ⎡#⎤ in the Coding toolbar. Alternatively, choose View > Code View Options > Line Numbers to toggle them on and off.

> ▶ **TIP:** The Coding toolbar is displayed by default on the left of Code view and the Code Inspector. If you can't see the Coding toolbar in Code view, choose View > Toolbars > Coding to turn it back on. The Coding toolbar cannot be turned off in the Code Inspector.

Line numbers refer to new lines created by pressing Enter/Return. By default, Dreamweaver soft wraps long lines in Code view. If you don't want Dreamweaver to wrap lines of code like this, you can toggle the option on and off by clicking the Word Wrap icon ⎡⇄⎤ in the Coding toolbar. Alternatively, choose View > Code View Options > Word Wrap.

> ✳ **NOTE:** Previous versions of Dreamweaver had an option to insert a newline character automatically after a specified number of characters (hard wrapping). This option no longer exists in Dreamweaver CS5.

Syntax coloring

Dreamweaver automatically colors different elements of PHP code to make them easier to identify. PHP tags and strings (text in quotation marks) are colored red, reserved keywords are green, functions are dark blue, and variables are a lighter blue. If part of your script is the wrong color, it's an almost certain sign that there's an error in your code; the most common cause is a missing or mismatched quotation mark.

Setting Dreamweaver Preferences

Many default options can be changed in the Preferences panel, which you can access from the Edit menu on Windows and the Dreamweaver menu in the Mac version. You can also open the Preferences panel by pressing Ctrl+U/Cmd+U.

Mac users should note that the conventional Mac shortcut, Cmd+comma (,) is assigned to a different command (Go to Line).

✱ NOTE: Dreamweaver syntax coloring doesn't support PHP heredoc and nowdoc syntax. This book doesn't use heredoc or nowdoc syntax. For more details, see http://docs.php.net/manual/en/language.types.string.php.

If you want to change the default colors used by Dreamweaver, select the Code Coloring category in the Preferences panel. Select PHP in the Document Type field, and click the Edit Coloring Scheme button to open the following dialog box.

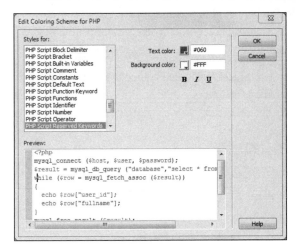

Don't be confused that the first item in the "Styles for" list is for a different server-side technology (ColdFusion Script Tag). Just click in the Preview pane at the bottom of the dialog box, and Dreamweaver automatically highlights the appropriate PHP value in the "Styles for" list.

- Select the type of element you want to change in the "Styles for" list or the Preview pane.

- Click the color box next to "Text color" to select a new color.

- Use bold, italic, or underlined text, or any combination of them to change text.

- "Background color" applies a background color only to the selected type of element.

- To change the background color of Code view, click OK to close the Edit Coloring Scheme for PHP dialog box, and then click the color box next to "Default background" in the Code Coloring category in the Preferences panel.

Syntax coloring is turned on by default. It can be toggled on and off by choosing View > Code View Options > Syntax Coloring.

Dreamweaver CS5 supports PHP syntax coloring and code hints in files that use the following filename extensions: .php, .php3, .php4, .php5, and .phtml. It also recognizes Smarty templates

(.tpl files) but treats them the same way as HTML files. Unless you have a specific reason for choosing a different filename extension, you should always use .php. However, if you need to use a filename extension that's not on the list, you can get Dreamweaver to recognize it by following the instructions found at http://go.adobe.com/kb/ts_tn_16410_en-us.

Balancing braces

Curly braces must always be in matching pairs, but there might be dozens or hundreds of lines of code between the opening and closing braces. Unlike some other editing programs, Dreamweaver does not automatically insert a closing brace when you type an opening brace, but Balance Braces is an indispensible visual guide.

With the insertion point anywhere between two braces, click the Balance Braces icon in the Coding toolbar to highlight the code enclosed by the braces.

Alternatively, choose Edit > Balance Braces, or press Ctrl+'/Cmd+' (single quotation mark).

Code collapse

When working on a long script, it's useful to be able to hide one or more sections of the code so you can see code that might be far from the section you're currently working on. To collapse a section of code, select it, and click the minus box at the top or bottom of the selection. In the Mac version, the minus boxes are replaced by a down triangle at the top and an up triangle at the bottom. Click either triangle to collapse the selected code.

The collapsed section of code displays just a few characters from the first line in a dark gray box. Hover your pointer over the gray box, and Dreamweaver displays the first ten lines as a tooltip to remind you what the collapsed section contains.

Dreamweaver remembers which sections of code have been collapsed, even when you close a file. When you reopen it, the collapsed sections remain closed.

To expand a collapsed section, click the plus box (or right-facing triangle on a Mac) next to the gray box. If the plus box or triangle isn't visible, click the gray box to bring it back into focus.

You can also expand all sections of collapsed code in a single operation by clicking the Expand All icon 🌟 in the Coding toolbar. Alternatively, press Ctrl+Alt+E/Opt+Cmd+E.

> ▶ **TIP:** The disadvantage of Expand All is that only the final section of code remains selected. If you want to collapse your code again, use your mouse to expand and collapse individual sections.

Split Code view

Another useful way to view different parts of the same script is to use Split Code view. This opens the current document in Code view with the Document window split vertically or horizontally. Both sides of the Document window scroll independently, allowing you to access completely different sections of the same page. To access Split Code view, choose View > Split Code.

> ✳ **NOTE:** You cannot drag and drop from one side of Split Code view to the other. Use copy or cut and paste.

Applying and removing comment tags

Comments are useful not only for documenting your scripts, but also to disable a section of code while troubleshooting.

When you click the Apply Comment icon 🗨, you are presented with the following choice of five styles of comments.

The only options of value in a PHP script are /* */ and //.

The final option, `<?php /*?> <?php */?>`, is of limited use because you cannot nest PHP tags inside a PHP code block. Its only purpose is to comment out a section of HTML inside a PHP page and prevent the affected section from being sent to the browser. By contrast, an HTML comment remains visible in the browser's source code view.

- To apply a multiline comment, select the code you want to comment out, click the Apply Comment icon, and choose Apply /* */ Comment from the menu.

- To apply a single-line comment, put the insertion point where you want the comment to begin, click the Apply Comment icon, and choose Apply // Comment.

By default, code that has been commented out is displayed in orange, making it easy to distinguish it from code that should be processed by the PHP engine.

The Remove Comment icon should really be called Remove Comment Tags. It removes the comment characters, but leaves everything else intact. It works like this:

- To remove the tags from a multiline comment, select the entire comment, including the /* at the beginning and the */ at the end. If you select less, nothing happens.

- To remove the tags from several multiline comments in a single operation, select at least from the first /* to the last */, and click the Remove Comment icon.

- Single-line comments embedded in multiline comments are not affected when the multi-line tags are removed.

- To remove a single-line comment tag, set the insertion point anywhere inside the comment, and click Remove Comment.

Single-line comment tags are removed *only* when nothing else (except whitespace) precedes them on the same line. For example, the two forward slashes will be removed from the following line, even if there are spaces before the comment tag:

```
// echo 'Hello, world!';
```

However, they will *not* be removed from the following line, because the comment doesn't affect the whole line:

```
echo 'Hello, world!'; // this is a comment
```

Live Code

As long as you have a testing server defined for your site (defining a site and a testing server is covered in Lesson 2), clicking the Live Code button in the Document toolbar displays the HTML output of dynamic code, including PHP and JavaScript, in Code view.

Document toolbar

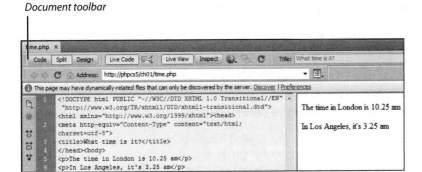

This is the same as using View Source in a browser without launching your page in the browser. Everything is done inside the Dreamweaver Document window.

If you can't see the Document toolbar, choose View > Toolbars > Document. You can also choose View > Live Code.

New and improved PHP features in Dreamweaver CS5

The features listed so far are all useful—essential, indeed—but would not be enough on their own to recommend using Dreamweaver CS5 as a serious PHP development environment. It's the following improvements that really make a difference:

- Expanded code hinting for PHP core functions, classes, and constants
- Code hints for custom functions and classes
- Site-specific code hints
- Automatic recognition of classes and objects
- Autocompletion of defined variables
- Real-time syntax checking
- Dynamically related files
- Live View navigation
- CSS inspection

Code hinting for PHP core functions, classes, and constants

Dreamweaver CS5 code hints now cover all core elements of PHP 5.2, namely:

- Approximately 1,900 core functions

- About 170 classes and interfaces, including 800 related methods and more than 200 class properties

- Nearly 2,000 constants

If you're wondering why PHP 5.3 isn't supported, it's because of the engineering time required to integrate the documentation into Dreamweaver. Yes, that's right—documentation. Dreamweaver automatically displays the relevant help page from the PHP manual for a built-in function or class.

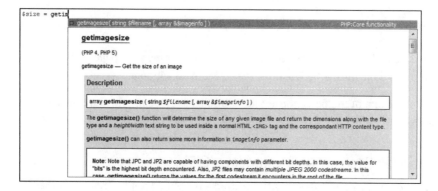

Most help pages include a description of the function or class with details of the arguments it takes, the values it returns, and the minimum version of PHP required. In addition, there are frequently code examples. And if that's not enough, clicking the link at the top left of the documentation takes you to the equivalent page in the PHP online manual, which contains the most up-to-date information, as well as comments and tips added by other users.

The way in which code hints are selected has also been improved in three important ways:

- Code hints are not case sensitive. You can type in lowercase, and Dreamweaver automatically converts the selected value to uppercase for constants and superglobals.

- Underscores are automatically inserted. When you type **$p**, Dreamweaver automatically suggests $_POST as one of the options.

- You don't need to start at the beginning. Dreamweaver constantly searches for substrings within code hints. For example, typing **sep** automatically selects all functions and constants that contain that sequence of letters, including the constants DIRECTORY_SEPARATOR and PATH_SEPARATOR.

With a little experimentation, you can create your own shortcuts for code that you use regularly. All you need to do is discover the sequence of characters that rapidly brings up the one you want. For example, typing **gesi** takes you instantly to getimagesize(). Dreamweaver recognizes the "ge" of "image" and the "si" of "size" as a unique sequence.

To activate code hints, press Ctrl+spacebar in a PHP code block. Even if you forget to do so before you start typing, press the same key combination *without* first pressing the spacebar, and Dreamweaver uses the preceding sequence of characters to select available choices.

> ● **TIP:** Mac users should note that the key combination to activate code hints is the same on both operating systems. Use Control+spacebar, not Cmd+spacebar.

As soon as Dreamweaver narrows down the available candidates, you can use your up and down arrow keys or your mouse to select the one you want. Press Enter/Return or double-click to insert the function or constant into your script.

Code hints for custom functions and classes

Dreamweaver CS5 doesn't stop at built-in functions. It's now capable of *code introspection*. This is just a fancy way of saying that Dreamweaver automatically inspects any custom functions or classes and builds code hints from them. Hints are available for functions and classes that are either declared in the same page or directly included in the page using one of the PHP include or require constructs. The following screenshot shows an example of custom code hints in action.

```
<?php require_once('scripts/date_functions.inc.php');

$date = md
        ▣ ftp_mdtm( resource $ftp_stream , string $remote_file )      PHP:Miscellaneous functions and classes
        ▣ ftp_rmdir( resource $ftp_stream , string $directory )       PHP:Miscellaneous functions and classes
        ▣ gmdate( string $format [, int $timestamp ] )               PHP:Core functionality
        ▣ gmp_hamdist( resource $a , resource $b )                   PHP:Miscellaneous functions and classes
        ▣ md5( string $str [, bool $raw_output = false ] )           PHP:Core functionality
        ▣ md5_file( string $filename [, bool $raw_output = false ] )  PHP:Core functionality
        ▣ mdecrypt_generic( resource $td , string $data )            PHP:Encryption and Compression
        ◉ mdy2mysql($input)                                          date_functions.inc.php
        ◉ MHASH_MD4                                       <global>   PHP:Encryption and Compression
        ◉ MHASH_MD5                                       <global>   PHP:Encryption and Compression
```

In this example, the file date_functions.inc.php contains a custom function called mdy2mysql(). Because it's included in the current page through require_once, Dreamweaver automatically includes it in code hints that are displayed when you type the letters **md**. The list of code hints also indicates where the function is defined, making it clear that it's a custom function.

When you select a custom function from the list of code hints, Dreamweaver displays the names of any arguments it expects.

```
<?php require_once('scripts/date_functions.inc.php');
                        mdy2mysql($input)
$date = mdy2mysql(
```

> **TIP:** Dreamweaver doesn't generate documentation for custom functions and classes. When designing your own functions and classes, it's a good idea to make them self-documenting by choosing meaningful names for functions, methods, and any arguments they take.

Site-specific code hints

If you're serious about working with PHP, you'll probably want to use a framework. A *framework* is a library of predefined functions and/or classes that perform common tasks. The advantage of a framework is that the code has usually been developed and tested by very experienced people. Instead of reinventing the wheel, you can build sophisticated applications by writing very little code. All the complicated code is in the framework files.

The framework that I chose to use in later lessons is the Zend Framework (ZF). The "minimal" version of ZF 1.10 contains more than 2,700 files in nearly 500 folders. Fortunately, ZF has an autoloader that accesses only those files that are needed for a particular purpose. Unfortunately, the ZF naming convention leads to class names, such as `Zend_File_Transfer_Adapter_Http`, that are a nightmare to type—and remember. This is where site-specific code hints come to the rescue.

Site-specific code hints are designed to generate code hints for third-party frameworks, including the three most popular content management systems, WordPress, Drupal, and Joomla! The code hints are generated through code introspection in the same way as for custom functions and classes. The difference is that you don't need to include the external files directly in the page you're working on. Once you have set up site-specific code hints, Dreamweaver scans the necessary files automatically and generates the code hints on the fly. Hints are available even if the definition file isn't directly linked to your page.

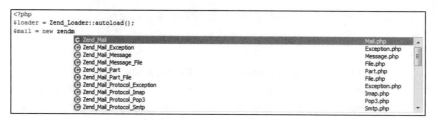

You'll learn how to set up site-specific code hints for WordPress, Drupal, or Joomla! in Lesson 4. The setup for other frameworks, including ZF, is covered in Lesson 7.

Automatic recognition of classes and objects

Most of the time, there's no need to press Ctrl+spacebar to get code hints for classes and objects. As soon as you enter a space after the keyword `new`, Dreamweaver presents you with code hints for all the classes it recognizes.

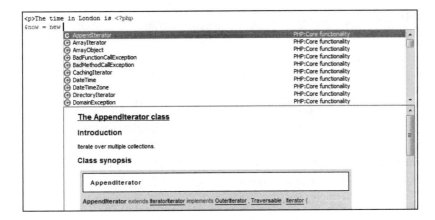

Typing -> after an object automatically brings up code hints for all public methods and properties associated with the object's class.

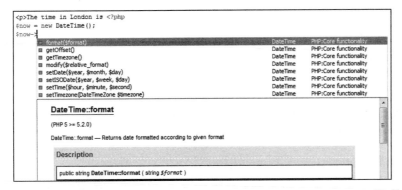

Similarly, typing the scope resolution operator—a double colon (::)—after a class name displays all static methods and properties associated with that class.

Controlling PHP code hints

Being provided with so many code hints is great, but what if you don't want or need them all? Dreamweaver CS5 gives you the option to disable some—or even all—of them.

To control which code hints are enabled, select the Code Hints category in the Preferences panel. Turn off those that you don't need by deselecting the appropriate checkbox in the Menus section. **Table 1.1** lists the PHP modules covered by each option.

Table 1.1	PHP Modules Covered by Code Hints
Option	**Modules covered**
Core functionality	Core functions, keywords, and superglobals, plus the following modules that are normally enabled in a standard configuration of PHP: Ctype, cURL, Date/Time, Filter, GD (images), JSON, Multibyte strings, MySQL, MySQL Improved, PDO (PHP Data Objects), PCRE (regular expressions), Reflection, Sessions, SPL (Standard PHP Library), SQLite, Tokenizer
Encryption and Compression	Bzip2, Hash, Mcrypt, Mhash, OpenSSL, Zip, Zlib
Other Databases	IBM DB2, LDAP, MS Sql, oci8 (Oracle Call Interface), ODBC, PostgreSQL
DOM & XML hints	DOM, SimpleXML, SOAP, WDDX, XML Parser, XML Reader, XML Writer, XML-RPC, XSL
Miscellaneous functions and classes	BC Math, Calendar, EXIF, GetText, GMP, IMAP, MemCache, Mimetype, Shared Memory, Sockets, Tidy

If you're not sure which to choose, deselect all except "Core functionality" and, possibly, "DOM & XML hints." The other options are mainly for specialist use. On the other hand, unless you find having them all turned on affects you adversely, just leave them all selected. The code hints are there to help you. The large number of code hints doesn't appear to slow down Dreamweaver, but this might vary depending on your computer's specifications and other programs running at the same time.

Autocompletion of defined variables

PHP variables begin with a dollar sign, so as soon as you type $, Dreamweaver CS5 pops up a list of predefined variables. In previous versions, this behavior was limited to PHP super-globals, such as $_POST and $_GET. In Dreamweaver CS5, you get your own variables, too. Continue typing, and the list of code hints narrows down the candidates. This is a major time-saver. Not only that but PHP variables are case sensitive, which helps to avoid problems with using, for example, $name in one place and $Name in another.

Experienced developers will be delighted to know that autocompletion is aware of *variable scope*. This is the principle that variables declared inside a function are not visible outside that function, nor are variables declared outside a function affected by what happens inside a function unless their values are explicitly passed to and returned by the function. In practice, this means that if you declare a variable called $total outside a function, $total will not be included in the autocompletion candidates while you are working inside a function. Similarly, if you declare a variable called $output inside a function, it will be among the candidates only within the scope of the function.

It should be noted, however, that there are some limitations with code hints for variables. Dreamweaver doesn't provide code hints for array keys. For example, let's say you have the following array:

```
$colors = array('black' => '#000', 'white' => '#FFF');
```

Dreamweaver will provide a code hint for $colors[, but after that, you're on your own. You need to type 'black' or 'white' followed by the closing square bracket manually.

Real-time syntax checking

When you begin typing a PHP script in Dreamweaver CS5, you'll immediately notice that the program gives you a syntax error. Even typing the first couple of characters of an opening PHP tag triggers an error message in the Info Bar at the top of the Document window and puts a red marker over the line number.

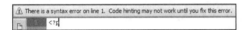

The red error markers remain visible even if you turn off line numbering. At first, this might seem like an overly aggressive attitude toward error checking, but if the marker doesn't disappear when you get to the end of a statement, you know immediately that an error needs to be corrected. Errors are much easier to identify and correct as you go. No more round trips to the testing server to discover that a semicolon is missing or a mismatched quote exists somewhere deep in your script.

The Syntax Error Alerts in Info Bar icon 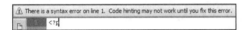 in the Coding toolbar toggles the display of error messages on or off. Alternatively, choose View > Code View Options > Syntax Error Alerts in Info Bar.

The only way to turn off the red markers next to lines with errors is in the Preferences panel— but you'll also lose other useful functionality. Select the Code Hints category, and deselect the "Object methods and variables" checkbox in the Menus section. This disables Dreamweaver's PHP and JavaScript knowledge engines, but as the name suggests, it also turns off code hints for objects and variables. In my view, it's a poor trade-off.

Although this real-time syntax checking is smart enough to spot something wrong with your script, it won't tell you what the problem is. That's up to you. But knowing where to look for the problem makes troubleshooting a whole lot easier.

> **TIP:** When you're working on a long script, the syntax checker might not clear the error markers immediately. Press Ctrl+./Cmd+. (period) to refresh syntax checking. You might also need to do this when switching to Code view if the page was originally opened in Design view.

Dynamically related files

When you open a PHP file in Dreamweaver CS5, a narrow strip (the Info Bar) appears at the top of the Document window. If you haven't yet defined a testing server, the Info Bar provides a link that opens the Site Setup dialog box (defining a site and testing server is covered in the next lesson). Otherwise, it informs you that the page might have dynamically related files that can only be discovered by the server.

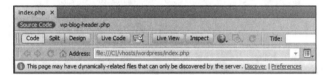

By default, Dreamweaver displays only directly linked files in the Related Files toolbar. To display dynamically related files, click the Discover link in the Info Bar. The first time you do this, you will see a warning that Dreamweaver will execute any scripts included in the page. This is just Adobe being ultracautious. All it means is that Dreamweaver will parse the PHP in the same way as if you loaded the page into a web browser. Unless you want to see this warning every time you use dynamically related files, select the checkbox to not show the warning again, and click OK.

Dreamweaver connects to your testing server (which needs to be running) and compiles a list of dynamically related files. This might take a few seconds, depending on the complexity of the page and your site. The dynamically related files are added to the Related Files toolbar in the order they are discovered. If there are too many to fit, click the double chevron at the right end to display a list of all the files.

Filtering dynamically related files: A basic WordPress site uses no fewer than 65 dynamically related files, so you need to filter them to maintain your sanity. To do so, click the funnel-shaped icon at the right end of the Related Files toolbar, as shown here.

You can toggle on and off the display of .css, .php, and .xml files. However, a WordPress site has so many .php files, you need to narrow down the list to the ones you want, as follows:

1 Click the funnel-shaped icon at the right end of the Related Files toolbar, and choose Custom Filter to open the Custom Filter dialog box.

2 Type a list of files or filename extensions separated by semicolons into the text field. There should be *no* space around the semicolons.

Using the Custom Filter disables the other filter options, so you need to include all the files you want to work with. For example, the basic structure of a WordPress site consists of index.php, header.php, sidebar.php, footer.php, and any style sheets.

Use this as your custom filter:

```
index.php;header.php;sidebar.php;footer.php;.css
```

You can also use an asterisk as a wildcard character. For example, wp* selects all files that begin with wp.

> **TIP:** Unfortunately, there's no way to save a custom filter setting. You need to type it in each time. If you find yourself using the same filter regularly, save it in a text file to copy and paste into the Custom Filter dialog box.

Setting Preferences for Related Files

By default, Dreamweaver searches for dynamically related files only if you tell it to do so. If you want it to search for them automatically—or to disable the feature altogether—you can do so in the Preferences panel.

1. Open Preferences by clicking the Preferences link in the Info Bar (it appears only in pages for which dynamically related files have not yet been discovered). Alternatively, choose Preferences on the Edit menu in Windows or the Dreamweaver menu on a Mac, and then select the General category from the list on the left.

2. The Enable Related Files checkbox controls *all* related files. If you deselect this option, it disables the feature completely and removes the Related Files toolbar from the top of the Document window.

3. Choose one of the three options in the Discover Dynamically-Related Files menu: Automatically, Manually (default), or Disabled. If you want to disable dynamically related files but keep directly related files, set the menu to Disabled but leave the Enable Related Files checkbox selected.

Live View navigation

Live View is a browser within the Dreamweaver Document window. It uses the WebKit browser engine, which also drives Safari and Google Chrome. Although you can't edit a page in Live View, you can use Split view and related files to edit the underlying code and styles, and see the effect instantly in the Document window.

When it was introduced in Dreamweaver CS4, Live View made it a lot easier to see how dynamic effects, such as rollovers, flyout menus, and CSS, would work. The big drawback was that you could see only the current page. Links didn't work, nor did any of the popular CMSs, such as WordPress, Drupal, or Joomla!, that rely on dynamically related files.

All that has changed in Dreamweaver CS5. Live View now works like an ordinary browser—well, almost. The only difference is that you need to hold down Ctrl/Cmd to follow a link. There is an option on the Live View Options menu to follow links continuously, but this applies only to the current page. You need to select it again for each new page.

▶ **TIP:** The Live View Options menu can also be accessed from the View menu. If you can't see the Browser Navigation Bar, choose View > Toolbars > Browser Navigation, or View > Live View Options > Show Browser Navigation Bar.

What makes Live View so powerful in Dreamweaver CS5 is that it follows links wherever they go, even if they lead to a live site on the Internet (assuming that you're connected). Code view also shows the source code for related files on external sites, although they are read-only.

In addition, you can log into password-protected pages. The following screen shot shows the Dashboard of a WordPress site, which can be accessed only by submitting a username and password.

Browser Navigation Bar   *Live View Options menu*

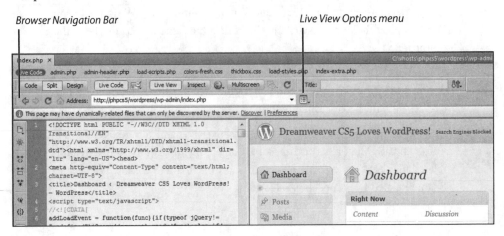

The icons on the Browser Navigation Bar work like an ordinary browser with Back and Forward arrows, Refresh, and Home—which takes you back to the page you originally loaded into the Document window. The Address text field remembers the URLs of pages you have loaded during the current session (but not those you have navigated to). This enables switching to another page without leaving Live View by simply clicking the down arrow at the right end of the Address field and selecting the URL. You can also type the URL of a remote site in the Address field to inspect it in Live View.

Live inspection of CSS layout

Yet another important new feature in Live View is CSS Inspect mode. Click the Inspect button on the Browser Navigation Bar, and mouse over the page. Dreamweaver highlights each page element as you pass over it, showing elements in blue, padding in violet, and margins in yellow.

Click the element in Live View to freeze the display. CSS Inspect mode combined with the CSS Styles panel or a style sheet selected from the Related Files toolbar provides a powerful way to inspect and edit CSS, particularly in a PHP site.

What You Have Learned

In this lesson, you have:

- Seen how PHP builds web pages dynamically and communicates with a database (pages 5–8)

- Explored Dreamweaver's tools that aid PHP development (pages 9–15)

- Examined the improved support for PHP code hints in Dreamweaver CS5 (pages 15–20)

- Seen the benefits of variable autocompletion and real-time syntax checking (pages 20–21)

- Learned how to access and filter dynamically related pages (pages 22–23)

- Seen how to navigate to other pages, including password-protected pages, in Live View (pages 24–25)

What You Will Learn

In this lesson, you will:

- Install a complete local testing environment, including a web server, PHP, MySQL, and phpMyAdmin

- Test the installation and make any necessary configuration changes

- See how to create virtual hosts

- Define a PHP site in Dreamweaver CS5

- See how to edit and back up your site definitions

Approximate Time

The time taken to complete this lesson will vary considerably depending on your setup and the choices you make. Allow yourself at least 2 hours.

Lesson Files

Media Files:

styles/examples.css

Starting Files:

None

Completed Files:

lesson02/site_check.php

lesson02/test.php

LESSON 2

Getting Ready to Develop with PHP

PHP code needs to be processed by a web server. You can upload your pages to your remote server to test them, but this is tedious and exposes all your mistakes in public. The solution is to create a dedicated testing environment on your local computer that consists of four elements:

- A web server—Apache or Microsoft Internet Information Services (IIS)
- PHP
- MySQL
- A graphical front end for MySQL called phpMyAdmin

This is not as difficult as it sounds. All the necessary software is free.

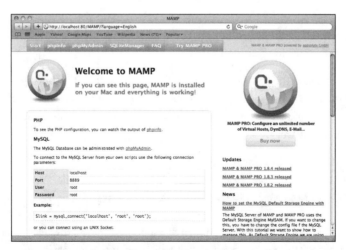

MAMP installs everything you need to develop with PHP on Mac OS X. Similar packages are available for Windows.

Setting Up a Local Testing Environment

PHP's roots lie in Linux, and it's designed in a modular fashion. This allows server administrators to decide which features to enable, rather like choosing optional extras when you buy a new car. The extra features normally need to be compiled into PHP at the time it's built. Compiling PHP from source requires specialist knowledge. Fortunately, all that has been taken care of for you by several all-in-one packages that install not only PHP with a rich range of features, but also a web server, MySQL, and phpMyAdmin.

Don't be confused by the need for a web server. It doesn't mean setting up a separate computer. A *web server* is simply a piece of software that sits on a computer waiting for requests for web pages and sends them back to a browser. MySQL is also a *database server*. Again, it's just a piece of software that responds to requests that query or alter the data stored in the database. For a local testing environment, everything can be installed on your existing computer. The servers normally run in the background, and consume very few resources. However, you can also start and stop the servers manually if needed.

No particular hardware specifications are required. If your computer can run Dreamweaver CS5, it's more than adequate. The basic installation on Windows occupies about 250 MB. On Mac OS X, you need roughly twice that amount of disk space. However, you also need space to store your files and databases. If you allocate 1 GB, that should be fine.

In 99 percent of cases, installation is quick and trouble free. When things go wrong, it's usually because you have previously tried and failed to install one or more of the components manually. The other common cause of problems is a software conflict. A web server listens for requests on port 80, and it can't run if another program on your computer is already using that port. If you can't identify the other program, it's a simple matter to switch the web server to a different port for testing purposes.

After you have installed the software, it's important to check that it's working correctly and that you have the right settings for a development environment. Finally, you need to define a site in Dreamweaver and tell it where to find the testing server. The site setup process has been simplified in Dreamweaver CS5.

Because the installation procedures might change during the lifetime of this book, it's best to follow the online instructions, because they will be updated to reflect any changes. The options for Windows and Mac OS X are different, so I'll deal with them separately.

✱ **NOTE:** If you have a PHP testing environment that supports a minimum of PHP 5.2 and MySQL 5.0, you're already good to go. Just check that your configuration settings match the recommendations in Table 2.1. If your versions are older, follow the instructions in Lesson 13 to export your existing data from MySQL, and make sure everything is completely uninstalled before reinstalling.

Options available for Windows

Windows users have the choice of several all-in-one packages or of integrating PHP into IIS.

Using an all-in-one package

The most popular all-in-one packages are

- **XAMPP.** www.apachefriends.org/en/xampp-windows.html

- **WampServer.** www.wampserver.com/en/

- **Easyphp.** www.easyphp.org

All use the Apache web server, which powers more than half of the active domains on the Internet. They also include PHP, MySQL, and phpMyAdmin. Some offer extra features, but they are not required for this book.

You can find my detailed installation instructions for installing XAMPP online in the Adobe Developer Connection at www.adobe.com/devnet/dreamweaver/articles/setup_php_02.html.

Integrating PHP with IIS

If you are already running IIS to develop with Active Server Pages (ASP) or ASP.NET, PHP can also be easily integrated into IIS using the Microsoft Web Platform Installer (WPI). This avoids a conflict with Apache trying to run on the same port as IIS. Details of how to obtain and use the WPI can be found online in the Adobe Developer Connection at www.adobe.com/devnet/dreamweaver/articles/setup_asp_02.html. If ASP or the .NET framework is already installed, just follow the instructions for using the WPI to install PHP.

If you use IIS, you will also need to install MySQL and phpMyAdmin. Follow the instructions at www.adobe.com/devnet/dreamweaver/articles/setup_php_03.html.

Options available for Mac OS X

Both Apache and PHP are preinstalled on Mac OS X. However, I do *not* recommend using them. Neither is enabled by default, and the version of PHP is missing some important features. You also need to install and configure MySQL and phpMyAdmin separately.

It's far simpler to install MAMP, which you can download from www.mamp.info/en/index.html. After downloading, just drag the MAMP icon from the disk image to your Applications folder. You'll find instructions on installing and configuring MAMP in the Adobe Developer Connection at www.adobe.com/devnet/dreamweaver/articles/setup_php_04.html.

Checking Your PHP Installation

When you're working with a PHP testing environment, there are two simple, yet important concepts that you need to understand:

- The web server's document root
- The URL for your testing environment

Both are directly related to each other. The *document root* (often called the *server root*) is the physical location where your web files are stored. The URL is the address you enter in a browser to test or view your pages. Remember that the PHP code needs to be processed, so you can't just open a file directly in the browser. It must always be accessed through a URL.

Locating the web server's document root

The location of the document root depends on which method you chose to install PHP. The default location for the most commonly used setups is as follows:

- **XAMPP.** C:\xampp\htdocs
- **WampServer.** C:\wamp\www
- **EasyPHP.** C:\EasyPHP\www
- **IIS.** C:\inetpub\wwwroot
- **MAMP.** Macintosh HD:Applications:MAMP:htdocs

If you installed Apache independently on Windows or use the preinstalled version on a Mac, the default location for the server root follows:

- **Windows 32-bit.** C:\Program Files\Apache Software Foundation\Apache2.2\htdocs
- **Windows 64-bit.** C:\Program Files (x86)\Apache Software Foundation\Apache2.2\htdocs
- **Mac OS X.** Macintosh HD:Library:WebServer:Documents

Assuming that you installed your testing environment on the same computer as you're working on, the URL for the document root is http://localhost.

✱ NOTE: If you're using MAMP and decide not to use the default Apache and MySQL ports, you need to use http://localhost:8888.

Testing PHP

If you installed PHP using an all-in-one package, you've probably already verified that PHP is working by clicking the phpinfo link in the setup screen. This displays a long page of details about your PHP configuration. If you see a page similar to the following screen shot, skip ahead to "Understanding the PHP configuration page."

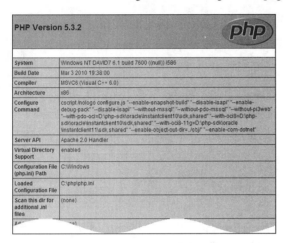

> **TIP:** The information displayed by the configuration page is generated dynamically by a function called phpinfo(), so it's perfectly normal if your page doesn't look exactly the same as shown here.

If you didn't use an all-in-one installation package, create a test page like this:

1 In Dreamweaver, choose File > New. This opens the New Document dialog box.

2 Select Blank Page, set Page Type to PHP, and set Layout to <none>. Click Create.

3 In the blank page that opens, switch to Code view, and delete everything in the page. You should be left with a completely blank file.

4 Type the following code into the file:

```
<?php phpinfo(); ?>
```

If you typed the code correctly, the Info Bar should report "No syntax errors."

5 Save the page as **test.php** in your server's document root. For example, if you're using IIS, the page should be saved in C:\inetpub\wwwroot.

6 Open a browser, enter **http://localhost/test.php** in the address bar, and load the page. You should see a page similar to the one shown at the beginning of this section.

If the page fails to load, check the following:

- Make sure there are no errors in your code. Copy lesson02/test.php to your server root, and use that instead.

- Make sure the web server is running.

- Save an HTML page in the server root, and test it using the localhost URL. If the browser displays the HTML page but not test.php, the problem lies with how PHP has been installed.

- Try a different browser. Your browser's security settings might be set too high to permit dynamic scripts to run locally.

- Turn off any firewall or security software temporarily. If that does the trick, adjust your firewall settings to allow *local* communication on port 80.

▼ **CAUTION!** Ensure that you allow access to port 80 only from the same computer or your local network. Permitting unrestricted access to port 80 is a security risk.

- If all else fails, seek help in an online forum, giving details of your setup and any error messages that appear onscreen.

Understanding the PHP configuration page

When you first start working with PHP, the details displayed by `phpinfo()` are nothing short of information overload. However, it's the first place you should check if your PHP scripts don't work as expected.

One of the most important pieces of information—Loaded Configuration File—is close to the top. This tells you where to find php.ini, the file that must be edited if any settings need to be changed.

▶ **TIP:** If you have previously installed PHP manually, it's possible that an old version of php.ini is being loaded. Always check Loaded Configuration File before editing php.ini. Otherwise, you could be making changes to a file that is being ignored by the web server.

The information displayed by phpinfo() is split into sections. Most relate to the different extensions that have been loaded or compiled into PHP. The most important section is PHP Core (in some versions, it's just Core). It contains nearly 100 settings. Most of the defaults are fine, but you need to check a handful of settings against the recommendations in **Table 2.1**.

Table 2.1 Recommended Testing Server Settings for PHP Core

Directive	Local Value
allow_url_fopen	On
allow_url_include	Off
display_errors	On
error_reporting	32767 (PHP 5.3) or 6143 (PHP 5.2)
file_uploads	On
log_errors	Off
magic_quotes_gpc	Off, but see "Deciding to use or not to use 'magic quotes'"
register_globals	Off
register_long_arrays	Off
safe_mode	Off
short_open_tag	Off
upload_tmp_dir	See "Setting a temporary upload directory"

The purpose of allow_url_fopen and allow_url_include is to control how PHP handles files accessed on another server. It's often very useful to access a remote file, for example, to extract the contents of a news feed or get details from an online weather service. That's why allow_url_fopen is turned on by default (the f in fopen stands for file). After opening the file, you are expected to process the content—including any security checks—before incorporating it into your own pages. However, including a remote file directly into a page or script without first checking it is potentially very dangerous, so allow_url_include is turned off by default—and should stay off. Security online is of paramount importance, so take a minute or so to read the sidebar "Security Should Be Your Top Priority."

Make a note of any settings that are different from those recommended in **Table 2.1**. Before explaining how to change them, I'll describe the purpose of some of them to help you decide which setting to use.

Security Should Be Your Top Priority

In the early days of PHP, the emphasis was on making things easy, which was why PHP became so popular. Unfortunately, making things easy for the developer also made it too easy for malicious attackers to exploit security loopholes. In recent years, PHP has tightened up security considerably—without sacrificing too much of the emphasis on the ease of development.

You might see recommendations in old books or online tutorials to turn on `register_globals` because it makes it easier to handle user input from forms. Under no circumstances should you do so. This was one of the biggest security loopholes in PHP. The setting was turned off by default in 2002, but many hosting companies turned it back on because it broke so many scripts. Fortunately, this trend has reversed, and `register_globals` will be removed from the next major version of PHP. So, even if you turn on this directive locally, your scripts will probably break online.

In the interests of security, you need to eliminate all errors from your scripts. That's why `display_errors` should be turned on and `error_reporting` set to the highest level in your local testing environment. PHP 5.3 introduced new categories of errors, which is why the value differs from PHP 5.2. I recommend turning off `log_errors` to avoid clogging up your disk with a large log file. It's much easier to deal with errors if they're displayed onscreen.

On a live website, displaying error messages gives attackers potentially useful information, so `display_errors` should be turned off. Nowadays, most hosting companies do this, but some don't, which is why local testing is so important. If `display_errors` is turned off, a mistake in your script frequently presents you with a blank screen, leaving you to scratch your head wondering what the problem is. If your hosting company gives you control of php.ini, the settings on your live website should be `display_errors = Off`, and `log_errors = On`.

If security is so important, why turn off `safe_mode`? Like `register_globals`, it was an early attempt to make things simple. It was well intentioned but didn't work as well as intended. It will be removed from the next major version of PHP.

Deciding to use or not to use "magic quotes"

The magic_quotes_gpc directive controls another misguided early attempt to make things easy for beginners. When this directive is turned on, PHP automatically inserts a backslash in front of single or double quotation marks submitted through a URL or online form. The idea of adding the backslashes was to prevent problems when inserting text into a database.

It was eventually realized that this caused more problems than the one it was intended to solve. As a result, magic_quotes_gpc is turned off by default in a new installation of PHP, and the directive is scheduled for removal. However, many scripts have been written on the assumption that PHP will insert backslashes in front of quotation marks, so a lot of hosting companies turn the setting back on. Consider the following scenarios:

- If magic_quotes_gpc is off on your remote server, make sure it's off locally as well.

- If magic_quotes_gpc is enabled on your remote server, and your hosting company allows you to change your own settings, turn it off on both servers.

- If your hosting company lets you control settings with an .htaccess file, turn off magic_quotes_gpc locally, and add the following line to .htaccess in the site root of your remote server:

    php_flag magic_quotes_gpc Off

- If magic_quotes_gpc is enabled on your remote server, and you have no way of turning it off, set the local value to "on."

Setting a temporary upload directory

When uploading files, PHP stores them in a temporary directory (folder) before you move them to their final destination. The all-in-one packages automatically create the necessary folder. However, you should check the value displayed for upload_tmp_dir, and make sure that a folder actually exists at the location indicated. If no folder exists, create one, and make sure it is writable by the web server.

> ✳ **NOTE:** If you're using IIS, right-click the folder, and choose Properties. Select the Security tab, and click Edit. Add the IUSR account to the "Group or user names" section. In IIS7, the account is called IIS_IUSRS. Give the account the following permissions: Read & execute, Read, and Write.

It doesn't matter where the folder is. As the name suggests, it is used only for temporary storage. As soon as the file has been moved to its ultimate location, PHP deletes the temporary file.

Checking other configuration settings

To work with this book, make sure the following sections are listed in the PHP configuration page:

- **date.** This controls date and time functions, automatically adjusting for time zones and daylight saving time.

- **filter.** Filter functions are used for validating email addresses and other user input. They were added in PHP 5.2.

- **gd.** This enables PHP to generate and modify images and fonts.

- **mysql.** PHP 5 offers several ways of supporting MySQL. This is the original one, which is used by Dreamweaver's PHP server behaviors.

- **mysqli.** This is a more recent way of connecting to MySQL. The "i" stands for improved. It requires a minimum of PHP 5.0 and MySQL 4.1.

- **PDO.** PHP Data Objects offer a software-neutral way of connecting to a database. Unlike mysql and mysqli, which are tied to MySQL, PDO can be used with a wide range of databases.

- **pdo_mysql.** This is the MySQL driver for PDO.

- **session.** Sessions maintain information connected to a user, for example, in a login system or shopping cart.

In the "date" section, make sure "Default timezone" is appropriate for your location. If it's wrong, you need to replace it with one of the values listed at http://docs.php.net/manual/en/timezones.php.

Also, check the value of session.save_path in the "sessions" section. It needs to point to a folder that exists and is writable. If it has no value or points to a nonexistent folder, you need to change the setting. The location of the folder is not important. It will be used by PHP to store temporary files similar to cookies.

You should now have a list of configuration settings that need changing. If there's nothing on the list, you're good to go, but it's still useful to know how to change your PHP configuration, which the next section explains.

Changing configuration settings

Most configuration changes can be made simply by editing php.ini. Each time the web server starts, it reads this file. So, all you need to do is restart your web server after editing php.ini, and your changes should take effect immediately. Editing php.ini is easy. It's written in plain text, so you can edit it with any text editor, such as Notepad or TextEdit. However, it's important to save the file as plain text and preserve the filename and `.ini` extension.

Editing php.ini

In Windows 7 or Vista, if your version of php.ini is in a subfolder of Program Files, you will not be able to save any changes to the file if you open it directly in Notepad. In the Windows Start menu, right-click Notepad, and choose "Run as administrator." In Notepad, choose File > Open, and set File Types to All (*.*) to navigate to php.ini and open it.

TextEdit in Mac OS X has a nasty habit of saving files in Rich Text Format (`.rtf` files) or adds a `.txt` filename extension if you're not careful. It's better to use a dedicated script editor, such as BBEdit. If you don't have a dedicated script editor, you can download TextWrangler, a free, cut-down version of BBEdit, from www.barebones.com/products/TextWrangler/.

Newcomers to PHP often take fright the first time they open php.ini. It's an extremely long document: Depending on which version of PHP you have installed, it might be more than 1,800 lines. The reason it's so long is not only because it covers numerous settings, but also because it contains detailed explanations of what the settings are for.

The best way to deal with php.ini is to make a list of the settings you want to change, and then use the Find option in your script editor to move quickly to the appropriate section of the file. Everything should go smoothly as long as you remember the following:

- Make a copy of php.ini as a backup in case anything goes wrong.

- Lines that begin with a semicolon (;) are comments. They are ignored by PHP.

- The lines you need to edit do not begin with a semicolon.

- A few directives are disabled by default. In these cases, you need to delete the semicolon at the beginning of a line to enable the directive.

- The comments in php.ini show several example settings. Before deleting the semicolon at the beginning of a line, always make sure there isn't another line farther down that contains the actual directive. If the same directive is repeated in php.ini, the lower one takes precedence.

For those directives that use On or Off, all you need to do is to change the value to the recommended one. For example, if `display_errors` is turned off, locate the following line:

```
display_errors = Off
```

Change it to this:

```
display_errors = On
```

Setting the level of error reporting

PHP gives you a high degree of control over the types of errors it reports. Older versions of PHP used to turn off the reporting of "notices," which are warnings about noncritical errors that don't prevent your script from working. It's now recognized that this was a bad idea, because failure to fix such errors can leave you exposed to security risks. You should set error reporting to the highest level, and make sure you eliminate all errors before deploying a PHP script on a live website.

The error reporting section of php.ini contains a lot of examples. Locate the line that begins like this:

```
error_reporting =
```

If you are running PHP 5.3 or later, use the following setting:

```
error_reporting = E_ALL | E_STRICT
```

If you are running PHP 5.2, use this:

```
error_reporting = E_ALL
```

▼ CAUTION! PHP is case sensitive. E_ALL and E_STRICT must be all uppercase. The character between E_ALL and E_STRICT in the setting for PHP 5.3 and later is a vertical pipe (|). On most keyboards, you type it by holding down the Shift key and pressing backslash (\).

Enabling other PHP extensions

The section "Checking other configuration settings" lists several PHP extensions needed for working with this book. All of them should be enabled by default if you used one of the all-in-one installation packages or used the Microsoft WPI to integrate PHP into IIS.

✱ NOTE: PHP extensions are optional features written in the C programming language that normally need to be compiled into PHP. They are not related to Dreamweaver extensions.

If you used a different installation or want to use other PHP features later, it's useful to know how to enable extra extensions. Unfortunately, *this works on Windows only*. On a Mac, extra extensions need to be compiled from source, a subject that is beyond the scope of this book.

Let's say, for example, that you want to work with the PostgreSQL database. If it's not already enabled, locate the Dynamic Extensions section in php.ini, and then find the following lines:

```
;extension=php_pdo_pgsql.dll
;extension=php_pgsql.dll
```

Remove the semicolon from the beginning of each of those lines to enable them. You must also check that the appropriate .dll files are in your PHP extensions folder. The location of the folder is listed as the value of extension_dir in the Core or PHP Core section of the PHP configuration page.

If you don't have the right .dll files, you can extract them from the Zip version of the PHP Windows binaries at http://windows.php.net/download/.

Activating configuration changes

After you have edited and saved php.ini, restart your local web server (Apache or IIS). Reload the PHP configuration page to check that it reflects your changes.

If your web server refuses to start, check the error log:

- In XAMPP, it's located at C:\xampp\apache\logs\error.log.

- In WampServer, click the WampServer icon, and access the Apache log from the menu.

- In Easyphp, right-click the icon in the task tray, and choose Log Files from the menu.

- If you installed Apache independently in Windows, the log is located at C:\Program Files\Apache Software Foundation\Apache2.2\logs\error.log. For 64-bit Windows, replace Program Files with Program Files (x86).

- In MAMP, the log is located at Macintosh HD:Applications:MAMP:logs:apache _error_log.

- If you are using the preinstalled version of Apache on a Mac, choose Applications > Utilities > Console. Any error message should be displayed at the bottom of Console Messages.

- For help with IIS errors, see http://msdn.microsoft.com/en-us/library/ms524984.aspx.

Using Virtual Hosts

After you have installed your local PHP testing environment and confirmed that it's working, you're ready to start developing dynamic websites with PHP. However, the default setup for a web server allows you to create only one website. Since most people usually develop or maintain more than one site, there are two ways you can handle this:

- **Create each new site in a subfolder of the server's document root.** This is the simplest approach because it involves no further setup. However, it prevents you from using links relative to the site root. See the sidebar "Using Links Relative to the Site Root" for an explanation of the implications of this.

- **Create a virtual host for each site.** This is how hosting companies manage shared hosting. It takes a little extra time to set up but has the advantage of providing a unique local domain for each site.

Using Links Relative to the Site Root

Internal links in a website can be created in two ways:

- **Relative to the document.** You can recognize this type of link in Code view by the fact that the `href` attribute contains only the name of the file if it's in the same folder. If the file is in a folder at a different level, the path to the file often begins with `../`, which indicates that the path begins one level up from the current folder.

- **Relative to the site root.** This type of link always begins with a forward slash, which represents the root folder, and is followed by the full path to the file.

By default, Dreamweaver creates links relative to the document, and it generates the correct link format. You can change this default either for an entire site or on an individual basis for each link.

In most cases, it doesn't matter which type of link you use. The exception is when you break your pages into modules and use PHP includes (SSI), for example, if you put your navigation menu into a separate file and include it in every page. Because the menu is likely to be included by files at different levels of the site hierarchy, links must be relative to the site root.

If you develop your site in a subfolder of the server's document root, you can't test your menu locally. This problem doesn't exist if you create a virtual host for each site.

Although creating a virtual host for each site does have advantages, it's not absolutely essential. I use both approaches in my local testing environment.

The following sections describe how to create virtual hosts. If you don't want to bother with virtual hosts at this stage, skip ahead to "Setting Up a PHP Site in Dreamweaver CS5."

✱ **NOTE:** IIS on Windows XP supports only virtual directories, which are treated as subfolders of the server root. If you are running Windows XP, you must use Apache if you want to create virtual hosts.

Creating virtual hosts

Creating virtual hosts consists of two stages:

- Editing your computer's hosts file
- Registering the virtual hosts in the web server

The hosts file tells your computer to look for certain domain names on your local system. When choosing names for virtual hosts in your testing environment, it's essential to avoid using the name of a real domain. Otherwise, your browser will always show the local version of the site rather than the live one on the Internet.

The naming convention that I use removes the top-level domain name. My main website is foundationphp.com. So, the domain name for local testing is just foundationphp. The advantage of using this technique is that you can easily edit the URL in the address bar of your browser, adding or removing the .com to switch between the live site and the local testing version.

The following sections describe the process of creating a virtual host on Windows and Mac OS X.

▼ **CAUTION!** Editing the various files needed to set up virtual hosts is very easy, but it's important to pay attention to spelling. The Apache directives are case sensitive and use hybrid words, such as ServerRoot. Incorrect spelling or spaces will prevent Apache from running. Pay careful attention to detail, and don't rush. Once you have learned how to do this, it should take only a few minutes to add new virtual hosts to your local testing environment.

Setting up virtual hosts on Windows

The hosts file is located in the Windows system files, so you need administrator privileges to edit it. These instructions apply to both Apache and IIS7:

1 From the Windows Start menu, choose All Programs > Accessories, and right-click Notepad. Choose "Run as administrator."

2 Choose File > Open, and navigate to C:\Windows\System32\drivers\etc.

3 Choose the option to display All Files (*.*), select "hosts," and click Open.

4 The hosts file contains a brief description of its purpose and some examples. Lines that begin with a hash or number sign (#) are treated as comments.

List the IP address and name of each virtual host on a separate line at the bottom of the file. The loopback IP address for your local computer is 127.0.0.1.

The first entry should be for localhost. So, if you want to create a virtual host called "phpcs5" for this book, the list at the bottom of the file should look like this:

```
127.0.0.1    localhost
```

```
127.0.0.1    phpcs5
```

5 Check if your version of hosts contains the following entry:

```
::1    localhost
```

This line can prevent virtual hosts from working correctly. Comment out the line by preceding it with a hash like this:

```
# ::1    localhost
```

6 Save and close the hosts file.

Registering virtual hosts in Apache on Windows

Before registering a virtual host in Apache, you need to decide where you want to store your virtual host files. I normally create a folder called "vhosts" at the top level of my C drive and create each virtual host in a subfolder. The following instructions assume that your virtual host is called phpcs5:

1 Create the folder for your virtual host at C:\vhosts\phpcs5.

2 Open the main Apache configuration file httpd.conf in Notepad.

In XAMPP, it's located at C:\xampp\apache\conf\httpd.conf.

3 Scroll to the bottom of the file to locate the following directive:

```
Include "conf/extra/httpd-vhosts.conf"
```

Lines that begin with a hash sign (#) are commented out. If there's a hash sign at the beginning of the line, delete the hash sign to enable the directive.

4 Save httpd.conf and close the file.

5 Open httpd-vhosts.conf in Notepad.

In XAMPP, it's located at C:\xampp\apache\conf\extra\httpd-vhosts.conf.

6 This file contains examples of how to define virtual hosts. If the examples are not commented out, delete them or add a hash sign at the beginning of each line to disable them.

7 Add the following code at the bottom of the file:

```
<Directory C:/vhosts>
  Order Deny,Allow
  Allow from all
</Directory>
```

This sets the correct permissions for the folder that contains the sites you want to treat as virtual hosts. If you chose a location other than C:\vhosts as the top-level folder, change the value in the first line. Notice that the pathname uses forward slashes rather than the Windows convention of backslashes. Surround the pathname in quotation marks if it contains spaces.

8 Locate the following directive:

```
NameVirtualHost *:80
```

Enable the directive by removing any hash signs at the beginning of the line.

9 Because virtual hosts replace the existing setup, you need to create a virtual host for localhost. Add the following code at the bottom of the file:

```
<VirtualHost *:80>
  DocumentRoot c:/xampp/htdocs
  ServerName localhost
</VirtualHost>
```

The value of DocumentRoot should point to your existing server root. Change the value as appropriate.

10 Do the same for your virtual host, using the appropriate values for DocumentRoot and ServerName. To set up phpcs5 as a virtual host at C:\vhosts\phpcs5, use the following:

```
<VirtualHost *:80>
  DocumentRoot c:/vhosts/phpcs5
  ServerName phpcs5
</VirtualHost>
```

11 Save httpd-vhosts.conf, and restart Apache. You should still have access to http://localhost. Any files that you store in C:\vhosts\phpcs5 will be accessible through http://phpcs5.

Registering virtual hosts in IIS7

Creating a new website in the Internet Information Services (IIS) Manager is the equivalent of creating a virtual host.

1 From the Windows Start menu, choose Control Panel > Administrative Tools > Internet Information Services (IIS) Manager.

2 Expand the tree menu in the Connections panel on the left, if necessary, and select Sites.

3 Right-click and choose Add Web Site to open the Add Web Site dialog box.

4 Type a name for the site in the "Site name" text field.

5 Click the button next to the "Physical path" text field to choose the folder where the files for the virtual host will be stored.

6 Type the name of the virtual host in the "Host name" text field.

7 Click OK. Your virtual host is ready for use.

Creating virtual hosts on Mac OS X

The simplest way to create virtual hosts on Mac OS X is to use MAMP PRO, the commercial version of MAMP, which automates the process. You can also do it manually.

Using MAMP PRO

Everything is done through the MAMP PRO console.

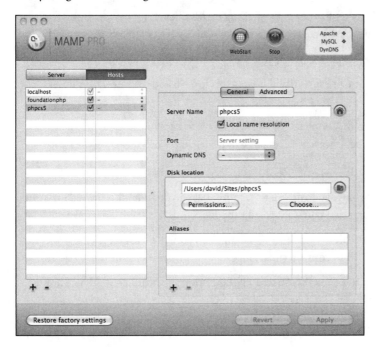

1 Click the Hosts button at the top left of the console, and then click the plus (+) button at the bottom left.

2 Type a name for the virtual host in the Server Name text field.

3 Click the Choose button under the "Disk location" text field, and navigate to the location where you want to store the virtual host files, creating a new folder, if necessary.

4 Click the Apply button.

5 Click OK when prompted to restart the servers.

Adding virtual hosts manually

If you don't want to purchase the commercial version of MAMP, you can edit the hosts file and the Apache configuration file manually. The hosts file is a hidden file, but you can edit it easily in BBEdit or TextWrangler (see the sidebar "Editing php.ini" earlier in this lesson).

> **TIP:** The preinstalled version of Apache in Mac OS X uses a different setup. If you're using the preinstalled version, follow the instructions at http://foundationphp.com/tutorials/vhosts_leopard.php. They were written for Mac OS X 10.5 but also apply to 10.6.

1 In BBEdit or TextWrangler, choose File > Open Hidden.

2 In the Open dialog box, set Enable to Everything or All Files. If there's an option to show hidden files, make sure it's selected.

3 Select Macintosh HD:private:etc:hosts, and click Open to open the hosts file.

4 The IP address and name of each virtual host needs to be listed on a new line at the bottom of the file.

Type 127.0.0.1 (this is the loopback IP address that refers to your local computer) followed by one or more spaces and the name of the virtual host:

```
127.0.0.1  phpcs5
```

As soon as you start typing, you will see a warning that the document is owned by "root." Click Unlock to confirm that you want to edit the file.

5 Save and close the hosts file. Because it's a system file, you will be asked to enter your Mac administrator's password to confirm the changes.

6 The next file you need to edit is the Apache configuration file httpd.conf. It's not hidden, so just choose File > Open, and select Applications:MAMP:conf:apache:httpd.conf.

7 Scroll to the bottom of the file and locate the following line:

```
# NameVirtualHost *
```

Delete the hash sign at the beginning of the line.

8 Because virtual hosts replace the existing setup, you need to create one for localhost and one for each virtual host that you want to add. Add the following code at the bottom of the file:

```
<VirtualHost *>
  DocumentRoot /Applications/MAMP/htdocs
  ServerName localhost
</VirtualHost>
```

```
<VirtualHost *>
  DocumentRoot /Users/your_name/Sites/phpcs5
  ServerName phpcs5
</VirtualHost>
```

For each virtual host, the value of DocumentRoot is the location of the folder that contains the site, and ServerName is the name of the virtual host. The preceding example assumes you are calling the virtual host "phpcs5," and that the files are in a folder called "phpcs5" in your personal Sites folder (replace your_name with the name of your Mac home folder). If any of the folder names contain spaces, wrap the path in quotation marks.

9 Save and close httpd.conf. When you restart Apache, you should still have access to http://localhost. Any files that you store in the phpcs5 folder will be accessible through http://phpcs5.

Setting Up a PHP Site in Dreamweaver CS5

Dreamweaver works on the basis of creating an exact copy of your website on your local computer. So, before you can do anything else, you need to tell the program a few basic details about the site. This process has been simplified in Dreamweaver CS5. All you need to do to get going is to give the site a name and tell Dreamweaver where you want to store the files on your local computer. Everything else can wait until you need it. However, for a PHP site, it's a good idea to define the testing server at the same time.

In theory, you can locate your PHP files anywhere on your computer, and Dreamweaver will copy them to the testing server whenever you use Live View or Preview in Browser. However, this results in two identical copies of every file; instead, it makes more sense to store your project files in the testing server's document root. You also need to tell Dreamweaver the URL of the testing server.

Both pieces of information depend on whether you chose to create a virtual host for the exercises in this book.

Using a virtual host

If you decided to create a virtual host, store your files in the folder you chose as the server root for the phpcs5 virtual host.

The URL will be http://phpcs5/.

Using a subfolder of the server root

If you decided not to create a virtual host, the local site folder and testing server folder will be a subfolder of your server root:

- **In XAMPP.** C:\xampp\htdocs\phpcs5

- **In WampServer.** C:\wamp\www\phpcs5

- **In Easyphp.** C:\EasyPHP\www\phpcs5

- **In an independent Apache installation on Windows.** C:\Program Files\Apache Software Foundation\Apache2.2\htdocs\phpcs5—add (x86) after Program Files for 64-bit Windows

- **In IIS.** C:\inetpub\wwwroot\phpcs5

- **In MAMP.** Macintosh HD:Applications:MAMP:htdocs:phpcs5

- **In the preinstalled Apache on Mac OS X.** Macintosh HD:Library:WebServer:Documents:phpcs5

The URL will be http://localhost/phpcs5/.

Creating the site definition

Use the following instructions to set up your PHP site for this book:

1 In Dreamweaver CS5, choose Site > New Site to open the Site Setup dialog box.

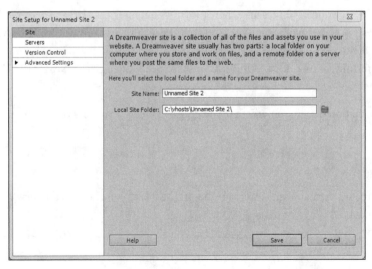

If you've used a previous version of Dreamweaver, you'll notice that the Basic and Advanced tabs (buttons on a Mac) have been eliminated.

2 In the Site Name text field, type a name for the site, for example, **PHP CS5**. This name is used internally by Dreamweaver to identify the site in the Files panel, so it should be descriptive and can contain spaces.

3 Click the "Browse for folder" icon next to the Local Site Folder text field, and select the folder where you will store the files for your site.

At this stage, you could just click OK, but it's best to set up the testing server at the same time.

4 Click Servers in the list on the left of the Site Setup dialog box to display the panel where you define the server(s) that you want the site to connect to.

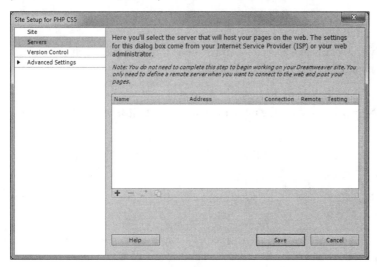

NOTE: Although the instructions at the top of the panel refer to the server that will host your pages on the web, this is also where you define the settings for a local testing server.

5 Click the plus (+) button at the bottom left of the panel to open another panel where you define the settings for the testing server.

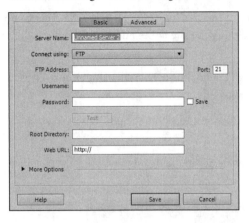

6 In the Server Name text field, type a descriptive name for the server, such as **Testing Server**.

7 Click the "Connect using" menu to view the options. For a local testing server, choose Local/Network to reduce the remaining text fields to just two: Server Folder and Web URL.

8 In the Server Folder text field, select the same folder as you used for Local Site Folder in step 3.

9 In the Web URL field, enter the URL for your local testing server. Make sure it ends with a trailing slash.

The following screen shot shows the settings for a virtual host called "phpcs5" located in C:\vhosts\phpcs5.

Use the appropriate values for whichever type of setup you're using.

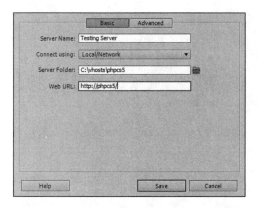

10 Click the Advanced button at the top of the dialog box to reveal separate sections for a remote server and a testing server.

11 Click the Server Model menu in the Testing Server section at the bottom of the dialog box, and choose PHP MySQL.

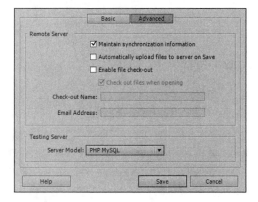

Click Save.

12 The testing server should now be listed in the Servers panel. Make sure the Remote checkbox is deselected and the Testing checkbox is selected.

Now that a server has been defined and is selected, the other buttons at the bottom of the panel become active. As the screen shot on the next page shows, the buttons allow you to add a new server and delete, edit, or copy the selected server.

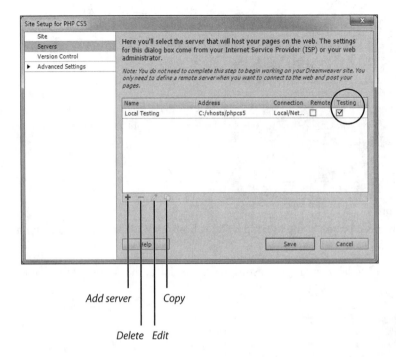

Add server

Copy

Delete Edit

13 Click Save to close the Site Setup dialog box.

Setting up multiple servers

If you've used a previous version of Dreamweaver, you'll have noticed that a major difference in CS5 is that there are no longer separate panels for defining your remote and testing servers. The Servers panel in the Site Setup dialog box lets you add as many servers as you like. This is mainly for the benefit of developers working in a team environment, where the individual developer might need access to more than one testing server—for example, one for initial tests and experiments, and another shared with the rest of the team for testing the entire website before it goes live.

The role of the server is determined by two items:

- The settings in the Advanced view of the server definition
- The checkbox selected in the Servers panel

The main difference between selecting the Remote or Testing checkbox is that Dreamweaver normally transfers files automatically to a testing server but expects you to initiate the upload to a remote server. Setting up and communicating with a remote server is covered in Lesson 13.

✳ NOTE: Although you can define multiple remote and testing servers, you can use only one of each at any given time. You cannot, for example, select the Remote checkbox for two servers and expect Dreamweaver CS5 to upload to both of them. The current version of Dreamweaver can access only one server at a time.

Testing your testing server

The final stage in preparing your local testing environment is making sure that the testing server works:

1 Copy the sample files for this book into the folder you designated as the Local Site Root.

2 In the Dreamweaver Files panel, expand the lesson02 folder, and double-click site_check.php to open it in the Document window.

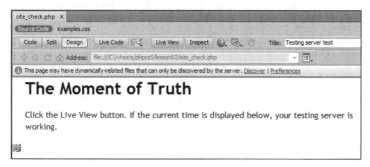

3 Click the Live View button. If everything is working OK, you should see a short message followed by the current time.

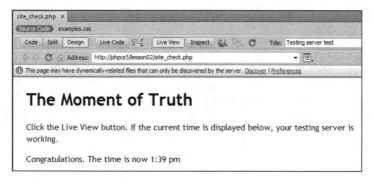

Don't worry if there's a slight delay. It usually takes Dreamweaver a few seconds to connect to the testing server the first time you use Live View after launching the program. On subsequent occasions, Live View normally displays the output of the testing server immediately.

4 Click the Live View button again to turn it off.

If everything worked, you're all set to start developing with PHP in Dreamweaver CS5.

If you got a blank screen or error message, check the troubleshooting hints in the next section.

Troubleshooting the testing server

If the test page failed to display correctly in Live View, try the following:

- Check that your local web server is running.

- Press F12/Opt+F12 to preview the page in a browser. If the page works in a browser but not in Live View, turn off any security software and try Live View again. It's possible that the security software is blocking access between the web server and Dreamweaver.

- Check the settings for Server Folder and Web URL in the Site Setup dialog box (see the next section, "Editing a site definition"). This is the most common mistake with setting up a testing server.

   Both fields *must* point to the same folder: Server Folder is the physical path; Web URL is the address a browser uses to get to the same folder.

Editing a site definition

If you have made a mistake or need to change any details of your site definition, you can open the Site Setup dialog box easily by choosing Site > Manage Sites. In the dialog box that opens, select the name of the site you want to modify, and click the Edit button.

- To edit the definition of a remote or testing server, select Servers from the list on the left of the Site Setup dialog box. Then select the server you want to edit, and click the Edit icon (it looks like a pencil).

- Select Version Control from the list on the left to set up a Subversion repository. Using Subversion is not covered in this book.

- Click the right-facing triangle next to Advanced Settings to reveal the other categories. The only section of interest to most people is Local Info.

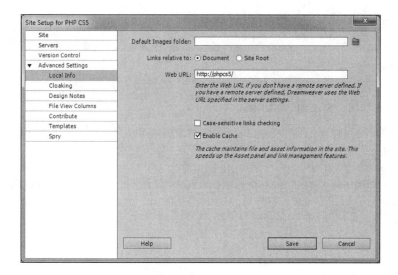

- Use the "Default Images folder" text field to define the default location for the site's images. Dreamweaver automatically copies images to this folder whenever you select an image outside the site root.

- Use the "Links relative to" radio buttons to set the default type of links for your site (see the "Using Links Relative to the Site Root" sidebar earlier in this lesson).

▼ **CAUTION!** If you select the option to use links relative to the site root, Dreamweaver uses a nonstandard function (virtual()) for PHP includes. This works only on Apache and can cause problems with some server behaviors. If you plan to make extensive use of Dreamweaver server behaviors, it's more advisable to use the default setting of links relative to the document and override this setting for individual links that need to be relative to the site root.

- By default, the "Case-sensitive links checking" checkbox is deselected. Since most PHP sites are hosted on Linux servers, which are case sensitive, it would seem like a good idea to enable this option. However, it's not as useful as it sounds, because it checks the letter case of internal links only when you run the Check Links Sitewide command from the Site menu.

- Enable Cache is selected by default. As the description beneath the checkbox explains, this speeds up certain features within Dreamweaver. The only reason for deselecting this option is if you have a site with a very large number of files. Once your site gets beyond a certain limit—the actual size depends on the amount of memory available on your computer—the cache has the opposite effect of slowing down Dreamweaver's responsiveness.

Click the Help button for details about the other options in the Site Setup dialog box.

When you have finished editing the site definition, click Save. Then click Done to close the Manage Sites dialog box.

Backing up and restoring site definitions

Computers and software occasionally fail, sometimes catastrophically. If you have more than a handful of sites, it's a major headache to set them up again in Dreamweaver after a crash unless you have taken the precaution of backing up your site definitions. Dreamweaver makes it easy to export the details of your sites to .ste files, which you should store in a safe location. If you suffer a crash—or simply want to move the definitions to another computer—you can restore the site definitions from the .ste files.

Here's how you do it:

1 Choose Site > Manage Sites to open the Manage Sites dialog box.

2 Shift-click or Ctrl/Cmd-click to select the sites for which you want to back up the definitions.

3 Click the Export button.

If any of your site definitions contain login information, Dreamweaver asks if you want to export the usernames and passwords. Your choice applies to all site definitions being exported.

4 Select a location to store the backup files. Just accept the name suggested by Dreamweaver, and click Save.

Dreamweaver creates a separate .ste file for each site definition. This is an XML file that contains the details stored in the Site Setup dialog box.

If you ever need to restore your site definitions or move them to a different computer, choose Site > Manage Sites, click the Import button, and select the .ste files of the sites you want to restore.

▼ **CAUTION!** The Manage Sites dialog box handles only the site settings, such as server details and the location of files. It does not create a backup of the files within a site. You need to do that separately. Similarly, selecting a site and clicking the Remove button removes only the site definition. It does not delete the site files from your computer. Back up your site definitions regularly. On Windows, they're stored in the Windows Registry, so restoring them is impossible without a backup. On Mac OS X, you can recover them from a copy of Macintosh HD:<username>:Library:Application Support:Adobe:Common:11:Sites:Site Prefs.

What You Have Learned

In this lesson, you have:

- Installed and tested a local PHP development environment consisting of a web server, PHP, MySQL, and phpMyAdmin (pages 28–32)

- Checked and changed the configuration settings, if necessary (pages 32–39)

- Learned the difference between links relative to the document and links relative to the site root (page 40)

- Seen how to create virtual hosts (pages 40–47)

- Defined and tested a PHP site in Dreamweaver CS5 (pages 47–54)

- Seen how to edit, back up, and restore site definitions (pages 54–56)

Where you go from here depends on your experience and interests. The next lesson provides an introduction to the most important features of PHP for the benefit of readers who are new to the subject or those who need a refresher. If you're familiar with PHP, you can jump ahead to Lesson 4 to experiment with WordPress.

What You Will Learn

In this lesson, you will:

- See how to embed PHP code in a page and store values in variables and arrays
- Discover how PHP gathers information from an online form
- Explore the use of conditional statements to make decisions
- Learn about functions, objects, and resources
- See how PHP handles arithmetical calculations
- Explore the use of loops for repetitive tasks
- Include external files into a web page
- Decode the mysteries of PHP error messages

Approximate Time

The time required for this lesson depends on your previous experience. Don't attempt to memorize everything on a first read through; instead, refer back to this lesson when you need to refresh your understanding of PHP.

Lesson Files

Media Files:

images/birds_of_a_feather.jpg
styles/examples.css
styles/include_examples.css

Starting Files:

lesson03/start/includes_start.php
lesson03/test_includes/year_01.inc.php

Completed Files:

lesson03/completed/function_01.php
lesson03/completed/function_02.php
lesson03/completed/function_03.php

lesson03/completed/function_04.php
lesson03/completed/function_05.php
lesson03/completed/function_06.php
lesson03/completed/function_07.php
lesson03/completed/get_01.php
lesson03/completed/get_02.php
lesson03/completed/includes_01.php
lesson03/completed/includes_02.php
lesson03/completed/includes_03.php
lesson03/completed/includes_04.php
lesson03/completed/includes_05.php
lesson03/completed/includes_06.php
lesson03/completed/includes_07.php
lesson03/completed/includes_08.php
lesson03/completed/loops_01.php
lesson03/completed/loops_02.php
lesson03/completed/loops_03.php
lesson03/completed/loops_04.php
lesson03/completed/loops_05.php
lesson03/completed/loops_06.php
lesson03/completed/loops_07.php
lesson03/completed/post_01.php
lesson03/completed/post_02.php
lesson03/completed/post_03.php
lesson03/completed/post_04.php
lesson03/completed/quotes_01.php
lesson03/completed/quotes_02.php
lesson03/completed/quotes_03.php
lesson03/completed/quotes_04.php
lesson03/completed/quotes_05.php
lesson03/completed/strings_01.php
lesson03/completed/strings_02.php
lesson03/completed/strings_03.php
lesson03/completed/time.php
lesson03/test_includes/header_01.html
lesson03/test_includes/header_02.html
lesson03/test_includes/year_02.inc.php
lesson03/test_includes/year_03.inc.php

LESSON 3

A Quick Crash Course in PHP

PHP makes a website dynamic through the ability to organize and manipulate information drawn from various sources, such as an online form, database, or even another website.

This lesson is aimed principally at readers who have no PHP experience, but it should also be a useful refresher if your knowledge is a little rusty or uncertain. It provides you with the basic knowledge that you need to start working with PHP. Skim each section, and work through the various exercises to get a basic feel for how different features work. Then move on to the rest of the book. Come back to this lesson when you need reminders of the language details.

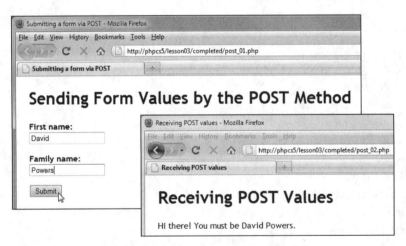

PHP captures and processes the input of online forms.

How PHP Makes Pages Dynamic

PHP uses a number of techniques common to most programming languages:

- *Variables* store information that isn't fixed or known in advance.

- *Arrays* store multiple values, usually of related information.

- *Conditional statements* make decisions, based on such things as the size of a number, the date, or whether something is true.

- *Functions* perform tasks, such as transforming and sorting information, or querying a database.

- *Operators* add, subtract, multiply, divide, and so on.

- *Loops* perform repetitive actions.

Embedding PHP code in a page

The web server needs to recognize PHP code so that it can process it and send the output to the browser. In addition to giving your pages a .php filename extension, you signal the start of any PHP code within a page by using the opening PHP tag, which looks like this:

```
<?php
```

⚠ CAUTION! There must be no space between any of the characters in the opening tag.

You also have the option of using short opening tags, which consist of the first two characters <?. Not all servers support short opening tags. To ensure that your scripts will work everywhere, stick to the full version <?php.

You signal the end of a PHP code block with a closing tag, which looks like this:

```
?>
```

You can have as many PHP code blocks as you like within a page, but you cannot nest them inside each other. In other words, this will work:

```
<?php
// some PHP code
?>
<p>A bit of HTML.</p>
<?php
// some more PHP code
?>
```

However, the following *won't* work:

```php
<?php
// some PHP code
<?php
// you cannot do this
?>
?>
```

❋ NOTE: To save space, most code examples in this book omit the opening and closing PHP tags except where they are needed to show the transition from HTML to PHP and back.

Using comments in PHP scripts

The examples in the preceding section contain lines beginning with two forward slashes. This is one of the ways of creating a comment in PHP. Comments are ignored by the PHP engine. They're simply for your benefit.

It's easy to forget what code is for, so it's a good idea to add brief comments to your scripts. There are three ways to do so in PHP:

- Everything following two forward slashes is ignored until the end of the line.
- Everything following a hash or number sign (#) is ignored until the end of the line.
- Everything between /* and */ is treated as a comment. This type of comment can stretch across multiple lines.

For example:

```php
// This is a comment
$name = 'David'; // This comment is alongside code

# This is another style of writing a comment
$name = 'David'; # This type of comment can also go alongside code

/* This is a comment that stretches
   across two lines. */
```

You can also create multiline comments by beginning each line with two forward slashes or the number sign.

In addition to reminding you—and others—what the code is intended to do, comments can be used to disable parts of a script. This is often necessary during testing or debugging problems.

Ending statements with a semicolon

PHP scripts are usually a series of *statements* or commands. Every statement *must* end with a semicolon like this (don't worry about the meaning of the code at the moment):

```
$name = 'David';
echo $name;
```

Forgetting the semicolon is one of the most common beginner's mistakes.

The semicolon is important, because—unlike JavaScript and ActionScript—PHP allows you to spread statements over multiple lines. As a general rule, PHP ignores whitespace within scripts, which means you can spread out and indent code for greater readability.

Taming the Unknown with Variables

What makes programming languages so powerful is their ability to handle unknown values. Whenever I visit Amazon.com, it always greets me with "Hello, David Powers" at the top of every page. The way it personalizes my visits is by using variables. A *variable* is a placeholder for a value you don't know in advance. The *name* of the variable remains constant, but its *value* can change.

We use variables all the time in everyday life:

- What's your *name*?
- What *day* is it?
- What's the *balance* of my bank account?

Variables are easy to recognize in PHP because they always begin with a dollar sign ($). You can name a variable almost anything you like, as long as it follows these rules:

- It must begin with a dollar sign.
- The first character after the dollar sign cannot be a number. It must be a letter or the underscore character (_). Acceptable letters include accented characters used in Western European languages (see the sidebar "Using Accented Characters in Variable and Function Names").
- Subsequent characters can also include the numbers 0–9.
- Spaces, hyphens, and other punctuation are not permitted.
- $this is a special variable reserved for use with PHP objects. You cannot assign your own value to it.

> ### Using Accented Characters in Variable and Function Names
>
> PHP 5 allows the use of characters between ASCII 0x7F and ASCII 0xFF in variable and function names. This range of characters includes symbols such as ©, £, and ¢, as well as the inverted question mark and exclamation point used in Spanish. Although it's perfectly valid to use these characters in naming variables and functions, the main purpose of permitting this range of characters is to allow the use of accented characters commonly used in Western European languages. So, for example, a Spanish developer could use $mañana as a variable to hold tomorrow's date.

So, you could create PHP variables to represent the previous examples from everyday life like this:

```
$name
$day
$balance
```

When naming variables, it's a good idea to use a meaningful name because it makes your code easier to read and understand, particularly when you come back to it six months later. Don't be tempted to use short, cryptic variables. The code hinting in Dreamweaver CS5 saves you the extra typing anyway.

If you need to combine multiple words in a variable name, either use an underscore to separate them, or use "camel" case (starting subsequent words with an uppercase letter). For example:

```
$first_name
$firstName
```

▼ **CAUTION!** PHP variables are case sensitive. $firstname and $firstName are treated as completely different values.

Assigning a value to a variable

You assign a value to a variable with the equals sign (=). The variable goes on the left of the equals sign, and the value goes on the right. But what sort of values can a variable have?

PHP is known as a *weakly typed language*. No, that doesn't mean it gets sand kicked in its face. In fact, it's one of the reasons that PHP is easy to learn. In many programming languages, you must specify what type of data a variable will be used for, and you can't change your mind later. With PHP, it doesn't matter. A variable can store any of the eight data types listed in **Table 3.1**.

Table 3.1 PHP Data Types	
Type	**Description**
Boolean	True or false
Float	A floating point number (the PHP documentation also refers to this data type as a double)
Integer	A whole number
String	Text
Array	An ordered collection of (usually related) values
Object	A sophisticated data type that can store and manipulate values
Resource	A reference to an external resource, such as a database result or file
NULL	A variable with no value

Being weakly typed makes it easy to handle form input. HTML forms pass all input values as text, but PHP is smart enough to recognize when a value from a form should be used as an integer or floating point number without you needing to change the data type explicitly.

When you assign any of the first three data types in Table 3.1 to a variable, the value is *not* enclosed in quotation marks. For example:

```
$love = TRUE;
$lie = FALSE;
$pi = 3.14159;
$answer = 42;
```

TRUE and FALSE are case-insensitive keywords, so the following are also correct:

```
$love = true;
$lie = false;
```

▶ **TIP:** With case-insensitive keywords, you can even mix uppercase and lowercase. So, TruE and FaLsE are also technically correct. However, it's best to choose one style, and stick to it. Consistency in writing code makes it easier to maintain and debug.

NULL is also a case-insensitive keyword. It's relatively uncommon to assign the NULL value directly to a variable, but if you want to destroy the value of a variable without destroying the actual variable, you can do it like this:

```
$novalue = NULL;
$novalue = null;
```

Assigning values to the other data types requires more detailed explanation.

Assigning text to a variable

PHP calls a block of text a *string*—a reference to the fact that text is usually composed of a string of characters. Strings must be enclosed in quotation marks. You can use either single or double quotation marks, but they must be in matching pairs. For example:

```
$title = 'Adobe Dreamweaver CS5 with PHP';
$author = "David Powers";
```

Because the entire string must be enclosed in quotation marks, you need to be careful when a string in single quotation marks contains any apostrophes. The apostrophe in the following example will cause an error:

```
$movie = 'Wayne's World';
```

PHP sees the apostrophe as matching the opening quotation mark. Everything else up to the semicolon is seen as garbage and prevents the script from running.

One way to get around this is to precede the apostrophe with a backslash—or *escape* it— like this:

```
$movie = 'Wayne\'s World';
```

However, this is ugly, and it becomes difficult to read if you have a long string with several apostrophes or single quotation marks. A more elegant—and readable—solution is to use double quotation marks around the whole string like this:

```
$movie = "Wayne's World";
```

Equally, if you want to use double quotation marks inside a string, the best way is to surround the entire string in single quotation marks like this:

```
$theater = 'I saw "Hamlet" last night.';
```

Sometimes, though, you can't avoid using a backslash to escape a quotation mark:

```
$theater = 'We saw "A Midsummer Night\'s Dream".';
```

However, the previous example is more readable than this:

```
$theater = "We saw \"A Midsummer Night's Dream\".";
```

The issue with single and double quotation marks doesn't end there. When used with ordinary text, it doesn't really matter which you use. But double quotation marks play a special role with variables and escape characters.

Using variables with quotation marks

Variables act as placeholders for values that you don't know in advance. The following examples use hard-coded variables in the same page. But imagine that the values have come from an online form or database.

The files quotes_01.php, quotes_02.php, and quotes_03.php in the lesson03/completed folder all contain the following variable definition:

```
$name = 'David';
```

The PHP command echo displays onscreen a string or the value of a variable that contains a string. The first file, quotes_01.php, uses echo with $name and no quotation marks like this:

```
<p><?php echo $name; ?></p>
```

It outputs the value of $name, as shown in the following screen shot.

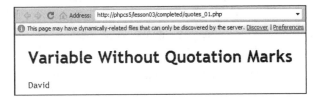

In quotes_02.php, $name is incorporated into a string that is enclosed in single quotation marks like this:

```
<p><?php echo 'Hello, $name.'; ?></p>
```

PHP treats anything enclosed in single quotation marks as literal text. As a result, $name is not treated as a variable but is displayed literally.

What happens, though, if you use double quotation marks? In quotes_03.php, $name is incorporated into the string like this:

```
<p><?php echo "Hello, $name."; ?></p>
```

This time the value of the variable is displayed.

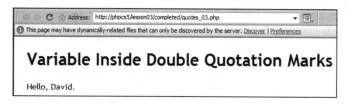

> **TIP:** The basic rule regarding the use of variables in strings is to use double quotation marks when embedding variables in a string.

Using array variables with quotation marks

Unfortunately, there's always an exception to a rule. Array variables, which are described later in this lesson, frequently use quotation marks to identify the array element to which they refer. In quotes_04.php and quotes_05.php, there's an array called $book that contains the name of the author and the title of this book. In quotes_04.php, the array variables are enclosed in the string like this:

```php
<p><?php echo "$book['title'] by $book['author']"; ?></p>
```

Although this fits the existing rules, it stops PHP in its tracks and produces an error that has caused many programmers to bang their heads on the keyboard.

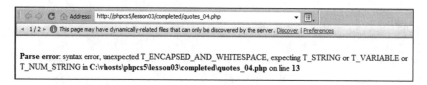

> **NOTE:** PHP error messages and how to interpret them are covered in "Understanding Error Messages" at the end of this lesson.

To embed array variables like this into a string, you need to wrap each variable in a pair of curly braces like this (the code is in quotes_05.php):

```php
<p><?php echo "{$book['title']} by {$book['author']}"; ?></p>
```

This results in the variables being interpreted correctly.

> **TIP:** If you're wondering where the double quotation marks around the title come from, they're defined in the array variable.

Using escape characters in strings

An *escape character* is a character that you want to be treated differently. For example, you've already seen how a backslash escapes an apostrophe or double quotation mark in a string. The only time you need to use an escape character inside single quotation marks is for an apostrophe or single quotation mark. All other escape characters occur only between double quotation marks. Those most commonly used are listed in **Table 3.2**.

Table 3.2 Escape Characters Used in Double-quoted Strings

Escape Sequence	Meaning
\"	Double quotation mark
\n	Newline character
\r	Carriage return
\t	Tab
\\	Backslash
\$	Dollar sign
\{	Opening curly brace
\}	Closing curly brace
\[	Opening square bracket
\]	Closing square bracket

Since newline characters, carriage returns, and tabs are ignored when a browser renders a web page, you might be wondering when you might use them. PHP can be used for many other tasks, not just for web pages. As a simple example, "\r\n" is used frequently in PHP scripts that send emails. You need a carriage return followed by a newline character between the headers of an email message.

Grouping Related Values in Arrays

An *array* is a special type of variable that can store multiple values. An array can contain anything, but arrays are normally used to group related items.

Creating a basic array

You create an array with the `array()` constructor. List the values between the parentheses, and separate them with commas. For example:

```
$friends = array('Tom', 'Dick', 'Harriet');
```

> ● **TIP:** American readers should note that the comma goes outside the quotation marks. The comma separates the values. The quotation marks are an integral part of a string.

The variable `$friends` refers collectively to Tom, Dick, and Harriet, but you also need a way of referring to each value—or *array element*. Each element is identified by its position in the array, which is known as the element's *key* or *index*.

You identify an individual array element by putting its key in square brackets after the variable name. In common with most programming languages, PHP counts the elements of an array from 0. So, Tom is `$friends[0]`, Dick is `$friends[1]`, and Harriet is `$friends[2]`.

To add an element to an array, use an empty pair of square brackets like this:

```
$friends[] = 'Amanda';
```

Amanda is now `$friends[3]`.

These numbers change if you reorder the array. For example, if you sort `$friends` alphabetically, Amanda becomes `$friends[0]`, and Tom becomes `$friends[3]`. Although this might sound confusing, it's no different from what happens when your reorder the `<li>` elements in an HTML ordered list. The only time you normally need to concern yourself with these numbers is when you're looking for an element in a particular position in an array.

An array that uses numbers to keep track of array elements is sometimes called an *indexed array*. Using numbers is sufficient in many cases. However, PHP also allows you to define your own array keys.

Creating an associative array

An array with user-defined keys is known as an *associative array*. You specify the key for each element as a string and assign its value using => (an equals sign followed immediately by a greater-than sign). For example, this is the $book array from the sample files for "Using variables with quotation marks":

```
$book = array('author' => 'David Powers',
              'title'  => '"Adobe Dreamweaver CS5 with PHP"');
```

Each element of the array can be identified by putting the key in quotes between square brackets after the variable name like this:

```
$book['author'] // value is 'David Powers'
$book['title']  // value is '"Adobe Dreamweaver CS5 with PHP"'
```

You can also add new values to the array by creating a new key like this:

```
$book['publisher'] = 'Adobe Press';
```

In all these examples, the values stored in the arrays are strings, but an array can store any type of legitimate value. You can mix different types of values in the same array, and even create an array of arrays—a *multidimensional array*. For example, you could create an array called $books in which each element is an associative array containing the author, title, and publisher of a book. To identify the author of the second book, you use both keys like this: $books[1]['author'].

Arrays play a big role in PHP. You use them a lot when handling the results of a database query. PHP has a large number of functions to manipulate arrays, not only sorting them, but also merging them and extracting values that occur in one array but not another. Also, as you'll see later in this lesson, PHP uses loops to perform repetitive tasks. If you want to perform the same task on a large number of items, it's very easy if they're stored in an array. You just tell PHP to loop through the array, and it performs the same task on each element automatically.

Some of the most useful arrays—the *superglobal* arrays—are built into PHP.

Getting useful information from superglobal arrays

The superglobal arrays are created automatically by PHP. The ones you'll use most often are $_POST and $_GET. As their names suggest, $_POST and $_GET automatically capture values sent by forms submitted using the POST and GET methods respectively. So, if you have a text input field in a form called "phone," its value can be retrieved from $_POST['phone'] or $_GET['phone'], depending on the method used to submit the form.

The following quick exercise demonstrates how $_POST and $_GET work:

1 In the Files panel, double-click post_01.php in lesson03/completed to open it in the Document window. The page contains a form with two text input fields.

2 Examine the form in Code view. The name attributes of the two input fields are first_name and family_name respectively.

3 Launch the page in a browser by pressing F12/Opt+F12.

4 Type your name and family name in the relevant fields, and click Submit.

5 The values you entered should be displayed in post_02.php, as shown in the screen shots on the first page of this lesson.

If you examine the PHP code in post_02.php, you'll see how the values were captured and displayed using the $_POST superglobal array:

```php
<?php echo "{$_POST['first_name']} {$_POST['family_name']}"; ?>
```

The files get_01.php and get_02.php work exactly the same way except that the form uses the GET method, and the values are captured and displayed using the $_GET superglobal array:

```php
<?php echo "{$_GET['first_name']} {$_GET['family_name']}"; ?>
```

Also note that when you use the GET method, the form input data is transmitted as a series of name/value pairs appended to the URL following a question mark. This is known as a *query string*.

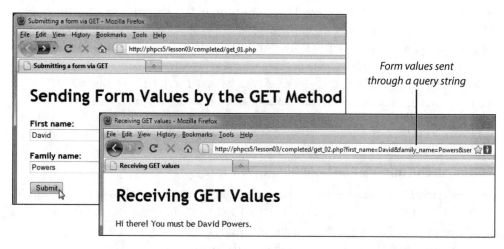

Form values sent through a query string

Deciding Whether to Use GET or POST

The GET method exposes input data as a query string appended to the URL, so you should never use it to submit sensitive data, such as passwords or credit card numbers. Also, Internet Explorer limits to roughly 2,000 characters the amount of data that can be transmitted through the GET method. The POST method, on the other hand, sends the data in the background and can handle a much larger volume. In practice, the default limit on a PHP server is 8 MB, with no individual piece of data exceeding 2 MB, although both limits can be changed by the server administrator.

The advantage of GET is that you can bookmark a URL that has a query string appended to it, making GET ideal for use in search forms. You can also add a query string to the URL in an ordinary link. As you'll see in later lessons, this can be very useful when working with a database. However, in most other cases, you should use the POST method.

Table 3.3 lists all superglobal arrays and provides a description of what they're used for. In addition to $_GET and $_POST, the most useful are $_FILES, $_SESSION, and $_SERVER. You'll work with each of these superglobals in later lessons.

Table 3.3   The PHP Superglobal Arrays

Array	Use
$_GET	Captures values passed through a query string at the end of a URL.
$_POST	Captures input data submitted through the POST method.
$_FILES	Contains files uploaded to the server along with information, such as filename, MIME type, and whether the upload was successful.
$_COOKIE	Gives access to cookies stored on the user's computer.
$_SESSION	Stores persistent variables for use with login systems, shopping carts, and so on. The variables are similar to cookies except that the values are stored on the web server instead of the user's computer.
$_SERVER	Gathers information from the web server about the current script, such as its filename and location. Not all servers support the full range of values.
$GLOBALS	Gives access inside a function to a variable defined outside in the "global scope." Its use is generally frowned upon these days as bad practice and is not used in this book.
$_REQUEST	A shortcut that contains the content of $_GET, $_POST, and $_COOKIE. Unless used with care, it can lead to security problems so is best avoided.
$_ENV	Contains information about the server environment. The range of information depends on the server.

Using Conditions to Make Decisions

The exercise in the preceding section loaded post_02.php in the browser when you submitted the form in post_01.php. Assuming you filled in both fields, it should have displayed your name in the second page. On a website, though, it's unwise to assume that visitors will always do what you want. Some might forget to fill in all fields. Others might deliberately try to fill your form with garbage or even try to hack into your system. You need to be prepared for every situation and use conditional statements to decide what happens.

A conditional statement works on a yes/no or true/false basis. The basic structure is very simple:

```
if (TRUE) {
    // do something
}
```

The condition is an expression placed in parentheses after the keyword if.

Decisions on what is true can be made in the following ways:

- Is something bigger, smaller, or equal to something else?

- Does a variable exist or have a value?

- A variable that has been set explicitly to TRUE or FALSE.

- A value that PHP treats implicitly as TRUE or FALSE.

If the condition equates to TRUE, the code inside the curly braces is executed. If the condition equates to FALSE, the code inside the braces is ignored.

Of course, you often want something else to happen if the condition fails. To specify a default action, you use the keyword else followed by another set of curly braces like this:

```
if (TRUE) {
    // do something
} else {
    // do something else
}
```

You're not limited to just two options. You can set a series of conditions, each of which is evaluated in turn. To set an alternative conditional test, use elseif followed by the condition in parentheses like this:

```
if (condition1) {
    // do something
```

```
} elseif (condition2) {
  // do something else
} else {
  // default action
}
```

✱ **NOTE:** The keyword elseif is normally written as one word, but you can also put a space between else and if.

Using comparisons to make decisions

Conditions based on comparative values use the conditional operators listed in **Table 3.4**. The last four should be familiar from regular math.

Table 3.4	Comparison Operators Used in PHP
Operator	**Meaning**
==	True if both values are equal.
!=	True if the values are not equal
===	True if both values are identical. To be identical, both values must be of the same data type. For example, 2 and '2' are equal, but not identical (the first one is an integer; the second one is a string).
!==	True if the values are not identical.
>	True if the first value is greater than the second value.
>=	True if the first value is greater than or equal to the second value.
<	True if the first value is less than the second value
<=	True if the first value is less than or equal to the second value.

As a trivial example, the following conditional statement displays specific content to a named individual and generic content to everyone else:

```
if ($name == 'David') {
  // show David's stuff
} else {
  // show generic content
}
```

Of course, there are a lot of Davids in this world, so you would need a more robust test in a real application. The key point is to understand that when comparing values, you need to use *two* equals signs, not one.

> **TIP:** Even experienced developers sometimes forget and use a single equals sign in a conditional statement. This always equates to TRUE because the assignment of value succeeds. If you find your conditional statements are producing unexpected results, there's a strong likelihood that you have used one equals sign instead of two.

Many decisions are based on numerical comparisons. A typical scenario in an e-commerce application might look like this:

```
if ($total < 100) {
    $delivery = 5;
} else {
    $delivery = 0;
}
```

Testing for multiple conditions

You can also test for multiple conditions. For example, in the e-commerce application, you might want to set a range of delivery charges. To test whether a value is within a specific range, you need to check that it's greater than the lower limit *and* less than the higher limit. The *logical operators* in **Table 3.5** allow you to combine tests as part of the same condition.

Table 3.5	Logical Operators in PHP
Operator	**Meaning**
&&	Equates to TRUE if both conditions are true. If the first condition is false, the second one is never tested.
||	Equates to TRUE if either condition is true. If the first condition is true, the second one is never tested.
!	Tests whether something is not true.

> **NOTE:** You can use *and* in place of &&, and *or* in place of \|\|. However, to avoid potential problems with rules that govern the order in which conditions are evaluated, it's advisable to stick with && and \|\|.

So, to set a different delivery charge for a total between 50 and 100, you would alter the conditional statement like this:

```
if ($total < 50) {
  $delivery = 5;
} elseif ($total >=50 && $total < 100) {
  $delivery = 3;
} else {
  $delivery = 0;
}
```

When setting a series of conditional statements, make sure they follow a logical order. PHP evaluates each one in sequence. Once it reaches a statement or set of conditions that equates to TRUE, it skips the rest. The order of your conditional statements can improve the efficiency of a script. If possible, test first for the most likely option.

The following exercise demonstrates the use of a conditional statement to determine what is displayed when a form is submitted:

1 Load post_01.php into a browser, and then submit the form without entering anything into either of the text fields. The second page displays, but the greeting looks rather odd. Because the text fields are empty, there's nothing after "You must be."

2 Click in the browser address bar, and press Enter/Return to load post_02.php without resubmitting the form. This time, you'll see the following ugly error messages.

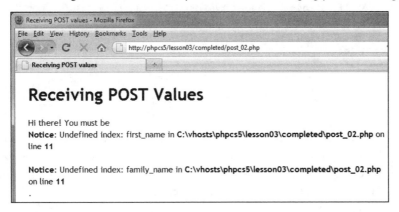

These messages tell you that $_POST['first_name'] and $_POST['family_name'] don't exist.

✳ **NOTE:** If you don't see any error messages, it means display_errors is turned off in your PHP configuration, or that error_reporting has been set to a lower level than the one recommended in Table 2.1 in the preceding lesson.

3 Load post_03.php into a browser. The page contains the same form but submits the data to a different page.

4 Click the Submit button without entering anything in either of the text fields. Instead of the ugly error messages, you should see a custom error message along with a link that takes you back to the form.

5 Click the link to return to post_03.php, and fill in both fields.

6 Click the Submit button. This time you should be greeted by name as in the previous exercise. The link back to the form is no longer displayed.

The PHP code that controls what is displayed in the page looks like this:

```php
<?php
if (empty($_POST['first_name']) || empty($_POST['family_name'])) {
?>
<p>Hey! You didn't fill in all the fields.</p>
<p><a href="post_03.php">Back to the form</a></p>
<?php } else { ?>
<p>Hi there! You must be <?php echo "{$_POST['first_name']}
{$_POST['family_name']}"; ?>.</p>
<?php } ?>
```

The first block of PHP code checks the condition using a function called empty() that checks whether a variable contains a value (functions are covered in the following section). The conditional statement uses ||, so it equates to TRUE if either text field is left empty. To display the error message and link only if *both* fields are empty, replace the || with &&.

Using the logical Not operator

The logical Not operator is an exclamation point (!), which you place directly in front of a value or condition. It converts a TRUE value to FALSE and vice versa.

The preceding exercise used `empty($_POST['first_name'])` to test if `$_POST['first_name']` was empty. If you precede this expression with an exclamation point, it tests the opposite. The following conditional statement tests whether `$_POST['first_name']` is *not* empty—in other words, it has a value:

```
if (!empty($_POST['first_name'])) {
  echo $_POST['first_name'];
}
```

So, if `$_POST['first_name']` is *not* empty, the code inside the curly braces displays the value. If `$_POST['first_name']` is empty, the condition equates to `FALSE`, and nothing happens.

What PHP regards as false

PHP treats the following values as being false or implicitly false:

- The keywords `FALSE` and `NULL` (both case insensitive)
- The number 0 (as an integer, floating point number, or the string `'0'`)
- An empty string (`''` or `""` with no space between the quotation marks)
- An empty array (one with no elements)
- A SimpleXML object created from empty tags

Everything else is considered true.

> **▼ CAUTION!** Unlike JavaScript, PHP treats –1 (minus one) as TRUE. It's also important to note that FALSE and NULL are keywords and should not be wrapped in quotation marks. Adding quotation marks converts them into a nonempty string, which is treated as TRUE.

Using Functions to Perform Tasks

A *function* performs a predefined task. A typical PHP installation has more than 1,500 built-in functions, putting a vast and powerful toolbox at your disposal. Some functions perform relatively simple tasks, such as converting a string to uppercase. Others make light work of complex operations, such as generating a thumbnail image. Most developers use only a small proportion of these functions, but it's useful to know they're available when you need them.

Functions always end with a pair of parentheses. Sometimes the parentheses remain empty, as in the case of the function that displays the details of your PHP configuration, `phpinfo()`.

However, you frequently pass values to a function by inserting them between the parentheses. For example, the preceding exercise used `empty()` to test whether `$_POST['first_name']` and `$_POST['family_name']` contained any values by passing each variable separately to the function like this:

```
empty($_POST['first_name'])
```

This is known as *passing an argument* to the function.

The `empty()` function takes just one argument. Other functions expect more arguments, some of which might be optional. When a function requires more than one argument, they should be separated by commas and *must be in the order that the function expects*. Remembering which arguments to use and in which order can be difficult, even for experienced programmers. Fortunately, Dreamweaver's code hints relieve you of the burden of trying to memorize everything.

✳ **NOTE:** When you pass a value to a function in a script, it's referred to as an "argument." However, in the function definition, it's called a "parameter." The difference is so subtle that most developers use the two words interchangeably. Throughout this book, I normally use "argument."

Some functions alter the value stored in the variable passed to them as an argument. For example, the `sort()` function changes the order of an array.

```
$letters = array('c', 'a', 'b');
sort($letters);
// array is now 'a', 'b', 'c'
```

However, in most cases, you need to capture any changes made by a function, either by reassigning the result of the function to the same variable or by assigning it to a new one. This allows you to preserve the original value if you need it for any reason.

The exercise files in lesson03/completed demonstrate how this works:

1 Open function_01.php in the Document window.

2 Switch to Code view. The page contains a mixture of HTML and PHP. The HTML is simply there to explain what's going on. If you concentrate on the PHP, it looks like this:

```
$name = 'David';
echo $name;
echo strtoupper($name);
echo $name;
```

The third line uses a function called `strtoupper()`. In spite of its outlandish name, it makes sense once you realize that it converts a *string* to *upper*case.

3 Switch to Design view, and click the Live View button. You should see that the value of $name has been converted to uppercase by strtoupper(), but the original value remains unchanged.

This type of behavior can be very useful in a situation where you need to compare two strings in a case-insensitive manner. If you convert both values temporarily to uppercase, you can compare them without losing their original spelling.

4 Open function_02.php and test it in Live View. This contains a similar mixture of HTML and PHP. The PHP code looks like this:

```php
$name = 'David';
$name_upper = strtoupper($name);
echo $name_upper;
echo $name;
$name = strtoupper($name);
echo $name_upper;
echo $name;
```

In this case, the value of strtoupper($name) is assigned to a new variable, $name_upper. When $name_upper and $name are displayed the first time, it should come as no surprise that the $name_upper is all uppercase, but $name remains unchanged. However, in the fifth line, strtoupper($name) is reassigned to $name. So, when $name_upper and $name are redisplayed, they are both in uppercase.

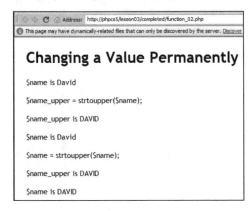

Reading the PHP documentation for a function

So, how do you know what arguments a function expects and whether you need to capture the result in a variable? RTFM. Depending on whom you ask and what mood they're in, this stands for "read the fine manual," "read the friendly manual," or something not quite so polite.

The PHP manual is both fine and friendly. Dreamweaver CS5 makes it even more so by putting most of it at your fingertips. By pressing Ctrl+spacebar in a PHP code block, you activate code hints. As you start typing, Dreamweaver narrows down the candidates. By the time you have typed **strtou**, you are presented with the code hint for `strtoupper()` and its page from the PHP documentation.

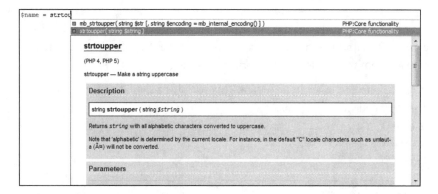

Immediately beneath the name of the function are the versions that support it with a brief explanation of what the function does. The function name at the top left is also a direct link to the same page in the online documentation. The rest of the page is divided into the following sections:

- **Description.** This not only describes the function in more detail, but also shows you the function signature.

  The *function signature* is a formal way of describing how to use a function, and learning how to read it will make your life a lot easier. You read it in conjunction with the next two sections in the documentation.

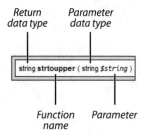

- **Parameters.** This section describes the parameters (arguments) that the function expects, if any (some functions don't take arguments). In the function signature, each parameter is displayed in italics and prefixed with a dollar sign. Most parameters have names that act as a clue. For example, `strtoupper()` expects a string, so the parameter is called *$string*. Functions that search for something usually have parameters called *$needle* and *$haystack*.

  In the case of `strtoupper()`, it's obvious that the data type of *$string* should be a string, but that's not always the case. So, the name of each parameter is preceded by the data type that it should be. The data type is always one of those listed in Table 3.1. The documentation abbreviates Boolean and integer as "bool" and "int" respectively. When more than one data type is acceptable, it's shown as "mixed."

  Some functions take optional arguments, which are shown in the signature in square brackets. Optional arguments always come at the end of the signature.

  If the function permanently changes the value of a variable passed to it—as in the case of `sort()`—the parameter name in the signature is prefixed by an ampersand like this: *&$array*.

- **Return Values.** Functions normally *return* a value. In the case of `strtoupper()`, the return value is an uppercase string. On the other hand, `sort()` returns a Boolean telling you whether the sort was successful. The return value is shown in the function signature as a data type to the left of the function name. Some functions don't return a value. In this case, the return data type is shown as "void."

- **Examples.** This provides one or more concrete examples of how to use the function and the type of output to expect. This is the really useful section of the documentation.

The online version of the documentation is organized according to categories. Two of the most useful are string functions and array functions. To access the documentation quickly from Dreamweaver, click the link at the top of the page that is displayed with the code hints to go to the same page in the online documentation. Click the link for related functions in the navigation menu on the left of the page to view a useful page with a one-line description of each function.

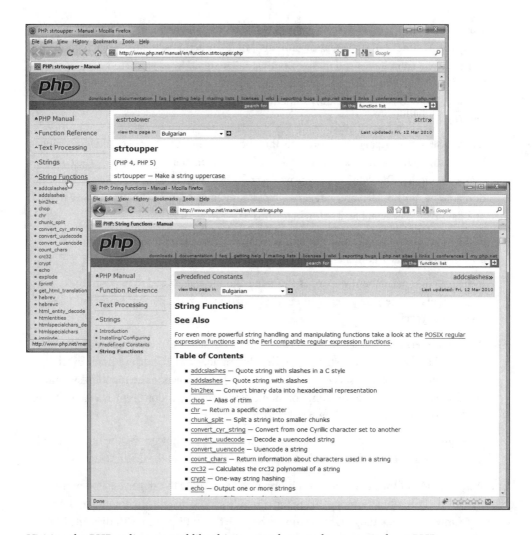

Visiting the PHP online manual like this is a good way to learn more about PHP.

Creating your own functions

With so many functions in core PHP, the idea of creating your own might sound odd. But this is what makes languages like PHP so powerful. Building your own functions is a way of combining existing functions to fit your needs. If you have a routine that needs to be repeated several times, a custom function saves time and effort. It also helps reduce mistakes. Once you have created and tested a function, you can use it repeatedly and be confident that it will always work the same way—and if there's an error, you need to correct it in only one place.

You define a function with the `function` keyword, followed by the name of the function, and a pair of parentheses. Any arguments go between the parentheses as a comma-separated list, and the code that you want the function to execute goes between a pair of curly braces.

You can name a function anything you like, following the same rules as a variable. It should contain only alphanumeric characters and the underscore, and shouldn't begin with a number. You also must avoid using the name of an existing function.

> **TIP:** If you choose a name that is already in use, PHP generates an error message telling you that you cannot redeclare the function of that name.

You saw how `strtoupper()` converts a string to uppercase. Another function called `strrev()` reverses the order of a string. Let's say that for some mad reason you need to reverse text and display it in uppercase. The PHP code in function_03.php passes a variable containing the title of this book first to `strrev()` and then to `strtoupper()` like this:

```
$title = 'Adobe Dreamweaver CS5 with PHP';
echo $title;
$title = strrev($title);
echo $title;
$title = strtoupper($title);
echo $title;
```

This does the job as expected.

If you need to do this repeatedly, you can modularize your script as a function like this:

```
function upBack($text) {
  $text = strrev($text);
  echo strtoupper($text);
}
```

Then all that's necessary is to pass the value to upBack() as an argument like this:

```
upBack($title);
```

✱ **NOTE:** This example is for illustrative purposes only. Using echo in a function is generally considered bad practice. You should normally return a value from a function as described next.

You can find the code in function_04.php. If you examine the page in Code view, you'll see that the function definition is at the bottom of the page, way after the function has already been used. As long as the function definition is in the same page, it doesn't matter where you define it, so it's often convenient to keep all function definitions together rather than mix them in with the rest of the script.

This function automatically displays the converted string, so the original value is preserved. However, to assign the result to a variable, you need to use the return keyword like this:

```
function upBack2($text) {
  $text = strrev($text);
  return strtoupper($text);
}
```

The code in function_05.php reassigns the value of upBack2($title) to the $title variable like this:

```
$title = upBack2($title);
```

As a result, $title now contains the value returned from upBack2(), permanently changing the string.

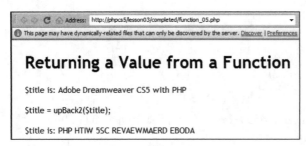

Understanding Variable Scope

Functions act rather like a black box. What happens inside the box is invisible to everything outside. Normally, when you pass a variable as an argument to a function, only the value is passed to the function. In the case of upBack2(), the value is passed as an argument to $text. Once the function completes its task, $text ceases to exist, and it is created again only if the function is reused.

The *scope* of a variable—in other words, where it can be used—depends entirely on where the variable is defined. A variable defined in a function or as one of its parameters is limited in scope to that function. It cannot be seen outside the function. Equally, a function has no knowledge of or influence over variables outside. In the example in function_06.php, there's no cause for confusion, because the external and internal variables have different names.

However, what happens if both variables have the same name? In function_07.php, $title has been changed to $text, and it's passed as an argument to upBack2(). If you test the page, you'll see the value of $text that was declared outside the function remains unchanged.

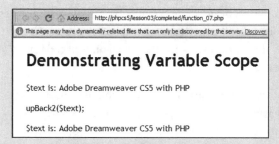

In a small script, it's easy to keep track of variable names. But as your project grows, you could easily end up reusing the same name for a variable that's used inside a function. By keeping the internal working of functions separate from everything else, variable scope reduces the need to worry about names clashing.

This change in the value of $title comes about only through capturing the return value. Forgetting to capture the return value of a function is a common beginner's mistake. The code in function_06.php shows what happens when the return value of upBack2($title) is not assigned to a variable.

As soon as a function encounters the return keyword, it processes the rest of the line and returns the value. Any other code inside the function is ignored.

Using Objects and Resources

The name "object" comes from *object-oriented programming* (OOP), a practice common in most modern programming languages. As projects get bigger, code becomes more complex. Mistakes become not only more likely, but also more difficult to detect. OOP tackles this problem by breaking down complex tasks into simple units—the idea being that small units of code are easy to maintain. Once a unit has been tested, you know it will produce reliable results.

OOP also promotes the reuse of code, so you're not constantly reinventing the wheel. The code that defines an object's features is called a *class*, which can be regarded as a blueprint for making objects. Some classes are built into core PHP, but you can also create your own, or use a third-party class library, such as the Zend Framework. What makes OOP attractive and powerful is that most classes can be extended, and the new class inherits all the features of its parent. As a result, objects are becoming an increasingly important part of PHP.

PHP is not an object-oriented language, but it does have strong support for OOP. Since the release of PHP 5 in 2004, many classes have been built into the language, and the Zend Framework that you will use later in this book is written entirely in OOP. At this stage, all you really need to know about objects is what they are and how to use them.

In practical terms, an object is a variable capable of storing multiple values—called *properties*—in the same way as an associative array. An object also has access to functions—called *methods*—that are directly associated with it.

Creating an object

You create—or *instantiate*—an object in a similar way to assigning the return value of a function to a variable. The function that creates an object is known as a class *constructor*. Like a function, the constructor may take a number of arguments. The difference is that the constructor is preceded by the keyword new.

A copy of the example from Lesson 1, time.php, is in lesson03/completed. It uses two core PHP classes, DateTime and DateTimeZone. The code begins like this:

```
$now = new DateTime();
```

This creates a DateTime object called $now. As the class name suggests, the object represents the current date and time. Closely related to the DateTime class is another one called DateTimeZone. To create a DateTimeZone object, you pass the constructor a string identifying the time zone like this:

```
$ldn = new DateTimeZone('Europe/London');
```

That creates a DateTimeZone object for the part of the world where I live. To create another one for the West coast of the United States, you can use this:

```
$westCoast = new DateTimeZone('America/Los_Angeles');
```

❋ **NOTE:** The PHP documentation lists all the valid time zones at http://docs.php.net/manual/en/timezones.php.

What's great about these two classes is that they are fully aware of daylight saving time, and they automatically adjust the time regardless of where your server is located. To set the time zone for a DateTime object, you use the DateTime class's setTimezone() method, and pass it a DateTimeZone object as its argument. The -> operator (a hyphen followed by a greater-than sign) gives you access to the methods and properties of an object.

So, you access the setTimezone() method like this:

```
$now->setTimezone($ldn);
```

The $now object is now set to UK time.

Another method of the DateTime class is format(). As its name suggests, it formats the date and/or time. Unfortunately, it takes as an argument an arcane set of modifiers, which even experienced users find impossible to remember (thank goodness the PHP documentation is built into Dreamweaver CS5).

You display the time using the 12-hour clock like this:

```
echo $now->format('g.i a');
```

To change the time zone to the West coast of the United States, you can pass an object to the setTimezone() method like this:

```
$now->setTimezone($westCoast);
```

Alternatively, you can create the DateTimeZone object directly as the argument to the setTimezone() method like this:

```
$now->setTimezone(new DateTimeZone('America/Los_Angeles'));
```

You can see how the time zone is changed by testing time.php in Live View or a browser.

> **NOTE:** The preceding screen shot, like the one in Lesson 1, was taken when the United States had already switched to daylight saving time but the UK had not, which explains why the time difference is seven hours rather than the normal eight.

The DateTime class doesn't have properties, but you access an object's properties in exactly the same way with the -> operator:

```
$someObject->someProperty
```

Using resources

A resource is a reference to something outside PHP, for example, a database connection or a file that you want to read or write to. In some cases, the result of a database query is also a resource.

You create a resource by assigning the result of a function to a variable. Once created, the resource is required as an argument to other functions that access the resource. For example, the fopen() function opens a file for writing like this:

```
$file = fopen('somefile.txt', 'w');
```

Assuming that the text you want to write to the file is contained in $contents, you pass both the resource and the text to the fwrite() function as arguments:

```
fwrite($file, $contents);
```

Finally, close the file by passing the resource to the fclose() function like this:

```
fclose($file);
```

You can't do anything directly with a resource on its own. But it provides an essential link to the file, database, or other resource that you're dealing with.

Using Operators for Calculations and Joining Strings

PHP is often used for e-commerce and other applications, such as mortgage calculators. A lot of the hard number crunching can be done with mathematical functions. There are nearly 50 of them in the core distribution of PHP, and you might have access to even more, depending on your configuration (for details, see http://docs.php.net/manual/en/refs.math.php).

Basic calculations use the arithmetic operators listed in **Table 3.6**.

Operator	Meaning	Example	Result
+	Addition	2 + 2	4
-	Subtraction (use the hyphen)	5 - 2	3
*	Multiplication	5 * 6	30
/	Division	5 / 2	2.5
%	Modulo division	5 % 2	1
++	Increment by 1	See text	
--	Decrease by 1	See text	

Table 3.6 PHP Arithmetic Operators

Modulo division finds the remainder of the division of one number by another. This can be very useful for working out whether a number is odd or even, because dividing by 2 always produces 1 or 0.

The operators that increase and decrease a value by 1 are used mainly in loops (see "Automating Repetitive Tasks" later in this lesson). They work in different ways, depending on where you put the two plus or minus signs.

When the operator comes after the variable, 1 is added or subtracted from the value *after* any other calculation has been performed. For example:

```
$i = 1;
$x = $i++ * 2; // $x is 2
$y = $i++ * 2; // $y is 4
```

In the first line, $i is assigned the value 1.

In the second line, $i is multiplied by 2, producing 2. After the calculation, $i is incremented by 1. Consequently, in the third line, $i is 2 when it is multiplied by 2, producing 4. Again, $i is incremented by 1 after the calculation, so if it's used later in the script, its value will be 3.

The opposite happens if the operator is placed before the variable like this:

```
$i = 1;
$x = ++$i * 2; // $x is 4
$y = ++$i * 2; // $y is 6
```

In this case, the value of $i is incremented by 1 *before* the calculation. So, in the second line, $i becomes 2 before being multiplied by 2, and in the third line, it's 3 before being multiplied.

Calculations involving more than two values are performed using the normal rules of arithmetical precedence. Multiplication and division are performed first, followed by addition and subtraction. For example:

```
$x = 10 + 2 * 5;
```

This results in $x being 20, not 60, because 2 is multiplied by 5 before being added to 10. If you want the addition to be performed first, you need to enclose that part of the calculation in parentheses like this:

```
$x = (10 + 2) * 5;
```

This results in $x being 60.

❋ NOTE: I have used numbers in most of these examples to make them easier to read. In a PHP script, they would often be replaced by variables. Yes, all those years of algebra in school are about to come flooding back!

It goes without saying that the arithmetic operators work with integers and floats. What might come as a surprise is that they also work with strings.

Using strings in calculations

As mentioned earlier, PHP is a weakly typed language, so it doesn't insist—like some other languages—on you specifying the type of data a variable contains. So, if your script uses a string in an arithmetical calculation, PHP obligingly converts it to a number, and you usually get the result you expected.

This flexible approach makes a lot of sense, because online forms submit all data as text—that is, even numbers submitted from a form are treated as strings. So, the following calculations work without problem:

```
$x = '2' * '2';      // $x is 4
$y = '3.4' * '2.6';  // $y is 8.84
```

Even though the values in these calculations are strings, the results are numbers: $x is an integer, and $y is a float. Within a PHP script, you don't really need to worry about the data type, but it might be important if you are transferring the PHP output to another application that requires a particular data type.

> **TIP:** For details of how to convert from one data type to another, see http://docs.php.net/manual/en/language.types.type-juggling.php.

If you have experience with JavaScript, the result of the following calculation might come as a surprise:

```
$addition = '2' + '2';
```

- In JavaScript, this produces 22, because the plus sign (+) is used not only for addition, but also to join two strings together.
- In PHP, the result is 4, because the plus sign is used only for addition.

You can see the different results in strings_01.php, where both results are calculated dynamically.

I'll explain in a moment how you join strings together in PHP, but there's one more detail you need to know about using strings in calculations. The file strings_02.php contains the following calculation:

```
$mayhem_or_harmony = '2 dogs' + '2 cats';
```

Again, PHP does its best to perform the calculation. If you test strings_02.php, you'll see the result is 4, and the `gettype()` function reveals that it's treated as an integer.

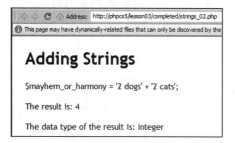

If you're familiar with JavaScript, what's happening here is similar to using `parseInt()` or `parseFloat()` to extract a number at the beginning of a string. Unlike JavaScript, PHP does the conversion automatically.

However, the number must be at the beginning of the string. If anything else precedes the number, PHP cannot extract it and silently converts the value to 0. And just in case you were wondering, `'two' + 'two'` is also 0.

Joining strings

As you have just discovered, PHP does not use the plus sign to join strings. Instead, it uses a period (.) or dot. Because of its size, it can be easy to miss in code, so it's a good idea to put a space on either side to make it easier to see. However, adding space around the period—or *concatenation operator*, to use its correct name—doesn't add any space to the resulting string.

> ✳ **NOTE:** Concatenation, a term frequently used in computer contexts, means linking together in a chain or series.

The code in strings_03.php looks like this:

```
$first_name = 'David';
$family_name = 'Powers';
$full_name = $first_name . $family_name;
echo $full_name;
```

Because the two strings are simply joined together, `$full_name` contains no space between my first and family names.

If you want space between concatenated strings, you need to add it. One way is to insert a space as a string like this:

```
$full_name = $first_name . ' ' . $family_name;
```

The alternative—and more convenient—solution is to enclose the variables in a pair of double quotation marks, and leave a space between them like this:

```
$full_name = "$first_name $family_name";
```

However, be careful when using array elements inside double quotation marks. As explained earlier in this lesson, you need to wrap array variables in a pair of curly braces (see "Using array variables with quotation marks").

Reassigning a result to the same variable

Very often, you need to perform a calculation and assign the result to the original variable, or you want to add more text at the end of a string. For example, if you want to double the number stored in a variable, you can do it like this:

```
$number = $number * 2;
```

This is a perfectly correct way of doing it. However, because reassigning the result of a calculation to the same variable is such a frequent requirement, you can use a shortcut by combining the two operators like this:

```
$number *= 2;
```

This does exactly the same as the preceding code: it multiplies $number by 2 and assigns the result back to $number.

Table 3.7 lists the combined operators and provides their meaning.

Operator	Example	Equivalent to
	Table 3.7 Combined Assignment Operators	
+=	$x += 2;	$x = $x + 2;
-=	$x -= 2;	$x = $x - 2;
*=	$x *= 2;	$x = $x * 2;
/=	$x /= 2;	$x = $x / 2;
%=	$x %= 2;	$x = $x % 2;
.=	$text .= ' more text';	$text = $text . ' more text';

Automating Repetitive Tasks

Most of us hate doing tedious, repetitive work. Fortunately, computers don't get bored—with the exception, perhaps, of Marvin, the paranoid android. That's a good thing, because dynamic websites need to do a lot of recurring tasks, such as searching through arrays to find the right element and displaying multiple results of a database search.

Loops are the answer to repetitive tasks. PHP uses four different loop structures:

- while
- do. . . while
- for
- foreach

They all repeat the same task until a particular condition is met. The reason for the different structures lies in how you want to use the loop.

Using a while loop

The `while` loop is the simplest. It looks like this:

```
while (condition is TRUE) {
  // do something
}
```

Any PHP code between the curly braces is repeated until the condition equates to `FALSE`. The code in loops_01.php demonstrates a simple `while` loop that displays the numbers 1–10 by using the increment operator like this:

```
$i = 1;
while ($i <= 10) {
  echo $i++ . '<br />';
}
```

CAUTION! The danger is forgetting to set a condition that will eventually be FALSE. This creates an infinite loop. It's all too easy to do. When writing this lesson, I forgot to increment $i inside the loop, so $i never reached 10, bringing my browser to a grinding halt until I closed it. Don't try it unless you enjoy looking at a blank screen.

Using a do. . . while loop

In a `do. . . while` loop, the condition comes at the end of the loop like this:

```
do {
  // do something
} while (condition is TRUE);
```

The effect is to ensure that the code inside the curly braces is executed at least once. The code in loops_02.php looks like this:

```
$i = 1000;
do {
  echo $i++ . '<br />';
} while ($i <= 10);
```

Since `$i` is 1000, the condition inside the parentheses will never be `TRUE`. So, the loop displays 1000 and immediately comes to an end.

The Dreamweaver server behaviors use this type of loop to display results from a database because Dreamweaver automatically retrieves the first row of the result ready for display. The code that retrieves subsequent rows is used as the condition, halting the loop when there are no more rows. If a `while` loop were used instead, the first row wouldn't be displayed.

Using a for loop

The `for` loop is slightly more complex, but it has the advantage of being almost impossible to create an infinite loop, because you create a counter, condition, and counter increment at the same time.

The code in loops_03.php displays the numbers 1–10 like this:

```
for ($i = 1; $i <= 10; $i++) {
  echo $i . '<br />';
}
```

Inside the parentheses, three statements separated by semicolons control how the loop operates:

- The first statement is executed before the loop begins. In this case, it initializes a counter variable.

- The second statement sets the condition that determines how long the loop should continue running.

- The final statement is executed at the end of each iteration of the loop. Here, it increases the counter by one.

In this example, the counter is initialized at 1. But it's more common to start at 0 because arrays are counted from 0, so you can use the size of the array as the condition. Although the counter is normally incremented by 1 in a `for` loop, you can use a different increment, such as `$i += 10`, or go in reverse order by starting the counter at a high number and decreasing it each time the loop runs. You can construct more complex `for` loops, but this is the most typical implementation.

> **TIP:** All these examples use `$i` as the counter variable. There's nothing magical about `$i`. It's a convention that dates back to the days when computer memory was very limited. If `$i` is already in use, most developers use `$j` and `$k` for subsequent counters.

Using a foreach loop

This final loop structure is used only with arrays and objects. The way you use it is by assigning each element to a temporary variable with the keyword *as*.

The code in loops_04.php shows how this works.

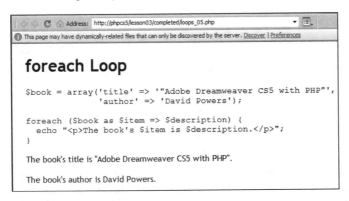

The temporary variable exists only inside the foreach loop and represents the current element each time the loop runs.

When dealing with associative arrays, the foreach loop uses the => operator to create separate temporary variables for the array keys and values like this:

```
foreach ($array_name as $key => $value) {
  // do something
}
```

The following example is in loops_05.php.

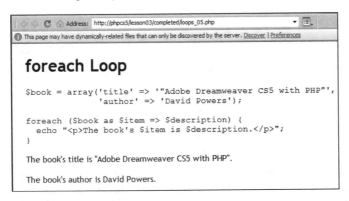

> ▼ **CAUTION!** Do not put a space between "for" and "each" in foreach. It must be written as a single word.

Breaking out of a loop

Sometimes, you might want to end the loop when a condition is matched, for example, when you find a particular value. To so do, you use the keyword break.

The code in loops_06.php is an adaptation of the while loop used earlier:

```
$i = 1;
while ($i <= 10) {
  echo $i++ . '<br />';
  if ($i == 5) {
    break;
  }
}
```

It displays only the numbers 1–4, because the loop is broken as soon as $i hits 5.

> **TIP:** If you're wondering why it doesn't display 5, remember that the value is increased by 1 after the current operation when the increment operator is placed after the variable. So, the script displays 4 and then increments $i to 5. The break keyword immediately stops the loop. So, 5 is never displayed.

However, you might simply want to skip a particular iteration of the loop rather than stop it altogether. In this case, the keyword to use is continue.

The code in loops_07.php looks like this:

```
$i = 1;
while ($i <= 10) {
  if ($i == 5) {
    $i++;
    continue;
  }
  echo $i++ . '<br />';
}
```

This displays the numbers 1–4 and 6–10. When the script encounters continue, it stops whatever it was doing and goes back to the top of the loop. You need to use continue before any code that you want to skip, so there's no point putting it at the end of the loop. You also need to ensure that any counter is incremented before using continue. If the counter wasn't incremented inside the conditional statement, $i would remain 5, sending it into an infinite loop.

Including External Files

The ability to include the contents of one file inside another is one of the biggest time-savers in PHP. You can store HTML or PHP elements that are used on multiple pages in external files, and any changes to an external file are automatically reflected in the pages that include them. The contents of the files are merged on the server, so are often referred to as *server-side includes* (SSI). However, in PHP, they're usually called includes or include files.

You can use the following commands to include one file inside another:

- `include`
- `include_once`
- `require`
- `require_once`

Why do you need four ways to do the same thing?

When you use `include`, the script tries to keep running even if the external file is missing. But when you use `require`, the script immediately stops if it can't find the external script. So, `require` is used in the sense of "mandatory."

The other two, `include_once` and `require_once`, include the external script only once. In large projects, there's a danger that several files will try to include the definition of a function or class. Attempting to do this more than once triggers a fatal error, so these commands prevent this from happening. When your include file contains a function or class definition, always use `include_once` or `require_once`. For anything else, `include` or `require` is fine.

To include an external file, use one of these commands followed by a string containing the *relative path* to the file. The string can optionally be enclosed in parentheses. So, both the following are valid:

```
include('../test_includes/header_02.html');
include '../test_includes/header_02.html';
```

Includes are so useful that it's important to understand how to use them correctly. The exercises in the following sections show how to avoid common pitfalls.

Including HTML files

This exercise shows how—and how not—to include an external HTML file as a PHP include. The external file contains a banner image, such as you might put at the top of every page in a website.

1 Open lesson03/start/includes_start.php in the Document window. The page contains some dummy text and has been given some basic styling with CSS. At the moment, it doesn't contain any PHP code, but by the end of these exercises, you will have included an HTML header <div> and some PHP code to update the copyright notice at the bottom of the page.

2 Switch to Split view, and locate the following code (around lines 9–11):

```
<body>
<div id="wrapper">
  <h1>Including HTML into a Page</h1>
```

3 Insert a blank line between the <div> tag and the opening <h1> tag, and type **<?php include** followed by an opening parenthesis and quotation mark:

```
<div id="wrapper">
<?php include('
  <h1>Including HTML into a Page</h1>
```

Don't worry about any warnings about syntax errors. They will disappear once you have finished the next steps.

4 With your insertion point to the right of the quotation mark, right-click, and choose Code Hint Tools > URL Browser. This brings up a small Browse icon.

5 Click the Browse icon to open the Select File dialog box, and browse to lesson03/test_includes/header_01.html.

6 By default, Dreamweaver uses links relative to the document. If you are using the default setting, select the file, and click OK (Choose on a Mac).

If your site uses links relative to the site root, set the "Relative to" menu in the Select File dialog box to Document. Then click OK (Choose).

7 Dreamweaver should have inserted the correct path to header_01.html next to the opening quotation mark. Complete the include command by typing a closing quotation mark and parenthesis followed by a semicolon and a closing PHP tag. The code in your page should now look like this:

```
<div id="wrapper">
<?php include('../test_includes/header_01.html'); ?>
  <h1>Including HTML into a Page</h1>
```

If necessary, compare your code with lesson03/completed/includes_01.php.

8 Save the page, and click in Design view. A banner image has been included, but the page's background color has changed. There's some stray text at the top and a closing </head> tag highlighted in yellow. Also, all the original text has disappeared, as shown in the following screen shot.

★ **NOTE:** If the banner image doesn't appear, choose Edit > Preferences (Dreamweaver > Preferences on a Mac), and click Invisible Elements in the Category list on the left side of the panel. Make sure that the "Show contents of included file" checkbox is selected.

9 Press F12/Opt+F12 to preview the page in a browser. In all probability, the page should display perfectly with a banner image at the top and the dummy text where you would expect it to be.

★ **NOTE:** Browsers are constantly evolving, so don't worry if the page doesn't display perfectly. There's an error in the way header_01.html has been included. Browsers tend to be forgiving of even the worst mistakes, but future browsers might not be as generous.

10 Return to Dreamweaver, and click header_01.html in the Related Files toolbar to see what's causing the problem. As the following screen shot shows, the file that has been included is a complete HTML document with its own DOCTYPE declaration, <html>, <head>, and <body> tags.

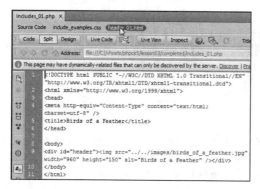

This is perhaps the most common mistake made with includes. An include file should contain *only* the code that you want to add to the other file. Nothing more.

Many people remain unaware of this problem, because browsers usually display the page correctly. In fact, older versions of Dreamweaver used to ignore it, but Design view now helps you by signaling something is wrong.

Apart from making it impossible to see your page correctly in Dreamweaver's Design view, using a full HTML document as an include file usually prevents JavaScript from working correctly. So, it's important to ensure that your HTML includes don't contain a duplicate DOCTYPE declaration and extra <html>, <head>, and <body> tags.

11 Change the path in the include command to point to header_02.html (this version is in completed/includes_02.php):

```
<?php include('../test_includes/header_02.html'); ?>
```

12 Save the page, and click in Design view to refresh its contents. The page should now look similar to the way it did in a browser.

13 Click header_02.html in the Related Files toolbar to examine its contents. You should see that it contains only the HTML code for the header <div>.

14 Change the path in the include command to use a link relative to the site root like this (this version is in completed/includes_03.php):

```
<?php include('/test_includes/header_02.html'); ?>
```

When you save the page and refresh Design view, it should look the same.

15 Click the Live View button or preview the page in a browser. Instead of the banner image, you should see a couple of ugly error messages telling you that there is "no such file or directory."

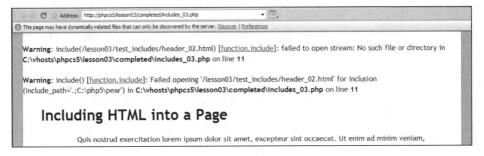

Although Dreamweaver is capable of recognizing a path relative to the site root in Design view, the PHP engine expects a path relative to the current document. There are other ways to specify the path to an include file, but this is the most convenient.

16 Change the path back to the way it was in step 11 (relative to the current document), so it's ready to be used in the next exercise.

Including PHP scripts

Although including HTML fragments in your pages is very useful, using includes for PHP scripts avoids repeating the same code every time you want to use a function or class. This exercise shows how to avoid common pitfalls with including PHP scripts. Continue working with the file from the preceding exercise. Alternatively, use lesson03/completed/includes_03.php.

1 In Split view, scroll to the copyright notice at the bottom. It looks like this:

```
<p>&copy; 2009 Birds of a Feather</p>
```

The problem is that it's out of date. Rather than manually updating the year, it's a good idea to do it with PHP.

2 Simply use the following code, which is in lesson03/test_includes/year_01.inc.php:

```
if (date('Y') > 2009) {
  echo '&ndash;' . date('y');
}
```

This uses the PHP date() function to get the current year in a 4-digit format and tests whether the result is greater than 2009. If it is, it displays an en dash followed by the current year in a 2-digit format.

✱ **NOTE:** This is an example of the importance of case sensitivity in PHP scripts. The argument passed to date() in the first line is an uppercase Y, which produces the year as four digits. In the second line, it's lowercase, which produces only the final two digits.

3 Include year_01.inc.php immediately after "2009" in the copyright notice, using the same technique as steps 3–7 in the preceding exercise.

Your code should now look like this (it's also in includes_04.php):

```
<p>&copy; 2009<?php include('../test_includes/year_01.inc.php'); ?>
Birds of a Feather</p>
```

4 Save the page, and click in Design view to refresh it.

If necessary, scroll down in Design view to see the copyright notice. The code has been included all right, but it's raw PHP code!

> © 2009if (date('Y') > 2009) { echo '-' . date('y'); } Birds of a Feather

5 Click year_01.inc.php in the Related Files toolbar to examine the include file. It contains the code listed in step 2, but it's not enclosed in PHP tags.

Of course, it's a deliberate mistake. But the include command is surrounded by PHP tags, so it's not unreasonable to assume that the include file will also be treated as PHP. As you can see, that doesn't happen. The PHP engine automatically switches to HTML mode when it encounters an include command, and it doesn't return to PHP until it encounters an opening PHP tag or it returns to the original page.

6 Add PHP tags around the code in year_01.inc.php like this:

```
<?php
if (date('Y') > 2009) {
  echo '&ndash;' . date('y');
}
?>
```

This code is also in test_includes/year_02.inc.php, which is included in completed/includes_05.php.

7 Save the include file, and refresh Design view. The PHP code is now replaced by a gold shield that indicates there's a PHP script at that point.

✱ **NOTE:** If you can't see the gold shield, choose Edit > Preferences (Dreamweaver > Preferences on a Mac), select the Invisible Elements category, and check that the Scripts checkbox is selected. Also, choose View > Visual Aids, and make sure Invisible Elements is selected.

8 Click Live View. The gold shield should be replaced by an en dash and the last two digits of the current year.

© 2009📄 Birds of a Feather ⟶ © 2009-10 Birds of a Feather

9 Turn off Live View, and open completed/includes_06.php in the Document window. For the last few steps of this exercise, I suggest you just look at the code rather than typing it out yourself.

At the bottom of the page, I have converted the code that displays the current year into a function like this:

```
<p>&copy; 2009<?php addYear(); ?> Birds of a Feather</p>
</div>
</body>
</html>
<?php
function addYear() {
  if (date('Y') > 2009) {
    echo '&ndash;' . date('y');
  }
}
?>
```

10 Test the page in Live View. It should display the current year as before.

11 Open completed/includes_07.php. This is the same as the previous page, but the function definition has been put in an include file:

```
<p>&copy; 2009<?php addYear(); ?> Birds of a Feather</p>
</div>
</body>
</html>
<?php include('../test_includes/year_03.inc.php'); ?>
```

12 Test the page in Live View. PHP throws a fatal error, reporting that addYear() is an undefined function.

> © 2009
> **Fatal error:** Call to undefined function addYear() in
> C:\vhosts\phpcs5\lesson03\completed\includes_07.php on line 20

The function has been defined, but it's in an external file. When a function is defined in the same page, it doesn't matter where you put it. But when the definition is in an external file, it must be included *before* the function is used.

13 Test completed/includes_08.php. The definition of *addYear()* is included above the DOCTYPE declaration. This time everything should work perfectly.

> **✱ NOTE:** In a static web page, nothing should come before the DOCTYPE declaration, because it switches browsers into quirks mode, preventing CSS styles from being rendered correctly. However, there is no problem putting a PHP code block above the DOCTYPE declaration— as long as it doesn't send any output to the browser. Although the *addYear()* function uses echo, nothing is sent to the browser until the function is used in the copyright notice.

Understanding Error Messages

In the early stages of working with PHP, you will become depressingly familiar with error messages. Understanding what the messages mean will speed up your learning process and make life a little less stressful.

PHP error messages consist of three parts:

- The type of error
- What went wrong
- Where it went wrong

Straightforward though that sounds, PHP error messages can be rather cryptic. The type of error and where it occurred are often the most useful.

The main types of errors are

- **Parse error.** This is a mistake in your code—usually a missing semicolon, a missing curly brace at the end of a loop or conditional statement, or mismatched quotation marks. Nothing will be displayed onscreen (apart from the error message) until you sort it out.

- **Fatal error.** This is usually caused by attempting to use a function or class that hasn't been defined. Everything up to that point is displayed, but the script stops dead when it reaches a fatal error.

- **Warning.** This is a serious error but not enough to prevent PHP from trying to display the page. One of the most common causes is a missing include file.

- **Deprecated.** This is a friendly warning from PHP that the code you are using will not work in the next major release of PHP. It might work now, but you had better start thinking about replacing it.

- **Notice.** This usually warns you that you're accessing a variable that hasn't been defined. It won't stop your application from working, but could be an important signal alerting you to a potential security risk.

Parse error messages are generally the most difficult to understand because they report something "unexpected" on a particular line. Most beginners search frantically for the problem on that line—usually in vain. When PHP tells you something was unexpected, it means something is missing *before* that point. Imagine you're driving on a road and the safety barrier is missing. You drive over the edge and end up in a ditch. That's unexpected, but the error isn't in the ditch. It's in the missing safety barrier.

So, when you get a parse error message, start at the line it reports, and *work backward*, looking for missing semicolons, braces, and quotation marks. If the error is reported on the last line of the page, it means that a closing brace is missing from a loop or conditional statement. Fortunately, the syntax error checking in Dreamweaver CS5 should help you spot such errors before you even test a page.

What You Have Learned

In this lesson, you have:

- Seen how to embed PHP code in a page (pages 61-63)

- Seen how to store values in variables (pages 63-66)

- Examined the difference between single and double quotation marks (pages 67-69)

- Explored the use of arrays to store multiple values (pages 70-73)

- Sent data to another page from an online form (pages 71-72)

- Discovered how conditions are used to make decisions (pages 74–79)

- Explored functions and objects (pages 79-91)

- Seen how PHP performs calculations and joins strings (pages 91-96)

- Discovered how loops perform repetitive tasks (pages 96-100)

- Included external HTML and PHP files in a web page (pages 101-108)

- Probed the mysteries of PHP error messages (pages 108-109)

There's a lot to absorb in this lesson, but hopefully it has fired up your enthusiasm (not dampened it) to get started with PHP. If you come from a design background, dealing with raw code can seem intimidating at first. I find that a good approach to PHP is to break down what you want to do into a series of small tasks, and then build a skeleton of comments outlining the logic. Then you can start fleshing it out with code. Make sure that each section works as expected, and before you know it, you'll have created a dynamic web page that does what you want.

What You Will Learn

In this lesson, you will:

- Examine the basic structure of Drupal, Joomla!, and WordPress
- Install WordPress 3.0 in your local testing environment
- Create a child theme based on the default WordPress Twenty Ten theme
- Use Live View, the CSS Styles panel, and Code Navigator to style WordPress
- Enable site-specific code hints for WordPress
- Edit a WordPress template

Approximate Time

This lesson takes approximately 2 hours 30 minutes to complete.

Lesson Files

Media Files:

lesson04/start/images/birds_bg_gradient.jpg
lesson04/start/images/cormorants.jpg
lesson04/start/images/cormorants-thumbnail.jpg
lesson04/start/images/screenshot.png
lesson04/start/images/seagulls.jpg
lesson04/start/images/seagulls-thumbnail.jpg

Starting Files:

lesson04/start/auth_keys.txt
lesson04/start/wordpress-3.0.zip

Completed Files:

lesson04/completed/functions.php
lesson04/completed/header.php
lesson04/completed/style.css

LESSON 4

Restyling a WordPress Site

Open source content management systems (CMSs), such as Drupal, Joomla!, and WordPress, take much of the hard work out of creating a dynamic website. WordPress claims—with some justification—that it takes only five minutes to install. The difficult part is trying to style a CMS to give it a unique look. That job is now considerably easier thanks to several new features in Dreamweaver CS5: navigable Live View, dynamically related files, CSS Inspect, and site-specific code hints.

Instead of constantly reloading the site in a browser to see the effect of your changes, you can now redesign your CMS entirely in the Document window. In this lesson, you'll adapt the default theme for a WordPress 3.0 site. The same basic principles apply to styling Drupal and Joomla!

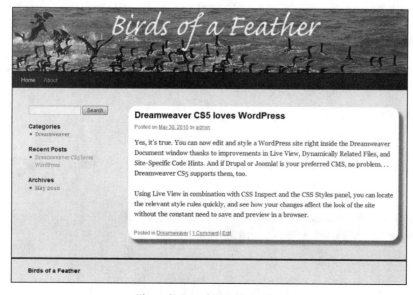

The redesigned WordPress site.

Understanding the Structure of a CMS

Before embarking on restyling a WordPress site, it's worth spending a few moments examining how a CMS like WordPress, Drupal, or Joomla! is structured. A bare-bones Drupal installation consists of more than 460 files in 58 folders; WordPress has nearly 800 files in 79 folders; and Joomla! weighs in at a whopping 3,913 files in 711 folders. Unlike a website built with HTML, these files don't contain any of the site's content. In fact, the only page that most users ever see is index.php.

With the exception of images and other media files, all the content is stored in a database. The job of the army of files is to insert, update, and delete content in the database, and to serve visitors to the site with the information they want to see. If you open index.php in any of the CMSs, you see just a handful of PHP commands. There's nothing recognizable as a web page. Each part of the final web page is generated separately. Different scripts handle the page header, menus, main content, and footer.

This mass of files can be intimidating, even if you have a good understanding of PHP. As a result, many designers opt for using third-party themes (or templates, as Joomla! calls them) to improve the look of their CMS. There are plenty of good themes and templates available, and the default Twenty Ten theme in WordPress 3.0 is very attractive. But with the help of Dreamweaver CS5, it's not difficult to do your own customization—providing you have a strong grasp of CSS.

With a CMS, it's important to apply security fixes as soon as they're released, so you need to install your custom files in a place where they won't be overwritten. The location depends on the CMS you're using:

- **Drupal.** Create two subfolders called **modules** and **themes** in sites/all. The themes folder is where you install third-party themes or create your own.

- **Joomla!** Create a subfolder in the templates folder.

- **WordPress.** Create a subfolder in wp-content/themes.

Although the instructions in this lesson concentrate on creating a WordPress theme, the same principles of editing the CSS apply to Drupal and Joomla!

▶ **TIP:** There's a tutorial by David Karlins on modifying Drupal themes with Dreamweaver CS5 at www.peachpit.com/articles/article.aspx?p=1590589.

Installing WordPress

The following instructions assume you have created a PHP local testing environment as described in Lesson 2, and that your web server and MySQL are running.

Setting up a MySQL database and user account

Before you can install WordPress, you need to create a MySQL database and user account. Both subjects are covered in greater detail in Lesson 5, but the following steps guide you through the process of setting up a WordPress database.

1 Load phpMyAdmin in your browser, and log in as the root user if necessary.

2 In the "MySQL localhost" section in the center of the screen type **wordpress** in the "Create new database" text field. Leave all other settings at their default, and click Create.

You should see a message that the database has been created. You don't need to create any tables. WordPress does it for you.

3 Click the Home icon 🏠 at the top left of the phpMyAdmin screen to return to the previous page. Then click the Privileges tab at the top of the screen.

⚠ **CAUTION!** Don't be tempted to click the Privileges tab on the previous screen. You must return to the phpMyAdmin welcome page to access the correct screen.

4 Click the "Add a new User" link halfway down the screen.

5 In the "Add a new User" section, type **wpuser** in the "User name" field.

6 Select Local from the Host menu to insert localhost in the Host field.

7 Type **P3@chp!T** in the Password field, and again in the Re-type field.

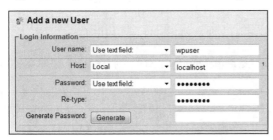

8 Scroll to the bottom of the page, and click Go.

phpMyAdmin reports that it has created the user and displays a page where you can edit the user's privileges. The first section, "Global privileges," gives the user the same privileges on all databases, which is insecure.

9 Scroll down to "Database-specific privileges" and select **wordpress** from the menu labeled "Add privileges on the following database."

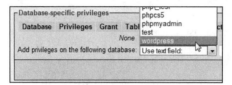

This loads a new screen where you define the database-specific privileges.

10 You need to select all checkboxes except the three in the Administration box. The quickest way is to click "Check all," and then deselect the three Administration checkboxes.

11 Click the Go button in the "Database-specific privileges" section.

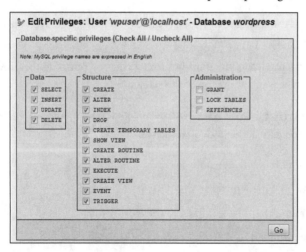

⚠ CAUTION! There are two Go buttons on this page. Make sure you click the top one.

You should see a message saying you have updated the privileges for 'wpuser'@'localhost'. You're now ready to install WordPress.

Adding WordPress to the phpcs5 site

Installing WordPress involves unzipping the files into the folder where you want to locate the CMS. This can be the site root or a subfolder. For this lesson, use a subfolder of the phpcs5 site you set up in Lesson 2. After extracting the files, you need to edit a configuration file filling in the details of the MySQL database. The rest of the installation process is automated.

1 Use lesson04/start/wordpress-3.0.zip or download the most recent version of WordPress from http://wordpress.org/.

2 Extract the files to the phpcs5 site root. This should create a folder called wordpress inside the phpcs5 site. The folder contains about 25 files and three subfolders: wp-admin, wp-content, and wp-includes.

3 Click the Refresh icon 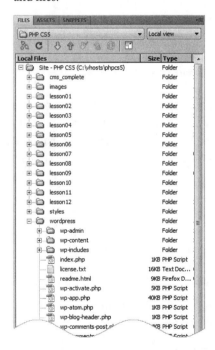 in the Dreamweaver Files panel to see the newly added folders and files.

4 Double-click wp-config-sample.php in the wordpress folder to open it in the Document window, and switch to Code view.

The first part of the script (around lines 18–34) defines the MySQL settings for the CMS. Replace the placeholder text in the first three lines with the name of the database, the user name, and password that you created in the previous section like this:

```
/** The name of the database for WordPress */
define('DB_NAME', 'wordpress');

/** MySQL database username */
define('DB_USER', 'wpuser');

/** MySQL database password */
define('DB_PASSWORD', 'P3@chp!T');
```

5 Scroll down to around line 45 to the following section of code:

```
define('AUTH_KEY',         'put your unique phrase here');
define('SECURE_AUTH_KEY',  'put your unique phrase here');
define('LOGGED_IN_KEY',    'put your unique phrase here');
define('NONCE_KEY',        'put your unique phrase here');
define('AUTH_SALT',        'put your unique phrase here');
define('SECURE_AUTH_SALT', 'put your unique phrase here');
define('LOGGED_IN_SALT',   'put your unique phrase here');
define('NONCE_SALT',       'put your unique phrase here');
```

This defines a series of measures designed to make it extremely difficult, if not impossible, for anyone to reuse cookies if the security of your site is breached. When creating your own WordPress site, you can use your own imagination to create unique character sequences, or you can use the automatic key generator at https://api.wordpress.org/secret-key/1.1/salt/.

For this lesson, use the values in lesson04/start/auth_keys.txt to replace the eight lines shown here.

✳ NOTE: In the event that the security of a live WordPress site is breached, you should replace these eight values and update the file on your remote server immediately.

6 Save wp-config-sample.php as **wp-config.php**, and close both files.

7 Launch your browser, and open wordpress/wp-admin/install.php in your phpcs5 site. The URL depends on how you set up your testing environment:

- **Virtual host.** http://phpcs5/wordpress/wp-admin/install.php

- **Localhost.** http://localhost/phpcs5/wordpress/wp-admin/install.php

✱ **NOTE:** If you are using the MAMP default ports on a Mac, add :8888 after phpcs5 for a virtual host, or after localhost.

8 The install page asks for some basic information to set up the site. Type **Birds of a Feather** in the Site Title field.

9 Leave username at the default admin.

10 Type **C0rm0R@nT** in both Password fields.

11 For a live site, you should use a real email address in Your E-mail, because it's used to send alerts about posts waiting for approval. It's also used if you forget your password. A dummy address is fine for testing.

12 Deselect the checkbox that allows your site to appear in search engines like Google and Technorati. You won't be deploying this exercise on the Internet.

13 Click Install WordPress. In a few moments, you'll see a screen telling you that WordPress has been installed and inviting you to log in as admin.

14 Click Log In to open the login screen. Type **admin** in the Username field and **C0rm0R@nT** in the Password field. It's also a good idea to select the Remember Me checkbox to avoid the need to type these details every time.

15 Click Log In to enter the WordPress Dashboard, the administration center for a WordPress site.

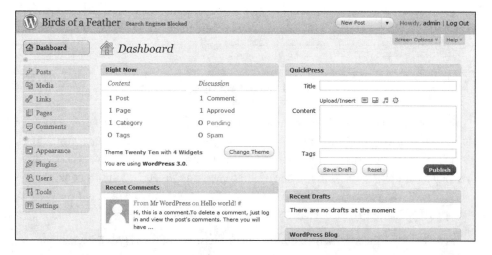

16 Click the name of the site (Birds of a Feather) next to the WordPress logo at the top of the page to view the front page.

Why Can't I See the Multiscreen Button?

The screen shot on the next page shows a Multiscreen button in the Document tool-bar, which isn't part of a default installation of Dreamweaver CS5. It comes from the HTML5 Pack that was released in May 2010, a month after Dreamweaver CS5 became available for purchase. Although the Multiscreen button isn't used in this book, the HTML5 Pack upgrades the version of the WebKit browser engine used in Live View to support CSS3 properties that are used later in this lesson.

If you don't see the Multiscreen button, check the status of the HTML5 Pack at http://labs.adobe.com/technologies/html5pack/. It's possible that during the lifetime of this book the pack's functionality will be added to Dreamweaver through the Adobe Updater. Download and install the HTML5 Pack using whichever method is available.

17 In Dreamweaver, double-click index.php in the wordpress folder to open it in the Document window. In Code view, there are just two lines of PHP code, together with a dozen or so lines of comments.

Switch to Design view, and click the Live View button. After a few moments, you should see the Birds of a Feather site in the Dreamweaver Document window. There are several files called index.php in a WordPress site. If you don't see the front page of the Birds of a Feather site in Live View, make sure you opened index.php in the top wordpress folder.

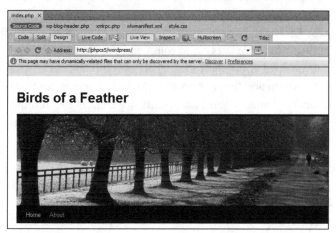

The default Twenty Ten theme in WordPress 3.0 has been designed to look good straight out of the box. But with the help of Dreamweaver CS5's new features, you'll learn how to develop your own theme to style WordPress.

Creating a WordPress Theme

Developing a WordPress theme from scratch requires considerable knowledge of CSS, HTML, PHP, and the WordPress application programming interface (API). The good news is that you can stand on the shoulders of others to adapt an existing theme as a *child theme*.

Child themes work on a similar principle to CSS. The child theme automatically inherits all the features of the existing theme, but you can decide which elements to override. The advantage is that the original files remain intact, so you can revert to the default if you change your mind or make a mistake. Also, if the parent theme is updated, you can replace all its files without worrying about losing your customizations because they're all stored in the child theme.

Most themes can be adapted as child themes. Before doing so, check the license. Some commercial themes have restrictions on how they can be used. The Twenty Ten theme used in the following exercises is released under the GNU General Public License (www.gnu.org/licenses/gpl.html), which means you are free to modify and redistribute it.

Preparing the files for a child theme

Themes consist of at least one style sheet and a number of WordPress templates. A WordPress template doesn't control a complete page. It's more like a Dreamweaver Library item in that it represents a fragment of a page. Each template is named after the part of the page it controls. For example, the Twenty Ten theme has templates called comments.php, footer.php, header.php, sidebar.php, and so on. If you open any of these files, you'll see a mixture of HTML and PHP. If you don't have any PHP experience, the code probably looks incomprehensible, but much of it is based on conditional statements. You'll gain plenty of experience with conditional statements in later lessons, so the code should be a lot easier to decipher by the time you have completed this book.

However, you don't really need to worry about the PHP code in the templates. A child theme requires only one file—a style sheet, which must be called style.css and reside in the child theme's top level folder. The child theme automatically uses the parent theme's templates and custom functions. In other words, at its simplest level, creating a child theme is just the WordPress way of attaching your own style sheet to an existing theme. But if you're feeling more ambitious, you can create your own templates and functions. When the active theme is a child theme, WordPress always looks first in the child theme's folder. If it finds the appropriate template or function there, it uses it. Otherwise, it uses the version in the parent theme's folder. For example, if you create your own version of header.php, WordPress uses it. But if you don't have your own version of footer.php, WordPress uses the one from the parent theme. This gives you the opportunity to experiment. You can copy a template file from the parent theme, and make some changes. If you like the result, you're on the way to developing your own theme. If it doesn't work, just delete the template file from your child theme's folder, and revert to the parent template.

Developing WordPress themes is a vast subject, so the exercises in this lesson only scratch the surface, but they demonstrate how quickly you can begin to style a WordPress site in Dreamweaver CS5.

1 In the Dreamweaver Files panel, expand the wordpress and wp-content folders, select the themes folder, right-click, and choose New Folder. Name the new folder **birds_phpcs5**. The new folder should be inside the themes folder at the same level as twentyten.

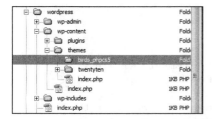

2 Expand the twentyten folder, and double-click style.css to open it in the Document window.

3 The first eight lines of style.css look like this:

```
/*
Theme Name: Twenty Ten
Theme URI: http://wordpress.org/
Description: The 2010 default theme for WordPress.
Author: the WordPress team
Version: 1.0
Tags: black, blue, white, two-columns, fixed-width, custom-header,
➥ custom-background, theme-options, threaded-comments, sticky-post,
➥ translation-ready, microformats, rtl-language-support, editor-style
*/
```

This tells WordPress what the theme is called, plus some basic information about the theme.

4 Choose File > Save As or press Ctrl+Shift+S/Shift+Cmd+S. In the Save As dialog box, navigate to the birds_phpcs5 folder, and save the file with the same name (style.css). When asked if you want to update links, click No.

5 Close the original style.css, and make sure you're working in the version in the birds_phpcs5 folder. The file path should be visible in the Browser Navigation toolbar.

Alternatively, click the Open Documents icon at the top of the Coding toolbar to reveal the file path.

6 The Theme Name comment must contain a unique name, which cannot consist only of numbers (that's why it's "Twenty Ten," not "2010"). When creating a child theme, you need to specify the parent theme as the child theme's template. Without these two changes, WordPress won't recognize your child theme. Changes to the remaining comments are optional. Amend the comments at the top of style.css like this:

```
/*
Theme Name: Birds of a Feather
Template: twentyten
Theme URI: http://foundationphp.com/phpcs5/
Description: Adaptation of the 2010 default theme for WordPress.
Author: David Powers, but mainly the WordPress team
Version: 1.0
Tags: purple, pink, blue, white, two-columns, fixed-width, custom-header,
➥ custom-background, theme-options, threaded-comments, sticky-post,
➥ translation-ready, microformats, rtl-language-support, editor-style
*/
```

The parent is identified by `Template` followed by a colon and its folder name.

7 Save style.css and close it.

8 This is sufficient for WordPress to identify the new theme, but it's a good idea to add an image to distinguish it from others in your Dashboard. The image should be about 300 pixels wide and must be called screenshot.png. Copy screenshot.png from lesson04/start/ images to the birds_phpcs5 folder. The child theme folder should now contain two files.

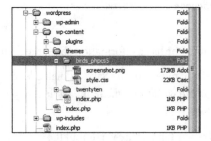

You'll add more files later, but that's sufficient for now.

▶ **TIP:** If you create a mockup of your final design in a graphics program, such as Fireworks or Photoshop, you can create screenshot.png by scaling the mockup and exporting it as a .png file. If it can't find screenshot.png, WordPress displays a text description of the theme.

Activating the child theme

The child theme needs to be activated before you can style it in Dreamweaver.

1 In your browser, log into the WordPress Dashboard. Depending on how you set up your testing environment, the URL should be one of the following:

- **Virtual host.** http://phpcs5/wordpress/wp-admin/

- **Localhost.** http://localhost/phpcs5/wordpress/wp-admin/

2 Expand the Appearance section in the column on the left of the Dashboard, and select Themes. The new Birds of a Feather theme should be displayed in the Available Themes section.

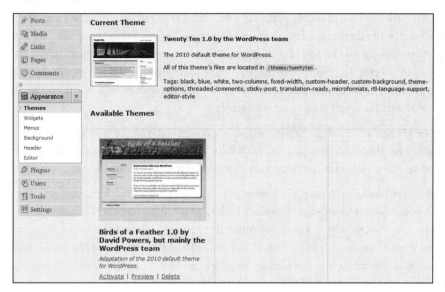

3 Click the Activate link for the Birds of a Feather theme. After a few seconds, Birds of a Feather is displayed as the Current Theme and Twenty Ten moves down to the Available Themes section.

4 Click the Widgets link in the Appearance menu to open the widget settings screen. The child theme inherits the default settings of the Twenty Ten theme. You can study all the options later. For now, remove the Recent Comments and Meta widgets from the Primary Widget Area by dragging them from the sidebar on the right back to the Available Widgets area.

5 Drag the Categories widget to move it just below the Search widget. The Primary Widget Area should now look like this:

6 Click the Background link in the Appearance menu. This allows you to set a background image and color for the site. However, it does this by generating a `<style>` block in the head of the page. It's better to use style.css to handle this, so leave this screen unchanged.

7 Click the Header link in the Appearance menu. This is one of the cleverest parts of the new Twenty Ten theme. It offers a choice of eight header images for your site. You can also upload your own images. The problem is that if your image isn't exactly the same size as used by Twenty Ten (940 × 198 pixels), you're prompted to crop it. WordPress doesn't crop your original, but instead makes a copy. If your image's height is less than 198 pixels, it's stretched. The result is often unsatisfactory.

The height and width of the header images are controlled by a custom function in the Twenty Ten theme. To change the default values, you need to override that function. Leave your browser open at the current page, and return to Dreamweaver.

8 Custom functions for WordPress themes are stored in a file called functions.php. If you attempt to redefine an existing function, PHP throws a fatal error, but WordPress overcomes this problem with a simple conditional statement. All the functions in the parent theme's functions.php file are wrapped in a conditional statement that checks whether a function of the same name has already been defined. If it hasn't, the parent theme defines the function. Otherwise, it uses the one defined by the child theme.

Choose File > New. Set Page Type to PHP, set Layout to <none>, and click Create. Switch to Code view, and delete all the HTML code inserted by Dreamweaver. You should have a completely blank page.

9 Add an opening PHP tag at the top of the new page, and save it as **functions.php** in the birds_phpcs5 folder.

10 Double-click functions.php in the twentyten folder to open it in the Document window. The file contains extensive comments that help you understand what the functions are for and how to override them.

11 Scroll down to around line 47 to locate the following code:

```
if ( ! isset( $content_width ) )
  $content_width = 640;
```

This defines the width of the main content `<div>` in the Twenty Ten theme. As you can see, the conditional statement sets the value to 640 (pixels) only if $content_width hasn't already been defined. So, to change the width to a different value, you need to add $content_width to functions.php in the child theme. Otherwise, this value is used.

12 The header image for Birds of a Feather is 20 pixels wider than the Twenty Ten images, so you can expand the content by the same amount.

Switch to the empty functions.php file you created for the child theme, and add the following code after the opening PHP tag:

```php
<?php
$content_width = 660;
```

13 Switch back to the Twenty Ten version of functions.php, and scroll down to locate the following line of code (around line 53):

```php
if ( ! function_exists( 'twentyten_setup' ) ):
```

This conditional statement checks whether a function called `twentyten_setup()` has already been defined. If it hasn't, it creates the function, which—as the name suggests—defines the default settings for the Twenty Ten theme.

❊ **NOTE:** This conditional statement ends with a colon rather than an opening curly brace. This is an alternative syntax for control structures. See http://docs.php.net/manual/en/control-structures.alternative-syntax.php.

14 To create your own default settings for the child theme, you need to copy the function definition to the version of functions.php in birds_phpcs5. The function definition begins like this (around line 75):

```php
function twentyten_setup() {

    // This theme styles the visual editor with editor-style.css to match
    ➥ the theme style.
    add_editor_style();
```

The final section of the function definition looks like this (around lines 171–178):

```php
        'sunset' => array(
          'url' => '%s/images/headers/sunset.jpg',
          'thumbnail_url' => '%s/images/headers/sunset-thumbnail.jpg',
          /* translators: header image description */
          'description' => __( 'Sunset', 'twentyten' )
        )
    ) );
}
```

Select the entire function description, and copy it to your clipboard.

15 Paste the function definition into functions.php in the birds_phpcs5 folder. If you copied and pasted the code correctly, Dreamweaver should display "No syntax errors" in the Info Bar at the top of the Document window.

16 Scroll down to locate this code (around line 35):

```
define( 'HEADER_IMAGE', '%s/images/headers/path.jpg' );
```

This defines the default header image for the Twenty Ten theme (the tree-lined path). To display a different image, change the filename like this:

```
define( 'HEADER_IMAGE', '%s/images/headers/cormorants.jpg' );
```

You'll add this and other images to the relevant folder shortly.

17 The next section of code defines the width and height of the header image. Change the width from 940 to **960** and the height from 198 to **150** like this:

```
define( 'HEADER_IMAGE_WIDTH', apply_filters(
➥ 'twentyten_header_image_width', 960 ) );
define( 'HEADER_IMAGE_HEIGHT', apply_filters(
➥ 'twentyten_header_image_height', 150 ) );
```

18 About 20 lines farther down is a long section of code that begins like this:

```
register_default_headers( array(
  'berries' => array(
  'url' => '%s/images/headers/berries.jpg',
  'thumbnail_url' => '%s/images/headers/berries-thumbnail.jpg',
  /* translators: header image description */
  'description' => __( 'Berries', 'twentyten' )
  ),
```

This passes a multidimensional array to `register_default_headers()`, a function new to WordPress 3.0, which defines the choice of header images offered by the theme. The default Twenty Ten images are all 940 pixels wide and 198 pixels high, so they won't fit the child theme.

The media files for this lesson contain two header images called cormorants.jpg and seagulls.jpg, together with two smaller versions called cormorants-thumbnail.jpg and seagulls-thumbnail.jpg. Change all instances of berries in the multidimensional array to **cormorants**, and cherryblossom(s) to **seagulls**. There are only two header images, so you need to delete the other six subarrays. When you have finished, the final section of functions.php should look like this:

```
register_default_headers( array(
  'cormorants' => array(
    'url' => '%s/images/headers/cormorants.jpg',
```

```
      'thumbnail_url' => '%s/images/headers/cormorants-thumbnail.jpg',
      /* translators: header image description */
      'description' => __( 'Cormorants', 'twentyten' )
   ),
   'seagulls' => array(
      'url' => '%s/images/headers/seagulls.jpg',
      'thumbnail_url' => '%s/images/headers/seagulls-thumbnail.jpg',
      /* translators: header image description */
      'description' => __( 'Seagulls', 'twentyten' )
   )
) );
}
```

19 Save functions.php and copy cormorants.jpg, cormorants-thumbnail.jpg, seagulls.jpg, and seagulls-thumbnail.jpg from lesson04/start/images to twentyten/images/headers. The images must go in the parent theme's folder because that's where `register_default_ headers()` expects to find them.

20 Return to the Header page in the WordPress administrative area. Click the Background link in the Appearances menu, and then click Header to reflect the changes you have made. The Custom Header section should now display the two Birds of a Feather header images, and the text in the Upload Image section should show the new default dimensions of 960 × 150 pixels.

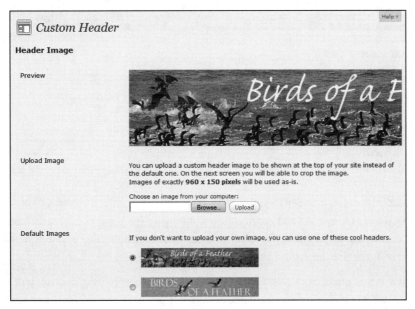

If necessary, compare your code with lesson04/completed/functions.php.

Styling the child theme

All that remains now is to adjust the styles to give the theme its own look. Most of the remaining tasks are done in Live View and the CSS Styles panel.

1 Close functions.php if it's still open, and create a new folder called **images** in the birds_phpcs5 folder. Copy birds_bg_gradient.jpg from lesson04/start/images to the new folder. You'll use this later as a background image to the new theme.

2 Double-click index.php in the main wordpress folder to open it in the Document window. Switch to Design view if necessary, and click Live View. The Birds of a Feather site should display with the new default header and the edited sidebar.

3 The header image is now wider than the menu bar. To fix that, click the Inspect button in the Document toolbar. As you move your pointer over Live View, you'll see different sections of the page highlighted. The content of an element is light blue or aqua, padding is mauve, and margins are yellow.

Notice that as you move from element to element, the currently highlighted element is also selected in the Tag selector at the bottom of the Document window. When your pointer is over the black menu bar below the header image, you should see <div#access> highlighted in the Tag selector. Click the menu bar to select it.

4 Selecting an element turns off the Inspect button, allowing you to move your pointer without highlighting other elements. Open the CSS Styles panel by clicking its tab or by choosing Window > CSS Styles. On Windows, you can also use the keyboard shortcut Shift+F11 (there is no Mac shortcut).

Make sure the Current button is selected at the top of the CSS Styles panel and that the Rules pane is visible in the middle section. If the middle section is titled About, click the Cascade icon as indicated in the following screen shot. You might need to close other panels and drag the panes inside the CSS Styles panel to see the rules and properties listed.

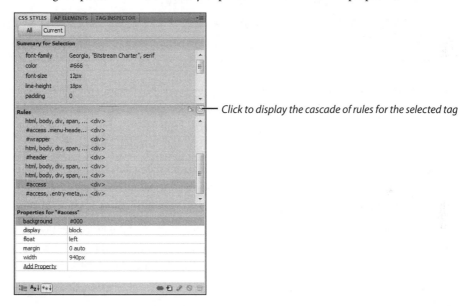

— *Click to display the cascade of rules for the selected tag*

The Rules pane displays all the style rules that affect the current selection. Sometimes you need to examine several rules before finding the right one, but on this occasion, it should be the one selected by Dreamweaver. It's the #access rule shown in the preceding screen shot.

Select #access in the Rules pane. This reveals that the width property is set to 940px. Click the value to edit it, and change the number to **960**. The px unit is controlled by a separate menu, so you don't need to change it.

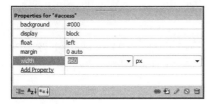

As soon as you press Enter/Return to confirm the edit, the menu bar in Live View expands to match the width of the header image.

5 Although the header image and menu bar are now the same length, there's a gap of about 20 pixels of white space on the left of both elements. Finding the cause of the gap is a process of elimination, but if you look farther down the page, you'll see there's a similar gap on both sides of the horizontal line above the footer.

Click the Inspect button again, position the pointer over the footer so that the full width below the horizontal line is highlighted, and click to select it.

6 In the Rules pane of the CSS Styles panel, #colophon is selected. Examining the Properties pane reveals nothing to help eliminate the gap on the left and right, so start moving up the cascade of rules in the Rules pane. The next property begins with #access.menu-header and has a width property of 940px. Change the number to **960** as you did in step 4.

As soon as you press Enter/Return, the white background expands to create the same gap on both sides of the header image, menu bar, and the horizontal line above the footer. This is progress, but the final design calls for the gap to be eliminated.

7 Click <div.hfeed#wrapper> in the Tag selector at the bottom of the Document window to reveal its properties in the CSS Styles panel. You'll see that the padding property is set to 0 20px. This adds 20 pixels of padding to both sides of the wrapper <div>.

Remove the padding by selecting it in the Properties pane of the CSS Styles panel and clicking the trash can icon at the bottom right of the panel.

The left and right sides of the heading image, menu bar, and horizontal line above the footer are now flush with the white background of the wrapper.

8 There's a large gap between the white background and the top of the page. It's caused by the margin-top property, which is set to 20px. Select margin-top in the Properties pane for #wrapper and click the trash can icon to delete it.

The entire contents of the page move up to eliminate the gap, leaving the white background flush with the top of the Document window.

9 With #wrapper still selected in the Rules pane of the CSS Styles panel, change the background property from #fff (white) to **#FAF2EF** (light pink).

> **TIP:** Hexadecimal values for colors are case insensitive. The Twenty Ten style sheet uses a mixture of uppercase and lowercase, indicating that it's almost certainly the work of more than one person. Color values can also be shortened to three characters if each even character is the same as the preceding odd one. Thus, #ffffff can be shortened to #fff, but #FAF2EF cannot be shortened.

10 The next step is to change the background of the whole page. Begin by selecting <body.home blog> in the Tag selector. The Rules pane selects the body, input, textarea style rule, which covers too many elements, so start moving up the list of rules. The next one, body, defines the background property, which is the one you need to change.

The background shorthand CSS property is difficult to define directly in the Properties pane of the CSS Styles panel, so select the property and click the Edit Rule icon at the bottom right of the panel to open the CSS Rule Definition dialog box.

11 The CSS Rule Definition dialog box should automatically select the Background category.

Change the value of Background-color from #f1f1f1 to **#E1DFE0**.

Click the Browse button next to the Background-image text box, navigate to the birds_phpcs5/images folder, and select birds_bg_gradient.jpg.

Set the Background-repeat menu to **repeat-x**.

When you click OK, the page background should change from light oatmeal to a vertical gradient that fades from light purple to a light gray.

12 Now comes a little bit of CSS magic—swapping the sidebar from right to left. The default style rule for the sidebar floats it to the right in a margin created by the main content. You can move the sidebar to the other side of the page by floating it left and giving it a large enough negative left margin to sit on the opposite side of the main content. But first, you need to adjust the margins of the main content.

Click the Inspect button and select the main content on the left of the page. The style rule that controls its margins is applied to the container <div>, so click <div#container> in the Tag selector at the bottom of the Document window. The Properties pane of the CSS Styles panel reveals that its margin property is set to 0 -240px 0 0. In other words, a space of 240 pixels has been created on the right for the sidebar. You need to move the space to the opposite side. Change the margin property to **0 0 0 240px**. This moves the main content to the right of the page, but pushes the sidebar below it.

> **TIP:** The Twenty Ten style sheet's use of a negative right margin on the container `<div>` is rather unconventional. It's needed because the `width` property of the `<div>` is set to `100%`. Using a negative value reduces the width and makes room for the sidebar. If you need to brush up on your knowledge of CSS, take a look at my book, *Getting StartED with CSS* (friends of ED, 2009, ISBN: 978-1-4302-2543-0).

13 Click the Inspect button again, and move your pointer until the whole of the sidebar is highlighted. Then select it. This selects `<ul.xoxo>` in the Tag selector. The rule that you want to edit is the next one up the page hierarchy. Click `<div.widget-area#primary>` in the Tag selector.

The Properties pane of the CSS Styles panel displays no styles, so move up the cascade in the Rules pane. The next one—`#primary, #secondary`—displays the rules that you need to change.

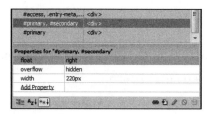

14 Change the value of `float` from right to **left**. The sidebar jumps to the left of the page but still below the main content.

15 Click Add Property, type **margin-left**, and set the value to **-1180px**. (That's *minus* 1180 pixels.) The sidebar is after the main content in the underlying HTML markup, but a combination of the left float and the large negative margin allows it to leapfrog over the main content and move into the correct position in the margin on the left.

16 Let's add a touch of CSS3 coolness to the main content. Click the Inspect button, move the pointer over the main content until it's highlighted, and click to select it. The Tag selector shows you have selected `<div.post-1 post type-post hentry category-uncategorized#post-1>`. Whew! That's a complex CSS selector. Fortunately, the Rules pane selects the lowest part of the cascade, the style rule for the `hentry` class, which currently sets only the `margin` property.

Although you could add the next set of CSS properties through the CSS Styles panel, it's a lot easier to work directly in the style sheet. The problem is that the style sheet contains more than 1,000 lines. A quick way to locate the correct rule is to use the Code Navigator.

Hold down the Alt key on Windows or Cmd+Opt on a Mac, and click anywhere in the "Welcome to WordPress" default post to invoke the Code Navigator, a context-sensitive tool for investigating styles that affect the area you clicked. Many rules affect this area, but you should find .hentry listed near the bottom of the panel, as shown in the following screen shot.

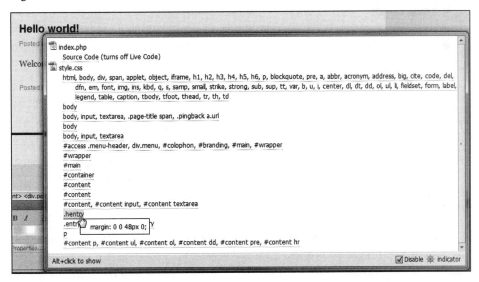

Click the .hentry link in the Code Navigator to open the style sheet in Split view. Using this technique positions the insertion point directly inside the .hentry style rule.

17 Amend the style rule like this:

```
.hentry {
  margin: 0 0 48px 0;
  padding:5px 5px 5px 15px;
  background-color: #FFF;
  -moz-border-radius: 20px;
  -webkit-border-radius: 20px;
  border-radius: 20px;
  -moz-box-shadow: 10px 10px 5px #888;
  -webkit-box-shadow:10px 10px 5px #888;
  box-shadow: 10px 10px 5px #888;
  border: 1px solid #eee;
}
```

The properties beginning with -moz and -webkit are browser-specific implementations of the CSS3 border-radius and box-shadow properties. Putting the properties in this order ensures that the effects will be maintained when the official properties are implemented by browsers.

If you refresh Live View by pressing F5 or clicking anywhere in Live View, you'll see the post now has a white background with rounded corners. In the Mac version of Dreamweaver, you'll also see a drop shadow as shown in the following screen shot.

> ✳ **NOTE:** The Windows version of Live View fails to render the drop shadow correctly. However, if you view the finished WordPress site in a recent version of Safari, Google Chrome, or Firefox, the drop shadow is rendered correctly on both Windows and Mac OS X. Internet Explorer 8 and earlier ignores the CSS3 properties and just displays a rectangular white background.

18 Save style.css.

Hopefully, by now you've got the picture. You use the Inspect button or Code Navigator in Live View to identify elements on the page and inspect the style rules that govern their display. The Tag selector at the bottom of the Document window shows you where the element resides in the document hierarchy. Most CSS properties are inherited, so you often need to go back up the hierarchy to find the element where a specific rule has been applied. The CSS Styles panel in Current mode also allows you to work back up the cascade of rules affecting the selected element.

Styling a web page requires patience and skill. If you have a good command of CSS, you'll find working in Live View with these tools make styling WordPress, Joomla!, or Drupal very similar to working with a static HTML page. This lesson has concentrated on styling the front page of a WordPress site, but Live View is navigable in Dreamweaver CS5. Just hold down Ctrl/Cmd while clicking a link, and you can inspect and style all pages and views within a CMS.

To round out this lesson, let's take a look at a WordPress template and make a slight change so that the text heading can be hidden from visual browsers. When editing CMS templates it's a good idea to set up site-specific code hints.

Enabling site-specific code hints for WordPress, Drupal, and Joomla!

WordPress, Drupal, and Joomla! use many custom functions to generate the content for each page. For example, WordPress provides the `bloginfo()` function (http://codex.wordpress.org/Template_Tags/bloginfo) to display information about your site. Dreamweaver uses code introspection to generate hints for your chosen CMS, speeding up editing page templates or functions.

The following instructions show how to enable site-specific code hints for WordPress in the phpcs5 site. The procedure is identical for Drupal and Joomla!

1 Make sure that the phpcs5 site is selected in the Files panel, and that the active document is from the same site or that all documents are closed.

2 Choose Site > Site-Specific Code Hints. As long as you haven't previously set up site-specific code hints for the same site, the Site-Specific Code Hints dialog box automatically recognizes not only which CMS is installed, but also the correct folder.

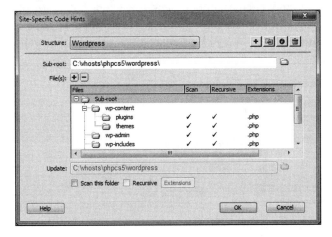

3 All that's necessary is to check that the Sub-root text field points to the folder that contains the top level of the CMS. If it doesn't, click the folder icon next to the Sub-root text field, and select the correct folder.

4 After checking the Sub-root text field, just click OK. That's all there is to it.

5 Dreamweaver inserts a file called dw_php_codehinting.config into the site root and automatically cloaks it to prevent it from being uploaded to your remote server when you use site synchronization to update your files. This file is used only in your local development environment.

Editing a WordPress page template

The first time you dive into a WordPress template can be a baffling experience, but the Twenty Ten theme is well commented. If you understand the HTML structure of the template you're working with, it's not too difficult to work out where to add custom features, such as a static paragraph, or remove elements that you don't want. As long as you make the changes to a template in a child theme, you can always delete the template and use the parent theme's default version if you make a mistake.

1 Open index.php in the top-level wordpress folder and click Live View to display the front page of the Birds of a Feather site.

2 Click Live Code to display in Split view the underlying HTML output generated by WordPress. Adjust Split view so you can see the code and "Just another WordPress site" at the top right of the page (you might need to scroll horizontally in Live View).

3 Click between the words "Just" and "another" in Live View. Depending on the size of your monitor, this should scroll Code view so that the equivalent HTML output is in the center with the insertion point between the two words, as shown on line 24 in the following screen shot:

```
18              <div id="branding" role="banner">
19                      <h1 id="site-title">
20                  <span>
21                      <a href="http://phpcs5/wordpress/" title="Birds of a
Feather" rel="home">Birds of a Feather</a>
22                  </span>
23              </h1>
24              <div id="site-description">Just another WordPress site</div>
25
26                      <img src=
"http://phpcs5/wordpress/wp-content/themes/twentyten/images/headers/cormorants.
jpg" width="960" height="150" alt="">
27                      </div><!-- #branding -->
```

You can't edit the output in Live Code, because it's dynamically generated by WordPress, but inspecting the output here gives you a good idea of what to look for when you open the WordPress template.

The text you clicked is in a <div> that has the ID site-description. You can also see on line 19 that the main heading has the ID site-title, and that the text is wrapped in a link that returns to the front page of the WordPress section of the site.

The final point to notice is that the alt attribute of the header image on line 26 is empty. The HTML specification requires all images to have alternative text (in the alt attribute), but it's recommended to use an empty string when the image is purely decorative. This redesign incorporates text into the image, so the same text should be inserted into the alt attribute in case the image is not displayed for any reason.

4 In the Files panel, double-click twentyten/header.php to open it in the Document window. Save the file as **header.php** in the birds_phpcs5 folder, and click No when asked if you want to update the links. Close the original version of header.php. You want to edit the copy in the child theme.

5 Scroll down to locate the following (it should be around line 54):

```
<div id="site-description"><?php bloginfo( 'description' ); ?></div>
```

This uses the WordPress bloginfo() function to display the site description ("Just another WordPress site").

6 Delete the entire line, and save header.php.

7 Switch back to index.php, and press F5 or click the Refresh icon ⟳ in the Document toolbar (not the Files panel) to update Live View. After a few moments, the text disappears from the top right of the page, and the corresponding code is removed from Live Code.

8 Switch back to header.php, and examine the code immediately above the line that you removed in step 6. It looks like this:

```
<?php $heading_tag = ( is_home() || is_front_page() ) ? 'h1' : 'div'; ?>
  <<?php echo $heading_tag; ?> id="site-title">
    <span>
      <a href="<?php echo home_url( '/' ); ?>" title="<?php echo esc_attr(
      ➡ get_bloginfo( 'name', 'display' ) ); ?>" rel="home"><?php
      ➡ bloginfo( 'name' ); ?></a>
    </span>
</<?php echo $heading_tag; ?>>
```

This code checks whether the current page is the site root or the front page of the WordPress section. If it is one of these, $heading_tag creates a pair of <h1> tags. Otherwise, it creates a <div>. It then creates a link to the front page of the WordPress site, which is wrapped around the site name.

9 The site name is already in the header image, so you don't want it displayed twice. However, you should leave it in the underlying code for search engines and screen readers for the blind. Edit the code like this to remove the link and <span> tags:

```
<?php $heading_tag = ( is_home() || is_front_page() ) ? 'h1' : 'div'; ?>
  <<?php echo $heading_tag; ?> id="site-title">
    <?php bloginfo( 'name' ); ?>
</<?php echo $heading_tag; ?>>
```

10 Save header.php, and refresh Live View in index.php. The text heading is still there, but it's no longer a link.

11 Click the Inspect button, select the Birds of a Feather text in Live View, and open the CSS Styles panel in Current mode. In the Rules pane, #site-title should be automatically selected. You know this is the style rule you want to change, because it's the ID selector for the element you just edited in header.php.

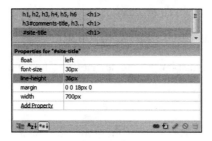

12 Select each of the properties in turn and click the trash can icon at the bottom right of the CSS Styles panel to delete them. Then click Add Property to add the position property, and set it to *absolute*.

Click Add Property again to add the top property, and set it to -1000px (minus 1000). The heading disappears from visual browsers but remains accessible to search engines and screen readers.

13 There's still a large gap at the top of the page, so click the Inspect button again, and select the area above the header image.

The #header rule is selected in the CSS Styles panel. Delete the padding property to remove the gap.

14 Click the header image in Live View to select the #branding img style rule, and delete the border-top property to remove the thick black border at the top of the page.

Save style.css to preserve the changes.

15 Return to header.php, and locate the following code, which inserts the header image (around line 63):

```
<img src="<?php header_image(); ?>" width="<?php echo HEADER_IMAGE_WIDTH;
➥ ?>" height="<?php echo HEADER_IMAGE_HEIGHT; ?>" alt="" />
```

You could hard code the value of the alt attribute, but that would mean changing the template if you decide to use the same theme for different sites. It makes more sense to use the WordPress API.

Position the insertion point between the quotation marks of the `alt` attribute, type an opening PHP tag followed by a space, and then press Ctrl+spacebar to bring up code hints. Type **bl**. Dreamweaver should select `bloginfo()`.

Press Enter/Return to autocomplete the function name. Dreamweaver automatically inserts the opening parenthesis. Complete the code by typing **'name'** followed by a closing parenthesis, semicolon, and closing PHP tag. The `alt` attribute should look like this:

```
alt="<?php bloginfo('name'); ?>"
```

16 Save header.php, and refresh Live View in index.php. When Live Code reloads, you should see "Birds of a Feather" in the `alt` attribute.

You can check your code against style.css and header.php in lesson04/completed.

What You Have Learned

In this lesson, you have:

- Examined the basic structure of Drupal, Joomla!, and WordPress (page 112)

- Installed WordPress 3.0 in your local testing environment (pages 113–119)

- Created a child theme based on the default WordPress Twenty Ten theme (pages 119–127)

- Used Live View, the CSS Styles panel, and Code Navigator to style WordPress (pages 128–134)

- Enabled site-specific code hints for WordPress (page 135)

- Edited a WordPress template (pages 136–139)

What You Will Learn

In this lesson, you will:

- See how a database stores information
- Understand the principles behind efficient database structure
- Explore the different data types stored in MySQL
- Define the database table for a user registration system
- Understand the effect of collation on how database records are sorted
- Pick the appropriate database engine
- Create MySQL user accounts and assign privileges
- Import existing data from an external file

Approximate Time

This lesson takes approximately 2 hours to complete.

Lesson Files

Media Files:

None

Starting Files:

None

Completed Files:

lesson05/states.sql

LESSON 5

Designing and Building Your Own Database

Having a content management system like WordPress build a database for you automatically is brilliant, but you're forced to use the structure your chosen CMS dictates. Often, the best solution is to create a database that suits your needs. Doing so in MySQL is remarkably easy.

What's not quite so easy is designing the database. Seemingly simple decisions can cause major headaches that are difficult to undo once the database has more than a few records. This lesson helps you avoid such mistakes and shows you how to build a database table for a user registration system, as well as how to import data from an external file.

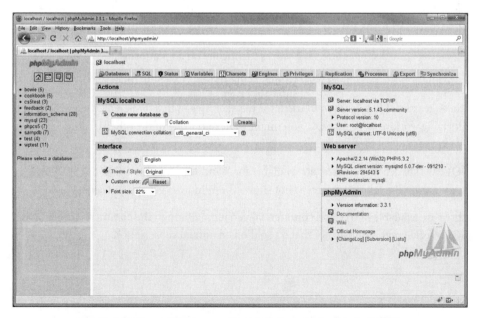

phpMyAdmin provides a convenient web-based interface to MySQL.

Working with MySQL

For many people, their first encounter with MySQL comes as something of a shock. It doesn't have a glossy user interface (UI). Because of its open source background, it's a command line program. Direct access to MySQL is through a Windows Command Prompt window or Terminal in Mac OS X. To make life easier, most people access MySQL through a third-party UI.

Choosing a UI for MySQL

You have a choice of UIs for MySQL, including:

- **phpMyAdmin** (http://phpmyadmin.net/)
- **MySQL Workbench** (http://dev.mysql.com/downloads/workbench)
- **Navicat** (http://navicat.com/)
- **SQLyog** (http://www.webyog.com/en/)

If you were to make your choice on looks alone, phpMyAdmin would almost certainly come last. It doesn't have the polished look of the others, but it's a solid workhorse maintained by dedicated volunteers who update it regularly. It might not look pretty, but it does everything you need for this book. It has several other advantages, namely:

- It's free.
- It's automatically installed by all-in-one packages like XAMPP and MAMP.
- It's a web-based application, so it works identically on all platforms.
- Most web hosts provide phpMyAdmin as the standard MySQL interface.

For these reasons, I have chosen to use it for the exercises in this book. Once you feel more comfortable working with MySQL, you might want to try one of the other UIs to see if the other features appeal to you.

MySQL Workbench and Navicat are available for Windows and Mac OS X, but SQLyog is Windows only. The following screen shot shows the Windows version of Navicat.

All three are available in free and commercial versions, although the commercial version of MySQL Workbench is unusual in that it's sold on an annual subscription.

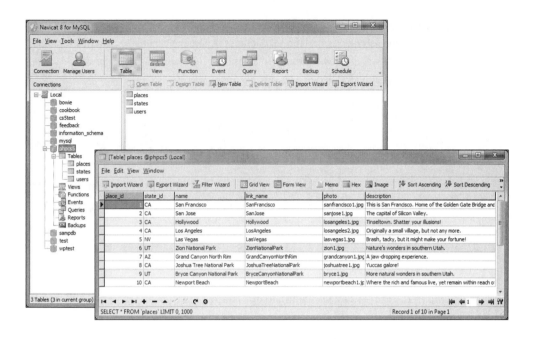

How a database stores information

Databases store information in rows and columns in a similar way to a spreadsheet. The problem with a spreadsheet is that all the data needs to be stored in a single table like this:

	name	state	link_name	photo	description
1	name	state	link_name	photo	description
2	San Francisco	California	SanFrancisco	sanfrancisco1.jpg	This is San Francisco. Home of the Golden Gate Bridge and Alcatraz.
3	San Jose	CA	SanJose	sanjose1.jpg	The capital of Silicon Valley.
4	Hollywood	California	Hollywood	losangeles1.jpg	Tinseltown. Shatter your illusions!
5	Los Angeles	Ca	LosAngeles	losangeles2.jpg	Originally a small village, but not any more.
6	Las Vegas	Nevada	LasVegas	lasvegas1.jpg	Brash, tacky, but it might make your fortune!
7	Zion National Park	Utah	ZionNationalPark	zion1.jpg	Nature's wonders in southern Utah.
8	Grand Canyon North Rim	Arizona	GrandCanyonNorthRim	grandcanyon1.jpg	A jaw-dropping experience.
9	Joshua Tree National Park	California	JoshuaTreeNationalPark	joshuatree1.jpg	Yuccas galore!
10	Bryce Canyon National Park	UT	BryceCanyonNationalPark	bryce1.jpg	More natural wonders in southern Utah.
11	Newport Beach	California	NewportBeach	newportbeach1.jpg	Where the rich and famous live, yet remain within reach of LA.

This often leads to the same information being recorded several times, which is not only repetitive, but can also lead to inconsistency. Each record in this spreadsheet lists the name of a state. But California has been entered in three different ways, and Utah appears fully spelled out and abbreviated as UT. These inconsistencies make searching more difficult.

What distinguishes data storage in MySQL from a spreadsheet is that MySQL is a *relational database*. You avoid inconsistency in a relational database by storing repetitive data in a separate table and building a relationship between the two tables. The following diagram shows the same data stored in two MySQL tables called `places` and `states`.

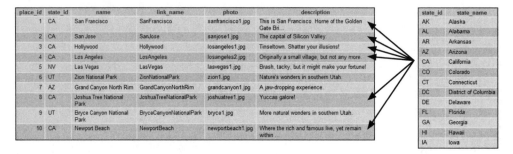

This is how the data is organized:

- Each record in the `places` table is identified by a unique number stored in the `place_id` column.

- The names of the states have been moved to a separate table that stores each state's United States Postal Service (USPS) abbreviation as `state_id` as well as the state's name spelled out in full.

- The relationship between the two tables is created by storing `state_id` in both tables.

At first glance, this might seem a cumbersome way of organizing the data, but the immediate gain is that it avoids the danger of someone entering "Missisipi" or "Massachusets" in the `places` table by mistake. Misspellings and inconsistent data are a major cause of database item search failures.

Separating the states into a table of their own has the added advantage of making it easier to store other details related to the state, such as time zone and the state tax rate. If you store the tax rate in the `places` table, you need to track down every entry to update it. By putting the state details in a separate table, you make the change in just one place.

The relationship between tables is managed using primary and foreign keys.

Managing relations with primary and foreign keys

Each record in a database table should have a unique identifier called a *primary key*. Usually, this is a number automatically assigned by the database when the record is inserted. The number is incremented by 1 for each new record. The places table uses this type of primary key and stores it in the place_id column. However, you can use any combination of letters and numbers as the primary key, as long as each one is unique. USPS state abbreviations are unique, so they act as the primary key in the states table.

You link the records by using the primary key from one table as a reference in the other table. When a primary key is used like this, it's known in the other table as a *foreign key*. Although a primary key can be used only once in its own table, it can be used many times as a foreign key.

The role of state_id can be summarized as follows:

- The state_id column is the primary key in the states table. Each value is unique.

- In the places table, state_id is a foreign key. Some values, such as CA and UT, are repeated several times.

This type of relationship—where a primary key from one table refers to multiple items in another table—is known as a *one-to-many relationship*. It can be represented diagrammatically like this:

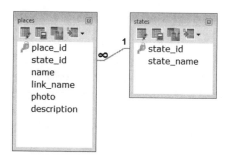

The key symbol next to place_id in the places table and state_id in the states table indicates they are the primary keys of their respective tables. The 1 indicates that each state_id in the states table is unique. The infinity symbol (∞) indicates that state_id can be repeated many times in the places table.

✳ NOTE: There's no standard for representing database relationships. However, you might come across another set of symbols known as Crow's Foot notation, which is explained in the sidebar "Using Crow's Foot Notation to Represent Relationships."

Using Crow's Foot Notation to Represent Relationships

There's a bewildering variety of ways to represent database relationships diagrammatically. You don't need to learn them, but it's useful to be able to recognize them if you encounter them elsewhere. The following diagram shows the relationship between the places and states tables using Crow's Foot notation. The name comes from the three-pronged link to the places table.

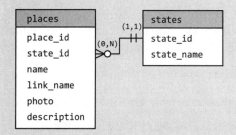

In a one-to-many relationship, the "one" side is represented by a vertical line through the link. The "many" side is represented by the three-pronged crow's foot. The relationship is further refined by a second vertical line on the "one" side and an empty circle on the "many" side. These indicate that a record must exist on the "one" side before it can be used as a foreign key on the "many" side.

It's quite common in a one-to-many relationship for there to be records on the "one" side that don't have corresponding records on the "many" side. For example, the states table lists all 50 states plus the District of Columbia, but the places table has records for only a handful of states. As more records get added to the places table, the number of times a state_id is used on the "many" side will change, but on the "one" side, the state_id will always be associated with only one record. This aspect of the relationship is reflected in the numbers in parentheses next to each table.

The (1,1) next to the states table means that state_id in the places table must refer to at least one—and only one—record in the states table. The (0,N) next to the places table means that state_id in the states table can refer to an unlimited number of records in the places table—or to none at all. Sometimes, the Crow's Foot symbols are used on their own, as are the numbers in parentheses.

Although one-to-many relationships are very common in database design, the task facing a database designer isn't always that simple. Here's a spreadsheet with details of several books.

1	author	title	publisher
2	David Powers	Adobe Dreamweaver CS5 with PHP	Adobe Press
3	Adobe Creative Team	Adobe Dreamweaver CS5 Classroom in a Book	Adobe Press
4	Michael Labriola, Jeff Tapper, Matthew Boles	Adobe Flex 4: Training from the Source	Adobe Press
5	Michael Labriola, Jeff Tapper	Breaking Out of the Web Browser with Adobe AIR	New Riders
6	David Powers	Getting StartED with CSS	friends of ED
7	Denise R. Jacobs	The CSS Detective Guide	New Riders

Each book has only one publisher, so it's easy to split the publishers' details into a separate table. But what about the authors? Some authors have written more than one book, and some books have more than one author. This is known as a *many-to-many relationship*.

The normal way to handle a many-to-many relationship is with an intermediate table that cross-references the primary keys in the other tables. The following diagram shows the same information distributed across four tables.

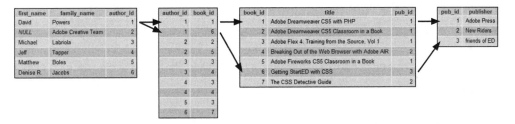

> ✱ **NOTE:** The normal convention is to put the primary and foreign key columns at the beginning of each table. The order has been changed in the preceding diagram to make the continuity of the relationships easier to follow.

Details of the authors, book titles, and publishers have been stored in separate tables called authors, books, and publishers. Each table has its own primary key: author_id, book_id, and pub_id respectively.

To find who wrote which book, a cross-reference table called author2book lists author_id and book_id in pairs as foreign keys. So, author_id 1 is associated with both book_id 1 and book_id 6. Each pair in the cross-reference table is unique, so it acts as a combined primary key.

The one-to-many relationship between the books and publishers tables is the same as in the earlier example. The pub_id column is the primary key of the publishers table and is stored as a foreign key in the books table.

The following diagram shows how the cross-reference table converts the many-to-many relationship into separate one-to-many relationships.

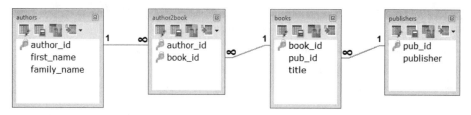

In addition, you can also have a *one-to-one relationship*, but this is relatively uncommon. Normally, data that goes logically together is stored in the same table. However, you might want to store data in a separate table for security reasons. For example, in a human resources database, an employee's salary details might be kept in a separate table that only payroll staff is permitted to access.

> **TIP:** If you have no previous experience working with databases, take some time to make sure you understand the principle of one-to-many and many-to-many relationships. They are indispensible to successful database design. At this stage, don't worry about how primary and foreign keys are generated. Part of the process is automatic. The rest is handled by using simple database queries.

Deciding how to organize your data

As you've already seen, relational databases don't store everything in one massive table. So, one of your first tasks is to decide on your table structure. There's no single "right" way to do it. Each database is different, but the following guidelines should help:

- Make a list of all the information you want to store in the database.
- Sort information into logical groups, and use them as the basis for tables. The ideal table should represent a single subject.
- If values are repetitive, consider moving them to a separate table.
- Use table columns to store only one piece of information for each record.
- Give each record a unique identifier (primary key).
- Cross-reference by storing the primary key as a foreign key in related tables.
- Simplify many-to-many relationships with a cross-reference table.

One of the main objectives in database design is to avoid repetition or redundancy. But if you're building a database that contains numerous addresses, what should you do about cities, districts, and street names? If you're not careful, you might end up with a highly fragmented structure that becomes a nightmare to maintain. It might make sense to store street names in a table devoted to a city or district rather than having separate tables for each one.

Perhaps the biggest mistake made by inexperienced database designers is putting more than one piece of information in a field. A *field* is the intersection of a column and a row, where a specific value, such as a primary key or the name of a state, is stored. Personal names should normally be separated into at least two fields: a person's family name and given names. If you want to store people's titles (Mr., Ms., Dr., and so on), they should go in a separate column. It's also common to have a column for suffixes (as in John Doe Jr. or John Doe III). You might even consider creating a separate column for middle names or initials.

> **TIP:** If in doubt, create a separate column for fields that store more than one piece of information. When displaying the results of a database search, it's easy to join fields together. Any item that will be used as a search term or for sorting results should go in a field of its own.

The places table shown earlier in "How a database stores information" has a photo column that could cause problems, because you might want to associate more than one photo with each record. A better solution might be to delete the photo column and store details of all photos in a separate table with a cross-reference table to match photos to various places.

Databases are capable of performing calculations, so there's no need to store the results of a calculation. For example, you don't need a column to store the tax-inclusive price of goods. The database can do the calculation for you. In fact, it's more efficient, because there's no need to recalculate all the values if the tax rate changes, and it avoids the risk of data corruption if you forget to recalculate when one of the values changes.

Naming databases, tables, and columns

You insert, update, delete, and search records in a database using Structured Query Language (SQL), which is based on natural language, so it's a good idea to use names that are meaningful when deciding on your table structure. Here are some useful naming practices:

- Use plural nouns, such as places, products, or members, for table names.
- Use singular nouns for column names.
- Do not use hyphens or spaces in names. Use an underscore to create hybrid names, such as first_name.

- Use lowercase only. The Windows version of MySQL converts all names to lowercase, which can cause problems when transferring data to a Linux server.

- Do not use any of the reserved words listed at http://dev.mysql.com/doc/refman/5.1/en/reserved-words.html.

> **TIP:** Some hosting companies insert hyphens in database names, even though they're invalid. Dreamweaver's server behaviors and phpMyAdmin automatically compensate for this by surrounding database, column, and table names with backticks (`). When writing your own SQL, you'll need to add the backticks. On some keyboards, the backtick is above the Tab key. On others, it's to the left of Z.

How Do You Pronounce SQL and MySQL?

Computing abounds with so many abbreviations and acronyms, it sometimes feels as though you're drowning in alphabet soup. There are two schools of thought about how to pronounce SQL. Some people spell it out as "Ess-Que-Ell," but most call it "sequel."

As a result, many people refer to MySQL as "my-sequel," but they're wrong. The official pronunciation is "My-Ess-Que-Ell." The "My" in MySQL is named after the daughter of Monty Widenius, one of the original creators of the database. So, now you know.

Deciding which data types to use

After you've decided on your table structure, you face one final hurdle—deciding which data type to use for each column. MySQL has no fewer than 36 to choose from!

Don't despair. This range of choices is mainly of interest to administrators of enterprise-level databases. In most cases, just a few data types are sufficient.

The basic data types fall into four categories:

- Numerical
- Strings
- Dates
- Geospatial data

Geospatial data is a highly specialized data type beyond the scope of this book. Let's take a look at the most frequently used data types for the other categories.

Storing numbers

Table 5.1 lists the three main data types used for storing numbers. If a column's data type is declared as UNSIGNED, negative numbers are not permitted.

Table 5.1	The Most Frequently Used Number Data Types in MySQL
Data Type	**Description**
INT	Stores integers.
FLOAT	Stores floating-point numbers.
DECIMAL	Stores fixed-point numbers.

The difference between FLOAT and DECIMAL lies in precision. FLOAT is considered an approximate value, whereas DECIMAL is a fixed-point number, not subject to rounding errors. Consequently, DECIMAL is particularly suited for use in storing currency values. When specifying DECIMAL as the data type, you need to set the maximum number of digits before and after the decimal point. If you fail to do so, it is treated as an integer.

> ▼ **CAUTION!** Prior to MySQL 5.0.3, DECIMAL was stored as a string, which meant it couldn't be used for calculations. If you are using an older version of MySQL, store currency values as cents, pence, or the smallest currency unit, and divide by 100 or the appropriate number to convert the value.

Storing strings

Strings normally refer to text, but in database terms, a string can also be a binary object, such as an image. **Table 5.2** lists the main string data types supported by MySQL.

Most text should be stored as CHAR, VARCHAR, or TEXT.

With CHAR and VARCHAR, you need to specify how wide you want the column to be. Text that exceeds the column width is truncated. The main difference between the two is that a CHAR column always occupies the space required for the full width, whereas a VARCHAR column uses only the amount necessary to store what's inserted. This means that a CHAR column ends up occupying unnecessary disk space if there's a lot of variation in the length of values being stored. However, CHAR columns tend to be faster.

Table 5.2   The Most Frequently Used String Data Types in MySQL

Data Type	Description
CHAR	Stores text in a fixed-width column. Maximum width: 255 characters. Trailing spaces are deleted. Accepts a default value.
VARCHAR	Stores text in a variable-width column. In theory, the maximum width of the column is 65,535 characters. Trailing spaces are preserved. Accepts a default value.
	In versions older than MySQL 5.0.3, the maximum width is 255 characters, and trailing spaces are deleted.
TEXT	Stores a maximum of 65,535 characters. Trailing spaces are preserved. Does not accept a default value.
BLOB	Stores binary objects up to a maximum of 64 KB. (BLOB stands for "binary large object.")
ENUM	Stores a single choice from a predefined list. Suitable for yes/no, male/female, and similar data, where only one choice is permitted.
SET	Stores zero or more values from a predefined list, up to a maximum of 64.

Since both VARCHAR and TEXT can store the same amount of characters in MySQL 5.0.3 or later, you might wonder if there's any advantage to one over the other. The advantage of VARCHAR is that it forces you to set a maximum width for the column, so you can limit the amount of material being stored. Here are some rules for using each data type:

- Use CHAR when you know all values will be the same length or there will be very little variation in length (e.g., phone numbers).

- Use VARCHAR for relatively short text that varies in length (e.g., product names, book titles, etc.).

- Use TEXT for longer text, such as articles and product descriptions. The maximum length (65,535 characters) is nearly 40 percent longer than this lesson.

Although BLOB is technically a string data type, I don't recommend its use. See the sidebar "Can I Store Images in a Database?" for an explanation.

That leaves the ENUM and SET data types. Although they are described as string data types, their values are actually stored as numbers, which makes them very fast and efficient (databases handle numbers more quickly than text). In both cases, you must define the list of acceptable values before using them. Although you can alter the table definition to add new values, attempting to enter a value that hasn't been preregistered results in the value being rejected.

Can I Store Images in a Database?

The short answer is "yes—but don't do it." There are several problems with storing images (or any other binary objects) in a database:

- Databases are best suited to the storage of text and numbers, which can be quickly searched and sorted. You can't search images. You can only search information that's been stored about them.

- Images tend to be large and cause your database tables to become bloated.

- If images are deleted, the database tables can quickly become fragmented.

- Databases store images as binary strings, so you need to store the image's MIME type separately and use a proxy script to display the image in a web page. If you fail to do so, you get a string of random characters instead of a picture.

Rather than storing images in a database, it is usually more efficient to store them in your web server's file system, and store only text details of each image in the database.

However, if you have a particular reason for storing images in a database, see my article on how to do so in the Dreamweaver Cookbook website at http://cookbooks.adobe. com/post_Upload_images_to_a_MySQL_database__PHP_-16609.html.

Instructions for creating the proxy script to display images stored in a database are at http://cookbooks.adobe.com/post_Display_an_image_stored_in_a_database__ PHP_-16637.html.

The ENUM data type is the database equivalent of a radio button in an online form. It's ideal for storing the results of multiple-choice questions where a single response must be selected. When defining the table, you list the acceptable values as a comma-separated list of strings. Because one value must be selected, you should also include an option to indicate nothing was selected. Technically speaking, you can store up to 65,535 options in an ENUM column. In practice, storing more than a handful is likely to become unmanageable in most situations.

If ENUM is the equivalent of the radio button, the SET data type can be compared to a checkbox group. Again, selections can be made only from a predefined list, which is limited to a maximum of 64 items. Some developers argue that the SET data type contravenes an important principle of database design, namely that you should not store more than one piece of information in a field. However, the way that MySQL stores SET columns is very similar to storing a foreign key.

The SET data type is useful for storing details of predefined options that are relatively stable. If the options are likely to change, it's better to store the values in a separate table and use a cross-reference table.

Storing dates and time

MySQL supports five data types for storing dates and time, all of which are listed in **Table 5.3**.

Table 5.3 Date and Time Data Types in MySQL	
Data Type	**Description**
DATE	Stores dates in YYYY-MM-DD format. All dates in the range from year 1000 to 9999 are accepted.
TIME	Stores hours, minutes, and seconds separated by colons. Valid range is '-838:59:59' to '838:59:59'.
DATETIME	Stores a combined date and time value in the format YYYY-MM-DD HH:MM:SS. Accepts the same range as DATE.
TIMESTAMP	Stores a combined date and time value in the same format as DATETIME but is limited to the range from 1970 to January 2038.
YEAR	When used with a 4-digit format, stores a year in the range 1901–2155. In a 2-year format, the range is 1970–2069.

The first thing to note about dates in MySQL is that they are stored in one format only: the year first, followed by the month number, and then the day of the month. This is the format recommended by the SQL specification and the International Organization for Standardization (ISO).

 TIP: Resistance is futile. Don't even think about trying to store dates in any other format. Some people try to get around this by storing dates in a VARCHAR column, thereby defeating most of the benefits of using a database, such as correct date sorting and date calculations. As long as you store your dates in YYYY-MM-DD format, you can use the MySQL DATE_FORMAT() function to display them in just about every way imaginable.

As you can see in Table 5.3, the range for TIME is not limited to the 24-hour clock, so its main purpose is to store durations rather than the current time.

A DATETIME column simply stores a combined date and time. If you don't specify the time, it defaults to 00:00:00.

A TIMESTAMP column stores a combined date and time in the same format as DATETIME, but it has automatic initialization and update properties. By default, a TIMESTAMP field is automatically set to the current date and time when you insert a new record, as long as you omit the field from the INSERT statement or set its value to NULL. The field is also automatically updated to the current timestamp whenever any other field in the record is changed. Only one TIMESTAMP column in a table can have these automatic initialization and update properties. By default, it's the first TIMESTAMP column in the table, but you can change this.

> ▼ **CAUTION!** MySQL timestamps record the date and time in a human-readable format unlike PHP, which stores timestamps as the number of seconds elapsed since January 1, 1970 (also known as the Unix Epoch). You cannot mix the two timestamps without converting one to the same format as the other.

Unless you need to store the year without any other part of the date, the YEAR data type is of limited interest. It's very easy to extract the year from a DATE, DATETIME, or TIMESTAMP field.

Creating a Database and Tables

After all that theory, it's time to achieve something practical. In this part of the lesson, I'll show you how to create a database and define a table to store the details for a user registration system.

Defining the database

For the exercises in this book, create a database called phpcs5 in your local testing environment. Even if you want to test these exercises on your remote server later, it doesn't matter if the database name is different. You can easily transfer tables and their associated data from one database to another.

1 Launch phpMyAdmin in your browser, and log in as the root user if necessary. You should see the phpMyAdmin welcome page, as shown in the screen shot on the first page of this lesson.

2 In the section labeled "MySQL localhost" in the center of the page, type **phpcs5** in the "Create new database" text field. Leave all the other settings at their default values, and click Create.

3 You should see a message telling you that the database has been created.

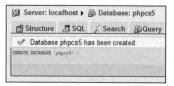

The screen also invites you to create a new table in the database. You'll do that in a moment, but first it's necessary to explain the meaning of collation.

Understanding how collation affects the sort order

The menu next to the "Create new database" field allows you to choose the default collation for the database. *Collation* is a technical term used in database design to specify the order in which results are sorted.

Collation is important if you work with languages other than English. If you work exclusively in English, you can ignore it entirely—well, almost. When phpMyAdmin displays the structure of a database or table, you'll notice that the Collation column is set to latin1_swedish_ci. Why the Swedish setting? MySQL was originally developed in Sweden, so its default collation is Swedish, which also happens to use exactly the same sort order as English.

However, in some languages, the traditional sort order is different from alphabetical order. For example, in Spanish, *LL* is treated as a separate character that comes after the letter *L*. The following screen shots show the difference.

Traditional Spanish   *Alphabetical order*

In the Traditional Spanish sort order, *llamar* comes after *loco*. But when sorted in alphabetical order, *llamar* comes first. The screen shot on the left was taken with collation set to utf8_spanish2_ci. The one on the right was taken with collation set to the default latin1_swedish_ci.

Collation can be set for the whole database, at table level, or for individual columns. If set at the database level or table level, that setting becomes the default for the whole database or table, but you can override the default for individual tables or columns.

The available options for collation depend on how MySQL has been set up, but the naming convention is easy to understand. Each name is composed of the following three elements separated by underscores:

- Encoding

- Language

- Case sensitivity: `bin` for binary, `ci` for case insensitive, and `cs` for case sensitive

✱ **NOTE:** Collation does not affect the encoding of data stored in MySQL. It is concerned solely with sort order.

Defining the users table

The `users` table for a user registration system needs to have at least five columns as follows:

- `user_id`

- `first_name`

- `family_name`

- `username`

- `password`

You might want to add other columns later, for example, to store the user's email address, but this will do for now.

1 If you left phpMyAdmin open on the page that confirmed the creation of the `phpcs5` database, skip to the next step.

If you need to relaunch phpMyAdmin, select `phpcs5` from the list of databases in the left column of the welcome page. This will open the Structure tab for the database and display the text fields for creating a new table.

2 In the section labeled "Create new table on database phpcs5," type **users** in the Name text field, and **5** in "Number of fields." Then click Go.

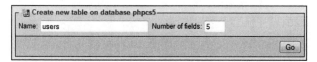

3 A huge matrix opens where you define the database table. There's a line for defining each table column.

This is perhaps the least user-friendly part of phpMyAdmin. The matrix is so large you will have difficulty seeing all of it onscreen without scrolling horizontally. In spite of this problem, it's quite easy to fill in.

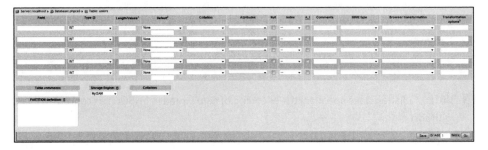

> **TIP:** When you create a table with only three columns, phpMyAdmin presents this matrix in a vertical layout, which makes it easier to see all options.

4 In the first row, type **user_id** in the Field text field.

5 Set the Type menu to INT. The first two fields should look like this:

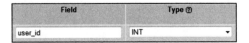

6 A primary key cannot be a negative number, so set the value of Attributes to UNSIGNED.

7 The user_id will be the primary key, so select PRIMARY from the Index menu.

8 You want the primary key to be automatically incremented, so select the A_I checkbox.

The values set in steps 6–8 should look like this:

9 The remaining columns are less complicated. Use the values shown in the following screen shot:

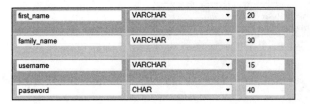

You don't know how long the values of `first_name`, `family_name`, or `username` will be. So, the data type needs to be VARCHAR. With this data type, you need to specify the width of the column in the Length/Values text field. It's a good idea to be generous in the size allocated. Otherwise, you run the risk that values will be truncated in the database.

Why use the CHAR fixed-width string data type for `password` and set its width at 40? Surely no one will have a password that long!

Passwords should not be stored in plain text, so the value will be encrypted as a 40-digit hexadecimal number.

10 Beneath the matrix in the center of the screen is a menu labeled Storage Engine. Make sure it's set to MyISAM (this is the default in XAMPP and MAMP).

For more details, see the sidebar "Choosing the Right Storage Engine."

11 Leave the remaining fields blank or at their default values, and click the Save button at the bottom right of the screen.

▼ CAUTION! Make sure that you click the Save button. The Go button adds an extra column to the matrix. If you click the Go button by mistake, type a dummy name in the Field text field, and set the Type menu to INT. Then click Save. This adds a column with the dummy name, which you can delete after saving the table definition.

12 After you have saved the table definition, phpMyAdmin presents you with a screen showing the settings for your new table. Check the values against the following screen shot.

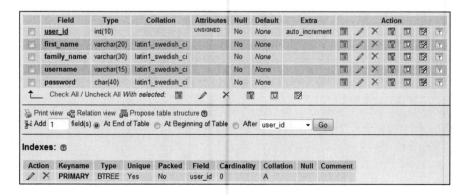

Choosing the Right Storage Engine

Choosing a storage engine in MySQL determines how your data is stored and retrieved. MySQL supports several storage engines, but the most widely used are MyISAM and InnoDB. MyISAM has been the default since MySQL 3.23, but it was announced in April 2010 that a new version of InnoDB would become the default from MySQL 5.5.

MySQL 5.5 was still in beta at the time this book was being prepared for publication. Moreover, many hosting companies don't offer support for InnoDB. Consequently, all the exercises in this book use MyISAM tables. Fortunately, choosing a storage engine isn't an irreversible decision. You can change a table's storage engine by selecting the Operations tab in phpMyAdmin and then selecting the new engine in the "Table options" section.

The main difference between the storage engines lies in InnoDB's added support for transactions and foreign key constraints.

A *transaction* is a series of database commands that must be executed as a group. If any part of the series fails, the transaction automatically undoes any changes. This is important in financial databases where money might be deducted from one account for transfer into another. If, for any reason, the money cannot be added to the second account, the whole transaction fails, and the money is restored to the original account.

A *foreign key constraint* keeps track of relationships between tables and prevents a record from being deleted if its primary key is still in use as a foreign key elsewhere.

If you installed the Windows Essentials version of MySQL and chose the Multifunctional Database option, your setup will default to InnoDB. You can change the default to MyISAM by editing C:\Program Files\MySQL\MySQL Server 5.x\my.ini in Notepad (launch Notepad by right-clicking it in the Start menu and selecting "Run as administrator"). Locate the following line:

```
default-storage-engine=INNODB
```

Change it to this:

```
default-storage-engine=MyISAM
```

Either restart your computer or restart the MySQL service by choosing Start > Control Panel > Administrative Tools > Services. Select MySQL in the Services panel, and click Restart.

Note that user_id is underlined, which indicates that it has been set as the table's primary key. This is confirmed by the Indexes section at the bottom.

You should also check that the Attributes field for user_id is set to UNSIGNED, and that Extra is set to auto_increment.

By default, phpMyAdmin sets Null to No, which means that a value must be entered in each field when adding a record to the table. This is exactly what you want for a user registration table. To make a column optional, select the Null checkbox in the definition matrix.

Collation for the text columns is set to latin1_swedish_ci. As explained in the previous section, this is the default for English. You don't need to change it unless you're working with a language that uses a special sorting order.

13 If any values are incorrect, you can edit the settings for individual columns by clicking the Edit icon ✎ in the appropriate row. This opens a similar screen to the matrix with the values for the selected column ready for you to edit.

If you need to delete a column—for example, if you created a dummy column after clicking Go by mistake—click the Delete icon ✕ in the appropriate row.

To edit or delete more than one column at the same time, select the checkbox next to each column name, and click the appropriate icon at the bottom of the structure table.

You'll start to populate this table with data in the next lesson. Before you do so, you should create dedicated user accounts for MySQL.

Creating MySQL User Accounts

When you connect to MySQL through phpMyAdmin in a local testing environment, you are logged in as the root superuser. The *root* user account has complete control over everything, including creating databases as well as deleting them. MySQL has no equivalent for the Windows Recycle Bin or Trash on a Mac. When something is deleted, it's gone forever.

The Web is a dangerous place, so you should never let a web page connect to MySQL as root. If you do, you run the risk of a malicious user finding a gap in your security and using it to destroy all your data. So, it's essential to create at least one user account with limited privileges.

For the exercises in this book, you should create two user accounts: one that can only retrieve information from the database and another with read/write privileges.

> ● **TIP:** When developing a database application for deployment on your live website, create one or more user accounts with the same username(s) and password(s) as assigned by your hosting company or server administrator. This will make it easy to test locally and deploy rapidly on your remote server.

Creating a user account with read/write privileges

The following instructions walk you through how to create a user account with the privileges to insert, update, and delete records, as well as to select them:

1 If necessary, launch phpMyAdmin in your browser, and log in as root.

If phpMyAdmin is already open, click the Home icon 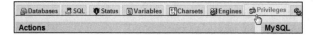 at the top left of the screen to return to the welcome page.

▼ **CAUTION!** To create a new user account, you must start on the phpMyAdmin welcome page. If you start from another page, you will be presented with different options.

2 Click the Privileges tab at the top of the page.

The "User overview" screen opens, which controls all user accounts.

If you have a new installation of MAMP on Mac OS X, continue with step 3. Otherwise, skip to step 4.

3 By default, MAMP allows anonymous access to MySQL. This is insecure, so you should remove the two anonymous accounts by selecting the checkboxes next to Any in the User column and then clicking Go.

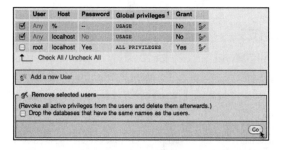

▼ **CAUTION!** Do not select "root." If you delete the root account, you will need to uninstall MAMP and start all over again.

4 The "User overview" screen should list the root superuser account, plus any other users already registered. (XAMPP creates a user called "pma" to support advanced features of phpMyAdmin beyond the scope of this book.)

Click the "Add a new User" link halfway down the page to open a new screen where you define the user.

5 In the Login Information section, type **cs5write** in the "User name" text field.

6 In the menu next to Host, select Local to insert "localhost" in the text field.

7 Type **Bow!e#CS5** in the Password and Re-type text fields.

For a database that will be deployed on a live website, you should choose a different password. "Bow!e#CS5" is only for the example files in this book. A strong password should contain a mixture of uppercase and lowercase letters, numbers, and special characters.

▼ **CAUTION!** Avoid using $ in a password, because PHP assumes that it's the beginning of a variable name when enclosed in double quotation marks.

The Login Information section should now look like this:

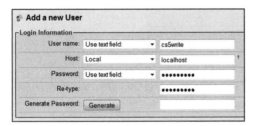

8 The remaining options on this page give the user privileges on all databases, which is potentially insecure. Leave the remaining options as they are, scroll down to the bottom of the page, and click Go.

You should see confirmation that you have added a new user.

9 Scroll down to the "Database-specific privileges" section, and select phpcs5 from the menu.

This loads the page where you specify the privileges for the cs5write user on the phpcs5 database.

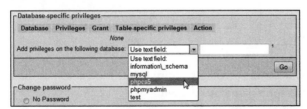

10 In the "Database-specific privileges" section, select the checkboxes for SELECT, INSERT, UPDATE, and DELETE. The meanings of these privileges are self-explanatory, but phpMyAdmin displays a tooltip as you hover over each one.

11 Click the Go button in the "Database-specific privileges" section to save the changes.

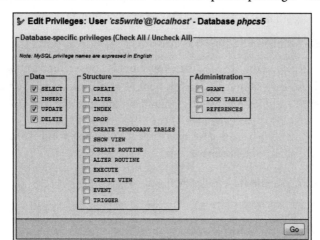

⚠ CAUTION! Often, several options are listed on a page in phpMyAdmin, each with their own Go button. Make sure you click the correct one.

This redisplays the same page with confirmation that you have updated the privileges for cs5write.

If you made any mistakes, you can correct them here, and then click Go to update the user account.

12 If everything is OK, click the Privileges tab at the top of the page.

This brings you back to the "User overview" page, where the cs5write user should now be listed.

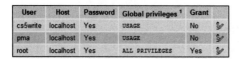

User	Host	Password	Global privileges [1]	Grant	
cs5write	localhost	Yes	USAGE	No	⚜
pma	localhost	Yes	USAGE	No	⚜
root	localhost	Yes	ALL PRIVILEGES	Yes	⚜

If you ever need to edit a user account's privileges, return to this page, and click the Edit Privileges icon ⚜ next to the appropriate user account.

Creating a view-only user account

Good security practice dictates that database users should have the fewest possible privileges to do what they need. Most web pages need only the ability to display records. So, using an account with read/write privileges for such pages opens a potential security gap. Close that gap by creating a second user account that has only the SELECT privilege on the phpcs5 database.

Repeat steps 4–12 in the previous section to create a user account called **cs5read** with the password **5T@rmaN**. In step 10, select only the SELECT checkbox.

> **TIP:** Some hosting companies allow only one user account on a MySQL database. In such circumstances, you are forced to use an account with read/write privileges for all your web pages. This means you must pay extra attention to security issues. Being alert to security is always a good thing, but a better alternative might be to move to a hosting plan that gives you greater control over setting MySQL user account privileges.

Importing Existing Data

Importing existing data into a MySQL database is very easy. The most common way is to use a .sql file. This is a text file that contains all the SQL instructions to build the database structure and then populate it with data.

Of course, someone needs to build the .sql file initially. You'll learn how to do so in Lesson 13.

Importing data from a .sql file

The following instructions show you how to import the list of USPS abbreviations and states from the example at the beginning of the lesson. You'll use the table you create here in lessons later in this book:

1 In the Dreamweaver Files panel, double-click lesson05/states.sql. It should open automatically in the Document window.

If Dreamweaver fails to recognize the .sql file type, right-click the file name, and select Open With > Dreamweaver.

You should see on the first line that the file is described as a SQL Dump. A *dump* is a text file that contains all the SQL commands to build and populate one or more database tables.

Lines that begin with a double-dash are treated as comments, as are sections of text enclosed between /* and */.

2 Scroll down to line 25, where you'll see a comment about the table structure for the `states` table. This is followed on line 28 by a SQL command that deletes the table if it already exists (DROP is the SQL command for deleting an entire column, table, or database). Lines 29–33 build the table and define its structure. Even without any knowledge of SQL, you should be able to follow what the commands are for. SQL is closely based on human language.

```
23
24   --
25   -- Table structure for table `states`
26   --
27
28   DROP TABLE IF EXISTS `states`;
29   CREATE TABLE IF NOT EXISTS `states` (
30     `state_id` char(2) NOT NULL,
31     `state_name` varchar(25) NOT NULL,
32     PRIMARY KEY (`state_id`)
33   ) ENGINE=MyISAM DEFAULT CHARSET=latin1;
34
35   --
36   -- Dumping data for table `states`
37   --
38
39   INSERT INTO `states` (`state_id`, `state_name`) VALUES
40   ('AK', 'Alaska'),
41   ('AL', 'Alabama'),
42   ('AR', 'Arkansas'),
43   ('AZ', 'Arizona'),
44   ('CA', 'California'),
45   ('CO', 'Colorado'),
46   ('CT', 'Connecticut'),
47   ('DC', 'District of Columbia'),
48   ('DE', 'Delaware'),
49   ('FL', 'Florida'),
          'Georgia'),
              ii'),
```

The SQL commands on lines 39–90 insert the values into the `states` table.

▶ **TIP:** Don't worry that you'll need to code this type of file by hand. MySQL has a utility program called `mysqldump` that's invoked by phpMyAdmin and does everything for you. Even with thousands of records, it takes only a few seconds to generate a `.sql` file.

3 Now that you have seen what a `.sql` file contains, you need to switch to phpMyAdmin and import the data.

In phpMyAdmin, make sure that you have selected the `phpcs5` database from the list on the left. Then click the Import tab at the top of the page.

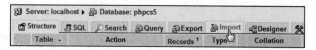

4 In the page that opens, click the Browse button in the "File to import" section, and use your operating system's dialog box to locate and select lesson05/states.sql. It doesn't matter if the file is still open in Dreamweaver.

5 Click Go. After a few seconds, you should see confirmation that the import was successful. The states table should also be listed together with the users table on the left of the page.

6 Click the states link on the left of the page to reveal the first 30 records in the newly imported table.

That's all there is to importing data from a .sql file. If the file contains more than one table, they will be imported in a single operation.

> **TIP:** If the import fails, it's likely to be caused by your server failing to understand some of the commented lines in the .sql file. Try removing all lines that begin with a double-dash, as well as all commands wrapped between /* and */.

What You Have Learned

In this lesson, you have:

- Taken a quick look at the most popular UIs for MySQL (pages 142–143)
- Seen how a relational database stores information (pages 143–144)
- Examined how primary and foreign keys build one-to-many, many-to-many, and one-to-one relationships between tables (pages 145–149)
- Studied best practices for naming databases, tables, and columns (pages 149–150)
- Explored the most important data types used in MySQL (pages 150–155)
- Created a database (pages 155–156)
- Seen the effect of collation on how records are sorted (pages 156–157)
- Defined a table for a user registration system (pages 157–161)
- Learned the difference between the MyISAM and InnoDB storage engines (page 160)
- Created MySQL user accounts and assigned privileges (pages 161–165)
- Imported existing data with a .sql file (pages 165–167)

What You Will Learn

In this lesson, you will:

- Create connection files for your MySQL user accounts
- Use an online form to insert records in a database table
- Build a login system and password-protect pages
- Encrypt passwords
- Display the results of a database query
- Use a repeat region to display multiple results
- Update and delete database records
- Hide part of the page and display a message when there are no results

Approximate Time

This lesson takes approximately 2 hours and 30 minutes to complete.

Lesson Files

Media Files:

styles/users.css

Starting Files:

lesson06/start/add_user.php
lesson06/start/delete_user.php
lesson06/start/login.php
lesson06/start/members_only.php
lesson06/start/restricted.php
lesson06/start/update_user.php
lesson06/start/user_list.php
lesson06/start/users.sql

LESSON 6

Generating PHP Automatically with Server Behaviors

A database without data is like a pub with no beer. Even with no PHP experience, Dreamweaver's built-in server behaviors can help you rectify the situation in next to no time. The server behaviors generate all the necessary code for basic database operations—processes that geeks with their love of acronyms sometimes refer to as CRUD (create, read, update, and delete).

By the end of this lesson, you will have used all the main server behaviors to create a simple user registration and login system. You'll also learn how to display, update, and delete existing records. Almost all the work will be done through dialog boxes, with only a minimal need to write code.

Dreamweaver server behaviors make it easy to insert records from a custom form.

What Server Behaviors Do

When Dreamweaver was first released in the late 1990s, the browser war between Netscape and Internet Explorer was at its height. A minefield of incompatibilities stood in the way of the average web designer trying to add dynamic features to a web page with JavaScript. So, Dreamweaver cut through the complexity by creating off-the-shelf scripts to solve common problems. A separate program called Dreamweaver UltraDev offered similar ready-made solutions for server-side functionality, which were merged into the core program in 2002 with the release of Dreamweaver MX. Everything is done through dialog boxes. Dreamweaver takes care of the rest.

This is a great boon for anyone who wants to create a database-driven site in a hurry, but you should be aware of the limitations of server behaviors. They provide only basic functionality. Apart from security improvements, they have remained essentially unchanged since they were first introduced. Adobe regards them more as a learning tool than as a production-level feature.

If you have no experience working with a database-driven site, this lesson will give you some useful insights to prepare you for later lessons. However, the rest of this book takes advantage of the enhanced PHP support in Dreamweaver CS5 to work with the Zend Framework, which offers a much wider range of features than server behaviors.

Connecting to the Database

Before you can use the server behaviors, you need to connect to the database with one of the MySQL user accounts you created in the previous lesson.

Each time a web page interacts with the database, MySQL verifies its credentials by checking the account's username and password. Rather than adding this information in every page, Dreamweaver creates a PHP file with the connection details, which server behaviors automatically include in the web page.

Creating a MySQL connection file

You need to create separate connection files for both user accounts: `cs5write` and `cs5read`. The process for both is identical:

1 In Dreamweaver, make sure you're in the PHP CS5 site that you're using for the exercises in this book, and open a PHP page in the Document window. Any page will do, even a blank PHP that hasn't been saved.

2 Open the Databases panel by clicking its tab or by choosing Window > Databases (Ctrl+Shift+F10/Shift+Cmd+F10).

If your site and testing server were set up as described in Lesson 2, you should see a list of four steps with check marks next to the first three.

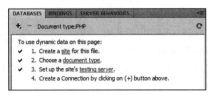

> **TIP:** If the check mark is missing from any of the steps, click the link in the first unchecked step. This opens the appropriate dialog box for you to set up the missing details. If your testing server wasn't running when you launched Dreamweaver, step 3 might be unchecked. Click the "testing server" link. This opens the Site Setup dialog box. Click Save to close it. This usually corrects the problem.

3 Click the plus (+) button at the top left of the Databases panel to open a menu with only one option: MySQL Connection.

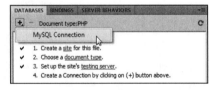

4 Click MySQL Connection to open the MySQL Connection dialog box. The options in the dialog box are fairly self-explanatory:

- "Connection name" not only identifies the connection, but is also used to create a PHP variable and the name of the connection file, so it should not contain any spaces or special characters, nor should it begin with a number.

- "MySQL server" is the location of the database server. For a local testing environment, enter **localhost**. If you are using MAMP with the default MAMP ports, enter **localhost:8889** instead.

- "User name" and "Password" are the name and password of the MySQL user account. The password used in the example files for cs5write is **Bow!e#CS5**.

- "Database" is the name of the database you want to connect to.

5 After filling in all the fields, click Test.

6 If everything is OK, you should see confirmation that connection was made successfully. Click OK to dismiss the confirmation alert, and then click OK in the MySQL Connection dialog box to create the connection file.

If you get an error message, consult the "Troubleshooting a MySQL connection" section.

7 Open the Files panel. You should see that Dreamweaver has created a new folder called Connections and inside is a PHP file with the same name as the connection you just created.

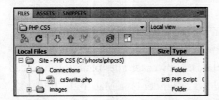

If you use Dreamweaver server behaviors on a live website, you need to upload the Connections folder to your remote server. Otherwise, your server behaviors won't work. Details of how to upload the necessary files are in Lesson 13.

8 Repeat the preceding steps to create another connection file for the cs5read user account. The password for cs5read in the example files is **5T@rmaN**.

⚠ CAUTION! For a live website, the location of the Connections folder is unimportant, as long as links to it are updated in files that use server behaviors. However, while you are developing a site in Dreamweaver, the Connections folder must remain in the site root for the server behavior dialog boxes to work. To avoid conflicts with your connection files, the Connections folder for the completed files for this lesson has been moved inside lesson06/completed.

Troubleshooting a MySQL connection

If you set up the testing server correctly in Lesson 2, everything should work. However, errors do happen. This checklist should help solve most problems:

- Check that your web server and MySQL are both running. If they are, turn off any security software temporarily, and try again.

- If that solves the problem, adjust your security software to allow local communication on port 80 for the web server and port 3306 for MySQL.

- Sometimes you will see an alert like this:

If your web server is running, read the URL in the second item very carefully. Dreamweaver uses a hidden folder called _mmServerScripts to communicate with MySQL. You normally can't see the folder in the Dreamweaver Files panel, but you can check for its existence using Explorer in Windows or Finder on a Mac. If the folder is in your site root, check the value of Web URL in your testing server definition (see "Creating the site definition" in Lesson 2). If you look closely at the preceding screen shot, you'll see that the URL uses "phpc5" instead of "phpcs5."

- MySQL error 2003 means that the MySQL server is not running or cannot be reached (probably because of a firewall restriction).

- The following error message is very common:

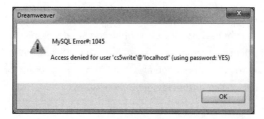

The error message tells you the name of the user, the MySQL server, and whether a password was used. Check all of them. Is the username right? Is the server correct? Is the password right? Passwords are case sensitive, so check that your CAPS LOCK key isn't turned on by mistake.

- If you are using MAMP, determine if you reset the Apache and MySQL ports or if you are using the MAMP defaults. If you are using the MAMP defaults, change "MySQL server" to **localhost:8889**.

- Occasionally, localhost fails to work on some systems. Try **127.0.0.1** instead (or **127.0.0.1:8889** if you're using the MAMP ports).

Inspecting the database in Dreamweaver

Once you have created the connection files successfully, the connections are listed in the Databases panel. If you expand one of them by clicking the tiny plus icon next to the connection name (it's a triangle in the Mac version), and then expand Tables, you can see the definition of each table and its columns.

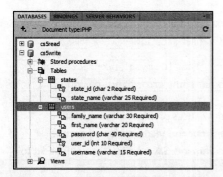

Dreamweaver lists the columns in alphabetical order, not in the order that they appear in the database. The primary key of each table is indicated by a small key icon to the left of the column name.

✴ **NOTE:** Although the Databases panel displays "Stored procedures" and Views, they are not supported by the PHP server behaviors.

Editing connection files

To edit a connection file, double-click the connection name in the Databases panel to reopen the MySQL Connection dialog box.

You can also edit a connection file by right-clicking its name in the Databases panel and choosing Edit Connection. The context menu also has options for testing and deleting a connection.

Using a dialog box to create the connection file is very convenient, but it's also a good idea to know what Dreamweaver is doing on your behalf. Let's take a quick look at the contents of a connection file:

1 Double-click cs5read.php in the Connections folder of the Files panel to open the file in the Document window.

2 Switch to Code view to examine the file. Apart from the PHP opening and closing tags, and some comments, it contains the following code:

```
$hostname_cs5read = "localhost";
$database_cs5read = "phpcs5";
$username_cs5read = "cs5read";
$password_cs5read = "5T@rmaN";
$cs5read = mysql_pconnect($hostname_cs5read, $username_cs5read,
➥ $password_cs5read) or trigger_error(mysql_error(),E_USER_ERROR);
```

The first four lines assign to variables the MySQL server address, the name of the database, and the username and password of the MySQL user account.

The final command creates the database connection, using the `mysql_pconnect()` function, and stores it as a resource in `$cs5read`. It also has some error handling code.

▶ **TIP:** On shared hosting, `mysql_pconnect()` sometimes causes problems. If your hosting company instructs you to use `mysql_connect()`, open your connection files and change `mysql_pconnect()` to `mysql_connect()` in the final command. Save the file(s) and upload it to your remote server.

3 Don't freak because your MySQL username and password are stored in plain text. To see what happens if anyone attempts to access this file, press F12/Opt+F12 to load it into a browser.

All you should see is a blank page.

4 Right-click, and select the option to view the page source. Again, it should be completely blank.

All PHP code remains on the web server. The connection file doesn't create any output that's sent to the browser, so your credentials are safe.

✱ **NOTE:** The only way anyone can access MySQL credentials stored this way is by hacking into a site's file system. Nevertheless, many developers prefer the added security of putting connection details outside the web server's document root. Dreamweaver server behaviors don't offer an easy way of doing this.

Inserting Records into a Table

Dreamweaver offers two ways of inserting records into a database table. One is with the Record Insertion Form Wizard, which does everything, including building the insertion form. The other is with the Insert Record server behavior, which uses a form that you build.

The wizard needs a new magic wand or book of spells. It does the job, but the form is ugly and you'll need to scrap everything and start again if you need to modify the form. It's more efficient to use the Insert Record server behavior with a form of your own. To save you time, I've already built one for you to practice with.

Using the Insert Record server behavior

The easiest way to use Dreamweaver's server behaviors for inserting and updating records is to give the input fields in your form the same names as the columns in the database table. However, some developers advocate using different names, because this makes it difficult for an attacker to guess the structure of your database. To show how to use the Insert Record server behavior both ways, the form for the following exercise has one text input field that uses a different name from its corresponding column.

✱ **NOTE:** For the remaining exercises in this lesson, you need to have created the users table in the phpcs5 database, as described in Lesson 5. If you need to rebuild the users table, you can import the table structure from lesson06/start/users.sql with phpMyAdmin.

1 In the Files panel, double-click lesson06/start/add_user.php and lesson06/start/login.php to open them in the Document window.

2 Choose File > Save As (Ctrl+Shift+S/Shift+Cmd+S) and save the files as **add_user.php** and **login.php** in lesson06/workfiles.

This opens a copy of each file in the new folder. Close the originals so you have clean copies if you make a mistake and need to start again.

3 Open Code or Split view to look at the underlying HTML. It contains a form with five text input fields. Three of them use the same name as columns in the users table: first_name, username, and password. The name attribute of the text input field for "Family name" has been changed to surname.

```
<body>
<h1>Sign Up ne..
<form id="form1" name="form1" method="post" action="">
    <fieldset>
        <legend>Just a few details and you&rsquo;re in</legend>
        <p>
            <label for="first_name">First name:</label>
            <input type="text" name="first_name" id="first_name" />
        </p>
        <p>
            <label for="surname">Family name:</label>
            <input type="text" name="surname" id="surname" />
        </p>
        <p>
            <label for="username">Username:</label>
            <input type="text" name="username" id="username" />
        </p>
        <p>
            <label for="password">Password:</label>
            <input type="password" name="password" id="password" />
        </p>
        <p>
            <label for="conf_password">Confirm password:</label>
            <input type="password" name="conf_password" id=
"conf_password" />
```

The id is required by the for attribute in the <label> tag to identify the correct form element. Another reason for this duplication is that an id must be unique within a page. However, radio button and checkbox groups use the same name for multiple elements. Dreamweaver appends an incremental number to the id of each element in radio button and checkbox groups that share a common name.

4 Open the Server Behaviors panel by clicking its tab, or choose Window > Server Behaviors (Ctrl+F9/Cmd+F9).

You should see a checklist of four items, with the first three checked off.

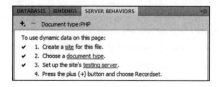

DATABASES | BINDINGS | SERVER BEHAVIORS

＋ – Document type:PHP

To use dynamic data on this page:
- ✔ 1. Create a <u>site</u> for this file.
- ✔ 2. Choose a <u>document type</u>.
- ✔ 3. Set up the site's <u>testing server</u>.
-   4. Press the plus (+) button and choose Recordset.

Why Does Dreamweaver Use Both "name" and "id"?

Dreamweaver inserts both name and id attributes in form elements. On the surface, this seems like unnecessary duplication. The name attribute has been deprecated on most HTML elements in favor of the id attribute. In other words, modern web standards specify that you should always use id instead of name. So why use both?

When a form is submitted, it's the name attribute, not id, that's used to identify the user input. If you leave out the name attribute, the form ceases to work.

5 Click the plus (+) button at the top left of the Server Behaviors panel, and then choose Insert Record from the menu that appears to open the Insert Record dialog box.

✱ **NOTE:** You can also insert server behaviors by choosing Insert > Data Objects or use the Data category of the Insert panel/bar. To avoid repetition, these instructions refer only to the menu in the Server Behaviors panel.

6 There is only one form, form1, in the page, so Dreamweaver selects it automatically in the "Submit values from" menu.

7 To insert records into the database, you need the cs5write connection.

Select cs5write in the Connection menu.

8 Dreamweaver might take a few moments to connect to MySQL and load details of the tables. When it's ready, it selects the first one in alphabetical order in "Insert table."

There are two tables in the phpcs5 database: states and users. Select users.

The Insert Record dialog box should now look like this:

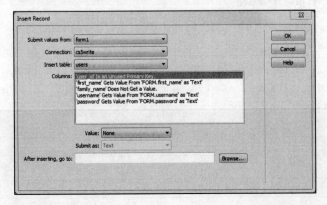

9 Look closely at the Columns section. The first item reports that user_id is "an Unused Primary Key." Although this might look wrong, it's not. When you defined the users table in the previous lesson, you set the user_id column to use auto_increment. This automatically assigns the next available number as the record's primary key, so there's no need to insert a value manually.

Most of the remaining entries match the name of each form element to the corresponding column in the table. Dreamweaver automatically recognizes the columns as being string data types, so the values will be submitted as text; that is, they will be wrapped in quotation marks.

There's one exception: The family_name column doesn't have a matching name in the form, so it's listed as getting no value. You need to fix that.

10 Select family_name in the Columns section. Click the Value menu below the Columns section, and select FORM.surname.

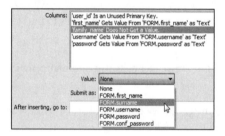

Dreamweaver should automatically detect that family_name is a string data type, so it sets "Submit as" to Text. That's all you need to do if you decide to use different names in your form and database tables.

11 To complete the Insert Record dialog box, you need to tell the server behavior which page to display after a record has been inserted.

Often, you want to display the insert form again. In such cases, just leave the "After inserting, go to" field blank.

However, in this case you want to send the user directly to the login page. Type **login. php** into the "After inserting, go to" field. Alternatively, click the Browse button and select lesson06/workfiles/login.php.

12 Check that the values in the Insert Record dialog box match those in the following screen shot, and click OK.

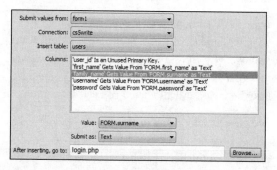

> ✴ **NOTE:** The Value and "Submit as" menus display the values related to whatever is selected in the Columns section.

13 The Server Behaviors panel now lists the Insert Record server behavior with details of the form name, MySQL connection, and table.

In Design view, the form is highlighted in aqua, indicating it's now dynamic.

> ➤ **TIP:** The highlighting can be distracting when you want to concentrate on the design of the page. Toggle the highlighting on and off by choosing View > Visual Aids > Invisible Elements.

14 Save the page, and switch to Code view. Dreamweaver has added more than 50 lines of PHP code above the DOCTYPE declaration. It has also added some PHP code in the action attribute of the opening `<form>` tag, as well as a hidden field at the bottom of the form.

Even if you don't understand the code, it's important to realize that all three parts are essential to this server behavior. Once you add a server behavior to a page, you need to be careful what you edit. Otherwise, you are likely to end up with PHP code that no longer works or behaves erratically.

A working copy of the page is in lesson06/completed/add_user.php.

Removing a Server Behavior Cleanly

A common mistake with server behaviors is deleting page elements in Design view without regard to the underlying code. If you make a mistake or decide you don't want a server behavior, do not attempt to remove it by editing Design view. Select the server behavior's listing in the Server Behaviors panel, and click the minus button at the top left of the panel. This removes the server behavior and all related code cleanly.

Edits made to server behaviors in Code view usually result in the server behavior being removed from the Server Behaviors panel, because Dreamweaver no longer recognizes it. The fact that a server behavior is not listed in the Server Behaviors panel is no guarantee that you haven't left behind code that could cause unpredictable results.

Testing the registration form

It's time to put everything to the test. In previous versions of Dreamweaver, you needed to launch the form in a browser to insert a record into a database, but now you can do it right inside the Document window:

1 With add_user.php open in Design view, click the Live View button, and enter some text in each field.

2 In Live View, you need to hold down a modifier key for links and form buttons to work. Hold down the Ctrl/Cmd key, and click the Sign me up! button.

✱ NOTE: There is nothing to check that the values entered in the password and confirmation fields are the same. You could use the Spry password widgets, but the check also needs to be made on the server. Lesson 7 deals with server-side validation.

3 If everything works OK, you should see the login page in Live View. If the login page doesn't load, see the sidebar "Why the Next Page Doesn't Always Load" on the next page.

4 Click the Live View button to toggle it off. You should be returned to add_user.php.

5 Open phpMyAdmin, and select the users table in the phpcs5 database from the list on the left of the page. You should see that the values you entered in the form have now been inserted in the database.

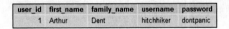

Note that the password is stored in plain text. Using a password text input field in a form only disguises the values that are entered. It does not encrypt the text. You'll fix that later.

Now that you have a username and password in the users table, you can create a login system and password-protect pages.

Creating a Login System

There are four User Authentication server behaviors in Dreamweaver:

- Log In User
- Restrict Access To Page
- Log Out User
- Check New Username

Why the Next Page Doesn't Always Load

If you have followed the instructions, the login page should have displayed correctly after the record was inserted into the database. However, it sometimes fails to do so because Dreamweaver uses the PHP `header()` function to redirect the user to the next page. This sends an HTTP header telling the browser to load a different page.

HTTP headers must be sent before any output to the browser, and if your testing server displays error messages (as recommended in Lesson 2), you should see a warning about "headers already sent." What confuses many people is that output to the browser can include any whitespace—such as spaces, tabs, or blank lines—outside the PHP tags, not only in the main script, but also in any include files, before the `header()` function is called. HTML comments and the Unicode byte order mark are also considered to be output.

If a server behavior fails to load the next page, check the following:

- Remove any whitespace before the opening PHP tag in the main page.

- Remove any whitespace before the opening PHP tag in any include files.

- If the include file contains only PHP code, remove the closing PHP tag. This is not only legitimate, it's the recommended practice.

- Make sure there is no HTML code before `header()` is used.

- Make sure that `echo` or `print` aren't used before `header()`.

- Choose Modify > Page Properties, and select the Title/Encoding category. Make sure that the Include Unicode Signature (BOM) checkbox is *not* selected.

- If you have set up your site to use links relative to the site root, Dreamweaver uses the `virtual()` function to include the MySQL connection file. The first line of the page should look similar to this:

```php
<?php virtual('/Connections/cs5write.php'); ?>
```

- Replace `virtual()` with `require_once()` and use a document-relative path to the connection file like this:

```php
<?php require_once('../../Connections/cs5write.php'); ?>
```

The first three are very useful, the last one is less so. The Check New Username server behavior prevents the insertion of duplicate usernames into the database, but it expects you to send the user to a different page if the username is already in use. Although you can get it to reload the registration page, it deletes all the values in the fields, forcing the user to type in everything again. Lesson 7 develops a more robust and user-friendly user registration system.

Applying the Log In User server behavior

The Log In User server behavior creates all the code to check the username and password. If it finds a match in the database, the user is redirected to a success page. If there's no match, the user is redirected elsewhere. You can designate a failure page, but it usually makes more sense to display the login form again. Follow these steps to apply Log In User:

1 Open lesson06/start/members_only.php in the Document window, and save a copy in lesson06/workfiles. Close the original file.

2 If lesson06/workfiles/login.php is closed, open it. You should now have your workfiles versions of login.php and members_only.php open.

3 With login.php as the active file in the Document window, click the plus button in the Server Behaviors panel, and choose User Authentication > Log In User to open the following dialog box.

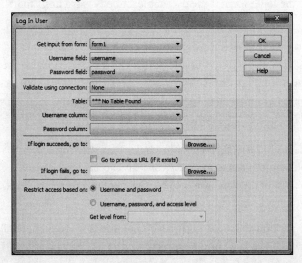

Dreamweaver normally fills in the first three items correctly. On a page that has more than one form, you might need to select the correct form in the "Get input from form" menu. Also, check that the correct values have been selected for "Username field" and "Password field."

4 A login form makes no changes to the database, so you should connect through the user account that has view-only privileges. In "Validate using connection," select cs5read.

Dreamweaver connects to MySQL and populates the Table menu with the names of the database tables.

5 Select the users table, and set "Username column" to username and "Password column" to password. The center section should look like this:

The next section is where you specify where the user should be redirected on success or failure.

6 Set the "If login succeeds, go to" field to **members_only.php**, and "If login fails, go to" to **login.php**. This will redisplay the login form if the username and password don't match a record in the database.

7 The "Go to previous URL (if it exists)" checkbox dictates what happens if a user has tried to visit a password-protected page without first logging in. The Restrict Access To Page server behavior remembers which page the user wanted to see. If this checkbox is selected, the user is sent to that page rather than to the default success page.

To see how this works, select "Go to previous URL (if it exists)."

8 The final section of the Log In User dialog box offers the choice of restricting access based on username and password only, or on username, password, and access level. If you choose the latter, you need to specify the database column that contains an access level, such as administrator or member.

The users table created in the previous lesson doesn't have a column to store such details, so leave the setting at the default "Username and password."

9 Click OK to insert the server behavior, and save login.php.

10 It's a good idea to test the server behavior before password-protecting any pages. Although you can do it in Live View, Dreamweaver has difficulty redirecting back to the login form if the username and password are invalid.

Press F12/Opt+F12 to launch login.php in a browser. Enter a nonexistent username and password, and click the Sign in button. The form should reload and clear both input fields. Ideally, an error message should be displayed, but the server behavior doesn't do that for you.

11 Enter the username and password that you stored in the database, and click Sign in. You should be taken to the members-only page.

A working copy of login.php is in lesson06/completed/login.php.

Password-protecting pages

The Dreamweaver Restrict Access To Page server behavior needs to be applied individually to each page that you want to protect. It cannot be applied simultaneously to multiple files or to an entire folder. Here's how to apply this server behavior:

1 Make a copy of lesson06/start/restricted.php in the lesson06/workfiles folder, and open it in the Document window.

2 In the Server Behaviors panel, click the plus button, and choose User Authentication > Restrict Access To Page. The following dialog box opens.

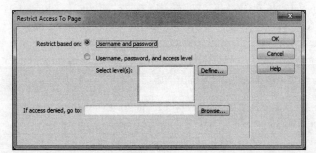

The default is to restrict access based on username and password only. If you want to restrict on the basis of access level as well, you need to click the Define button to specify the value(s) stored in the specified column of the database table, for example, administrator or member. After defining the values, you need to select them in the "Select level(s)" text area.

The users table doesn't have a column for access levels, so there's nothing to define or select. Use the default "Username and password."

3 When someone attempts to access a restricted page, you want to send them to the login form, so enter **login.php** in the "If access denied, go to" field.

4 Click OK to insert the server behavior, and save the page.

5 Repeat steps 2–4 with members_only.php.

6 Select the second paragraph in members_only.php, and create a link to restricted.php. Save the page.

7 Launch login.php in a browser, and log in with the username and password you stored in the users table. You should be taken to members_only.php.

8 Click the link to restricted.php. The server knows you are logged in, so it gives you access.

How the Server Knows You're Logged In

The Web is a stateless environment. Although you can navigate through the pages of a website, the server treats each request independently. Information can be passed from one page to another, but then it's wiped from the server's memory. To keep track of a user, the server can send a small piece of code called a cookie that's stored in the browser. However, cookies can hold only a limited amount of information, and storing them in the browser makes them vulnerable.

In common with other programming languages, PHP uses sessions to keep track of information related to a user. When a session is initiated, the server sends a cookie containing a random string to the user's browser. This allows the server to recognize the user with each new request. All the information about the user is stored as session variables on the web server. By storing the information on the server, it's more secure. Also, a much larger amount of information can be handled.

After someone logs in successfully, the Log In User server behavior stores the username in a variable called $_SESSION['MM_Username']. The Restrict Access to Page server behavior uses this to determine whether a user can view a protected page. For PHP sessions to work, cookies must be enabled in the user's browser.

Logging out users

In theory, a PHP session should expire after 24 minutes or when the browser is closed, whichever is sooner. Closing the browser is effective, but the 24-minute time limit is less reliable. Although you can't guarantee that visitors will log out, the Log Out User server behavior makes it easy to add a log out link to a page by following these steps:

1 If necessary, open workfiles/members_only.php in Design view.

2 Place the insertion point at the end of the second paragraph, and press Enter/Return to insert a new paragraph.

3 Click the plus button in the Server Behaviors panel, and choose User Authentication > Log Out User. The following dialog box opens.

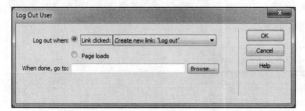

The radio buttons let you choose to log out when a link is clicked or when the page loads. You then specify where the user should be redirected.

4 Leave the radio button options set to the default to create a new link, and select login.php as the destination for "When done, go to."

5 Click OK to insert the server behavior and the log out link.

6 Save the page, and press F12/Opt+F12 to load the page in a browser. The server should still recognize you as being logged in.

If you are sent to the login form instead, log in to access members_only.php.

7 Click the "Log out" link.

You should be taken to the login form.

8 Edit the browser address bar to try to access members_only.php again. You should be taken straight back to the login form.

> ✱ **NOTE:** Attempting to use the browser back button should also result in the login form being displayed. However, some older browsers display the previous page again. This doesn't represent a security risk, because following any link to another protected page results in being sent back to the login form, requiring the user to log in again.

9 Without logging in, try to access restricted.php. You should be sent back to the login form.

10 Log in again. This time when you click the Sign in button, you should be taken directly to restricted.php instead of the default success page.

This is the result of selecting "Go to previous URL (if it exists)" in the Log In User dialog box.

Working copies of members_only.php and restricted.php are in the lesson06/completed folder.

Encrypting passwords

Storing passwords in plain text in a database is considered insecure. If anyone manages to compromise the database, everyone's password is exposed. The Log In User server behavior doesn't support encryption, but all it needs is a couple of quick edits to the code:

1 Open add_user.php in Code view. The first few lines of code look like this:

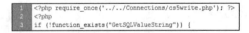

```
1   <?php require_once('../../Connections/cs5write.php'); ?>
2   <?php
3   if (!function_exists("GetSQLValueString")) {
```

The code on line 1 includes the MySQL connection file, and the server behavior code begins on line 2. Just in case you want the ability to change the server behavior's settings later, it's a good idea to add your own PHP code where it won't affect Dreamweaver's ability to recognize the server behavior.

2 Position the insertion point at the end of line 2, after the second opening PHP tag, and press Enter/Return to insert a new line.

3 Beginning on the line you just inserted, add the following code:

```
if (isset($_POST['password'])) {
  $_POST['password'] = sha1($_POST['password']);
}
```

Many server behaviors, such as Insert Record, use a self-processing form. Instead of submitting the form to another page, the server behavior reloads the same page and uses a PHP conditional statement to execute code only if the form has been submitted. When the insert form is first loaded into the browser, the conditional statement fails, so the code that inserts a record into the database is ignored. When the form is submitted, the conditional statement equates to TRUE, and the insert operation continues.

The code you just inserted works in a similar way. It uses the PHP isset() function to determine whether $_POST['password'] exists. If it does, the value is passed to sha1() to encrypt it, and the result is reassigned to $_POST['password'].

As explained in Lesson 3, the $_POST array is created automatically by PHP, but $_POST['password'] exists only if a form with an input element called password has been submitted using the POST method. So, $_POST['password'] doesn't exist when the page first loads, so this section of the code is ignored. But when the form is submitted, $_POST['password'] is encrypted using the sha1() function, which converts the value to a 40-digit hexadecimal string.

4 Select the code you just inserted, and copy it to your clipboard.

5 Open login.php, and paste the code into the same location as you did in add_user.php, immediately above the server behavior code. The first six lines of the page should now look like this:

```
<?php require_once('../../Connections/cs5read.php'); ?>
<?php
if (isset($_POST['password'])) {
  $_POST['password'] = sha1($_POST['password']);
}
if (!function_exists("GetSQLValueString")) {
```

6 Save add_user.php and login.php, and launch add_user.php in a browser.

7 Create a new user with a different username and password, and click the Sign me up! button.

8 When the login form appears, log in using the new username and password. It should work the same as before you made the changes in add_user.php and login.php.

9 Click the "Log out" link, and try to log back in using the first username and password. This time, it should fail, because the password wasn't encrypted when it was stored.

10 Open phpMyAdmin, and browse to the users table. You should see that the password for your second user is stored in encrypted form.

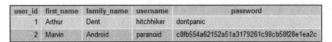

user_id	first_name	family_name	username	password
1	Arthur	Dent	hitchhiker	dontpanic
2	Marvin	Android	paranoid	c8fb554a62152a51a3179261c98cb58f28e1ea2c

Working copies of the amended files are in lesson06/completed/add_user_encrypt.php and lesson06/completed/login_encrypt.php. The code has also been amended so that the pages redirect to each other and to members_only_encrypt.php.

Displaying, Updating, and Deleting Records

To update or delete a record from a database, you first need to find it. The Dreamweaver server behavior that finds records in a database is called Recordset. It creates a SELECT query to find all matching records and stores the database result as a resource that can be used to display the information held in each row and column of the results. You can then use the primary key of each result to identify the record you want to update or delete.

Selecting records with the Recordset server behavior

The following instructions show how to retrieve a complete list of records in the users table, using the Recordset dialog box in Simple mode:

1 Make a copy of lesson06/start/user_list.php in your workfiles folder, and open it in Design view. The page contains an HTML heading and a skeleton table with two rows and four columns like this:

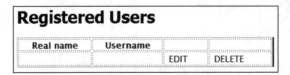

2 In the Server Behaviors panel, click the plus button, and choose Recordset to open the Recordset dialog box.

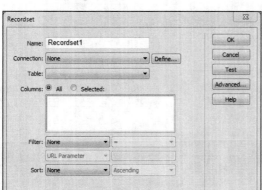

✱ NOTE: If the Recordset dialog box has different options from those shown here, click the Simple button on the right. It's in the same place as the Advanced button in the preceding screen shot.

3 Dreamweaver automatically fills the Name field with Recordset1. This value is used to create several PHP variables, so it's better to replace it with something more meaningful. Because it will be used as a variable, it should contain no spaces or special characters, and must not begin with a number.

Replace Recordset1 in the Name field with **getUsers**.

4 The Recordset server behavior doesn't alter records, so select cs5read in the Connection menu.

5 When Dreamweaver has populated the Table menu, select users. You should now see a list of the table columns in the Columns section. By default, the All radio button is selected, so the column names are grayed out.

6 Click the Selected radio button to activate the Columns section, and Shift-click to select all the columns except password.

7 You want to retrieve all records in the table, so leave Filter at the default value of None.

8 To sort the results by family name, select family_name from the Sort menu. This automatically sets the menu to the right to Ascending. If you select Descending, the results are returned in reverse order.

The settings in the Recordset dialog box should now look like this:

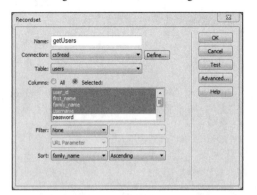

9 Click the Test button. This should display the results of the SQL query that Dreamweaver is building for you in the background. As long as you have some records in the table, you should see something similar to this:

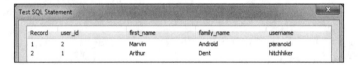

If you get an error message, check the settings in the Recordset dialog box.

10 Click OK to close the Test SQL Statement panel, and then click OK in the Recordset dialog box.

11 Save user_list.php. If you test the page in Live View or a browser, you'll see no difference. The Recordset server behavior gets the results from the database, but that's all. It's up to you to decide how to use them.

Leave user_list.php open and ready for the next section, where you'll display the first record in the second row of the table.

Using the Bindings panel to display database results

The code created by the Recordset server behavior extracts the first row of results from the database query so they're ready for display. All that's necessary is to drag them from the Bindings panel into your page:

1 With user_list.php still open from the previous section, open the Bindings panel by clicking its tab, or by choosing Window > Bindings (Ctrl+F10/Cmd+F10).

2 You should see the getUsers recordset listed there. If necessary, click the plus icon or triangle next to the recordset name to reveal the names of the columns you selected from the users table.

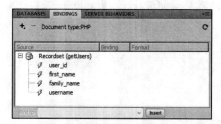

3 Select first_name in the Bindings panel, and drag it into the first cell of the second row of the table in Design view. This inserts a dynamic text object into the table like this:

The dynamic text object identifies the recordset and column name, making it easy to recognize.

TIP: If you have difficulty dragging and dropping, position the insertion point in Design view where you want the dynamic text object to go. Then select the column name in the Bindings panel, and click the Insert button at the bottom right of the panel.

4 Click to the right of the dynamic text object, and press the spacebar once to insert a space next to it.

5 Drag family_name from the Bindings panel and drop it next to the first_name dynamic text object. Alternatively, just select family_name in the Bindings panel, and click the Insert button.

6 Use either method to insert a dynamic text object for username in the second cell. The page should now look like this:

Don't worry that the `first_name` and `family_name` dynamic text objects are stacked on top of each other. Dynamic text objects are placeholders that give no indication of how they will look when the page is displayed in Live View or a browser. In this case, each dynamic text object represents a single word, but in a blog or product catalog, a dynamic text object could represent several paragraphs.

7 Save the page, and click Live View. You should see the first result from the database query displayed in place of the dynamic text objects.

8 Turn off Live View, and leave user_list.php open and ready for the next section, where you'll amend the page to display all results from the database.

If you want to check your code so far, compare it with lesson06/completed/user_list01.php.

Using the Repeat Region server behavior to display multiple results

The Repeat Region server behavior creates a `do. . . while` loop (see Lesson 3) to loop through multiple results from a database query. The server behavior gives you the option to display all results or limit them to a maximum number:

1 Click anywhere in the second table row, and then click `<tr>` in the Tag selector at the bottom of the Document window to select the whole row.

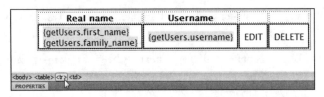

▶ **TIP:** Using the Tag selector is the most accurate way of selecting HTML elements. If you drag across the table cells, you might not select the `<tr>` tags in the underlying code. Failure to select the complete row results in the page falling apart when you apply the Repeat Region server behavior.

2 Click the plus button in the Server Behaviors panel, and choose Repeat Region to open the following dialog box.

There's only one set of database results on the page, so Dreamweaver selects the correct value for Recordset.

The radio buttons let you choose to display a specific number of records. The default is 10, but you can edit this. Alternatively, you can display all records.

3 There are only a couple of records in the users table at the moment, so leave the settings at their default values, and click OK.

4 In Design view, you should see a gray border around the second table row with a tab at the top left indicating that it's a repeat region.

5 Save the page, and click Live View. You should see both records displayed.

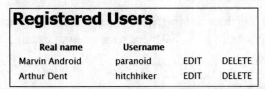

If you weren't careful, your table might end up looking like this:

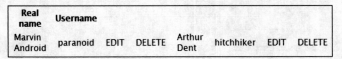

That's what happens if you don't select the whole table row correctly before applying a Repeat Region server behavior.

You can compare your code with lesson06/completed/user_list02.php.

Creating links to select specific records

To update or delete records, you need to filter the results to select the record you want. As explained in Lesson 5, each record in a database should have a primary key as its unique identifier. You use the primary key to select a specific record:

1 Copy lesson06/start/update_user.php and lesson06/start/delete_user.php to the workfiles folder.

2 Continue working with user_list.php from the preceding exercise. In Design view, select the text EDIT in the second table row. This will become a link to update_user.php.

3 Click the Browse for Folder icon in the Property inspector, and select update_user.php in the Select File dialog box. Do *not* click OK yet, because you need to add a query string at the end of the URL.

4 Click the Parameters button next to the URL field to open the Parameters dialog box.

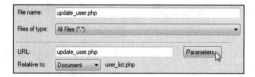

5 Type **user_id** in the Name field on the left of the dialog box

6 Click the Value field next to the value you have just entered. This reveals a lightning bolt icon on the right of the Value field (it's circled in the following screen shot). Click this icon to open the Dynamic Data dialog box.

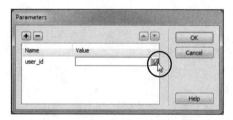

⚠ CAUTION! This is the point where many people go wrong. The lightning bolt icon appears next to each field when selected. It's vital that you click the one to the right of the Value field, not the Name field.

7 Expand the getUser recordset, if necessary, and select user_id.

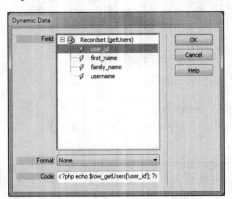

8 Click OK to close the Dynamic Data dialog box. Then click OK in the Parameters and Select File dialog boxes to close them.

9 Open Code view to check the link that has been created. It should look like this (it's around line 76):

```
<a href="update_user.php?user_id=<?php echo $row_getUsers['user_id'];
➡ ?>">EDIT</a>
```

The query string and associated PHP code has been highlighted. This adds a question mark followed by user_id= after the filename. The PHP code that follows inserts the user_id of the current record.

If your code doesn't look like this, delete the link and repeat steps 2–8 to get it right. If this part is wrong, nothing else will work.

10 Back in Design view, select the text DELETE in the fourth cell of the second row, and create a link to delete_user.php, adding a query string in the same way as for EDIT. The code for the link should end up looking like this:

```
<a href="delete_user.php?user_id=<?php echo $row_getUsers['user_id'];
➡ ?>">DELETE</a>
```

11 Save user_list.php, and test it by clicking the Live Code button. This launches Live View and simultaneously opens Split view to reveal the output of the PHP code. You should see something similar to this:

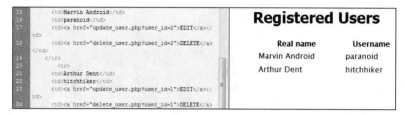

The query strings display user_id= followed by the primary key of each record. This value will be used to identify which record to update or delete.

12 Click Live View to switch off both Live Code and Live View.

You can compare your code with lesson06/complete/user_list03.php.

Loading a record into the update form

Updating a record involves the following stages:

1 Retrieve the record and use it to populate the input fields of the update form.

2 Make any changes in the update form.

3 Submit the form to update the database.

This means you need to start the task with the Recordset server behavior. This time, you use a filter to get the record you want. The value passed through the query string that you created in the preceding section acts as the filter.

1 Open update_user.php in the Document window, click the plus button in the Server Behaviors panel, and choose Recordset.

2 Use the following settings in the Recordset dialog box.

The Recordset server behavior only needs SELECT privileges, but you'll add the Update Record server behavior later, so use the cs5write connection.

The sha1() function used earlier in the lesson to encrypt the password performs one-way encryption. In other words, there's no way to decrypt the password, so there's no point in displaying it in the update form.

The user_id sent through the query string is used to select the correct record, so the Filter settings tell the SQL query to match the user_id column with the URL Parameter user_id.

Only one record will be selected, so Sort is set to None.

3 Click OK to close the Recordset dialog box. You now need to populate the form fields with the results of the recordset.

4 Select the "First name" text field in Design view. Open the Bindings panel, and select first_name in the getUser recordset. Make sure that "Bind to" at the bottom of the Bindings panel is set to input.value (this should happen automatically), and click Bind.

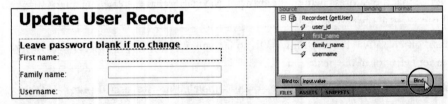

This inserts a dynamic text object for first_name in the text input field.

▶ **TIP:** If you're good at dragging and dropping, you can drag the value from the Bindings panel and drop it on the text input field in Design view. Dreamweaver automatically binds the dynamic text object to the value attribute of the <input> tag.

5 Repeat step 4 with the "Family name" and Username text fields, selecting family_name and username in the Bindings panel respectively. You should now have dynamic text objects in the first three text fields.

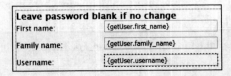

6 Save update_user.php, and switch to user_list.php.

7 Launch Live View. Hold down the Ctrl/Cmd key, and click one of the EDIT links. You should see the update form with the first three fields populated from the database.

Notice that the Address field in the Browser Navigation Bar displays the query string with the user_id at the end of the URL.

8 Turn off Live View. If everything is OK so far, you're ready to apply the Update Record server behavior in the next section.

You can compare your code with lesson06/completed/update_user01.php.

Using the Update Record server behavior

Using the Update Record server behavior is very similar to the Insert Record server behavior. However, you'll need to do some hand coding to handle the password. If nothing is entered in the Password text field, you need to use the existing value. Otherwise, you encrypt the new one and use that.

1 You need to store the value of the primary key in the form so that the Update Record server behavior knows which record to update.

With update_user.php open in Design view, position the insertion point anywhere inside the form, and choose Insert > Form > Hidden field.

2 In the Property inspector, change the name of the hidden field to user_id. Then click the lightning bolt icon next to Value to open the Dynamic Data dialog box.

3 Select user_id from the getUser recordset in the Dynamic Data dialog box, and click OK. This is the same procedure you used before when creating the query string for the EDIT and DELETE links.

4 Click the plus button in the Server Behaviors panel, and choose Update Record to open the Update Record dialog box.

You need to use the cs5write connection, and select the users table. As with the Insert Record server behavior, you need to set the family_name column to get its value from FORM.surname.

The important difference is that the Update Record server behavior picks up the primary key from the hidden form field. Select user_id in the Columns section, and check that it selects the record using FORM.user_id.

Set "After updating, go to" to user_list.php.

Check that the values match the following screen shot, and click OK.

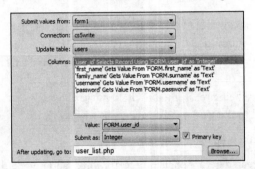

It's a good idea to save the page at this point in case you make a mistake in the following steps.

5 Switch to Code view, and cut the following lines of code to your clipboard. Use the line numbers in the screen shot only as a guide. The code might be in a slightly different location in your page.

```php
58  $colname_getUser = "-1";
59  if (isset($_GET['user_id'])) {
60    $colname_getUser = $_GET['user_id'];
61  }
62  mysql_select_db($database_cs5write, $cs5write);
63  $query_getUser = sprintf("SELECT user_id, first_name, family_name, username FROM users WHERE user_id = %s", GetSQLValueString($colname_getUser, "int"));
64  $getUser = mysql_query($query_getUser, $cs5write) or die(mysql_error());
65  $row_getUser = mysql_fetch_assoc($getUser);
66  $totalRows_getUser = mysql_num_rows($getUser);
```

This is the code created by the Recordset server behavior. It needs to come before the Update Record server behavior code, because you need the value of the password column in case it is to be reinserted in the database.

6 Scroll up to the following location, and paste the code on the blank line between the closing curly brace and the line beginning $editFormAction.

```
30      return $theValue;
31    }
32  }
33
34  $editFormAction = $_SERVER['PHP_SELF'];
```
———— *Paste code here*

7 Insert a blank line after the code you just pasted, and add the following:

```
if (isset($_POST['password']) && empty($_POST['password'])) {
  $_POST['password'] = $row_getUser['password'];
} else {
  $_POST['password'] = sha1($_POST['password']);
}
```

This conditional statement starts by checking if $_POST['password'] has been set. If it has, it means the update form has been submitted. If the field was left empty, the value already stored in the database is reassigned to $_POST['password']. But if the field isn't empty,
$_POST['password'] is encrypted before being reassigned to the same variable. This ensures that the correct value is passed to the Update Record server behavior code.

8 Save update_user.php, and test it by launching user_list.php.

Click the EDIT link for the user you created before encrypting passwords, and update the user's password.

9 If you check in phpMyAdmin, you'll see that the password has now been encrypted. Test the username and password in login.php, and you should be able to log into members_only.php.

A working update form is in lesson06/completed/update_user.php.

Using the Delete Record server behavior

By default, the Delete Record server behavior assumes you just want to delete the selected record without asking for confirmation. This seems a foolhardy approach, because there's no way to recover a record once it has been deleted. Fortunately, it's quite easy to modify the default behavior using these steps:

1 With delete_user.php open, click the plus button in the Server Behaviors panel, and choose Recordset. Create a recordset using the same settings as in step 2 of "Loading a record into the update form."

2 Use the Bindings panel to add dynamic text objects next to Name and Username. This will identify the record about to be deleted.

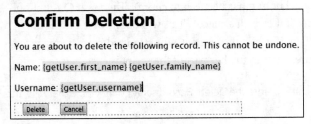

3 Click inside the red outline of the form, and insert a hidden field.

✳ **NOTE:** In Windows, Dreamweaver's visual aids display a form with a dotted outline in Design view, as shown in the preceding screen shot. The Mac version uses a solid outline.

Name the field user_id, and set its value to user_id from the getUser recordset in the same way as you did for the update form.

4 Click the plus button in the Server Behaviors panel, and choose Delete Record. Use the following settings in the Delete Record dialog box.

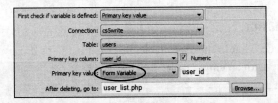

By default, "Primary key value" is set to URL Parameter. This deletes the record as soon as the page loads. You *must* change this to Form Variable.

5 Click OK to apply the Delete Record server behavior.

6 All that remains is to wire up the Cancel button.

In Code view, insert a new line *before* this code (it should be on line 3):

```
if (!function_exists("GetSQLValueString")) {
```

7 In the space you just created, add the following code:

```
if (isset($_POST['cancel'])) {
  header('Location: user_list.php');
  exit;
}
```

The name attribute of the Cancel button has been set to cancel. The isset() function checks the $_POST array to see if it contains cancel. This will be the case only if the Cancel button has been clicked. If it has, the header() function redirects the page to user_list.php, and exit ensures that no further part of the script is executed.

⚠ **CAUTION!** This redirect must come before the Delete Record server behavior. Otherwise, the record will still be deleted.

8 Test the page in a browser or Live View by launching user_list.php and clicking one of the DELETE links (hold down Ctrl/Cmd if using Live View). You should see the details of the record in delete_user.php.

9 Click the Cancel button. When you're redirected to user_list.php, the record is still listed.

10 Click the DELETE link again, and click Confirm this time. When you're redirected to user_list.php, the record is no longer listed. If you check in phpMyAdmin, you'll see that it's no longer in the database.

You can compare your code with lesson06/completed/delete_user.php.

Using the Show Region server behavior

At the moment, you should have one record left in the users table. But what happens if you delete the last record? Try it. You end up with an empty table.

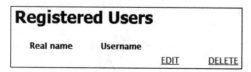

This looks odd. It would be much better if you could display a message that no records were found. The Show Region server behavior can fix that for you.

1 With user_list.php open in Design view, click to the right of the table, press Enter/Return to insert a new paragraph, and type **No records found**.

2 Select the whole paragraph by clicking <p> in the Tag selector at the bottom of the Document window.

3 With the paragraph still selected, click the plus button in the Server Behaviors panel, and choose Show Region > Show If Recordset Is Empty.

4 This launches a dialog box that asks you to select the recordset. There's only one on this page, so just click OK. This surrounds the paragraph with a gray border and a Show If tab at the top left.

5 Click anywhere inside the table, and click <table> in the Tag selector to select the whole table.

6 With the table selected, click the plus button in the Server Behaviors panel, and choose Show Region > Show If Recordset Is Not Empty.

7 Again, you're asked to select the recordset. There's only one, so just click OK. The table is surrounded by a gray border with a Show If tab.

8 Test the page. If there are no records in the users table, you should see this:

> **Registered Users**
>
> No records found

9 If you add another record to the users table, the "No records found" message will be hidden, and the new user listed.

You can compare your code with lesson06/completed/user_list_showif.php.

Evaluating the Server Behaviors

If you have no previous PHP experience and working with a database, the server behaviors are extremely impressive. They enable you to put together a database-driven site with a minimum of effort. This lesson has covered the main server behaviors. The only important one that has been omitted is the Recordset Navigation Bar, which inserts eight separate server behaviors in a single operation. It allows you to spread a long series of database results over multiple pages and navigate back and forth through them.

✱ **NOTE:** The Recordset Navigation Bar is not listed on the Server Behaviors panel menu. To insert one, choose Insert > Data Objects > Recordset Paging > Recordset Navigation Bar. The dialog box has only two options: the recordset you want to use and a choice of text or images for the navigation links. After inserting the navigation bar, you need to style it with CSS.

Using the server behaviors and the techniques taught in this lesson, you can achieve a great deal. For example, the EDIT and DELETE links use the same technique as you would use for a product list. By incorporating the product's primary key in a link, you can load a page to display the product's details. Instead of loading the details into an update form, you can load them into a normal page and use dynamic text objects to display them. In fact, delete_user.php does exactly that. To display images, store the filename in the database, and bind a dynamic text object to the src attribute of an <img> tag.

Impressive though they are, server behaviors have considerable drawbacks that become apparent the more you use them. Here are some of the main problems:

- There's only one validation server behavior, Check New Username, and it's not very user friendly.
- The User Authentication server behaviors don't support password encryption.
- Every time a page is loaded, a connection is made to the database, even if it's not needed.
- Recordsets are often created when they're not needed.
- The code is in the same page as the HTML, making it difficult for a designer and programmer to work simultaneously on different aspects of a site.
- A lot of identical code is embedded in each page. It would be more efficient to put it in external files.
- Much of the code is inflexible. As soon as you want to do anything different, you need to customize the code or write your own.
- The server behaviors are tied to MySQL. They cannot be adapted for use with any other database.

Perhaps the biggest problem with the server behaviors is that they raise unrealistic expectations. Being able to create a basic database-driven site without touching any of the underlying code leads beginners to expect server behaviors to do everything. They then start trying to work out how to do something and hit a brick wall. This has led to demands for improved server behaviors that perform more sophisticated operations, such as server-side validation, file uploading, and sending emails. In fact, a suite of advanced server behaviors, the Adobe Dreamweaver Developer Toolbox (ADDT), was available until its withdrawal from sale in April 2009. ADDT had many passionate fans, but the code it produced was inflexible and difficult to edit.

The difficulty with server behaviors is that they need to anticipate which options the user will want. The wider the range of options the more complex the code needs to be. To keep the code manageable, server behaviors offer only basic functionality. Judging from the decision to discontinue ADDT and not add new server behaviors to Dreamweaver CS5, the role of server behaviors is likely to decline. They're great for doing a quick mockup of a database-driven website or for a very simple site. For anything else, you need something more robust. The remaining lessons will use the Zend Framework to show you how to build more sophisticated solutions without needing to write masses of code.

> **TIP:** If you want to learn more about customizing Dreamweaver's PHP server behaviors, there's in-depth coverage in my book, *The Essential Guide to Dreamweaver CS4 with CSS, Ajax, and PHP* (friends of ED, 2008, ISBN: 978-1-4302-1610-0). Although it's written for the previous version of Dreamweaver, the server behaviors work identically in Dreamweaver CS5.

What You Have Learned

In this lesson, you have:

- Created MySQL connection files (pages 171–177)
- Used the Insert Record server behavior to insert records in the users table (pages 177–183)
- Created a login system with the Log In User server behavior (pages 183–187)
- Protected pages with the Restrict Access To Page server behavior (pages 187–188)
- Created a link to log out from the protected part of a site (pages 188–190)
- Encrypted passwords (pages 190–192)
- Selected records with the Recordset server behavior (pages 192–194)
- Used the Bindings panel to display the results of a recordset (pages 194–196)
- Displayed multiple results in a repeat region (pages 196–197)
- Created links to select specific records (pages 198–200)
- Updated and deleted records (pages 200–206)
- Hidden part of the page and been shown a message when a recordset is empty (pages 206–207)

What You Will Learn

In this lesson, you will:

- Install the Zend Framework and set up site-specific code hints
- Alter a database table to add a unique index and extra columns
- Validate user input on the server with Zend_Validate
- Preserve user input and display error messages when input fails validation
- Create reusable code with Dreamweaver's Server Behavior Builder
- Check for duplicate usernames
- Insert user input into a database with Zend_Db
- Create a login system with Zend_Auth

Approximate Time

This lesson takes approximately 3 hours to complete.

Lesson Files

Media Files:

    styles/users.css
    styles/users_wider.css

Starting Files:

    lesson07/start/add_user.php
    lesson07/start/login.php
    lesson07/start/members_only.php

Completed Files:

lesson07/completed/add_user.php
lesson07/completed/add_user01.php
lesson07/completed/add_user02.php
lesson07/completed/add_user03.php
lesson07/completed/login.php
lesson07/completed/members_only.php
lesson07/completed/scripts/library.php
lesson07/completed/scripts/library_magic_quotes.php
lesson07/completed/scripts/restrict_access.php
lesson07/completed/scripts/user_authentication.php
lesson07/completed/scripts/user_authentication01.php
lesson07/completed/scripts/user_registration.php
lesson07/completed/scripts/user_registration01.php
lesson07/completed/scripts/user_registration02.php
lesson07/completed/scripts/user_registration03.php

Validating Input on the Server

Using JavaScript for validation is not enough on its own, because it takes only a few seconds to turn off JavaScript in a browser, rendering your validation script useless. Before inserting user input into a database, you must validate it on the server with a server-side language, such as PHP.

In this lesson, with the help of a powerful third-party script library—Zend Framework— you'll create a robust user registration system that validates input on the server. This involves writing your own PHP code rather than relying on Dreamweaver to generate it for you. Any inconvenience is more than made up for in greater functionality, and the process is simplified by site-specific code hints.

You'll also use Dreamweaver's Server Behavior Builder to speed up the insertion of frequently used PHP code.

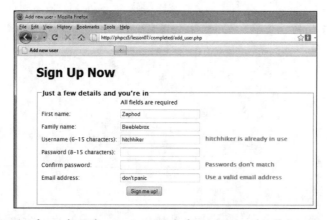

The registration form alerts the user to errors before inserting details into the database.

Introducing the Zend Framework

The Zend Framework (ZF) is a huge open source library of PHP scripts. The "minimal" version of ZF 1.10 consists of more than 2,700 files in nearly 500 folders, and is more than 22 MB in size. Of course, size isn't everything. In fact, you might wonder why you need so many files to do a few basic tasks, such as inserting and updating records in a database, uploading files, and sending emails.

Frameworks provide a wide range of options, many of which you might never use. For example, ZF has 14 components that access different e-commerce services on Amazon.com. Most developers never use them, but they're indispensible if you have an Amazon affiliate account. Instead of writing a script of mind-numbing complexity, you can query the Amazon database with just a few lines of code.

Most tutorials assume you want to use ZF to build a web application using the Model-View-Controller (MVC) design pattern, which divides data handling (the model), output (the view), and conditional logic (the controller) among separate scripts. Unless you have considerable PHP experience, the MVC design pattern can be confusing, so this book takes a different approach, offering a gentler introduction to ZF.

ZF is a *loosely coupled* framework, which means each part is designed to work with minimal dependency on other parts. You can use just a few components without needing to learn the whole framework. But should you decide later to adopt MVC, your knowledge of key ZF components will speed up the transition.

Here are the main components you'll be using in the remaining lessons:

- Zend_Auth to check user credentials
- Zend_Db to communicate with a database
- Zend_File to upload files
- Zend_Loader to load ZF classes automatically
- Zend_Mail to send emails and attachments
- Zend_Paginator to page through a long series of database results
- Zend_Service_ReCaptcha to prevent spam input
- Zend_Validate to validate user input

The exercises continue using MySQL, but Zend_Db makes the code more flexible. Changing just one or two lines allows you to switch to Microsoft SQL Server, PostgreSQL, or another database system.

ZF has a number of other factors in its favor:

- Its principal sponsor is Zend Technologies, the company founded and run by PHP core contributors.

- Leading software companies, including Adobe, Google, and Microsoft, have contributed components or significant features. Adobe contributed Zend_Amf, which acts as a gateway between PHP and the Flash Player, using the binary Action Message Format (AMF).

- ZF was designed from the outset to use PHP 5 objects. Many frameworks were originally designed for compatibility with PHP 4, which is less efficient.

- The next major version of ZF is being designed to enhance interoperability with other frameworks, such as Symfony.

> **TIP:** ZF is an object-oriented framework. If you're not familiar with PHP objects, now is a good time to review "Using Objects and Resources" in Lesson 3.

Installing the Zend Framework

The CD accompanying this book contains ZendFramework-1.10.6-minimal.zip. Alternatively, download the most recent version from http://framework.zend.com/download/latest. Choose the Minimal version of ZF, which contains all the files you need. Some download links require you to establish a Zend account. Like ZF, this is free and does not entail any obligations.

To install ZF, simply unzip the file to a suitable location on your hard disk. It's more efficient to locate it outside the phpcs5 site root, so it's accessible to all sites in Dreamweaver. Create a folder called php_library at the top level of your C drive on Windows or in your home folder on a Mac, and unzip ZF there.

Two folders, bin and library, are inside the main folder. The framework is in a subfolder of library called Zend. Each component has a corresponding .php file in the Zend folder plus a folder of its own.

There's no need to open the files, but if you do, you'll see that each file is extensively commented, which partly explains why the framework is so big. As you gain more experience, you'll discover a lot of useful information in these comments. Sometimes they help explain features that are not fully documented.

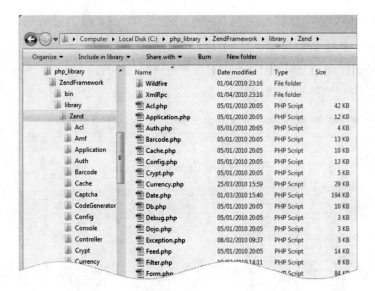

> **TIP:** The ZF documentation at http://framework.zend.com/manual/en/ is extensive and contains many examples. Unfortunately, much of it is written on the assumption that you are using the MVC design pattern. It also expects you to have a solid understanding of PHP. However, considerable efforts have been made to improve it.

Setting up site-specific code hints for ZF

In Lesson 4, you learned how to create site-specific code hints for WordPress, Drupal, and Joomla! Dreamweaver automatically recognizes the structure of these CMSs. With other frameworks, including ZF, you need to tell Dreamweaver where to find the files and which ones you want to scan to generate code hints. You don't need the WordPress code hints again in this book, so the following instructions show how to set up a separate structure for ZF hints. This replaces the existing version of dw_php_codehinting.config in the phpcs5 site, but you can easily switch between different sets of code hints by selecting them in the Structure menu of the Site-Specific Code Hints dialog box.

> **TIP:** You can also follow these steps in the final section of my Adobe TV video about PHP code hints at http://tv.adobe.com/watch/learn-dreamweaver-cs5/using-php-code-hinting-in-dreamweaver-cs5.

1 In the Dreamweaver Files panel, select the PHP CS5 site.

2 Make sure the active file in the Document window is from the current site, or close all files.

3 Choose Site > Site-Specific Code Hints.

4 Make sure the Structure menu is set to <New from Blank>.

5 Click the "Select sub-root folder" icon next to the Sub-root text box, and navigate to the library folder one level above the Zend folder.

✴ **NOTE:** The sub-root folder must be at least one level higher than any files or folders that you want to scan.

6 Click Select. Because the folder is outside the site root, Dreamweaver displays the following alert.

Just click OK.

7 Click the plus (+) button above the File(s) area to open the Add File/Folder dialog box.

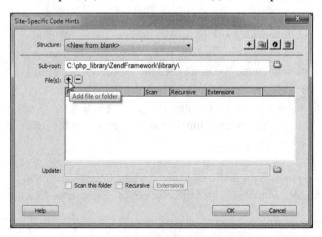

8 Click the "Select folder" icon next to the File/Folder text box, and select the Zend folder.

9 The Recursive checkbox tells Dreamweaver whether to scan all subfolders. If you select the checkbox for the Zend folder, code hints are enabled for the entire framework. Because ZF contains so many files and folders, scanning all of them is not a good idea, so leave the checkbox deselected.

10 To make the scanning process more efficient, click the plus button above the Extensions area, and type **.php** in the highlighted section. This tells Dreamweaver to scan only .php files.

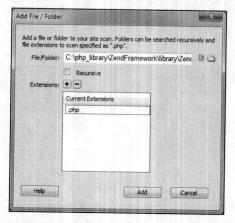

11 Click Add, and repeat steps 7–10 to add the following folders, all of which are subfolders of Zend: Auth, Captcha, Db, File, Loader, Mail, Paginator, and Validate. When setting up each folder, select the Recursive checkbox and add .php to the Extensions list.

You also need to add the Service folder and one of its subfolders, ReCaptcha. The Service folder contains many subfolders, so select the Recursive checkbox only for the ReCaptcha subfolder.

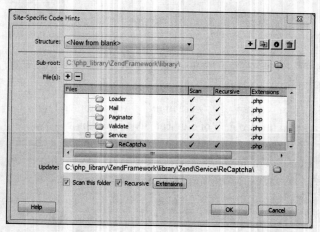

If you forget to select the Recursive checkbox or add the .php filename extension, you can change the options using the checkbox and button at the bottom of the Site-Specific Code Hints dialog box.

12 Save the configuration by clicking the Save Structure icon at the top right of the dialog box 🔳.

13 Type **Zend** in the Name text box (you can use any name except Custom, Drupal, Joomla, or WordPress), and click Save.

14 Click OK to close the Site-Specific Code Hints dialog box. This inserts a file called dw_php_codehinting.config in the site root. Dreamweaver uses this to scan the ZF folders and create code hints for the selected components.

> **TIP:** The folders are scanned in reverse alphabetical order each time you launch Dreamweaver. This process shouldn't slow down the program, but if you select the whole framework, it can take several minutes before all code hints are ready for use.

Improving the Registration Form

The registration form created in Lesson 6 has serious flaws. There's no control over the values entered in each input field. If you submit the form without filling in any of the fields, MySQL stops you, but the server behavior code leaves you with this unhelpful message and no way to get back to the form.

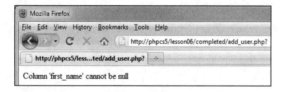

This is MySQL's way of saying that first_name is a required field, but you need a better way of conveying that message to the user.

What's more, a series of blank spaces is accepted as valid input, so you could end up with a completely blank record. There's also the problem of duplicate usernames, not to mention setting a minimum length for the password. The registration form needs to check all the user input before attempting to insert it into the database and to redisplay the form with error messages if validation fails, as shown in the following diagram.

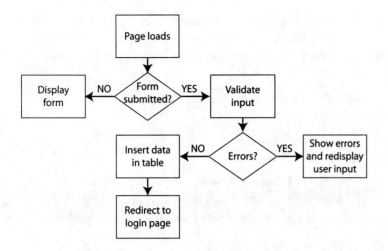

Additionally, there's the question of forgotten passwords. In Lesson 8, you'll learn how to send users an email to reset their password, so you need to add extra columns to the users table—one to store email addresses and the other for a security token.

There's a lot to fix. Let's start by updating the users table.

Adding a unique index to the users table

A *unique index* prevents duplicate values from being inserted in a database column. Adding an index to a column is quick and easy in phpMyAdmin.

1 Open phpMyAdmin, and select the users table in the phpcs5 database.

2 If you have any records with duplicate usernames, click the Delete icon 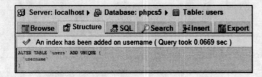 next to the record you want to delete. Leave at least one record in the table, because you need it for testing later.

3 Click the Structure tab at the top left of the screen to display the definition of the users table.

4 Click the Unique icon in the Action section of the username row. When the page reloads, you should see confirmation that an index has been added to username. The SQL command used to create the index is displayed immediately below. Check that it says `ADD UNIQUE`.

5 If you clicked the wrong icon and created a different type of index or a unique index on the wrong column, click the Details link at the bottom of the page to reveal the Indexes section, and delete the index you have just created; then repeat step 4 to add a unique index on username.

Leave phpMyAdmin open with the Structure tab selected to continue with the instructions in the next section.

Adding extra columns to the users table

It takes only a couple of minutes to add a column to a database table in phpMyAdmin. Changing the structure of a database is simple, but it should normally be done only in the development stage. Once you start filling the database with records, you risk losing data or having incomplete records.

1 With the Structure tab of the users table selected in phpMyAdmin, locate "Add field(s)" toward the bottom of the screen. Type **2** in the text field, leave the "At End of Table" radio button selected, and click Go.

⬛ **NOTE:** The other radio buttons let you specify where the new column(s) are to be inserted. If you select the After radio button, phpMyAdmin inserts the new column(s) in the middle of the table after the column chosen from the list.

This presents you with a matrix where you define the two new columns. Because there are only two, the options are listed vertically, which makes them easier to see.

2 For the email column, type **email** in Field, set Type to VARCHAR, and Length/Values to **100**.

The token will be a randomly generated, fixed-length string. For the other column, type **token** in Field, set Type to CHAR, and Length/Values to **32**. Also select the Null checkbox to make this column optional.

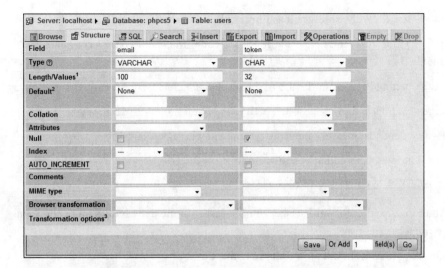

3 Click Save. The revised table structure should look like this:

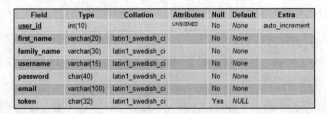

Field	Type	Collation	Attributes	Null	Default	Extra
user_id	int(10)		UNSIGNED	No	None	auto_increment
first_name	varchar(20)	latin1_swedish_ci		No	None	
family_name	varchar(30)	latin1_swedish_ci		No	None	
username	varchar(15)	latin1_swedish_ci		No	None	
password	char(40)	latin1_swedish_ci		No	None	
email	varchar(100)	latin1_swedish_ci		No	None	
token	char(32)	latin1_swedish_ci		Yes	NULL	

▼ **CAUTION!** If you click Go instead of Save, phpMyAdmin adds the options for another column. Give the column a dummy name, and select INT as Type. After you click Save, delete the unwanted column by clicking the Delete icon ✕ in the table structure.

There is no need to update the existing record(s) in the users table. They can be deleted after you have tested the script later in this lesson.

Loading ZF class files

Before you can use ZF classes and objects, you need to include the definition files into each page. With such a large framework, it would be cumbersome to include each file individually, so ZF provides an autoloader. This loads only those class definitions that are needed for the current script. For it to work, you need to add the library folder to your include_path, where PHP looks for include files.

1 Create a new PHP file, and save it as **library.php** in lesson07/workfiles/scripts.

2 Switch to Code view, and delete all the HTML code. You should have a completely blank file.

3 Add an opening PHP tag at the top of the file. Do *not* create a matching closing PHP tag.

4 On the next line, assign the absolute path to the library folder to $library.

The value depends on your operating system and where you saved ZF.

- On Windows, it should look similar to this:

```
$library = 'C:/php_library/ZendFramework/library';
```

You can use either forward slashes or backslashes in the path, but it's more common to use forward slashes.

- On Mac OS X, it should look something like this:

```
$library = '/Users/username/php_library/ZendFramework/library';
```

Note that the path begins with a forward slash. Replace **username** with your own Mac username.

✱ NOTE: This path needs to be changed when you upload the site to your remote server, but it's in only one file, so it's not a major problem.

5 The value of include_path is specified in php.ini, but you don't always have access to php.ini on shared hosting, so you can use the set_include_path() function to change it on the fly. Add the following code on the next line:

```
set_include_path(get_include_path() . PATH_SEPARATOR . $library);
```

Rather than overwriting the existing value of include_path, you need to add $library to it. The existing value is retrieved by get_include_path(). Each path needs to be separated by a semicolon on Windows or a colon on Mac/Linux. To make the code portable between different operating systems, the constant PATH_SEPARATOR inserts the appropriate separator automatically. Everything is joined with the concatenation operator (a period or dot).

▶ TIP: Press Ctrl+spacebar to invoke code hints to speed up the creation of this line of code and ensure its accuracy.

6 To use the autoloader, you need to include the class file for Zend_Loader_Autoloader like this:

```
require_once('Zend/Loader/Autoloader.php');
```

This is the only ZF file that you need to load explicitly. You don't need to use a fully quali-fied path to the Zend folder, because the code in the previous step added its parent folder, library, to the PHP include_path.

7 Now invoke the autoloader like this:

```
$loader = Zend_Loader_Autoloader::getInstance();
```

Technically speaking, you don't need to assign the result to a variable, but it's useful to do so to check that everything is working correctly.

8 To test your script so far, add the following:

```
if ($loader) {
   echo 'OK';
} else {
   echo 'We have a problem';
}
```

9 Save library.php, and click Live View to test the page. If everything is OK, you should see OK onscreen. If you see "We have a problem," read the error message(s). The most likely cause is a mistake in the path to the library folder. Also, check the spelling of all the func-tions and make sure PATH_SEPARATOR is all uppercase.

10 Once everything is working, remove the conditional statement that you added in step 8. You can also remove the $loader variable from step 7. The code in your page should look like this (the value of $library depends on your setup):

```
<?php
$library = 'C:/php_library/ZendFramework/library';
set_include_path(get_include_path() . PATH_SEPARATOR . $library);
require_once('Zend/Loader/Autoloader.php');
Zend_Loader_Autoloader::getInstance();
```

Do *not* add a closing PHP tag. See the sidebar, "Omitting the Closing PHP Tag," for an explanation.

Connecting to the database with Zend_Db

In ZF, all communication with a database is done through a Zend_Db object. This is similar to setting up a MySQL connection for Dreamweaver's server behaviors, but it has two signifi-cant advantages:

- A Zend_Db object doesn't connect to the database until it's needed. This puts less strain on the database than a Dreamweaver MySQL connection, which always connects, even if the script doesn't need it.

Omitting the Closing PHP Tag

When a script ends with PHP code, the closing PHP tag ?> is optional. In fact, the ZF coding standard actually forbids its use in pages that contain only PHP code. Leaving out the closing PHP tag prevents problems with the "headers already sent" error (see the sidebar "Why the Next Page Doesn't Always Load" in Lesson 6) and prevents a lot of hair tearing.

Dreamweaver CS5 supports the omission of the closing PHP tag. However, as you'll see in Lesson 8, leaving out the closing tag of an include file sometimes switches Design view into CSS quirks mode. If this hinders you, add a closing tag, but make sure it's not followed by any whitespace or newline characters.

The closing tag should always be used if HTML follows the PHP script in the *same* page. It's OK if the HTML is in a parent page. The PHP engine automatically switches back to HTML mode at the end of an include file.

- Zend_Db has several adapter subclasses that connect to different database systems. To connect to a different database, just create a Zend_Db object using the appropriate subclass. Normally, this involves a single line of code unless your SQL uses database-specific functions.

Since most pages require a database connection, it makes sense to instantiate the Zend_Db object in the same file that loads the ZF classes.

1 To connect to a database, you need to supply the location of the database server, the username and password of the account you want to use, and the name of the database. You pass these details as an associative array (see "Creating an associative array" in Lesson 3) to the Zend_Db constructor, using the array keys 'host', 'username', 'password', and 'dbname'.

Create an array for the cs5write user account at the bottom of library.php like this:

```
$write = array('host'     => 'localhost',
               'username' => 'cs5write',
               'password' => 'Bow!e#CS5',
               'dbname'   => 'phpcs5');
```

> **TIP:** It's not essential to indent an associative array and line up the => operators like this, but it makes your code easier to read and debug.

2 Create another array for the cs5read account directly below.

```
$read  = array('host'     => 'localhost',
               'username' => 'cs5read',
               'password' => '5T@rmaN',
               'dbname'   => 'phpcs5');
```

3 Your choice of Zend_Db adapter depends on the database you want to use and the PHP configuration of your remote server. If your remote server supports pdo_mysql, use this:

```
$dbWrite = new Zend_Db_Adapter_Pdo_Mysql($write);
```

If your remote server supports only mysqli, use this:

```
$dbWrite = new Zend_Db_Adapter_Mysqli($write);
```

> **TIP:** You don't need to type out the whole class name. As explained in Lesson 1, Dreamweaver's code hints ignore underscores and recognize substrings within names. Typing **pdomy** takes you directly to Zend_Db_Adapter_Pdo_Mysql. Just press Enter/Return as soon as it's highlighted. Also, be careful when passing $write as the argument to the constructor. Because it's an array, Dreamweaver automatically adds an opening square bracket, which you need to remove.

4 Create another object for the cs5read account, using the appropriate adapter:

```
$dbRead = new Zend_Db_Adapter_Pdo_Mysql($read);
```

Or

```
$dbRead = new Zend_Db_Adapter_Mysqli($read);
```

5 Because a Zend_Db object doesn't connect to the database until it's needed, it's a good idea to make a test connection to ensure your code is OK. Add these conditional statements at the end of library.php:

```
if ($dbWrite->getConnection()) {
  echo 'Write OK<br />';
}
if ($dbRead->getConnection()) {
  echo 'Read OK';
}
```

When you type the -> after the object, code hints should show you the methods it can use. The getConnection() method has a self-explanatory name. If each connection is OK, the conditional statements display confirmation. If there's a problem, you'll see a fatal error similar to this:

> **Fatal error:** Uncaught exception 'Zend_Db_Adapter_Exception' with message 'SQLSTATE[28000] [1045]
> Access denied for user 'cs5write'@'localhost' (using password: YES)' in
> C:\xampp\php\PEAR\Zend\Db\Adapter\Pdo\Abstract.php:144 Stack trace: #0
> C:\xampp\php\PEAR\Zend\Db\Adapter\Pdo\Mysql.php(96): Zend_Db_Adapter_Pdo_Abstract->_connect() #1
> C:\xampp\php\PEAR\Zend\Db\Adapter\Abstract.php(304): Zend_Db_Adapter_Pdo_Mysql->_connect() #2
> C:\vhosts\phpcs5\lesson07\completed\scripts\library.php(20): Zend_Db_Adapter_Abstract->getConnection() #3
> {main} thrown in **C:\xampp\php\PEAR\Zend\Db\Adapter\Pdo\Abstract.php** on line **144**

Don't panic. The important information is in the second line, which says access was denied for cs5write and that a password was used. This normally means the password was wrong.

Another possible cause is choosing the wrong adapter class. It's easy to mix up Zend_Db_Adapter_Pdo_Mssql with Zend_Db_Adapter_Pdo_Mysql. The former is for Microsoft SQL Server. If you make this mistake, the error message is likely to tell you that the mssql driver is not installed. If it is installed, you might be trying to connect to the wrong database server.

Check your code, paying particular attention to spelling and case sensitivity.

6 After verifying that your connections are working, delete the code you added in step 5. It's not needed any more.

Leave library.php open to continue working with it in the next section.

✱ **NOTE:** For details of the Zend_Db adapter classes for other databases, see http://framework. zend.com/manual/en/zend.db.adapter.html.

Handling exceptions with try and catch

ZF is an object-oriented framework. If an error occurs in any part of the script, it *throws an exception*. Unlike an ordinary PHP error, which displays the error message at the point in the script where it occurs, an exception can be handled in a different part of the script. If you look closely at the first line of the fearsome error message in the preceding screen shot, you'll see it refers to an "uncaught exception." When you throw something, it needs to be caught.

To prevent this sort of unsightly error message, you should always wrap object-oriented code in try and catch blocks like this:

```
try {
  // main script
} catch (Exception $e) {
  echo $e->getMessage();
}
```

The main script goes between the curly braces of the `try` block, where PHP tries to run the code. If all is well, the code is executed normally, and the `catch` block is ignored. If an exception is thrown, the script inside the `try` block is abandoned, and the `catch` block runs instead.

Objects can define many different types of exceptions, so you can have different `catch` blocks to handle each type separately. The `Exception` in the parentheses after `catch` indicates it's a generic `catch` block to handle all exceptions. The exception is assigned to the variable `$e` so you can access any messages it contains. At the moment, the `catch` block just uses `echo` and the `getMessage()` method to display the error message. When the script is ready to be deployed in a real site, you replace the code in the `catch` block with a more elegant way of handling the problem, such as displaying an error page.

You need to wrap most of the code in library.php in a `try` block, and add a `catch` block at the bottom of the page.

1 Position the insertion point at the end of the following line, and press Enter/Return to insert a blank line:

```
require_once('Zend/Loader/Autoloader.php');
```

2 On the new line, type **try**, followed by an opening curly brace.

3 Select all the code on the following line to the bottom of the page, and click the Indent Code icon ⬚ in the Coding toolbar to indent the code in the `try` block.

4 Add a new line at the bottom of the page, and insert the closing brace of the `try` block, together with a `catch` block like this:

```
} catch (Exception $e) {
    echo $e->getMessage();
}
```

5 Save library.php. You can compare your code with lesson07/completed/library.php.

Using Zend_Validate to check user input

The standard way of validating user input on the server is to create a series of conditional statements to test if a value meets certain criteria. For example, if you want to check whether a password contains between 8 and 15 characters, you can use the PHP function `strlen()`, which returns the length of a string, like this:

```
if (strlen($_POST['password']) >= 8 && strlen($_POST['password']) <= 15) {
    // it's valid
}
```

This works, but it doesn't check what characters are used in the password. Pressing the space-bar eight times passes this test. So, you need to add other conditional statements to make sure all criteria are met.

Zend_Validate works in a similar way but provides a set of commonly used validators. Each subclass has an easily recognizable name that makes your validation script much easier to read, and you don't need to become an expert in PHP functions to ensure that user input matches your requirements. **Table 7.1** lists the most commonly used subclasses. Each one is prefixed by Zend_Validate_, so Alnum becomes Zend_Validate_Alnum.

For example, to check that a string is 8–15 characters, use Zend_Validate_StringLength like this:

```
$val = new Zend_Validate_StringLength(8,15);
```

This instantiates a Zend_Validate_StringLength object, setting its minimum and maximum values to 8 and 15 respectively, and assigns it to $val.

To check whether $_POST['password'] contains between 8 and 15 characters, pass it as an argument to the isValid() method like this:

```
$val->isValid($_POST['password'])
```

If $_POST['password'] contains 8–15 characters, this returns TRUE. Otherwise, it returns FALSE.

Normally, if a validation test fails, you want to generate an error message. Do this by using a conditional statement with the logical Not operator (see "Using the logical Not operator" in Lesson 3) like this:

```
$val = new Zend_Validate_StringLength(8,15);
if (!$val->isValid($_POST['password'])) {
  $errors['password'] = 'Password should be 8-15 characters';
}
```

Adding the logical Not operator looks for a value that is *not* valid, so the error message is assigned to $errors['password'] only if $_POST['password'] is *not* 8–15 characters.

This validation test is fine as far as it goes, but it has the same problem as the earlier example: It checks only the number of characters. Pressing the spacebar 8–15 times still passes valida-tion. You need to combine validators. One way is to use a series of conditional statements, but ZF offers another solution—chaining validators.

Table 7.1   Commonly Used Validation Classes

Class	Description
Alnum	Checks that the value contains only alphabetic and number characters. Whitespace characters are permitted if TRUE is passed as an argument to the constructor.
Alpha	Same as Alnum except numbers are not permitted.
Between	Accepts a value between minimum and maximum limits. Constructor requires two arguments, which can be numbers or strings, to set the limits. By setting an optional third argument to TRUE, the value cannot be equal to either the maximum or minimum.
CreditCard	Checks whether a value falls within the ranges of possible credit card numbers for most leading credit card issuers. Does *not* check whether the number is genuine.
Date	Checks not only that a date is in the 'YYYY-MM-DD' format, but also that it's a valid date. For example, '2010-2-30' fails because it's not a real date, although it's in the right format.
Digits	Accepts only digits. The decimal point and thousands separator are rejected.
EmailAddress	Validates an email address. Has the option to check whether the hostname actually accepts email, but this slows down performance. On Windows, this option requires PHP 5.3 or later.
Float	Accepts a floating point number. The maximum value is platform-dependent.
GreaterThan	Checks that a value is greater than a minimum. Constructor takes a single argument to set the minimum value.
Identical	Checks that a value is identical to the value passed as an argument to the constructor.
Int	Accepts an integer.
LessThan	Checks that a value is less than a maximum. Constructor takes a single argument to set the maximum value.
NotEmpty	Checks that a value is not empty. Various options can be set to configure what is regarded as an empty value, offering greater flexibility than the PHP empty() function.
PostCode	Checks that a value conforms to the pattern for a postal or zip code. The pattern is determined by passing a locale string to the constructor, for example, 'en_US' for the United States or 'en_GB' for the UK.
Regex	Validates against a regular expression passed as an argument to the constructor.
StringLength	Checks the length of a string. The constructor accepts one, two, or three arguments. The first sets the minimum length, the second optionally sets the maximum length, and the third optionally specifies the encoding. Alternatively, these values can be presented as an associative array using the keys 'min', 'max', and 'encoding'.

Chaining validators to set multiple criteria

To test for more than one criterion, create a generic `Zend_Validate` object, and use its `addValidator()` method to add each new test. You can instantiate each validator separately, and then pass it as an argument to `addValidator()` like this:

```
$val = new Zend_Validate();
$val1 = new Zend_Validate_StringLength(8, 15);
$val2 = new Zend_Validate_Alnum();
$val->addValidator($val1);
$val->addValidator($val2);
```

However, it's simpler to instantiate each validator directly as the argument to `addValidator()` like this:

```
$val = new Zend_Validate();
$val->addValidator(new Zend_Validate_StringLength(8, 15));
$val->addValidator(new Zend_Validate_Alnum());
```

You can even chain the `addValidator()` methods one after the other like this:

```
$val = new Zend_Validate();
$val->addValidator(new Zend_Validate_StringLength(8, 15))
    ->addValidator(new Zend_Validate_Alnum());
```

Notice that there is no semicolon at the end of the second line, and the second `->` operator isn't prefixed by the `$val` object. Indenting it like this makes the code easier to read, but you could place it immediately after the closing parenthesis at the end of the first `addValidator()` method.

✱ NOTE: Chaining methods like this will be familiar to readers with jQuery experience. Unfortunately, Dreamweaver CS5's code hints don't support chaining methods, so the code in this book always uses separate statements to apply methods to ZF objects.

All three sets of code perform the same task: `$val` tests for a string 8–15 characters long that contains only letters and numbers, with no spaces.

Armed with this knowledge, you can validate the input of the registration form.

Building the validation script (1)

The user registration form from Lesson 6 has been modified to add a text input field for the email address and some hints for the user. The style sheet has also been changed to make room for error messages.

1 Copy add_user.php from lesson07/start to lesson07/workfiles.

2 It's more efficient to use an external file for the validation code so you can reuse the code for other projects. Choose File > New, and create a new PHP page. Save it as **user_registration.php** in lesson07/workfiles/scripts.

3 In the file you just created, switch to Code view, delete the HTML code inserted by Dreamweaver, and add an opening PHP tag at the top of the page. This page will contain only PHP, so it shouldn't have a closing PHP tag.

4 After the opening PHP tag, initialize an array to store error messages:

```
$errors = array();
```

5 When the form is first loaded, there's nothing to process, so the $_POST array is empty. An empty array is treated as FALSE (see "What PHP regards as false" in Lesson 3), so you can use this to ensure that the validation script is run only when the form is submitted. Add a conditional statement like this:

```
if ($_POST) {
  // run the validation script
}
```

6 The validation script needs access to the ZF files. Include library.php by adding it between the curly braces of the conditional statement:

```
require_once('library.php');
```

7 Add try and catch blocks inside the conditional statement created in the previous step:

```
if ($_POST) {
  // run the validation script
  require_once('library.php');
  try {
    // main script goes here
  } catch (Exception $e) {
    echo $e->getMessage();
  }
}
```

8 The first input field you need to validate is first_name. Personal names are alphabetic, so Zend_Validate_Alpha seems like a good choice. Add the following code inside the try block:

```
try {
  // main script goes here
  $val = new Zend_Validate_Alpha(TRUE);
  if (!$val->isValid($_POST['first_name'])) {
    $errors['first_name'] = 'Required field, no numbers';
  }
} catch (Exception $e) {
```

By passing TRUE as an argument, this permits spaces.

9 Before going any further, it's a good idea to test the script so far. Save user_registration. php, and switch to add_user.php.

Include user_registration.php by inserting space above the DOCTYPE declaration and adding the following code:

```
<?php
require_once('scripts/user_registration.php');
?>
```

10 To display error messages next to each input field, you need to add a pair of <span> tags with a PHP conditional statement in between.

Locate the following line in Code view:

```
<input type="text" name="first_name" id="first_name" />
```

> **TIP:** It's a good idea to work in Vertical Split view (choose View > Split Vertically and click Split in the Document toolbar). Select the input field in Design view to highlight the <input> tag in Code view.

11 Add the following code after the <input> tag:

```
<input type="text" name="first_name" id="first_name" />
<span>
<?php
if ($_POST && isset($errors['first_name'])) {
  echo $errors['first_name'];
}
?>
</span>
</p>
```

The conditional statement begins by checking $_POST. If the form has been submitted, it equates to TRUE, so the next test is applied. The isset() function checks the existence of a variable. $errors['first_name'] is created only if the validation test fails, so $errors['first_name'] is displayed if the form has been submitted and the first_name field failed validation.

The <span> tags remain empty if there isn't an error, so it might seem more logical to include them inside the conditional statement. They have been left outside to act as a hook for a custom server behavior that you'll create later in this lesson to insert error messages for the other fields.

12 Save add_user.php, and click Live View or press F12/Opt+F12 to test it. Start by leaving the "First name" field blank. Submit the form, and remember to hold down the Ctrl/Cmd key if you're in Live View. If all your code is OK, you should see an error message next to the "First name" field.

Sign Up Now

Just a few details and you're in
All fields are required

First name: [   ] Required field, no numbers

13 Now try typing your own name and resubmitting the form. The error message disappears.

14 Type some numbers and resubmit. The error message reappears.

15 Click inside the field, and press the spacebar several times before resubmitting the form. The error message disappears. You still have the problem of an empty field.

Unfortunately, the NotEmpty validation class doesn't have an option to handle this. Also, personal names sometimes include a hyphen or apostrophe. The best solution is to use a *regular expression*—a pattern for matching text.

16 Turn off Live View, if necessary, and switch back to user_registration.php. Change the validator from Alpha to Regex like this:

```
$val = new Zend_Validate_Regex('/^[a-z]+[-\'a-z ]+$/i');
```

This regular expression—or regex, for short—makes sure the value begins with at least one letter and is followed by at least one more letter, hyphen, apostrophe, or space.

This is fine for English. If you need to accept accented letters or names written in a different script, such as Japanese or Chinese, use the following:

```
$val = new Zend_Validate_Regex('/^\p{L}+[-\'\p{L} ]+$/u');
```

This line performs the same task, but also accepts Unicode letter characters.

▶ **TIP:** Regular expressions are used widely for matching text in PHP and other programming languages. Learn how to build your own regexes by following my tutorial series in the Adobe Developer Connection at www.adobe.com/devnet/dreamweaver/articles/regular_expressions_pt1.html.

17 Save user_registration.php, and test the "First name" field again. It now accepts names with spaces, hyphens, and apostrophes but rejects numbers and values that don't begin with a letter.

The second regex accepts names like Françoise, Дмитрий, and 太郎.

You can compare your code with lesson07/completed/add_user01.php and lesson07/completed/scripts/user_registration01.php.

Building the validation script (2)

The rest of the script follows a similar pattern: You need a validator for each input field and need to add a message to the $errors array if the value fails the test. Sometimes a validator can be reused, but if it's no longer appropriate, you can overwrite it by assigning a new one to the same variable.

1 The surname input field can use the same validator as first_name, so add the following code immediately after the first_name test in user_registration.php:

```
if (!$val->isValid($_POST['first_name'])) {
  $errors['first_name'] = 'Required field, no numbers';
}
if (!$val->isValid($_POST['surname'])) {
  $errors['surname'] = 'Required field, no numbers';
}
} catch (Exception $e) {
```

2 The next input field to validate is username. A username should consist of letters and numbers only, and should be 6–15 characters long. This requires two tests, so you need to create a Zend_Validate object, and chain the validators. You don't need the existing validator, so you can overwrite it.

Add the following code immediately after the code you entered in the previous step (and still inside the try block):

```
$val = new Zend_Validate();
$length = new Zend_Validate_StringLength(6,15);
$val->addValidator($length);
$val->addValidator(new Zend_Validate_Alnum());
if (!$val->isValid($_POST['username'])) {
  $errors['username'] = 'Use 6-15 letters or numbers only';
}
```

This starts by creating a generic Zend_Validate object ready for chaining. Next, a StringLength validator—with a minimum of 6 characters and a maximum of 15—is created and assigned to $length.

In the third line, the addValidator() method chains $length to $val.

Then the Alnum validator is chained to it. By not passing an argument to Alnum, no whitespaces are allowed.

Why use different ways of chaining the validators? Surely the StringLength validator could have been passed directly as an argument to addValidator() in the same way as Alnum, right? It could, but the password field needs to be a minimum of 8 characters.

Assigning the StringLength validator to its own variable lets you change the minimum value ready for reuse.

3 On the line immediately after the code you just inserted, type **$length->**. As soon as you type the -> operator, Dreamweaver code hints display the methods available to a StringLength validator. Type **s**. The code hints display a number of methods that begin with "set."

```
25        $errors['username'] = 'Use 6-15 letters or numbers only';
26    }
27    $length->s;
28    } catch (Exc ▣ getMessageVariables()
29    echo $e->c ▣ getObscureValue()
30    }         ▣ getTranslator()
31    }         ▣ isValid($value)
              ▣ setDisableTranslator($flag)
              ▣ setEncoding($encoding)
              ▣ setMax($max)
              ▣ setMessage($messageString, $messageKey)
              ▣ setMessages(array $messages)
              ▣ setMin($min)
```

4 Use your arrow keys to scroll down to setMin($min) and press Enter/Return or double-click. Set the value to **8**, and type a closing parenthesis and semicolon. The finished line should look like this:

```
$length->setMin(8);
```

This resets the minimum number of characters required by the StringLength validator to 8. The maximum remains unchanged at 15.

▶ **TIP:** Many ZF classes have methods that begin with "get" and "set" to find out or change the values of an object's properties.

5 Now that you have changed the minimum required by the StringLength validator, you can create the validation test for the password input field. It's almost exactly the same as for username. Add this immediately after the line you just entered:

```
$val = new Zend_Validate();
$val->addValidator($length);
$val->addValidator(new Zend_Validate_Alnum());
if (!$val->isValid($_POST['password'])) {
   $errors['username'] = 'Use 8-15 letters or numbers only';
}
```

This allows any combination of letters and numbers. For a more robust password, use the Regex validator. There's a regex for a strong password that requires a mixture of uppercase and lowercase characters and numbers at http://imar.spaanjaars.com/QuickDocId. aspx?quickdoc=297. In the comments on the same page, there's an even stronger one that requires at least one special character.

6 To check that both password values are identical, use the Identical validator. This code goes immediately after the code in the preceding step:

```
$val = new Zend_Validate_Identical($_POST['password']);
if (!$val->isValid($_POST['conf_password'])) {
  $errors['conf_password'] = "Passwords don't match";
}
```

You want to check that $_POST['conf_password'] is identical to $_POST['password'], so $_POST['password'] is passed as the argument to the Identical validator.

▼ **CAUTION!** The error message contains an apostrophe, so the string needs to be enclosed in double quotation marks.

7 The final test is for the email. Add this after code in the previous step:

```
$val = new Zend_Validate_EmailAddress();
if (!$val->isValid($_POST['email'])) {
  $errors['email'] = 'Use a valid email address';
}
```

8 Save user_registration.php. You'll come back to it later to add the code that inserts the user's details in the database. If you want to check your code so far, compare it with lesson07/completed/scripts/user_registration02.php.

Preserving input when validation fails

Ever submitted an online form only to be told there's an error, and all your input has been wiped out? Not much fun is it? Good validation and form design preserves the user's input if there's an error. It's quite simple to do. The input is stored in the $_POST or $_GET array, depending on the method used to submit the form (most of the time, it's POST). All that's necessary is to assign the appropriate element of the $_POST or $_GET array to the value attribute of the input field.

1 In add_user.php, locate the first <input> tag in Code view. It looks like this:

```
<input type="text" name="first_name" id="first_name" />
```

2 The <input> tag doesn't have a value attribute, so you need to add one, and use PHP to assign its content like this:

```
<input type="text" name="first_name" id="first_name"
value="<?php if ($_POST && $errors) {
  echo htmlentities($_POST['first_name'], ENT_COMPAT, 'UTF-8');
}?>" />
```

The PHP code block inside the quotation marks of the value attribute is controlled by a conditional statement that checks the $_POST and $errors arrays. The $_POST array is empty unless a form has been submitted, so the code inside the curly braces is ignored when the page first loads.

The $errors array is declared at the top of user_registration.php, so it always exists, but elements get added to it only if the validation script finds any problems with the user input. Consequently, $errors will equate to TRUE only if the form has been submitted and at least one error has been found.

If both tests equate to TRUE, the code passes $_POST['first_name'] to a function called htmlentities() and uses echo to display the result. You could use echo on its own, but displaying raw user input in a web page is a security risk. The htmlentities() function sanitizes the input by converting characters that have a special meaning in HTML into HTML entities. For example, the angle brackets in <script> are converted to < and >, which prevent an unauthorized script from running in your web page.

Often, htmlentities() takes just one argument—the string you want to convert. The second and third arguments have been added because htmlentities() uses Latin1 (iso-8859-1) as its default encoding. ENT_COMPAT is a constant that specifies preserving single quotation marks and converting only double ones. The third argument specifies UTF-8 (Unicode) as the encoding. This preserves accented or nonalphabetic characters.

3 Save add_user.php, type anything in the "First name" field, and submit the form. The validation script detects errors in the other fields, so $_POST and $errors are no longer empty arrays. The value you entered is redisplayed.

You can compare your code with lesson07/completed/add_user02.php.

Dealing with unwanted backslashes

In add_user.php, test the "First name" field with a name that contains an apostrophe, such as **O'Toole**. If magic quotes (see Lesson 2) are turned on, the apostrophe is preceded by a backslash like this when it's redisplayed:

```
┌─ Just a few details and you're in ──────────────
│                         All fields are required
│  First name:            O\'Toole
```

If you see a backslash in front of the apostrophe, add the following code after the `catch` block at the bottom of scripts/library.php (you can copy and paste it from lesson07/completed/scripts/library_magic_quotes.php):

```
if (get_magic_quotes_gpc()) {
  $process = array(&$_GET, &$_POST, &$_COOKIE);
  while (list($key, $val) = each($process)) {
    foreach ($val as $k => $v) {
      unset($process[$key][$k]);
      if (is_array($v)) {
        $process[$key][stripslashes($k)] = $v;
        $process[] = &$process[$key][stripslashes($k)];
      } else {
        $process[$key][stripslashes($k)] = stripslashes($v);
      }
    }
  }
  unset($process);
}
```

When you test the page again, the backslash should have been removed.

> ✱ **NOTE:** This script comes from the PHP manual at http://docs.php.net/manual/en/security.magicquotes.disabling.php and is the least efficient way of dealing with magic quotes. You need to add the script to library.php only if there is a backslash in front of the apostrophe and you cannot use any other method of disabling magic quotes (see "Deciding to use or not to use 'magic quotes'" in Lesson 2).

Creating your own server behaviors

Now you need to fix the redisplay of user input and error messages for the remaining input fields. Doing it all by hand is tedious. But take a look at what's happened in add_user.php. In Design view, Dreamweaver has added what looks like a dynamic text object in the "First name" input field. The Server Behaviors panel also lists a Dynamic Attribute.

Does this mean Dreamweaver has a server behavior that you can you use here? No, but it does have the Server Behavior Builder, which lets you create your own.

1 With add_user.php open in the Document window, open the Server Behaviors panel by clicking its tab or choosing Window > Server Behaviors (Ctrl+F9/Cmd+F9). Click the plus button at the top left of the panel, and choose New Server Behavior.

2 In the New Server Behavior dialog box, make sure "Document type" is set to PHP MySQL, and type **Redisplay on Error** in the Name field. Leave the checkbox deselected, and click OK.

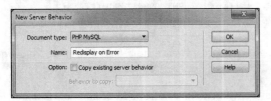

🔆 **NOTE:** Selecting the "Copy existing server behavior" checkbox lets you choose a server behavior on which to base a new one. However, you can do this only with server behaviors you have created yourself. You cannot use one of Dreamweaver's built-in server behaviors.

This opens a large dialog box where you define the new server behavior.

3 Click the plus button labeled "Code blocks to insert" to open the Create a New Code Block dialog box. Accept the name suggested by Dreamweaver, and click OK. This lists the code block in the top pane and inserts some placeholder text in the "Code block" section.

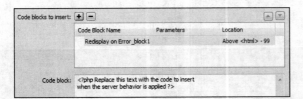

4 Replace the placeholder text with the PHP code that you added to the <input> tag's value attribute in step 2 of "Preserving input when validation fails." Here it is again:

```php
<?php if ($_POST && $errors) {
  echo htmlentities($_POST['first_name'], ENT_COMPAT, 'UTF-8');
}?>
```

5 If you leave the code like this, the server behavior would always use $_POST['first_name']. To make it editable, you need to replace first_name with a parameter.

Delete `first_name` but not the surrounding quotation marks. Make sure your insertion point is between the quotation marks of `$_POST['']`, and click the Insert Parameter in Code Block button.

6 In the "Parameter name" field, type **Field Name**, and click OK. The code in the "Code block" section should now look like this:

```php
<?php if ($_POST && $errors) {
  echo htmlentities($_POST['@@Field Name@@'], ENT_COMPAT, 'UTF-8');
}?>
```

The @@ surrounding the parameter name tell Dreamweaver to replace the value when you use the server behavior.

7 You now need to tell the server behavior where to insert the code when you use it. You want to use it in the `value` attribute of an `<input>` tag.

Set "Insert code" to Relative to a Specific Tag. An option called Tag appears.

8 Select "input" from the Tag menu.

9 Set "Relative position" to "As the Value of an Attribute." This opens up yet another option labeled Attribute.

10 Select "value" from the Attribute menu. The settings in the Server Behavior Builder dialog box should now look like this:

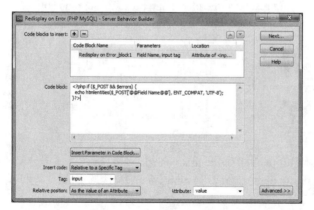

11 Click Next at the top right of the dialog box to open the dialog box that defines the options that will appear in the new server behavior's dialog box.

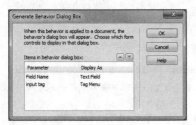

12 The values suggested by Dreamweaver are fine. Just click OK to complete the creation of the Redisplay on Error server behavior.

13 Create another custom server behavior to display the error messages. The process is the same, so the following instructions provide only the main points.

Click the plus button in the Server Behaviors panel, and choose New Server Behavior. Call it **Display Error Message**.

14 Create a new code block, and accept the default name. Replace the placeholder text with the following code:

```php
<?php if ($_POST && isset($errors['@@Field@@'])) {
  echo $errors['@@Field@@'];
} ?>
```

This is the same as the code used to display the error message next to the "First name" field except both instances of `first_name` have been replaced by the parameter `@@Field@@`.

15 The error message is displayed inside a `<span>` tag, so use the following settings at the bottom of the panel:

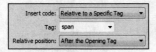

16 Click Next, accept the default settings in the next dialog box, and click OK.

Finishing the registration form

The custom server behaviors make it easy to preserve user input and display error messages. As long as you use an array called $errors to store error messages, they can be used in any page, not just this one.

> **TIP:** You could make the server behaviors more flexible by using a parameter for the $errors array. However, consistency in coding is a virtue, and using a fixed variable keeps the code simple.

1 With add_user.php open in Design view, select the "Family name" field in the registration form.

2 Click the plus button in the Server Behaviors panel, and choose "Redisplay on Error" to open the dialog box for your new server behavior.

3 Type **surname** in the Field Name field. The correct value should already be selected for "input tag."

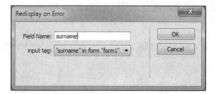

4 Click OK. Dreamweaver inserts a dynamic text object in the field. It also lists "Redisplay on Error" in the Server Behaviors panel. Dreamweaver should also recognize the code in the "First name" field and list that as a "Redisplay on Error" server behavior.

> **NOTE:** Don't worry if the hand-coded version isn't recognized as a "Redisplay on Error" server behavior. Differences in spacing and new lines could affect Dreamweaver's ability to recognize it as the same.

5 Repeat steps 1–4 with the Username and "Email address" fields, typing **username** and **email** respectively in Field Name.

6 You can't apply the server behavior to the password fields. There's no point in doing so anyway, because password fields don't display user input.

7 Save add_user.php, and test the new server behavior by typing values in all fields except the password fields and submitting the form. The lack of passwords causes validation to fail and redisplays the values you entered.

> ✳ **NOTE:** If your page doesn't work as expected, compare your code with add_user03.php in lesson07/completed. The most likely problem is a mistake in the "Code block" section of the Server Behavior Builder or in the parameter. You can edit a custom server behavior by clicking the plus button in the Server Behaviors panel and choosing Edit Server Behavior. To rebuild a server behavior from scratch, select its name in the Edit Server Behavior dialog box, and click Remove.

8 The error messages are displayed in <span> tags. In Design view, position the insertion point immediately to the right of the "Family name" input field, right-click, and choose Insert HTML.

This displays a small window for you to add an HTML tag. Type **sp** to highlight span, and press Enter/Return to insert an empty pair of <span> tags.

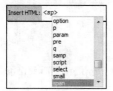

9 Open Split view to make sure the insertion point is between the opening and closing <span> tags. If it isn't, move it there by clicking between them.

10 Click the plus button in the Server Behaviors panel, and choose Display Error Message to open the dialog box for the other new server behavior.

11 Type **surname** in Field. The value of "span tag" should be "span [1]." The span doesn't have an id attribute, so Dreamweaver uses an array to identify it, counting from zero. So, this is the second <span> in the page.

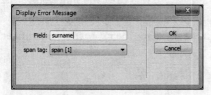

12 Repeat steps 8–11 for the remaining input fields. As long as the insertion point is between the opening and closing <span> tags, the Display Error Message dialog box selects the correct value for "span tag." The value you type in Field should match the name attribute of each input field, namely: **username, password, conf_password,** and **email**.

13 Save add_user.php, and test the page by typing a few letters in the "Confirm password" field only. When you submit the form, confirm that error messages are displayed next to each field.

```
┌─Just a few details and you're in──────────────────────────────────┐
│                         All fields are required                   │
│   First name:          [                    ]  Required field, no numbers  │
│                                                                   │
│   Family name:         [                    ]  Required field, no numbers  │
│                                                                   │
│   Username (6-15 characters): [              ]  Use 6-15 letters or numbers only │
│                                                                   │
│   Password (8-15 characters): [              ]  Use 8-15 letters or numbers only │
│                                                                   │
│   Confirm password:    [                    ]  Passwords don't match       │
│                                                                   │
│   Email address:       [                    ]  Use a valid email address   │
│                        [ Sign me up! ]                            │
└───────────────────────────────────────────────────────────────────┘
```

This completes add_user.php. Compare your code with lesson07/completed/add_user. php if the page doesn't work as expected.

Using a variable in a SELECT query

The final part of the form input that needs to be validated before you can register the user in the database is the username. At the beginning of this lesson, you added a unique index to the username column, so the database rejects any attempt to insert the same value more than once. To avoid this, you need to check the database and display an error message if the username already exists.

Zend_Db offers several different ways of querying a database. In this case, the simplest way is to write your own SQL query. All you're interested in is whether the username exists in the database, so selecting user_id is sufficient. To find the user_id for the username "hitchhiker," the basic SQL query looks like this:

```
SELECT user_id FROM users WHERE username = 'hitchhiker'
```

SQL is designed to emulate human language, so the meaning should be obvious. By convention, the SQL commands are written in uppercase. The names of columns and tables are not enclosed in quotation marks, but string values are. So, this selects the values in the user_id column from the users table, where the value in the username column equals "hitchhiker."

For this validation script, you want to match the value that comes from $_POST['username'], but you have no idea what this contains. It could be an attempt to hack into your database.

So, you need to sanitize the value that's inserted into the SQL. One way of doing this with Zend_Db is to use the quoteInto() method, which takes two arguments:

- The first argument is the SQL statement with a question mark used as a placeholder for the variable containing the user input.

- The second argument is the variable you want to use.

This sanitizes the value and wraps it in the necessary quotation marks.

To execute a SELECT query, you pass the SQL query to the fetchAll() method, which returns an array containing all the results.

Checking for duplicate usernames

Now that you know the basics of querying the database, you can fix the validation script so that it checks for a duplicate username.

1 The section in user_registration.php that validates the length and characters in the username ends with the following conditional statement (it should be around lines 19–21):

```
if (!$val->isValid($_POST['username'])) {
  $errors['username'] = 'Use 6-15 letters or numbers only';
}
```

If the username fails this validation test, there's no need to check the database; if the username passes, you need to make sure it's not a duplicate. This is an either/or situation, so it calls for an else block to be added to the original conditional statement like this:

```
if (!$val->isValid($_POST['username'])) {
  $errors['username'] = 'Use 6-15 letters or numbers only';
} else {
  // check the database for duplicate username
}
```

All the code in the following steps goes inside the else block.

2 Use the quoteInto() method to build the SQL statement with a question mark placeholder, and pass the variable to it as the second argument:

```
$sql = $dbRead->quoteInto('SELECT user_id FROM users WHERE username = ?',
➥ $_POST['username']);
```

$dbRead is one of the Zend_Db objects you created in library.php earlier in this lesson to connect to the database.

3 Execute the query by passing $sql to fetchAll(), and capture the result like this:

```
$result = $dbRead->fetchAll($sql);
```

4 The fetchAll() method returns an array of results. PHP treats an array that contains any elements as TRUE. If a match is found, the username is a duplicate, so you can create an error message like this:

```
if ($result) {
  $errors['username'] = $_POST['username'] . ' is already in use';
}
```

If no match is found, $result is empty, which PHP treats as FALSE, so the code inside the braces is ignored.

5 Save user_registration.php, and test add_user.php by entering a username that already exists in the database. If your database table is empty, you can add a record by selecting the users table in phpMyAdmin and clicking the Insert tab at the top of the page. When you submit the form with a duplicate username, you'll see the error message.

You can compare your code with lesson07/completed/scripts/user_registration03.php.

Inserting the user details with Zend_Db

Inserting a record in a database with Zend_Db is very easy. You don't need any SQL. Just create an associative array using the column names as the keys, and pass the table name and array as arguments to the insert() method.

You can now finish the user registration process:

1 If the user input passes all the validation tests, the $errors array is empty. You can use this to control whether to insert the data in the users table. Add this conditional statement at the end of the validation sequence, just above the catch block:

```
if (!$val->isValid($_POST['email'])) {
  $errors['email'] = 'Use a valid email address';
}
if (!$errors) {
  // insert the details in the database
}
} catch (Exception $e) {
```

PHP implicitly treats an empty array as FALSE. The logical Not operator (an exclamation point) reverses a Boolean value, so this effectively means "if there are *no* errors." If the $errors array is empty, the condition equates to TRUE, and the details will be inserted into the database.

All the remaining code goes inside this conditional statement.

2 Create an associative array of the column names and values. You don't need an array element for `user_id`, because MySQL automatically inserts the next available number for the primary key. The array should look like this:

```
$data = array('first_name'  => $_POST['first_name'],
              'family_name' => $_POST['surname'],
              'username'    => $_POST['username'],
              'password'    => sha1($_POST['password']));
```

Zend_Db automatically sanitizes the values before inserting them into the database. The password is the only value that receives special treatment. It's passed to the `sha1()` function for encryption.

3 To insert the data, you need to use the `Zend_Db` object with read/write privileges. Add this line after the array you have just created:

```
$dbWrite->insert('users', $data);
```

The first argument to the `insert()` method is a string containing the name of the table you want to use, and the second argument is the data array.

4 That's all there is to inserting the data. After the data is inserted, redirect the user to the login page with the `header()` function like this:

```
header('Location: login.php');
```

✳ NOTE: Strictly speaking, you should use a full URL when redirecting a page, but all current browsers accept a relative URL. Using this shortcut is acceptable for local testing, but you should replace this with a fully qualified URL when deploying your pages on a live site. See http://docs.php.net/manual/en/function.header.php.

5 Save user_registration.php, and copy lesson07/start/login.php to your lesson07/workfiles folder.

6 Test add_user.php to enter a new user in the database. If there are no errors, you will be taken to login.php. You can compare your code with lesson07/completed/scripts/user_registration.php.

Authenticating User Credentials with Zend_Auth

The end result of the improved registration form that you just created is the same as Dreamweaver's built-in Insert Record server behavior—it inserts user details in the database. Dreamweaver's User Authentication server behaviors can still be used to control access to pages. However, ZF makes it easy to create scripts to authenticate user credentials. Using external files for the scripts that control access and log out users simplifies their inclusion in any page.

Controlling user access with Zend_Auth

The Zend_Auth class creates a *singleton* object, which means that only one instance can exist at a time. In practical terms, the only difference is that you use getInstance() instead of the new keyword like this:

```
$auth = Zend_Auth::getInstance();
```

Zend_Auth is capable of using a variety of authentication methods. When the user credentials are stored in a database, authentication is done by an adapter called Zend_Auth_Adapter_DbTable, which takes the following five arguments:

- A Zend_Db object that connects to the database

- The name of the table that contains the user credentials

- The name of the column that contains the username

- The name of the password column

- The encryption, if any, to be applied to the password

The fifth argument uses a question mark as a placeholder for the password. The users table uses sha1() encryption, so you create an adapter like this:

```
$adapter = new Zend_Auth_Adapter_DbTable($dbRead, 'users', 'username',
➥ 'password', 'sha1(?)');
```

When a user logs in, pass the username and password to the adapter like this:

```
$adapter->setIdentity($_POST['username']);
$adapter->setCredential($_POST['password']);
```

To check whether the user's credentials are valid, pass the adapter to the Zend_Auth object's authenticate() method:

```
$result = $auth->authenticate($adapter);
```

Finally, if the login succeeds, store the user's details like this:

```
if ($result->isValid()) {
  $storage = $auth->getStorage();
  $storage->write($adapter->getResultRowObject(
    array('username', 'first_name', 'family_name')));
}
```

The array passed as an argument to the getResultRowObject() method is a list of the database fields you want to store. Dreamweaver's built-in Log In User server behavior stores only the username and access level, if any. Zend_Auth gives you access to as much information about the user as you want—provided, of course, it's stored in the database.

> ✴ **NOTE:** The getStorage() and write() methods store the user's details as a Zend_Auth_Storage_Session object, which is essentially just another way of storing session variables.

You restrict access to pages by using the hasIdentity() method, which returns TRUE if the user has logged in.

To access details of a logged-in user, use the getIdentity() method like this:

```
$auth = Zend_Auth::getInstance();
if ($auth->hasIdentity()) {
  $identity = $auth->getIdentity();
}
```

The details can then be accessed as properties of $identity, for example:

```
$identity->first_name
```

To log out a visitor, use the clearIdentity() method.

Creating the login script

The Log In User server behavior that you used in Lesson 6 sends the user to another page on failure or displays the login form again without explanation. This time you'll display an error message so the user knows what's happened.

1 Create a new PHP page, and save it as **user_authentication.php** in lesson07/work-files/scripts. The page will contain only PHP code, so delete the HTML inserted by Dreamweaver, and add an opening PHP tag.

2 To control the error message, create a FALSE Boolean variable:

```
$failed = FALSE;
```

If the login fails, this will be reset to TRUE and display the message.

3 The login script should run only if the form is submitted. Add a conditional statement to include library.php if the $_POST array equates to TRUE:

```
if ($_POST) {
  require_once('library.php');
  // check the user's credentials
}
```

4 The script uses objects, so add `try` and `catch` blocks inside the conditional statement, and get an instance of `Zend_Auth` in the `try` block.

```
try {
  $auth = Zend_Auth::getInstance();
} catch (Exception $e) {
  echo $e->getMessage();
}
```

▶ **TIP:** A quick way to select the code hint for Zend_Auth is to press Ctrl+spacebar, and type **dau**. This selects Zend_Auth immediately. Press Enter/Return to insert it, and then type two colons to bring up a code hint for getInstance().

The rest of the script goes inside the `try` block.

5 Create a `Zend_Auth_Adapter_DbTable` object. A quick way to select its code hint is by typing **hada** after the new keyword. This takes five arguments, but Dreamweaver helps you by highlighting the current argument in bold.

```
Zend_Auth_Adapter_DbTable(Zend_Db_Adapter_Abstract $zendDb, $tableName, $identityColumn, $credentialColumn, $credentialTreatment)
DbTable($dbRead, |
```

The code for this line should look like this:

```
$adapter = new Zend_Auth_Adapter_DbTable($dbRead, 'users', 'username',
➥ 'password', 'sha1(?)');
```

6 Set the identity and credential values for the adapter. They come from the `username` and `password` values in the `$_POST` array:

```
$adapter->setIdentity($_POST['username']);
$adapter->setCredential($_POST['password']);
```

7 Pass the adapter to the `authenticate()` method of the `Zend_Auth` object, and save the result in a variable:

```
$result = $auth->authenticate($adapter);
```

8 Use the `isValid()` method to determine whether the user's credentials are correct. If they are, store the details, and use `header()` to redirect the user to members_only.php. If the login attempt fails, reset `$failed` to TRUE. The code looks like this:

```
if ($result->isValid()) {
  $storage = $auth->getStorage();
  $storage->write($adapter->getResultRowObject(array(
    'username', 'first_name', 'family_name')));
  header('Location: members_only.php');
```

```
   exit;
} else {
   $failed = TRUE;
}
```

⚠ CAUTION! Relative links in include files are treated as relative to the page that includes them, not to the location of the include file. Although this script is in the scripts folder, it will be included in login.php, which is in the same folder as members_only.php. So, the relative link that redirects the user on success needs to be relative to login.php, not to user_authentication.php.

Testing the login script

To use the login script, include it above the DOCTYPE declaration of the login page, and add a conditional statement to show an error message if the login fails.

1 Copy login.php and members_only.php from lesson07/start to lesson07/workfiles.

2 Include user_authentication.php in login.php by adding the following above the DOCTYPE declaration:

```
<?php
require_once('scripts/user_authentication.php');
?>
```

3 In Design view, insert a new paragraph after the Members Only heading, and type **Login failed. Check username and password.**

With the insertion point anywhere in the paragraph, choose warning from the Class menu in the Property inspector. This turns the text bold red.

4 Switch to Code view, and wrap the paragraph you just created in a conditional statement like this:

```
<?php if ($failed) { ?>
<p class="warning">Login failed. Please check username and password.</p>
<?php } ?>
```

The script in user_authentication.php sets $failed to FALSE and changes it to TRUE only if a login attempt fails, so this prevents the error message from being shown unless the user's credentials are rejected.

▶ TIP: Some developers feel obliged to convert HTML in conditional statements to strings and use echo to display it. It's not necessary, and makes the code harder to write.

5 Save login.php, and test it in Live View or a browser. When the page first loads, the error message is not displayed. Try to log in using an invalid username or password. The error message is displayed.

6 Click "Sign in" without typing anything in either field. You get the following message: "A value for the identity was not provided prior to authentication with Zend_Auth_Adapter_DbTable."

This comes from the catch block. Failing to enter anything in the Username field has caused Zend_Auth to throw an exception. This is more elegant than the lengthy error message you get without try and catch, but it's not something you want to show visitors to your site.

7 Switch back to user_authentication.php, and add another conditional statement inside the existing one near the top of the script:

```
if ($_POST) {
  if (empty($_POST['username']) || empty($_POST['password'])) {
    $failed = TRUE;
  } else {
    require_once('library.php');
```

This uses empty() to test if $_POST['username'] or $_POST['password'] contains a value. If either is empty, $failed is reset to TRUE. The authentication script is now inside an else block that is executed only if $_POST['username'] and $_POST['password'] both have values.

8 A red marker on the last line of the script reminds you that you need to add a closing curly brace to match the opening one of the else block. Technically speaking, the missing brace goes between the last two braces at the bottom of the script, but you can put it on the final line, and the red marker goes away.

9 Save user_authentication.php, and test the login form again without filling in the fields. This time you get your custom error message in red.

10 Test the login form with a registered username and password. When you click "Sign in," you are taken to members_only.php.

You can compare your code with lesson07/completed/login.php and lesson07/completed/scripts/user_authentication01.php.

Password-protecting pages

Building the login script was the complex part. To restrict access to a page, you use the hasIdentity() method, which returns TRUE or FALSE. If the user is logged in, you retrieve his or her details with getIdentity(). Otherwise, you redirect the user to the login page.

1 Create a PHP page, and save it as **restrict_access.php** in lesson07/workfiles/scripts. Delete the HTML inserted by Dreamweaver.

2 The script is so short; here it is in its entirety:

```php
<?php
require_once('library.php');
try {
  $auth = Zend_Auth::getInstance();
  if ($auth->hasIdentity()) {
    $identity = $auth->getIdentity();
  } else {
    header('Location: login.php');
    exit;
  }
} catch (Exception $e) {
  echo $e->getMessage();
}
```

This includes library.php and creates an instance of Zend_Auth. The conditional statement checks whether the user is logged in. If it succeeds, the user's details are stored in $identity. Otherwise, the page is redirected to login.php, and exit ensures that the script comes to an immediate halt, preventing the protected page from being displayed.

3 To password-protect members_only.php, just include this script above the DOCTYPE declaration like this:

```php
<?php
require_once('scripts/restrict_access.php');
?>
```

Assuming you're already logged in, you need to log out before you can test this. For that, you need a logout button and script, which is coming up next.

Creating a logout system

Zend_Auth makes logging out easy with the clearIdentity() method. You can add the necessary code to user_authentication.php, and use a link to login.php to log out the user. A query string at the end of the link triggers the logout.

1 Create a new paragraph in members_only.php, and type **Log Out.**

2 Select the text, and link to login.php. Add **?logout** to the end of the link. You can do this in the Link field of the Property inspector or in Code view. Save members_only.php.

3 Switch to user_authentication.php, and add the following code at the bottom of the page:

```
if (isset($_GET['logout'])) {
  require_once('library.php');
  try {
    $auth = Zend_Auth::getInstance();
    $auth->clearIdentity();
  } catch (Exception $e) {
      echo $e->getMessage();
  }
}
```

Values passed through a query string are in the $_GET array. This uses isset() to see if $_GET['logout'] exists. If it does, the ZF files are included, an instance of Zend_Auth is created, and the clearIdentity() method performs the logout. That's all there is to it. The session variables storing the user's details are deleted automatically.

✳ NOTE: If you're wondering why the script doesn't use the earlier instance of Zend_Auth, it's created only when the login form is submitted. You could shorten the code slightly by including the ZF files and creating the Zend_Auth instance outside the conditional statements. However, neither is needed when the login form first loads, so this is more efficient, albeit at the expense of a few extra lines of code.

4 Save user_authentication.php, and load members_only.php in a browser or Live View. If the page displays, click the "Log out" link. You will be taken to the login form.

5 Log in, and click the "Log out" link again.

6 Now try to access members_only.php directly. You will be denied access and taken to the login form.

Displaying a logged-in user's details

The code in restrict_access.php calls the getIdentity() method and stores the user's user-name, first name, and family name as properties of $identity. This makes it possible to greet a user by name after logging in.

1 In Code view, amend the beginning of the first paragraph in members_only.php like this:

```
<p>Hi, <?php echo "$identity->first_name $identity->family_name"; ?>.
➥ You're in!
```

The column names are treated as properties of $identity, allowing you to access the information they contain about the user with the -> operator.

2 Save members_only.php, and log back in to be greeted by name.

> ## Welcome to the Clubhouse
>
> Hi, Arthur Dent. You're in! This is where the cool guys and gals hang out.
>
> Log out.

What You Have Learned

In this lesson, you have:

- Installed the Zend Framework (pages 214–215)

- Set up ZF site-specific code hints (pages 215–218)

- Altered a database table to add a unique index and extra columns (pages 219–220)

- Created a library file to load ZF classes and connect to the database (pages 221–227)

- Validated user input on the server with Zend_Validate (pages 227–236)

- Redisplayed user input when errors are detected in server-side validation (pages 236–237)

- Removed unwanted backslashes inserted by "magic quotes" (pages 237–238)

- Used Dreamweaver's Server Behavior Builder (pages 238–241)

- Displayed error messages when input fails validation (pages 242–244)

- Used a variable in a SELECT query to check for duplicate usernames (pages 244–246)

- Inserted user input into a database with Zend_Db (pages 246–247)

- Created a login system with Zend_Auth (pages 247–252)

- Password-protected pages with Zend_Auth (page 253)

- Created a logout system (pages 253–254)

- Displayed a logged-in user's details (pages 254–255)

What You Will Learn

In this lesson, you will:

- Compare the features of `mail()` and `Zend_Mail`
- Set up a default transport for `Zend_Mail`
- Create a new server behavior based on an existing one
- Incorporate a reCAPTCHA widget in a form to prevent spam
- Send the contents of a feedback form to your mail inbox
- Examine how the `$_POST` array treats different form elements
- Build an email-based system to reset user passwords or unsubscribe

Approximate Time

This lesson will take approximately 2 hours and 30 minutes to complete.

Lesson Files

Media Files:

styles/users.css
styles/users_wider.css

Starting Files:

lesson08/start/comments.php
lesson08/start/forgotten.php
lesson08/start/inquiry.php
lesson08/start/reset.php
lesson08/start/scripts/library.php
lesson08/start/scripts/process_comments.php
lesson08/start/scripts/request_reset.php
lesson08/start/scripts/reset_password.php

LESSON 8
Zending Email

Sending the contents of a feedback form by email is one of the most practical uses of PHP, so it's often the first project newcomers tackle. It's also full of traps for the unwary. The validation techniques you learned in the previous lesson should protect you from most problems, including a malicious exploit known as email header injection.

In this lesson, you'll use `Zend_Mail` and other ZF components to process feedback forms, and to prevent robots from attempting to submit. You'll also improve the user registration system from Lesson 7 by using email to allow users to change a forgotten password or unsubscribe.

*The Zend Framework makes it easy to process
feedback forms and prevent spam.*

How PHP Handles Email

PHP doesn't have the capability to transmit email. It acts as an intermediary, handing the content of the message and email headers to the web server's mail transport agent (MTA). PHP's role ends as soon as the MTA accepts the mail, so you have no way of tracking it. If the mail fails to arrive, the problem could lie anywhere along the route, so it's important to ensure that information passed to the MTA—such as the destination and return email addresses—is accurate.

Using the core mail() function

The basic method of sending email with PHP is to use the `mail()` function, which takes the following arguments, all of which must be strings:

- **Address(es) of the recipient(s).** Email addresses can be in either of the following formats:

```
'david@example.com'
'David Powers <david@example.com>'
```

  If you want to send the same email simultaneously to several addresses, they should be in a comma-separated string like this:

```
'David Powers <david@example.com>, Arthur Dent <hitchhiker@invalid.com>,
➥ another@example.com'
```

⚠ CAUTION! On Windows servers, avoid formatting the recipient's address as `'David Powers <david@example.com>'`, because it might not be correctly processed when passed to the MTA. It's safer to use the email address on its own.

- **Subject.** This is the subject line that appears in the recipient's inbox.

- **Message body.** This must be a single string.

- **Additional email headers.** Headers can be used to specify the return address, the addresses of other recipients (Cc and Bcc), encoding, and so on. Each header must be separated by a carriage return and newline character. This argument is optional.

⚠ CAUTION! On Windows servers, blind copies (Bcc) are treated as normal recipients, so all other recipients can see the address.

- **Additional parameters.** Although this argument is optional, many hosting companies now require its use as an anti-spam measure. It normally consists of your email address prefixed by `-f`, for example: `'-fdavid@example.com'`.

The following code shows a simple example of using mail():

```
$to = 'david@example.com';
$subject = 'PHP mail test';
$message = 'This is a test of the PHP mail() function.';
$headers = "From: webmaster@example.com\r\n";
$headers .= 'Cc: another@example.com';
$success = mail($to, $subject, $message, $headers);
if ($success) {
  echo 'Mail sent';
} else {
  echo 'Problem sending mail';
}
```

The message in this example is hard-coded, but it would normally come from user input when a feedback form is submitted.

This code is in lesson08/completed/mail_test.php. If you want to try it, replace the dummy email addresses with genuine ones. Upload the file to your remote server, and load it in a browser. If all goes well, you should see "Mail sent" and the test mail should arrive soon afterwards in your inbox.

If your hosting company requires the fifth argument to mail, add your email address preceded by -f like this:

```
$success = mail($to, $subject, $message, $headers, '-fyou@example.com');
```

▼ **CAUTION!** This script is unlikely to work in a local testing environment unless you have a mail server installed and configured. In the past, it was common to edit php.ini to point the SMTP directive at your Internet service provider's (ISP) mail server. However, most ISPs now reject mail unless you log in with a username and password. The mail() function doesn't support authentication.

The mail() function offers limited functionality. By default, it sends email in plain text and cannot handle attachments. Also, mail() opens a connection to the MTA each time, making it inefficient to send large amounts of email in a loop.

Perhaps the most serious problem comes from incorrect use. A popular technique is to use the additional headers argument to insert the user's email address in a Reply-to header. This is very convenient, because it means you can click the "Reply to" button in your email program to respond to the person who sent the message. But if you allow unfiltered user input in this argument, it exposes you to *email header injection*, whereby an attacker injects spurious headers into the email, effectively turning your website into a spam relay.

Using Zend_Mail

The Zend_Mail component offers a convenient wrapper around the mail() function, adding extra functionality and security. It can also send multiple emails in a single connection, making it more efficient.

Setting the default transport for Zend_Mail

By default, Zend_Mail hands the message and headers to the web server's MTA. If you don't need to supply the fifth argument to mail(), all you need to do is to create a Zend_Mail object, and use it directly.

If you need to supply the fifth argument to mail(), you need to create a Zend_Mail_Transport_Sendmail object first, and pass your return address preceded by -f as an argument to the constructor. Then you set the object as the default transport for Zend_Mail like this:

```
$transport = new Zend_Mail_Transport_Sendmail('-fyou@example.com');
Zend_Mail::setDefaultTransport($transport);
```

Zend_Mail also offers you the option to connect to any other mail server using simple mail transfer protocol (SMTP). To do so, you need to create an instance of Zend_Mail_Transport_Smtp, which expects two arguments: the host name of the SMTP server and an array containing your authentication details.

Zend_Mail_Transport_Smtp supports three types of authentication: login, plain, and CRAM-MD5, all of which expect a 'username' and 'password' value in the configuration array. Again, after creating the object, you set it as the default transport like this:

```
$mailhost = 'smtp.example.com';
$mailconfig = array('auth'     => 'login',
                    'username' => 'me@example.com',
                    'password' => 'topsecret');
$transport = new Zend_Mail_Transport_Smtp($mailhost, $mailconfig);
Zend_Mail::setDefaultTransport($transport);
```

▼ **CAUTION!** Although CRAM-MD5 is hyphenated, the hyphen must be omitted in the configuration array. The authentication type is case insensitive, so use 'auth' => 'crammd5' for servers that employ this method.

Preparing the email for sending

To prepare the email for sending, you must first create an instance of the Zend_Mail class like this:

```
$mail = new Zend_Mail();
```

By default, emails use Latin1 encoding (iso-8859-1), which is fine for unaccented English but is unsuitable for most other languages. To specify a different encoding, such as UTF-8, pass the name of the encoding as a string to the Zend_Mail constructor like this:

```
$mail = new Zend_Mail('UTF-8');
```

You then build the message and add the necessary headers using Zend_Mail methods. **Table 8.1** lists the most useful methods.

Table 8.1   The Most Useful Zend_Mail Methods

Method	Description
addBcc()	Adds a recipient as a blind copy without revealing the recipient's name and email address to others. Does *not* work on Windows servers. Takes 1 or 2 arguments: the email address, and optionally the recipient's name. To add multiple recipients, pass an array of email addresses as the argument. You can also use an associative array with the recipients' names as the array keys and the email addresses as the values.
addCc()	Adds a recipient to whom the email is copied, exposing the name and email address to other recipients. Takes the same arguments as *addBcc()*.
addHeader()	Used for adding an email header for which a dedicated method doesn't exist. Requires two arguments: the header name and its value. A Boolean value (TRUE or FALSE) can be passed as an optional third argument to specify whether the header can have multiple values.
addTo()	Adds a recipient to whom the email is addressed. Takes the same arguments as *addBcc()*.
createAttachment()	Adds an attachment. Takes up to five arguments. Only the first one, the file to be attached, is required. The optional arguments set the MIME type, disposition, encoding, and filename (in that order). By default, attachments are treated as binary objects (application/octet-stream) and transmitted in base64 encoding. Attachments are covered in Lesson 9.
send()	Sends the email using the default mail transport. To use a different transport, pass a Zend_Mail_Transport_Sendmail or Zend_Mail_Transport_Smtp object as an argument.
setBodyHtml()	Creates the HTML body of an email. Pass the HTML to the method as a single string.
setBodyText()	Creates the plain text body of an email. Expects the message as a single string.
setFrom()	Sets the From header. Expects an email address, and optionally the sender's name.
setReplyTo()	Sets the Reply-To header. Expects an email address, and optionally the sender's name.
setSubject()	Sets the email subject.

The process of composing and sending an email with the methods listed in Table 8.1 is very similar to mail(). This is how you would rewrite the example in "Using the core mail() function":

```
$mail->addTo('david@example.com', 'David Powers');
$mail->setSubject('PHP mail test');
$mail->setBodyText('This is a test of the PHP mail() function.');
$mail->setFrom('webmaster@example.com', 'Zend_Mail Test');
$mail->addCc('another@example.com');
$mail->send();
```

You can also chain the methods like this:

```
$mail->addTo('david@example.com', 'David Powers')
    ->setSubject('PHP mail test')
    ->setBodyText('This is a test of the PHP mail() function.')
    ->setFrom('webmaster@example.com', 'Zend_Mail Test')
    ->addCc('another@example.com')
    ->send();
```

Unfortunately, Dreamweaver CS5 code hints don't support chaining methods, so this book uses the more verbose style.

Stopping Spam with a CAPTCHA

If you don't want your inbox inundated with spam, it's a good idea to employ a technique to prevent automated programs—or web bots—from submitting your online forms. Several methods are available, but one that has become widely accepted is a CAPTCHA (Completely Automated Public Turing Test To Tell Computers and Humans Apart). Most CAPTCHAs present the user with a random string of characters that must be typed correctly into a text field.

Choosing a CAPTCHA

The Zend_Captcha component offers three main alternatives:

- The Zend_Captcha_Figlet class produces a FIGlet text (see www.figlet.org), which displays characters as ASCII art, as shown in the following screen shot:

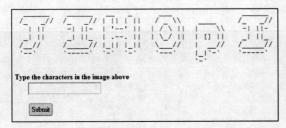

- The Zend_Captcha_Image class relies on the PHP GD extension to generate a .png image using TrueType or Freetype fonts like this:

- The Zend_Captcha_ReCaptcha class uses the reCAPTCHA online service (http://recaptcha.net/) to generate images of two words that cannot be read correctly by optical character recognition (OCR) software and displays them in a stylized box like this:

Zend_Captcha_Figlet is the easiest to use, but the ASCII art is ugly and unlikely to fit in with the design of many websites. Zend_Captcha_Image produces a more elegant result, but the characters are hard to read not only for spam bots, but also for humans, defeating the whole purpose of a CAPTCHA.

The same problem sometimes affects the images produced by the reCAPTCHA online service, but they have the advantage—for native speakers of English, at least—of using real words that users are more likely to be able to guess correctly. Other advantages of reCAPTCHA are that the interface automatically provides options for the user to refresh the images if they're difficult to read or to get an audio challenge instead. Also, using reCAPTCHA helps digitize books, newspapers, and old-time radio shows. The challenge always contains two words, one of which cannot be deciphered by software. The other word is already known. If the user provides the correct answer for the known word, there's a high likelihood that the other one will be correct. If several people provide the same answer, the digitization software can be taught to recognize it. Since the service is free, it's the solution chosen for this lesson.

Setting up to use reCAPTCHA

To use reCAPTCHA, you need a pair of software keys—one public and one private. It's quick and easy to obtain the keys:

1 Go to http://recaptcha.net/whyrecaptcha.html, and click the Sign up Now! button.

2 Create a username and password, and follow the instructions to set up an account. The only information you need to provide is an email address and the domain name of the site where you plan to use reCAPTCHA.

3 To test reCAPTCHA on your local computer, select the option to enable the key on all domains (global key), and click Create Key.

4 The public and private keys are random strings of characters. Copy them to a text file, and save the file outside your site root. If you forget the keys, you can always log back into the reCAPTCHA site to retrieve them.

Using Zend_Service_ReCaptcha

Zend_Captcha_ReCaptcha relies on another class, Zend_Service_ReCaptcha, which does all the hard work for you. The code required to display and verify a reCAPTCHA challenge is remarkably simple.

To display a challenge, instantiate a Zend_Service_ReCaptcha object with the public and private keys, and then use the object's getHtml() method to display it:

```
$recaptcha = new Zend_Service_ReCaptcha($public_key, $private_key);
echo $recaptcha->getHtml();
```

The challenge and response are automatically submitted in the $_POST array as $_POST['recaptcha_challenge_field'] and $_POST['recaptcha_response_field'].

To check whether the user answered the challenge correctly, pass these values to the object's verify() method, and store the result. You can then use the result's isValid() method to test the response like this:

```
$result = $recaptcha->verify($_POST['recaptcha_challenge_field'],
➥ $_POST['recaptcha_response_field']);
if (!$result->isValid()) {
  // response was incorrect
}
```

Processing User Feedback

In this section, you'll use Zend_Mail to process a simple feedback form that contains two text input fields and a text area, as well as a reCAPTCHA. The validation and error message techniques are the same as in the previous lesson, so the instructions concentrate mainly on the new features.

Creating a mail connector script

To test email from a local testing environment, you need to instantiate a Zend_Mail_Transport_Smtp object to connect to your ISP. Because this is likely to be used in multiple pages, the script should be in an external file. No connection is made to the mail server until a message is actually sent, so you could put the code in library.php. However, the following instructions use a separate file:

1 Create a new PHP file, and save it as **mail_connector.php** in lesson08/workfiles/scripts. The file will contain only PHP code, so remove the default HTML code inserted by Dreamweaver.

2 At the top of the file, insert an opening PHP tag, and assign the SMTP address of your ISP account to a variable like this:

```
$mailhost = 'smtp.example.com';
```

Use the same address as for outgoing email in your regular email program.

3 Create an array with your email login details like this:

```
$mailconfig = array('auth'     => 'login',
                    'username' => 'me@example.com',
                    'password' => 'topsecret');
```

Use the values for your own email account. In most cases, the value of 'auth' should be 'login', but use 'plain' or 'crammd5' as appropriate.

If your email account uses a secure connection, add 'ssl' => 'ssl' or 'ssl' => 'tls' to the array, depending on the protocol used by your ISP. If your ISP uses a nonstandard port, add a 'port' element to the array.

4 Create an instance of Zend_Mail_Transport_Smtp and set it as the default transport like this:

```
$transport = new Zend_Mail_Transport_Smtp($mailhost, $mailconfig);
Zend_Mail::setDefaultTransport($transport);
```

5 Save mail_connector.php.

Basing a new server behavior on an existing one

The start files for this exercise include a form script that already contains most of the error checking code. The Redisplay on Error and Display Error Message server behaviors that you created in Lesson 7 have been applied to the Name and Email text input fields. The Display Error Message server behavior has also been applied to the Comments text area, but the content of a text area goes between the opening and closing `<textarea>` tags, so you need to create a new server behavior to deal with text areas. The PHP code is almost identical to the Redisplay on Error server behavior, so you can base the new one on it like this:

1 Open lesson08/start/comments.php, and save a copy in lesson08/workfiles. Close the original, and leave the copy open in the Document window.

2 Click the plus button in the Server Behaviors panel, and choose New Server Behavior. Type **Redisplay Text Area** in the Name field, and select the "Copy existing server behavior" checkbox. Choose Redisplay on Error from the list of server behaviors you created in the previous lesson.

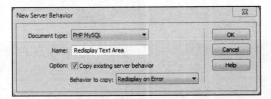

3 Click OK to open the dialog box where you define the server behavior. Because you're basing the new server behavior on an existing one, all fields are already filled in. You just need to make a few changes.

4 Edit the PHP code in the "Code block" section to remove all new lines, and change `Field Name` to **Text Area** like this:

```php
<?php if ($_POST && $errors) {echo htmlentities($_POST['@@Text Area@@'],
➥ ENT_COMPAT, 'UTF-8');}?>
```

▼ **CAUTION!** The code is spread over two lines here because of the limitations of the printed page, but it's necessary to put all the code on a single line. Otherwise, Dreamweaver cannot distinguish it from the existing server behavior. Changing the parameter is not enough on its own.

5 Select "textarea" from the Tag menu at the bottom left of the dialog box.

6 Set "Relative position" to "After the Opening Tag." The Attribute menu disappears when you do this. The settings should now look like this:

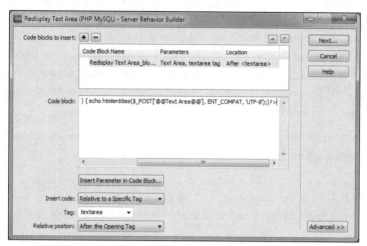

7 Click Next. You should see the following alert:

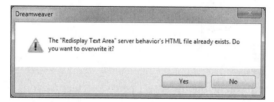

The HTML file creates the dialog box for the server behavior. You need to overwrite it so the new server behavior has its own dialog box.

Click Yes, and skip to step 9.

Continue with step 8 if you see this warning instead:

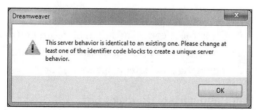

8 Removing the new lines from the PHP in step 4 should be sufficient to distinguish this server behavior from the original. However, Dreamweaver might still have difficulty, depending on how the original server behavior code was formatted. To get around this, change the PHP code in the "Code block" section like this:

```
<?php if (!empty($_POST) && $errors) {echo htmlentities(
➥ $_POST['@@Text Area@@'], ENT_COMPAT, 'UTF-8');}?>
```

Replacing $_POST with !empty($_POST) is just another way of testing that the form has been submitted. It's more verbose but achieves the same effect and should enable Dreamweaver to distinguish the different server behaviors.

Go back to step 7 before continuing with the next step.

9 Dreamweaver displays its suggested options for the server behavior dialog box. They're fine, so just click OK.

10 Select the Comments text area in Design view in comments.php, click the plus button in the Server Behaviors panel, and choose Redisplay Text Area. Type **comments** in the Text Area field, and click OK to insert the PHP code in the text area.

11 Open Split view to check the code that has been inserted. It should be highlighted if the text area is still selected in Design view. Dreamweaver normally moves the closing </textarea> tag onto a new line, as shown on line 36 in the following screen shot.

```
35    <textarea name="comments" id="comments" cols="45" rows="5"><?php if ($_POST &&
      $errors) {echo htmlentities($_POST['comments'], ENT_COMPAT, 'UTF-8');}?>
36    </textarea>
```

12 The new line creates unwanted space at the beginning of the text area, so you need to edit Code view to remove it and close the gap between the closing PHP and </textarea> tags like this:

```
35    <textarea name="comments" id="comments" cols="45" rows="5"><?php if ($_POST &&
      $errors) {echo htmlentities($_POST['comments'], ENT_COMPAT, 'UTF-8');}?></textarea>
```

13 Save comments.php, and leave it open for the next section.

Incorporating reCAPTCHA into the validation script

To save time and space, the validation script for the text fields and text area is in the start files for this lesson. It uses Zend_Validate in the same way as in Lesson 7. The only difference is that the conditional statement that checks whether the form has been submitted is inside the try block. This is because you need to instantiate a Zend_Service_ReCaptcha object every time the page loads.

This is how you add a reCAPTCHA widget to the validation script and form:

1 Copy library.php and process_comments.php from lesson08/start/scripts to lesson08/workfiles/scripts. Close the originals, and work with the copies.

2 Switch to comments.php, and include process_comments.php by adding the following code above the DOCTYPE declaration:

```
<?php
require_once('scripts/process_comments.php');
?>
```

> ❊ **NOTE:** Unlike previous external scripts, process_comments.php has a closing PHP tag. This is because the try and catch blocks are not wrapped in a conditional statement. Without a closing tag, Dreamweaver treats the PHP code as text above the DOCTYPE declaration, causing problems with Design view.

3 Save comments.php to add process_comments.php to the Related Files toolbar. Click process_comments.php in the Related Files toolbar to access it for editing in Split view.

> ▶ **TIP:** Editing related files in Split view allows you to keep the web page visible in Design view, speeding up testing in Live View. If you prefer to edit files in separate tabs, Dreamweaver keeps both versions in sync. What you see as a related file in Split view is exactly the same as the file in its separate tab, so there's no danger of getting the two mixed up. Choose the workflow that suits you best.

4 A Zend_Service_ReCaptcha object is responsible for displaying the reCAPTCHA widget and checking the answer, so it needs to be instantiated before the conditional statement that runs only if the form has been submitted. Add the highlighted code at the beginning of the try block, using your own public and private keys.

```
try {
    $public_key = 'Your_reCAPTCHA_public_key';
    $private_key = 'Your_reCAPTCHA_private_key';
    $recaptcha = new Zend_Service_ReCaptcha($public_key, $private_key);
    if (isset($_POST['send'])) {
```

The code that displays the widget will be added to comments.php later.

5 Checking the answer belongs with the validation script. Create a new line after the "validate the user input" comment, and insert the code there:

```
// validate the user input
$result = $recaptcha->verify($_POST['recaptcha_challenge_field'],
➥ $_POST['recaptcha_response_field']);
if (!$result->isValid()) {
  $errors['recaptcha'] = 'Try again';
}
$val = new Zend_Validate_Alnum(TRUE);
```

The original challenge and the user's input are transmitted through the $_POST array. The verify() method checks that both values are the same.

6 Save process_comments.php, and switch to the source code of comments.php.

Zend_Service_ReCaptcha generates all the HTML and CSS for the reCAPTCHA widget, so you need to insert the code inside the form without any formatting. The form elements in comments.php are in paragraphs, so the code to display the reCAPTCHA widget needs to go between the paragraphs containing the Comments text area and the submit button, as shown on line 44 in the following screen shot:

```
40     <?php if ($_POST && isset($errors['comments'])) {
41        echo $errors['comments'];
42     } ?>
43     </span></p>
44     <?php echo $recaptcha->getHtml(); ?>
45     <p>
46        <input type="submit" name="send" id="send" value="Send Comments" />
47     </p>
```

Even though $recaptcha is defined in a different page, Dreamweaver generates code hints for it because process_comments.php is a related file.

7 Save comments.php, make sure you're connected to the Internet, and click Live View. You should see a reCAPTCHA challenge added to the feedback form, as shown in the screen shot on page 258 (the first page of this lesson).

8 Click Live Code, and examine the huge amount of HTML and JavaScript that has been added to the page. The Zend_Service_ReCaptcha object adds its own CSS as a <style> block in the <head> of the page.

The reCAPTCHA widget is around line 144 in a <div> with the ID recaptcha_widget_ div. Use this ID in your CSS to make adjustments to the margins around the <div>. The styles in users_wider.css give the widget the same margins as paragraphs inside the form like this:

```
form p, #recaptcha_widget_div {
  margin:0 0 10px 205px;
}
```

9 Leave all the fields blank, and test the page in Live View by holding down Ctrl/Cmd and clicking Send Comments (the modifier key is needed for links and forms to work in Live View). At the top of the Document window, you'll see a message that reads "Missing response field" but no error messages next to the input fields.

This is because Zend_Service_ReCaptcha has thrown an exception. When this happens, the try block is abandoned, and only the catch block is executed. "Missing response field" is the message generated by the exception.

10 To prevent an exception from being thrown when the reCAPTCHA challenge is left blank, you need to modify the code in process_comments.php like this:

```
if (empty($_POST['recaptcha_response_field'])) {
  $errors['recaptcha'] = 'reCAPTCHA field is required';
} else {
  $result = $recaptcha->verify($_POST['recaptcha_challenge_field'],
  ➥ $_POST['recaptcha_response_field']);
  if (!$result->isValid()) {
    $errors['recaptcha'] = 'Try again';
  }
}
```

This uses empty() to check the reCAPTCHA field. If it hasn't been filled in, a message is added to the $errors array. The code that verifies the response is wrapped in an else block and is executed only if the field is not empty.

11 Save process_comments.php, and test the form again leaving the fields blank. The script no longer throws an exception, so the error messages are displayed next to each form field.

12 To display the $errors['recaptcha'] message, amend the code that displays the reCAPTCHA widget like this:

```
<?php if (isset($errors['recaptcha'])) {
  echo "<p><span>{$errors['recaptcha']}</span></p>";
}
echo $recaptcha->getHtml(); ?>
```

Technically speaking, the <span> is redundant. It has been added here so that the error message is styled the same way as the others. The string is wrapped in double quotation marks to display the value of $errors['recaptcha'], which needs to be wrapped in curly braces because it's an array element (see "Using array variables with quotation marks" in Lesson 3).

Sending the feedback by email

The email should be sent only if there are no errors in validation. So the script that builds the message and sends the email goes in the conditional statement at the end of the validation script. You build the message by concatenating the user input into a single string, together with labels to indicate which fields it comes from. For HTML email, the string needs to contain the HTML tags as well.

1 In process_comments.php, locate the following conditional statement (it should be around lines 30–32):

```
if (!$errors) {
 // create and send the email
}
```

All the mail processing code goes between the curly braces of this conditional block.

2 Include the mail connector script, and create a Zend_Mail object like this:

```
require_once('mail_connector.php');
$mail = new Zend_Mail('UTF-8');
```

Passing UTF-8 to the Zend_Mail constructor ensures that accented or nonalphabetic characters will be rendered correctly.

3 Use the Zend_Mail methods described earlier in "Using Zend_Mail" and Table 8.1 to set the recipient's address, the From header, and subject. Use your own email addresses in the addTo() and setFrom() methods:

```
$mail->addTo('me@example.com', 'David Powers');
$mail->setFrom('another@example.com', 'Zend Mail Test');
$mail->setSubject('Comments from feedback form');
```

▼ CAUTION! If possible, use different email addresses for addTo() and setFrom(). Both should be genuine email addresses. For setFrom() use the email address connected with the username and password in your mail connector script. Using a different email address could result in the email being rejected when the mail server attempts to forward it. Zend_Mail has no knowledge of what happens after handing the message to the server, so you won't have any way of knowing its fate.

4 Because the user's email address has been validated, you can safely use it to set the Reply-To header like this:

```
$mail->setReplyTo($_POST['email'], $_POST['name']);
```

5 Since the user's name and email have been included in `Reply-To` header, you could just send the value of `$_POST['comments']` as the body text. However, that doesn't demonstrate how to build a longer email message. Create the body for a plain text version like this:

```
$text = "Name: {$_POST['name']}\r\n\r\n";
$text .= "Email: {$_POST['email']}\r\n\r\n";
$text .= "Comments: {$_POST['comments']}";
```

Again, this uses strings enclosed in double quotation marks so that the values of the variables are incorporated. The email specification requires each line to end with a carriage return and newline character. The \r\n\r\n at the end of the first two lines use escape sequences to insert the appropriate characters (see Table 3.2 in Lesson 3).

CAUTION! The second and third lines in the preceding code block use the combined concatenation operator (a period followed by an equals sign) to add more text to the variable. If you omit the period, each new line overwrites the previous one.

6 For such a simple feedback form, you probably wouldn't want to send it as HTML email, but you build the message body in exactly the same way, adding the HTML tags to the string like this:

```
$html = '<html><head><title>';
$html .= $mail->getSubject();
$html .= '</title></head><body>';
$html .= "<p><strong>Name: </strong><a href='mailto:
➥ {$_POST['email']}'>{$_POST['name']}</a></p>";
$html .= '<p><strong>Comments: </strong>' . nl2br($_POST['comments']) .
➥ '</p>';
$html .= '</body></html>';
```

This creates the HTML for the email. The second line uses the `Zend_Mail getSubject()` method to retrieve the email's subject line to go inside the `<title>` tags.

The user input is embedded in two paragraphs. In the first one, the user's email is turned into a link for the name. In the second one, the value of `$_POST['comments']` is passed to the PHP `nl2br()` function, which converts newline characters into HTML `<br />` tags. You can't use a function inside a string, so the string is built in three parts and joined together by the concatenation operator.

CAUTION! If you omit the closing PHP tag from process_comments.php, Dreamweaver interprets the HTML tags in this string as part of the page markup, preventing Design view from displaying the form.

7 After building the message body, add the plain text and HTML versions to the email like this:

```
$mail->setBodyText($text, 'UTF-8');
$mail->setBodyHtml($html, 'UTF-8');
```

Adding the character set as the second argument is optional, but it's a good idea to ensure that the input is handled correctly.

> **TIP:** Not everyone likes HTML mail, and some people set their email program to reject it. When using Zend_Mail, you should always use setBodyText() to create a plain text version, even if you want most recipients to see the HTML version. If you send both HTML and plain text, recipients will see the message in their preferred format.

8 You're now ready to send the email. The send() method returns a Boolean value indicating whether it succeeded. You can capture this value to preserve the user's input and redisplay it in the form if the mail can't be sent. Add the following code to the mail processing script:

```
$success = $mail->send();
if (!$success) {
    $errors = TRUE;
}
```

Normally, form fields are cleared when a form is submitted. You want this to happen if the email is sent successfully, but setting $errors to TRUE results in the Redisplay on Error server behavior code preserving the input. This gives the user the option to retry later without needing to fill in every field again.

9 Save process_comments.php, and switch to the source code in comments.php. Add the following mixture of PHP and HTML to display the results of submitting the form:

```
<form id="form1" name="form1" method="post" action="">
  <?php if (isset($success) && !$errors) { ?>
  <p>Thank you. Your comments have been sent.</p>
  <?php } elseif (isset($success) && $errors) { ?>
  <p>Sorry, there was a problem. Please try later.</p>
  <?php } ?>
  <p>All fields are required</p>
```

The first conditional statement uses isset() to check whether $success exists. The variable is created only when the email is sent, which in turn can happen only if there are no errors. So, if $success exists, and $errors is FALSE, the mail must have been sent successfully. If, on the other hand, $success exists, but $errors is TRUE, it means an attempt was made to send the email, but it failed.

10 Finally, the moment of truth. Save comments.php and load it into a browser. Fill in all the fields, and click Send Comments. If all your code is correct, you should receive an email in your inbox after a short while. As the following screen shot shows, setting the character set of the email to UTF-8 supports languages other than unaccented English.

You can compare your code with lesson08/completed/comments.php and lesson08/completed/scripts/process_comments.php.

What happens if the email doesn't arrive?

Troubleshooting email problems is notoriously difficult. Emails normally travel around the Internet in seconds. Sometimes, they take several hours or never arrive at all. This can happen for a variety of reasons:

- Incorrect settings on the mail server
- Rejection by a mail server
- Network problems
- System failure
- Overaggressive spam filtering

If the problem lies with your mail connector script, the processing script should throw an exception. Analyze the message. The most likely cause is that you have used the wrong authentication type or that your login details are incorrect.

If submitting the form doesn't result in an exception being thrown, try using different email addresses.

If email still doesn't arrive, amend your mail connector script to use Zend_Mail_Transport_Sendmail, as described in "Setting the default transport for Zend_Mail," and upload all the files to your remote server. It should work when you test it from there.

Processing Other Form Elements

The simple feedback form in comments.php uses only text input fields and a text area. Other form elements need to be handled slightly differently. The form in lesson08/start/inquiry.php contains all types of input elements. In addition to the text input fields and text area, it contains a checkbox group, a radio button group, a single-choice <select> menu, and a multiple-choice <select> list.

Examining the $_POST array

As you saw in previous lessons, the values of form elements are passed through the $_POST or $_GET array depending on which method was used to submit the form. In the absence of a form being submitted or a query string being appended to the URL, the $_POST and $_GET arrays exist but contain no elements. Because PHP treats an empty array as FALSE, you can use if ($_POST) to test whether a form has been submitted by the POST method. When you submit a form, elements are created in the $_POST array for the submit button and each text field or text area. Even if nothing is entered in the fields, the array elements exist, so the $_POST array—as opposed to individual elements—is no longer empty; therefore, PHP implicitly treats it as TRUE.

Checkboxes, radio button groups, and multiple-choice <select> lists behave differently. The following exercise illustrates what happens when you include them in a form:

1 Copy lesson08/start/inquiry.php to lesson08/workfiles, and switch to Code view.

2 Add the following code between the closing `</form>` and `</body>` tags:

```
<pre>
<?php if ($_POST) {
  print_r($_POST);
} ?>
</pre>
```

This checks if the form has been submitted. If it has, `print_r()` displays the contents of the $_POST array. The `<pre>` tags make the output easier to read.

3 Save the page, click Live View, and submit the form leaving all the fields blank. The contents of the $_POST array are displayed like this:

```
Array
(
    [name] =>
    [email] =>
    [howmany] => 0
    [comments] =>
    [send] => Send Inquiry
)
```

Only two elements have values: howmany and send, the single-choice `<select>` menu and submit button respectively. The two text input fields and the text area are included in the array but don't have any values.

The checkboxes, radio buttons, and multiple-choice `<select>` list weren't selected in the form, so they aren't even registered in the $_POST array.

4 It's unusual for a radio button group not to have a default value. Switch off Live View, and select the No radio button in Design view. In the Property inspector, set "Initial state" to Checked. This inserts `checked="checked"` in the first radio button's `<input>` tag.

5 Save the page, and test it again by submitting the form without changing any of the fields. This time, `[dogs]` => n is added to the array.

6 With Live View still active, select all the checkboxes, and Shift-click to select all values in the "Special interests" list. Resubmit the form. This is the result:

```
Array
(
    [name] =>
    [email] =>
    [destinations] => national parks
    [dogs] => n
    [howmany] => 0
    [interests] => walking
    [comments] =>
    [send] => Send Inquiry
)
```

All the checkboxes and values in the multiple-choice <select> list were selected, but only the last ones are included in the $_POST array.

The problem is that PHP treats the name attributes of form elements as strings. If more than one element has the same name, only the last one is selected. Fortunately, the solution is simple: get PHP to treat multiple-choice form elements as an array by adding an empty pair of square brackets at the end of their name attributes (see "Creating a basic array" in Lesson 3).

7 In Code view, add a pair of square brackets at the end of the name attribute in each of the checkboxes and in the multiple-choice <select> list. The first checkbox should look like this:

```
<input name="destinations[]" type="checkbox" id="destinations_coast"
➥ value="coast" />
```

You need to do this in all three checkboxes. The multiple-choice <select> list has only one name attribute. Its opening tag should look like this:

```
<select name="interests[]" size="4" multiple="multiple" id="interests">
```

▼ **CAUTION!** Do **not** add square brackets at the end of the name attribute for single-choice <select> menus. The square brackets are required only for form elements that permit multiple choices.

8 Save inquiry.php, and test the form again, selecting all the checkboxes and values in the multiple-choice <select> list. This time, all the values are included in the $_POST array.

```
Array
(
    [name] =>
    [email] =>
    [destinations] => Array
        (
            [0] => coast
            [1] => city
            [2] => national parks
        )

    [dogs] => n
    [howmany] => 0
    [interests] => Array
        (
            [0] => cycling
            [1] => gourmet
            [2] => surfing
            [3] => walking
        )

    [comments] =>
    [send] => Send Inquiry
)
```

$_POST['destinations'] and $_POST['interests'] are now subarrays, so you need to treat them differently from other elements of the $_POST array.

To summarize:

- When no default value is set for a radio button group, it is omitted from the form's data if the user fails to select a value.

- A single-choice <select> menu is always included in the form's data.

- Multiple-choice <select> lists and checkboxes are excluded from the form's data if the user fails to select a value.

- To get all the values from multiple-choice <select> lists and checkbox groups, append an empty pair of square brackets to their name attributes.

- When using a single checkbox or checkboxes with unique name attributes, do *not* append square brackets. They are needed only when multiple checkboxes share the same name.

- The id attribute of each element must be unique within the page, even when multiple elements share the same name. Dreamweaver normally handles this automatically by appending an incremental number to the id attribute, but you should always verify this yourself. Duplicate id attributes in the same page cause serious problems with JavaScript.

Rather than give step-by-step instructions for completing inquiry.php, the following sections describe the basics of dealing with each type of form element. They also give instructions for creating six custom server behaviors to speed up the redisplay of user input when a form is submitted with errors.

Handling checkboxes

The value attribute of a checkbox <input> tag is optional. If omitted, the default value for a selected checkbox is "on." Using this default makes sense only for single checkboxes, for example one that asks for agreement to terms and conditions. When using a checkbox group that shares the same name attribute, you need to assign a unique value attribute to each one, as in inquiry.php.

When validating checkboxes, always verify the relevant element is in the $_POST array. The square brackets are not part of the name attribute. They simply tell PHP to treat the group as an array. Check for $_POST['destinations'], *not* $_POST['destinations[]']. So, to ensure that at least one checkbox is selected:

```
if (!isset($_POST['destinations'])) {
  $errors['destinations'] = 'Please choose at least one';
}
```

The values of a checkbox group with a common name are treated as a subarray, even if only one checkbox is selected. To convert the array to a string, use the PHP implode() function, which takes two arguments: the character(s) you want to use as a separator and the array. Add the following code to turn $_POST['destinations'] into a comma-separated string prefixed with a label:

```
if (!isset($_POST['destinations'])) {
  $errors['destinations'] = 'Please choose at least one';
} else {
  $_POST['destinations'] = 'Destinations: ' . implode(', ',
➥ $_POST['destinations']);
}
```

To format the subarray in a more sophisticated manner, use a foreach loop (see "Using a foreach loop" in Lesson 3) inside the else block.

The following instructions describe how to create a custom server behavior to reselect checkboxes when a form is submitted with errors:

1 Choose New Server Behavior from the Server Behaviors panel menu.

2 Name the server behavior **Redisplay Checkbox**.

3 Create a code block, and enter the following code in the "Code block" section:

```
<?php if ($_POST && $errors && isset($_POST['@@Group Name@@']) &&
➥ in_array('@@Value@@', $_POST['@@Group Name@@'])) {
  echo 'checked="checked"';
} ?>
```

The parameters @@Group Name@@ and @@Value@@ represent the name attribute of the checkbox group and the selected value respectively.

The if statement checks four conditions: the form has been submitted, there are errors, the checkbox group is in the $_POST array (using isset()), and the selected value is in the subarray (using in_array()).

If all conditions are met, checked="checked" is inserted.

> **TIP:** If you're not familiar with the functions, use Dreamweaver's code hints to display the documentation, and study the examples given there.

4 The checked="checked" attribute needs to be added inside the checkbox <input> tag, so use the following options at the bottom of the dialog box where you define the server behavior:

5 Click Next, and accept the default suggestions for the new dialog box.

To use the Redisplay Checkbox server behavior, select the checkbox in Design view, and choose Redisplay Checkbox from the Server Behaviors panel menu.

Type the name of the checkbox group in the Group Name field and the value in the Value field. As long as the correct checkbox is selected in Design view, the "input/checkbox tag" menu will be set to the correct value.

⚠ CAUTION! The Value field must use exactly the same spelling as the checkbox's `value` attribute, including any mixture of uppercase and lowercase characters.

Handling radio button groups

Radio button groups permit only one choice. It's generally a good idea to set a default value to ensure the data is always included in the $_POST array. If you don't set a default, you need to use `isset()` in the same way as for checkboxes to verify whether a value has been selected.

To redisplay radio button group values when a form is submitted with errors, you need to build two server behaviors: one for the default setting and another for all other buttons in the same group. It's easier to build the second one first, and then base the server behavior for the default value on it. The following instructions explain how:

1 Choose New Server Behavior from the Server Behaviors panel menu, and name the server behavior **Redisplay Radio Button**.

2 Create a code block with the following code:

```php
<?php if ($_POST && $errors && $_POST['@@Radio Group@@'] == '@@Value@@') {
  echo 'checked="checked"';
}?>
```

The parameters @@Radio Group@@ and @@Value@@ represent the `name` attribute of the radio button group and the selected value respectively. The `if` statement tests three conditions: the form has been submitted, errors exist, and the value in the $_POST array represents the selected value. Because only one value can ever be selected in a radio button group, it's always a string.

3 Use the following settings for the options at the bottom of the dialog box:

> **CAUTION!** Do **not** select input/radio as the value for Tag, because this inserts the same code in all radio buttons that belong to the same group. You need to insert different code in the default radio button's <input> tag.

4 Click Next, and accept the default suggestions for the new dialog box.

5 Choose New Server Behavior from the Server Behaviors panel menu to create the server behavior for the default radio button.

6 In the New Server Behavior dialog box, type **Set Default Radio Button** in the Name field. Select the "Copy existing server behavior" checkbox, and choose Redisplay Radio Button from the "Behavior to copy" list. Click OK.

7 Edit the code block like this:

```
<?php if (!$_POST || ($_POST && !$errors) || ($_POST && $errors &&
➥ $_POST['@@Radio Group@@'] == '@@Value@@')) {
  echo 'checked="checked"';
}?>
```

The if statement now handles three possible scenarios:

- The $_POST array is empty—in other words, the form hasn't yet been submitted. The radio button is set as the group's default.

- The form has been submitted and there are *no* errors, so the radio button needs to be reset as the default.

- The form has been submitted with errors, and this was the selected value.

The conditions for each scenario are separated by the || logical operator, but multiple conditions are wrapped in parentheses to ensure they are evaluated together.

> **CAUTION!** Don't forget the extra closing parenthesis after '@@Value@@'.

8 Leave the options at the bottom of the dialog box unchanged, and click Next.

9 Click Yes to overwrite the existing HTML file, and accept the default suggestions for the server behavior's dialog box.

To apply the new server behaviors, select the radio button in Design view, click the plus button in the Server Behaviors panel, and choose Set Default Radio Button for the default button or Redisplay Radio Button for other buttons. The options in the dialog box are the same as for checkboxes.

✱ NOTE: When using the Set Default Radio Button server behavior, make sure "Initial state" in the Property inspector is set to Unchecked for all radio buttons. The server behavior takes care of adding the necessary code when the page is viewed in a browser or Live View.

Handling single-choice <select> menus

A single-choice <select> menu always transmits a value when a form is submitted. The value attribute is not required in the <option> tags, but if it's omitted, the text between the opening and closing <option> tags is automatically used instead. It's common practice for the first option to be something like "Select One." If you want to make a selection required, set the value of the first <option> tag to 0 like this:

```
<select name="howmany" id="howmany">
  <option value="0">-- Select one --</option>
```

In your validation script do this:

```
if ($_POST['howmany'] == '0') {
  $errors['howmany'] = 'Please make a selection';
}
```

To redisplay the selected value when a form is submitted with errors, you need to create two server behaviors in the same way as for a radio button group: one to set the default value and the other for the remaining <option> tags. Call them **Set Default Option** and **Redisplay Select Option**. Again, it's simpler to base the default one on the server behavior for the remaining tags. You should be familiar with creating new server behaviors by now, so I'll just provide the basic settings.

The code block for Redisplay Select Option looks like this:

```
<?php if ($_POST && $errors && $_POST['@@Select Menu@@'] == '@@Value@@') {
  echo 'selected="selected"';
}?>
```

Use the following settings for the options at the bottom of the dialog box:

The suggested options for the server behavior's dialog box are fine.

Amend the code block for Set Default Option like this:

```php
<?php if (!$_POST || ($_POST && !$errors) || ($_POST && $errors &&
➥ $_POST['@@Select Menu@@'] == '@@Value@@')) {
  echo 'selected="selected"';
}?>
```

The conditional logic here is identical to the Set Default Radio Button server behavior. All other options remain the same. Click Yes when asked if you want to overwrite the HTML file.

Unfortunately, you can't select <option> tags in Design view to apply either server behavior. Even if you select a specific tag in Code view, Dreamweaver lists all <option> tags on the page as an indexed array, as shown here:

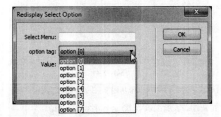

This makes no distinction between the single-choice <select> menu and the multiple-choice list, so you need to be careful when applying these server behaviors. As with radio buttons, leave "Initially selected" in the Property inspector deselected, and use the server behaviors to set the default value.

> **TIP:** It helps if you keep Code view or Split view open, so you can check that the code is being inserted into the correct <option> tag. If you still find it too confusing, save the PHP code in the Snippets panel (choose Window > Snippets), and edit the parameters manually. On Windows, you can also press Shift+F9 to open the Snippets panel. There is no keyboard shortcut in the Mac version because of a conflict with Exposé.

Handling multiple-choice <select>lists

Multiple-choice <select> lists are similar to checkbox groups in that they are excluded from the $_POST array if nothing is selected, and their values are submitted as a subarray when at least one item is selected. You verify and handle their values in exactly the same way as a checkbox group.

To redisplay selected values when a form is submitted with errors, create a new server behavior called **Redisplay Multi-Options**. Use the following code block:

```
<?php if ($_POST && $errors && isset($_POST['@@Select List@@'])) &&
➥ in_array('@@Value@@', $_POST['@@Select List@@'])) {
 echo 'selected="selected"';
} ?>
```

Because multiple-choice `<select>` lists work in the same way as checkbox groups, this code uses the same conditional logic as Redisplay Checkbox. The only difference is that it inserts `'selected="selected"` instead of `'checked="checked"`.

Use the same options in the Server Behavior Builder dialog box as for the single-choice `<select>` menu server behaviors.

Resetting Forgotten Passwords

A common problem with user registration systems is that people tend to forget their passwords. When you encrypt a password with the `sha1()` function, as in Lessons 6 and 7, it's a one-way operation—there's no way to decrypt it. So you need a way for users to reset their passwords. Just putting an update form online isn't sufficient. You need to ensure the right person is changing the password. A simple, yet effective method is to generate a security token, store it in the database, and email it to the user.

This project brings together many of the techniques you have learned: validation, interaction with a database, and email. To save time, the start files contain the basic structure so that you can concentrate on the new features.

Updating records with Zend_Db

Updating records with `Zend_Db` doesn't involve writing SQL. The `update()` method of a `Zend_Db_Adapter` object with read/write permissions—for this book, `$dbWrite`—does it all for you. The method takes three arguments:

- The table name
- An associative array of the column names and update values
- An expression that identifies the record(s) to be updated

The associative array uses the column names as the array keys. For example, the following array updates the password and token columns, setting them to the value in $_POST['password'] and NULL respectively:

```
$data = array('password' => $_POST['password'], 'token' => NULL);
```

If you have SQL experience, the third argument is the equivalent of the WHERE clause, but you don't need to use the keyword WHERE. For example, to update the record in the users table for user_id 2, the three arguments passed to update() look like this:

```
$dbWrite->update('users', $data, 'user_id = 2');
```

It's safe to include known values directly in the third argument, but if the values come from user input, you need to use quoteInto() to protect your database from SQL injection. For example, to insert an email address from user input into the third argument, you need to prepare it like this:

```
$where = $dbWrite->quoteInto('email = ?', $_POST['email']);
$dbWrite->update('users', $data, $where);
```

Alternatively, use the following syntax adapted from array notation:

```
$where['email = ?'] = $_POST['email'];
$dbWrite->update('users', $data, $where);
```

Normally, the key of an array element should be a number or a string that contains only alphanumeric characters. However, Zend_Db permits this unconventional syntax as a handy shortcut.

Because the third argument accepts an array, you can apply multiple criteria to identify the record being updated, like this:

```
$where['email = ?'] = $_POST['email'];
$where['username = ?'] = $_POST['username'];
$dbWrite->update('users', $data, $where);
```

This updates the record in the users table where the email column matches $_POST['email'] *and* the username column matches $_POST['username'].

* **NOTE:** Using a multiple-value array as the third argument to the update() method is the equivalent of using the AND operator in a SQL WHERE clause. To use the OR operator to specify alternative criteria, you need to build the third argument as a string.

If the third argument to the update() method is omitted, *all* records in the table are updated in the same way.

Using SQL functions with Zend_Db

As a security measure, Zend_Db converts values in data arrays to strings and escapes special characters. Consequently, you can't include a SQL function—such as CURDATE() for the current date—directly in a data array. Instead, you need to wrap SQL functions in a Zend_Db_Expr object like this:

```
$data = array('password' => $_POST['password'],
              'registered' => new Zend_Db_Expr('CURDATE()'));
```

To use a SQL function in the third argument to the update() method, do this:

```
$today = new Zend_Db_Expr('CURDATE()');
$where = "start_date > $today";
```

Building the reset request script

Before tackling the code for the reset request script, let's take a look at the decision chain it needs to employ. The following illustration outlines the process.

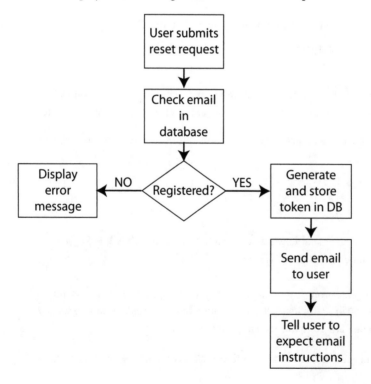

The reset request form has a single input field for the user's email address. The processing script needs to check if the email address is registered in the database. If it isn't, an error message is displayed and no further processing is necessary.

If the email address exists in the database, the processing script retrieves the user's details and generates a security token, a 32-character string that should be impossible to guess. The user's record in the database is updated by storing the token. At the same time, an email is sent to the user with a link to the password reset page. The user's primary key and the security token are appended to the link as a query string and will be used to verify the user's identity. Sending the link directly to the user's registered email address should ensure only the user can reset the password.

This part of the project finishes by displaying a message onscreen telling the user to expect an email with details of how to reset the password.

There's a lot going on, but it requires fewer than 40 lines of PHP code:

1 Copy request_reset.php from lesson08/start/scripts to lesson08/workfiles/scripts. The file already contains the following code:

```php
$errors = FALSE;
$result = FALSE;
if ($_POST) {
  require_once('library.php');
  require_once('mail_connector.php');
  try {

  } catch (Exception $e) {
  echo $e->getMessage();
  }
}
```

Only one error message is needed, so $errors is simply set to FALSE. If the email address fails validation or isn't registered, it will be reset to TRUE.

The other Boolean value, $result, determines whether to show the request form or a message telling the user to expect email instructions. It's initially set to FALSE and is used later in the script to store the result of the database query. If no record can be found in the database, it remains FALSE. Otherwise, it holds an array of the user's details, which PHP implicitly treats as TRUE.

2 Before searching for the email in the database, you need to validate the user's input. Add the following code inside the try block:

```php
$val = new Zend_Validate_EmailAddress();
if (!$val->isValid($_POST['email'])) {
  $errors = TRUE;
}
```

3 If the email address passes validation, you can use it to query the database. Add the following code to build the SQL query and execute it:

```
if (!$errors) {
  $sql = $dbRead->quoteInto('SELECT user_id, first_name, family_name,
  ➥ email FROM users WHERE email = ?', $_POST['email']);
  $result = $dbRead->fetchRow($sql);
}
```

This is a SELECT query, so the read-only account uses the quoteInto() method that you learned about in Lesson 7 to incorporate user input into the SQL. The query selects four columns from the users table by listing their names as a comma-separated list after the SELECT keyword.

In Lesson 7, you used fetchAll() to execute the query, but this time fetchRow() is used instead. See the sidebar "Choosing Between fetchAll() and fetchRow()" for an explanation of the difference.

Choosing Between fetchAll() and fetchRow()

The main difference between the fetchAll() and fetchRow()methods is that fetchAll() retrieves every matching row from the database, whereas fetchRow() gets just the first one. In Lesson 7, all you were interested in was whether there was a match in the database, so it didn't matter which method you used. However, it does matter when you want to access the values.

The fetchRow() method retrieves only one row and stores the results as a simple associative array, using the column names as array keys like this: $result['user_id'].

When you use fetchAll(), the results are always stored as a multidimensional array with a subarray for each row—even if there's only one row. You normally access the results of fetchAll() with a foreach loop like this:

```
foreach ($result as $row) {
  // handle each row
}
```

Inside the loop, you access each field by its column name like this: $row['user_id'].

If you don't use a loop, you need to specify the subarray number (counting from 0) like this: $result[0]['user_id'].

4 If the email isn't in the database, the fetchRow() method returns FALSE. So, if there's no result, you need to set $errors to TRUE. Otherwise, you can carry on with the reset request. Add the highlighted code *inside* the conditional statement you created in the previous step:

```
$result = $dbRead->fetchRow($sql);
if (!$result) {
    $errors = TRUE;
} else {
    // update database and send mail
}
}
```

5 If the email exists in the database, you need to create a security token and update the user's record to store it in the database. Insert the following code inside the else block:

```
$token = md5(uniqid(mt_rand(), TRUE));
$data = array('token' => $token);
$dbWrite->update('users', $data, "user_id = {$result['user_id']}");
```

The first line of new code uses a typical PHP shortcut by passing functions as arguments to other functions. The uniqid() function generates a unique ID based on the current time. It takes two optional arguments designed to randomize the value. The first of these is mt_rand(), which generates a random number. Finally, uniqid() is wrapped in md5(), an encryption function that produces a 32-character hexadecimal string. Don't worry if you find the details confusing. Just accept that the value assigned to $token should be impossible for anyone to guess.

The second line creates an associative array that assigns $token to the name of the database column where it's to be stored.

The third line uses the $dbWrite database object with read/write privileges to update the user's record. The third argument uses the user_id primary key from the database result to identify the record to be updated. Because $result['user_id'] is an array element, you need to wrap it in curly braces to incorporate it into the double-quoted string. The value contained in $result['user_id'] is the record's primary key, which is an automatically incremented integer, so it's safe to use directly in the third argument. Also, because it's a number, the value doesn't need to be in quotation marks.

6 Now, you need to send an email to the user with a link to the password reset page. Add the following script inside the `else` block, using your own email address in the `setFrom()` method:

```
$mail = new Zend_Mail('UTF-8');
$mail->addTo($result['email'], "{$result['first_name']}
➥ $result['family_name']}");
$mail->setSubject('Instructions for resetting your password');
$mail->setFrom('webmaster@example.com', 'DW CS5 with PHP');
$link = "http://phpcs5/lesson08/workfiles/reset.php?id=
➥ {$result['user_id']}&token=$token";
$message = "Use the following link to reset your password. This link
➥ can be used once only. $link";
$mail->setBodyText($message, 'UTF-8');
$mail->send();
```

Creating and sending an email was covered in detail earlier in this lesson, so this code should be easy to understand.

The values from the database result are used to set the recipient's address by passing the email address as the first argument to `addTo()` and enclosing the `first_name` and `family_name` values in a double-quoted string as the second argument. This personalizes the address with the recipient's real name—or at least the one registered in the system.

The `$link` variable contains the URL of the password reset page with a query string that contains the user's primary key and the security token. The `$link` variable is then incorporated in the `$message` string and passed to `setBodyText()`. This sends a plain text message only.

7 Save request_reset.php, and copy forgotten.php from lesson08/start to lesson08/workfiles. The code in forgotten.php contains two conditional statements that control the HTML displayed onscreen.

Use `require_once()` above the DOCTYPE declaration to include scripts/request_reset.php, and load forgotten.php into a browser. You should see the reset request form.

Forgotten Your Password?

Enter the email address you used when registering.

Email address: [   ]

[Submit]

8 Test the page by typing a false email address into the text field and clicking Submit. You should see an error message displayed below the form.

> ## Forgotten Your Password?
>
> Enter the email address you used when registering.
>
> Email address: [   ]
>
> [Submit]
>
> Sorry, there is no record of that address.

9 Type your own email address in the field, and submit the form. Assuming that your address is registered in the database, the form should disappear, and you are presented with the following message:

> ## Request Received
>
> An email has been sent to your registered address with instructions for resetting your password.

The different messages are controlled by the conditional statements in forgotten.php. An if. . . else statement uses the value of $result to determine whether to show the form or the message in the preceding screen shot. The error message is controlled by the value of $errors.

10 If the gods of cyberspace are smiling on you, you should receive an email similar to this:

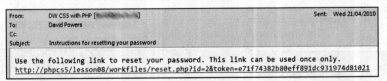

You're ready to move on to the script that resets the password. You can compare your code with lesson08/completed/scripts/request_reset.php.

If you see the success message in step 9 but don't receive an email, the most likely causes are network problems or the email being rejected by the mail server. Using a dummy address in the setFrom() method is a common cause of rejection, because the email is perceived as spam.

Building the password reset script

The script that resets a user's password needs to perform a couple of checks before updating the record in the database. First, it needs to verify the user_id and security token. If they don't match, there's no point in going any further. If they're OK, the next task is to validate the new password, using the same technique as in Lesson 7. If the password is acceptable, the script can finally update the user's record. The following illustration outlines the decision chain.

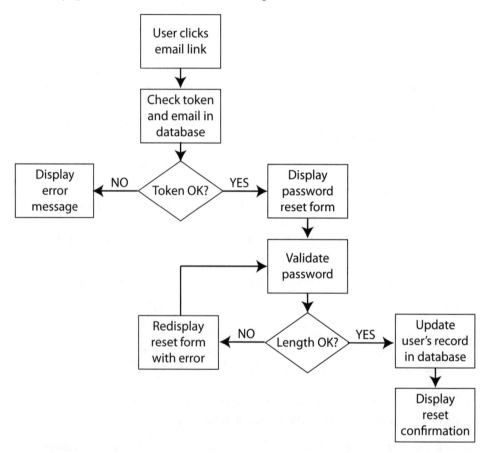

Again, there's a lot going on, but the final script is just 45 lines.

1 Copy lesson08/start/reset.php to lesson08/workfiles, and examine the code in Split view. In Design view, you can see there are three blocks of HTML: confirmation that the password has been reset, an error message, and a form with two password fields. The Display Error Message server behavior has been applied to <span> tags next to the password fields. As in forgotten.php, a series of conditional statements controls what is displayed.

2 Copy lesson08/start/scripts/reset_password.php to lesson08/workfiles/scripts. This contains the following basic code:

```
session_start();
$_SESSION['nomatch'] = TRUE;
$errors = array();
$success = FALSE;
require_once('library.php');
try {

} catch (Exception $e) {
  echo $e->getMessage();
}
```

The script needs to keep track of the user's identity to update the correct record in the database. You could store the details in hidden form fields, but it's more secure to use session variables, which remain on the server. So, the script initiates a session with `session_start()` and creates a session variable called `$_SESSION['nomatch']`, which is set to TRUE. `$_SESSION['nomatch']`, `$errors`, and `$success` control what is displayed in reset.php.

The script needs to access the database each time the page loads, so library.php is included right away.

3 Switch back to reset.php and include scripts/reset_password.php using `require_once()` above the DOCTYPE declaration.

4 Locate the opening <form> tag (around line 21). It currently looks like this:

```
<form id="form1" name="form1" method="post" action="">
```

The `action` attribute tells the browser the address of the script that processes the data when the form is submitted. If there's no address, the form is assumed to be self-processing—in other words, it submits the data to the same page. This form is self-processing but with a subtle difference.

The user accesses this page from the email link, which appends a query string to the URL. If you leave the form's `action` attribute blank, the query string remains in the URL when the form is submitted, creating a problem for the processing script. The query string must be removed.

PHP conveniently stores the base URL without the query string in a superglobal variable called $_SERVER['PHP_SELF']. Use echo to insert the page's URL in the action attribute like this:

```
<form id="form1" name="form1" method="post" action="<?php echo
➥ $_SERVER['PHP_SELF']; ?>">
```

When the form is submitted, the query string will be stripped from the URL.

> ▶ **TIP:** If you ever need the query string, it's contained in another superglobal variable called, as you might expect, $_SERVER['QUERY_STRING'].

5 Save reset.php, and switch to reset_password.php, where the rest of the code needs to go.

6 When the user clicks the email link, you need to check that the values in the query string match a record in the database. Create a conditional statement to check if the $_GET array contains id and token. If it does, use them to build a SELECT query. Add the following code in the try block:

```
if (isset($_GET['id']) && isset($_GET['token'])) {
  $id = $dbRead->quote($_GET['id']);
  $token = $dbRead->quote($_GET['token']);
  $sql = "SELECT user_id FROM users WHERE user_id = $id AND token =
  ➥ $token";
  $result = $dbRead->fetchRow($sql);
}
```

Variables from the $_GET array are insecure, so they need to be sanitized before they can be inserted into a SQL query. In previous files, you used the quoteInto() method to insert user input in a SQL query. Unfortunately, this can't be used with multiple values. Instead, use the quote() method to sanitize $_GET['id'] and $_GET['token'], and assign them to variables.

The sanitized variables can then be incorporated into the SQL query in a double-quoted string. Although the token column uses a string data type, there is no need to wrap $token in quotation marks. The quote() method takes care of that for you.

The query is passed to fetchRow() and the result stored as $result.

7 If the user's ID and security token match a record in the users table, you need to reset $_SESSION['nomatch'] to FALSE and to store the ID and token in session variables. It's also recommended to regenerate the session with session_regenerate_id() after a user's status has changed, such as being correctly identified. Add this conditional statement immediately after the line that fetches the database result:

```
  $result = $dbRead->fetchRow($sql);
  if ($result) {
    session_regenerate_id();
    $_SESSION['user_id'] = $_GET['id'];
    $_SESSION['token'] = $_GET['token'];
    $_SESSION['nomatch'] = FALSE;
  }
}
```

8 Save reset_password.php, and load reset.php into a browser. Because you accessed the page directly, $_SESSION['nomatch'] is TRUE, so this is displayed:

Error

Sorry, there was an error. Make sure you used the complete URL in the email you received. The URL can be used to change your password only once. If necessary, submit another request.

9 Now, use the link in the email you received. This time you are shown the password reset form.

10 The rest of the code in reset_password.php goes in a conditional statement that executes the code only if the form has been submitted. The conditional statement needs to be inside the try block immediately above the catch block:

```
if (isset($_POST['reset'])) {
  // password reset code goes here
}
} catch (Exception $e) {
```

The name attribute of the submit button is reset, so this ensures the code is run only if the $_POST data comes from the password reset form.

11 Before updating the user's record, you need to validate the password. Add this code inside the conditional statement you created in the previous step:

```
$val = new Zend_Validate();
$val->addValidator(new Zend_Validate_StringLength(8,15));
$val->addValidator(new Zend_Validate_Alnum());
if (!$val->isValid($_POST['password'])) {
  $errors['password'] = 'Use 8-15 letters or numbers only';
}
$val = new Zend_Validate_Identical($_POST['password']);
if (!$val->isValid($_POST['conf_password'])) {
  $errors['conf_password'] = "Passwords don't match";
}
if (!$errors) {
  // update the password
}
```

This code was explained in "Building the validation script (2)" in Lesson 7.

12 The final section of code goes after the "update the password" comment in the conditional statement at the end of the code in the previous step:

```
$data = array('password' => sha1($_POST['password']),
              'token'    => NULL);
$where['user_id = ?'] = $_SESSION['user_id'];
$where['token = ?'] = $_SESSION['token'];
$success = $dbWrite->update('users', $data, $where);
unset($_SESSION['user_id']);
unset($_SESSION['token']);
unset($_SESSION['nomatch']);
```

This prepares the data array for the update() method, encrypting the new password with sha1() and setting the token column to NULL. To ensure that the correct record is updated, both $_SESSION['user_id'] and $_SESSION['token'] are matched against their respective columns in the users table.

The result of the update operation is stored in $success. If it fails, $success is FALSE. If it succeeds, the update() method returns the number of records affected. Since one record has been updated, PHP treats this as TRUE. $success is used to control the display of the success message in reset.php.

Regardless of the result, all session variables related with the script are unset.

13 Save reset_password.php, and test the form in reset.php. If your password fails validation, error messages are displayed, but the reset form remains onscreen. If your password meets the validation criteria, you should see the following message onscreen:

Password Reset

Your password has been successfully reset. Please log in with your new password.

Of course, in a real application, you should link to the login page, use header() to redirect the user, or include the login form on the current page.

You can compare your code with lesson08/completed/scripts/reset_password.php.

Unsubscribing Registered Users

As well as providing a way for users to reset their passwords, you also need to give them the opportunity to unsubscribe. Fortunately, this doesn't mean writing a huge amount of code. Most of it is already covered by the password reset scripts. All you need to do is to generate a slightly different email message that directs the user to a page that requests confirmation. The confirmation page should also give the user the opportunity to cancel the request to unsubscribe.

The different email message is generated by amending request_reset.php like this (the code is in lesson08/completed/scripts/request_reset_unsub.php):

```php
$mail = new Zend_Mail('UTF-8');
$mail->addTo($result['email'], "{$result['first_name']}
{$result['family_name']}");
$mail->setFrom('webmaster@example.com', 'DW CS5 with PHP');
if (isset($_POST['unsub'])) {
  $mail->setSubject('Instructions for unsubscribing');
  $link = "http://phpcs5/lesson08/completed/confirm_unsub.php?id=
➥ {$result['user_id']}&token=$token";
  $message = "Use the following link to unsubscribe. $link";
} else {
  $mail->setSubject('Instructions for resetting your password');
  $link = "http://phpcs5/lesson08/workfiles/reset.php?id=
➥ {$result['user_id']}&token=$token";
  $message = "Use the following link to reset your password. This link
➥ can be used once only. $link";
}
$mail->setBodyText($message, 'UTF-8');
$mail->send();
```

This checks for the existence of $_POST['unsub'], which is the name of the submit button in lesson08/completed/unsubscribe.php, and it generates a different subject line and body text. Otherwise, the code is identical to request_reset.php.

The page that asks for confirmation of the request to unsubscribe has two submit buttons: confirm and cancel. The code that handles these buttons can be found in lesson08/completed/ scripts/reset_password_unsub.php, which simply adds two extra conditional statements to reset_password.php:

```
if (isset($_POST['confirm'])) {
  $where['user_id = ?'] = $_SESSION['user_id'];
  $where['token = ?'] = $_SESSION['token'];
  $success = $dbWrite->delete('users', $where);
}
if (isset($_POST['cancel'])) {
  $data = array('token' => NULL);
  $where['user_id = ?'] = $_SESSION['user_id'];
  $where['token = ?'] = $_SESSION['token'];
  $dbWrite->update('users', $data, $where);
}
```

The first conditional statement is executed if the confirm button is clicked. It uses the Zend_Db_Adapter object's delete() method, which takes two arguments: the table name and an argument that identifies which record(s) to delete. You identify the target record(s) in the same way as for the update() method.

The second conditional statement runs if the cancel button is clicked. It uses the update() method to set the value of the token column to NULL.

The unsubscribe request and confirmation pages are unsubscribe.php and confirm_unsub.php in lesson08/completed.

What You Have Learned

In this lesson, you have:

- Compared the features of `mail()` and `Zend_Mail` (pages 259–263)

- Set up a default transport for `Zend_Mail` (page 266)

- Edited the Redisplay on Error server behavior to create a new one for text areas (pages 267–269)

- Incorporated a reCAPTCHA widget in a feedback form (pages 270–272)

- Sent the contents of the feedback form to your mail inbox (pages 273–276)

- Examined how the `$_POST` array treats different form elements (pages 277–280)

- Created six new server behaviors to redisplay user input in checkboxes, radio button groups, and `<select>` elements (pages 280–286)

- Learned how to update records with `Zend_Db` (pages 286–287)

- Learned how to use SQL functions with `Zend_Db` (page 288)

- Built an email-based system for users to reset their passwords or unsubscribe (pages 288–300)

LESSON 9

What You Will Learn

In this lesson, you will:

- Build a basic form for uploading files

- Create a local folder to test scripts for file uploads

- Use Zend_File_Transfer to copy files to a specified location

- Check the type and size of files before transferring them

- Remove spaces from filenames

- Give users the option to overwrite or rename files that have the same name

- Attach files to an email

Approximate Time

This lesson takes approximately 2 hours and 30 minutes to complete.

Lesson Files

Media Files:

images/bryce1.jpg
images/bryce2.jpg
images/lasvegas1.jpg
images/lasvegas2.jpg
styles/users_wider.css

Starting Files:

lesson09/start/send_attachments.php
lesson09/start/upload_test_multi.php
lesson09/start/scripts/library.php
lesson09/start/scripts/mail_connector.php
lesson09/start/scripts/process_attachments.php

Completed Files:

lesson09/completed/send_attachments.php
lesson09/completed/upload_test.php
lesson09/completed/upload_test_01.php
lesson09/completed/upload_test_02.php
lesson09/completed/upload_test_03.php
lesson09/completed/upload_test_multi.php
lesson09/completed/scripts/get_attachments.php
lesson09/completed/scripts/library.php
lesson09/completed/scripts/process_attachments.php
lesson09/completed/scripts/process_upload_01.php
lesson09/completed/scripts/process_upload_02.php
lesson09/completed/scripts/process_upload_03.php
lesson09/completed/scripts/process_upload_04.php
lesson09/completed/scripts/process_upload_05.php
lesson09/completed/scripts/process_upload_06.php
lesson09/completed/scripts/process_upload_07.php

LESSON 9

Uploading Images and Other Files

In addition to communicating with a database and sending email, another important use of PHP is uploading files to your web server. Implementing file uploads is relatively simple, but you need to be careful about the size and types of files that you allow to be uploaded. The web server also needs permission to write to the file system.

In this lesson, you'll learn how to upload files to your web server through an online form, as well as how to reject files that are too large or that don't match a specified type. You'll also learn how to attach files to an email.

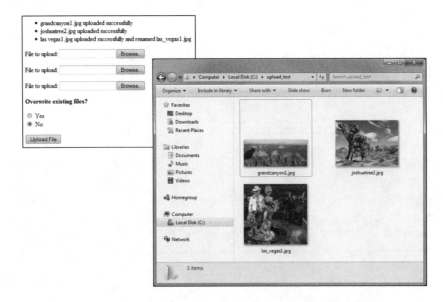

Zend_File_Transfer *makes it easy to validate and upload files.*

Understanding How PHP Uploads Files

Uploading files to a web server can refer to two different processes. The first is carried out by the web developer logging into the server using FTP (file transfer protocol) to upload the web pages and other assets that make up the site. The other process involves users uploading files, such as photos for a blog, from an online form. Although PHP can handle FTP, this lesson concentrates exclusively on uploading files from a form in a web page.

This type of file upload uses the POST method, which doesn't require authentication. As a result, you must implement your own security measures. Although the upload process uses the POST method, the files are handled by a separate superglobal array called $_FILES.

The $_FILES array is actually a multidimensional array. The key for the top-level array is the name attribute of the form field. If you have a form field called upload_file, the uploaded file and all its details are stored in a subarray called $_FILES['upload_file'], which contains the following elements:

- **$_FILES['upload_file']['name']**. The file's original name
- **$_FILES['upload_file']['type']**. The file's declared MIME type
- **$_FILES['upload_file']['tmp_name']**. A temporary name assigned to the file until it's moved to its final destination
- **$_FILES['upload_file']['size']**. The file's size in bytes
- **$_FILES['upload_file']['error']**. A code indicating whether the upload succeeded or the reason for failure

When the file is uploaded from the form, PHP moves it to a temporary location before transferring it to its final destination. The user has no direct control over where the file is ultimately stored. Everything needs to be handled by your script, which must rename and store the file immediately. Otherwise, the temporary file is destroyed, leaving you with nothing.

There's no point in saving an incomplete file, or if it has an unacceptable MIME type, or is too big. A file of the same name overwrites the existing one without warning, so your script needs to check if there's already a file of the same name at the target destination. It's also important to make sure that an attacker isn't trying to trick the script to work on a file to which it should have no access, such as the web server's password file.

To remain secure, you need to do quite a lot of checking. For this reason, you won't work directly with the $_FILES array, but you'll use the Zend_File component, which works in tandem with Zend_Validate_File subclasses to perform the necessary checks.

Creating an Upload Form

An online form needs a separate file field for each file that will be uploaded. You also need to add enctype="multipart/form-data" to the opening <form> tag. Dreamweaver adds this automatically when you insert a file field in a form.

Create a simple file upload form for the exercises in this lesson:

1 In Dreamweaver, create a new PHP file, and save it as **upload_test.php** in lesson09/workfiles.

2 Insert a form by choosing Insert > Form > Form or by clicking the Form icon ▣ in the Forms category of the Insert panel/bar.

3 Press Enter/Return to create two paragraphs inside the form.

4 Press the up arrow once to move the insertion point back into the first paragraph inside the form.

5 Insert a hidden form field by choosing Insert > Form > Hidden field or by clicking the Hidden Field icon ▣ in the Forms category of the Insert panel/bar.

6 With the hidden field still selected, type **MAX_FILE_SIZE** in the text field on the left of the Property inspector, and type **51200** in the Value field.

This sets the name attribute of the hidden field to MAX_FILE_SIZE. The 51200 in the Value field is the maximum size expressed in bytes (1024 bytes = 1 KB), so this sets the maximum to 50 KB. It's possible to bypass the limit set by a hidden field, so you need to validate the size on the server as well. But setting the limit here improves the user experience for most people. If the selected file exceeds the specified size, PHP won't even attempt to upload it.

⚠ **CAUTION!** MAX_FILE_SIZE must be in uppercase. It's also essential for the hidden field to come before the file field in the form for it to work.

7 Insert a file field by choosing Insert > Form > File Field or by clicking the File Field icon ▣ in the Forms category of the Insert panel/bar. This opens the Insert Tag Accessibility Attributes dialog box.

8 Type **upload_file** in the ID field and **File to upload:** in the Label field. Leave the other options at their default values, and click OK to insert the file field in the form.

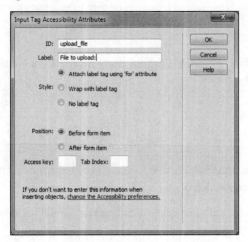

9 Move the insertion point into the second paragraph inside the form, and choose Insert > Form > Button or click the Button icon in the Forms category of the Insert panel/bar.

10 In the Input Tag Accessibility Attributes dialog box, type **upload** in the ID field. Leave all other options at their default values, and click OK. This inserts a submit button into the form.

11 With the submit button still selected, change the Value field in the Property inspector to **Upload File**. The form should look like this in Design view:

The shield to the left of the "File to upload:" label indicates the location of the hidden form field.

▶ **TIP:** If you don't see a shield indicating a hidden form field in Design view, choose Edit > Preferences (Windows) or Dreamweaver > Preferences (Mac), and select the Invisible Elements category. Make sure the "Hidden form fields" checkbox is selected. Also choose View > Visual Aids, and make sure there's a check mark next to Invisible Elements.

12 Save the page, and press F12/Opt+F12 to preview the form in a browser. How the form is rendered depends on your default browser.

If you're using Firefox or Internet Explorer, the form looks like this:

In a WebKit-based browser, such as Safari or Google Chrome, however, the form looks quite different.

13 Click Browse or Choose File depending on which browser you're using. Navigate on your local file system to a file—it doesn't matter which one.

In Firefox or Internet Explorer, the full file path is displayed and remains editable in the input field.

In a WebKit-based browser, only the name of the file is displayed, and it cannot be edited, as shown in the following screen shot.

✲ **NOTE:** These differences don't affect the way files are uploaded, but they need to be taken into account when designing your forms.

You can check your code against lesson09/completed/upload_test_01.php.

Using Zend_File for Uploads

To upload files using the POST method, you need to create an instance of the Zend_File_Transfer_Adapter_Http class. The cumbersome name is due to plans to support other transfer protocols, such as FTP and WebDAV (Web-based Distributed Authoring and Versioning), in the future.

Creating a local folder for testing uploads

The most convenient way to learn how to use Zend_File is by testing locally. As far as PHP is concerned, it's simply transferring the file from one location to another. Create a folder called **upload_test** on your local computer. It doesn't matter where it is, but a good location would be at the top level of your C drive on Windows or in your Mac home folder.

✱ **NOTE:** The upload_test folder is different from the folder described in "Setting a temporary upload directory" in Lesson 2. Files are automatically deleted from the temporary upload directory after they have been moved to their ultimate destination.

The web server needs permission to write to the upload_test folder. What action you have to take—if any—depends on your setup:

- **Apache on Windows.** You don't need to do anything.

- **IIS on Windows.** Right-click the folder, and choose Properties.

  Select the Security tab, and click Edit.

  Add the IUSR account (IIS_IUSRS in IIS7) to the "Group or user names" section. Give the account the following permissions: Read & execute, Read, and Write.

- **Mac OS X.** Select the folder in Finder, and choose File > Get Info or press Cmd+I.

  Expand the Sharing & Permissions section, click the padlock icon at the bottom right of the Get Info panel to unlock the settings, and enter your Mac administrator password when prompted.

  Change the Privilege for "everyone" from "Read only" to Read & Write, as shown in the following screen shot, and click the padlock icon again to save the settings.

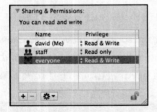

Creating a basic upload script

To test that you have configured PHP and the upload_test folder correctly, create the following bare minimum script, which sets the upload destination and transfers the file:

1 Create a new PHP file, and save it as **process_upload.php** in lesson09/workfiles/scripts. Strip out the default HTML code, and add an opening PHP tag.

2 Add a conditional statement that checks for the existence of $_POST['upload'] to ensure that the script runs only if the Upload File button has been clicked. Inside the conditional statement, include library.php with require_once(), and create a try and a catch block. The code should look like this:

```
if (isset($_POST['upload'])) {
  require_once('library.php');
  try {

  } catch (Exception $e) {
  echo $e->getMessage();
  }
}
```

3 Inside the try block, create a variable to store the full path of the upload_test folder.

If you used the suggested locations, the code should look like this:

- **Windows**

  ```
  $destination = 'C:/upload_test';
  ```

- **Mac OS X**

  ```
  $destination = '/Users/username/upload_test';
  ```

Replace **username** with your Mac username. Note that the path begins with a forward slash.

The reason for storing the path in a variable at the top of the script is to avoid the danger of errors when reusing the value later. If you decide to move the location of the upload folder, you make the change in this one place rather than needing to search through your whole script to find each instance.

4 Create an instance of the Zend_File_Transfer_Adapter_Http class, and use the object's setDestination() method to specify the location of the upload folder:

```
$uploader = new Zend_File_Transfer_Adapter_Http();
$uploader->setDestination($destination);
```

5 Use the receive() method to upload the file:

```
$uploader->receive();
```

6 Save process_upload.php, and switch to the page that contains the upload form, upload_test.php.

7 Use require_once() to include process_upload.php above the DOCTYPE declaration in upload_test.php.

8 Save upload_test.php, and click Live View or launch the page in a browser.

9 Use the Browse or Choose File button to navigate to a file on your local computer. Make sure you choose a file that's less than 50 KB, such as one of the files in the images folder for this book. If you choose a larger file, the upload won't work, and you won't see any error message.

10 Remember to hold down Ctrl/Cmd if you're in Live View, and click Upload File. The filename should disappear from the form or form field.

11 Use Explorer (Windows) or Finder (Mac) to examine the contents of the upload_test folder. If your code and configuration were correct, you should see the file you selected listed there.

You can check your code against process_upload_01.php in lesson09/completed/scripts.

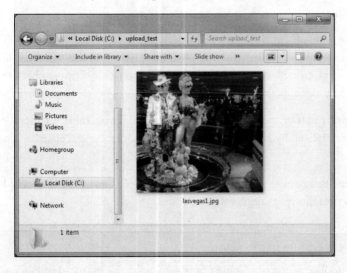

What if the file isn't transferred?

The following checklist should help troubleshoot problems if the file you selected hasn't been copied to the upload_test folder:

- Check your PHP configuration by running phpinfo(), as described in Lesson 2. Make sure file_uploads in the PHP Core or Core section is set to On.

- Farther down in the same section, check the value of upload_tmp_dir. Make sure it refers to a folder that exists, and that it is writable by the web server (use the same settings as in "Creating a local folder for testing uploads").

- If either setting needs to be changed, refer to "Changing configuration settings" in Lesson 2.

- If the permissions on the upload_test folder are incorrect, the script throws an exception and displays "The given destination is not writeable."

- If you misspelled the path to the upload_test folder, the script displays "The given destination is no directory or does not exist."

- Double-check the size of the file you selected. If it's greater than 50 KB, PHP doesn't even attempt to upload the file.

- Check the value of the MAX_FILE_SIZE hidden field in the form. Did you accidentally set it to a lower value?

- If you tested the form in Live View, did you remember to hold down the modifier key when clicking Upload File? Try testing the page in a browser.

Validating uploaded files

The basic script in process_upload.php is all you need to upload a file with Zend_File, but it's very rudimentary and—above all—insecure. Although MAX_FILE_SIZE prevents oversized files from being uploaded, it can be circumvented. It's vital for your server-side script to check that the file isn't too big or of an unacceptable type.

You validate file uploads with a set of special subclasses of Zend_Validate. **Table 9.1** lists the main ones, all of which are prefixed by Zend_Validate_File_. So, for example, Count becomes Zend_Validate_File_Count.

To use one or more of these validators, you apply the addValidator() method to the uploader object. The method takes the following arguments:

- **Validator.** This can be either an instance of a validation class or the short name of the validation class as a string, for example 'Count'.

- **Break on failure.** A Boolean value specifying whether to break the validation chain on failure. If set to FALSE, all tests are carried out, allowing you to report all reasons for failure. If set to TRUE, no further tests are carried out.

- **Options.** Classes indicated in Table 9.1 with an asterisk accept multiple values either as a comma-separated string or as an array. For example, the options for ExcludeExtension can be presented as 'exe,zip' or as array('exe', 'zip'). This argument is optional for IsCompressed and IsImage.

- **File(s).** This argument optionally specifies which file(s) the test should be applied to. Use an array of the file field name attributes to specify multiple files. If this argument is omitted, all uploaded files are normally tested. However, no further tests are carried out after the first file that fails validation.

	Table 9.1 Useful File Validation Classes
Class	**Description**
Count	Checks the number of files uploaded. If initialized with a string or an integer, the value is used as the maximum acceptable. Also accepts an array with the keys 'min' and 'max'.
ExcludeExtension *	Excludes files that have specified filename extensions. List the extensions without a leading period (for example, 'exe', not '.exe'). By default, filename extensions are treated as case insensitive. Checks only the extension used, not the file's MIME type.
ExcludeMimeType *	Excludes files of specified MIME types. You can specify whole groups by using just the first part of the MIME type. For example, 'image' excludes *all* images.
Exists *	Checks whether the file exists in specified folder(s).
Extension *	Does the opposite of ExcludeExtension by specifying acceptable filename extension(s).
FileSize	Checks the aggregate size of all files uploaded in the same operation, not the size of individual files. If initialized with a string or an integer, the value is used as the maximum acceptable. Also accepts an array with the keys 'min', 'max', and 'bytesize'. Values can be specified as strings using kB and MB, or as integers representing the number of bytes. If the files fail validation, the size is displayed as a string using kB or MB. To display the size in bytes, set 'bytesize' to FALSE. Values are converted using 1024 as the base value.
ImageSize	Checks the dimensions of images. Accepts an array with the keys 'minheight', 'maxheight', 'minwidth', and 'maxwidth', all of which are optional (but you must specify at least one). The array keys are case sensitive. Values should be integers.
IsCompressed *	Checks whether files use a compressed archive type, such as .zip. If no filename extension(s) or MIME type(s) are specified, any type of compressed archive is accepted.
IsImage *	Checks whether files are images. Setting filename extension(s) or MIME type(s) limits the acceptable types.
MimeType *	Does the opposite of ExcludeMimeType by specifying acceptable types.
NotExists *	Checks that the file doesn't exist in specified folder(s).
Size	Similar to FileSize except that it is used for single files.
WordCount	Checks the number of words in uploaded text files. If initialized with a string or an integer, the value is used as the maximum acceptable. Also accepts an array with the keys 'min' and 'max'. The limits apply individually to each file.

You don't normally need to do anything to verify whether the file(s) passed validation; the receive() method automatically does it for you. However, you can test individual files by passing the filename to the isValid() method.

The getMessages() method returns an array of error messages. You can also access an array of error codes using the getErrors() method.

▼ **CAUTION!** Although the IsCompressed and IsImage validation classes correctly identify valid file types and reject invalid ones, they generate blank error messages (correct as of ZF 1.10.4).

Displaying validation messages for a single file

Let's put some of the theory from the preceding section into practice by improving the code. Continue working with the files from the previous exercise. Alternatively, copy upload_test_01.php and process_upload_01.php from the lesson09/completed and lesson09/completed/scripts folders and save them in your workfiles folder for this lesson. When saving the files, strip the _01 from the end of the filenames. Also, adjust the path to the upload_test folder if necessary.

1 With upload_test.php the active document, click Live View or launch the page in a browser.

2 Click the Browse or Choose File button, and select a file on your local computer that's bigger than 50 KB, the maximum set by MAX_FILE_SIZE.

3 Click Upload File, remembering to hold down Ctrl/Cmd if you're in Live View. The filename disappears from the form, but there's no indication of what happened.

If you check the upload_test folder, the file isn't there. PHP didn't even attempt to transfer the file, because it exceeded the maximum size. This isn't very user friendly, so you need to give the user some feedback.

4 Exit Live View, if necessary, and switch to process_upload.php. Amend the code that executes the transfer like this:

```
$success = $uploader->receive();
if (!$success) {
  $messages = $uploader->getMessages();
}
```

This assigns the return value of $uploader->receive() to $success. If the file transfer fails, $success will be FALSE, causing the code in the conditional statement to be executed and storing any error messages in $messages.

Even if there's only one message, getMessages() returns an array. So, you need to loop through the array to display the results to the user.

5 Switch to upload_test.php, and add the following code above the form:

```
<body>
<?php
if (isset($messages)) {
  echo '<ul>';
  foreach ($messages as $item) {
    echo "<li>$item</li>";
  }
  echo '</ul>';
}
?>
<form action="" method="post" enctype="multipart/form-data" name="form1"
➥ id="form1">
```

The conditional statement checks whether $messages has been set. If it has, echo is used to insert an opening <ul> tag, and a foreach loop (see "Using a foreach loop" in Lesson 3) assigns each message in the array to $item and displays it between a pair of <li> tags. After the loop ends, the closing </ul> tag is inserted, displaying the error messages as an unordered (bulleted) list.

6 Save both pages, and test the upload form again with a file that exceeds 50 KB. This time you should see an error message at the top of the form.

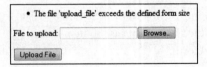

Unfortunately, the error message isn't as clear as it might be. Still, it's a start.

7 Choose a file that's smaller than 50 KB, and click Upload File. If you check the upload_test folder, it should have been transferred, but the form gives you no feedback. You need to create a message that can be displayed when the transfer succeeds.

8 Amend the conditional statement that checks the success of the transfer like this:

```
if (!$success) {
  $messages = $uploader->getMessages();
} else {
  $filename = $uploader->getFileName(NULL, FALSE);
  $messages[] = "$filename uploaded successfully";
}
```

The getFileName() method is designed to work with both single and multiple file uploads. It takes two arguments, both of which are optional.

- The first argument is a reference to the file. If omitted or set to NULL, the method returns the name of a single file as a string, or the names of multiple files as an array.

- The second argument determines whether to include the full path. By default, it's set to TRUE. Setting it to FALSE returns only the filename.

Both arguments are optional, but you can't set the second argument without the first one. The first line in the else block gets the filename without the path and assigns it to $filename. There's only one file being uploaded, so the value of $filename is a string.

The second line in the else block embeds $filename in a doubled-quoted string and assigns it to $messages[]. The empty square brackets make it an array element. You need to make it an array so that the loop you created in step 5 can handle it correctly.

9 Save process_upload.php, and test the form again, choosing a file that's less than 50 KB. This time, the form should report the name of the file and that it has been transferred successfully.

10 To improve the upload script, add some validation. The first test you should add is to make sure the file doesn't exceed the maximum file size, just in case someone tries to evade the MAX_FILE_SIZE setting in the upload form.

Because the upload form handles only one file upload, it doesn't make any difference whether you use the FileSize or the Size validation class. However, it's a good idea to get into the habit of using the right one: FileSize controls the aggregate size of all files uploaded in a single operation, whereas Size deals only with the size of an individual file. So, in this case, it's Size that you need.

To limit the maximum size of the uploaded file to 50 KB, add the highlighted code just before calling the receive() method:

```
$uploader->setDestination('C:/upload_test');
$uploader->addValidator('Size', FALSE, '50kB');
$success = $uploader->receive();
```

The default ZF style is to use kB (with a lowercase *k*) and leave no space between the number and unit. However, the third argument is a case-insensitive unit and accepts a space between the number and unit.

11 One of the most common uses of file uploads is for images. Ideally, you should be able to use the IsImage validation class to verify that the upload is indeed an image. However, at the time of this writing, it generates a blank error message when you attempt to upload an invalid file. The solution is to use the MimeType validation class instead.

Add another validator like this:

```
$uploader->addValidator('Size', FALSE, '50kB');
$uploader->addValidator('MimeType', FALSE, 'image');
$success = $uploader->receive();
```

Using 'image' on its own as the third argument accepts any type of image.

12 Save process_upload.php, and test the form again. If you select an image that's smaller than 50 KB, you'll see a message informing you that the upload was successful. However, if you select a different type of file, you get an error message like this:

- The file 'time.php' has a false mimetype of 'text/html'

File to upload: [   ] Browse...

[Upload File]

For a technically savvy user, this is fine, although it might be confusing for other users. See "Customizing error messages" later in this lesson.

13 Add another validation test to check the minimum height and width of the image like this:

```
$uploader->addValidator('MimeType', FALSE, 'image');
$uploader->addValidator('ImageSize', FALSE, array('minheight' => 500,
➥ 'minwidth' => 1000));
$success = $uploader->receive();
```

The minimum height and width values are specified by passing an array as the third argument, using the case-sensitive keys 'minheight' and 'minwidth'. Both values have been set deliberately high to trigger an error.

14 Save process_upload.php, and test the upload form again. If you select any of the files in the images folder for this book, you should see error messages similar to this:

- Minimum expected width for image 'longbeach1.jpg' should be '1000' but '400' detected
- Minimum expected height for image 'longbeach1.jpg' should be '500' but '208' detected

File to upload: [   ] Browse...

[Upload File]

15 As a final series of tests, change the minimum height and width values to **50** and **100** respectively, and add a validator to ensure the uploaded file doesn't overwrite an existing one with the same name. Change the code like this:

```
$uploader->addValidator('ImageSize', FALSE, array('minheight' => 50,
➥ 'minwidth' => 100));
$uploader->addValidator('NotExists', FALSE, $destination);
$success = $uploader->receive();
```

The third argument of the `NotExists` validator is the path to the upload folder.

16 Save process_upload.php, and test the upload form again to upload an image. As long as it matches all the criteria, you'll see a success message.

If, on the other hand, the file has already been uploaded, you'll see an error message like this:

> • The file 'joshuatree1.jpg' does exist
>
> File to upload: [   ] [Browse...]
>
> [Upload File]

Again, the message is probably OK for a technically savvy user but might confuse others. A better solution is to give the file a unique name and inform the user of the new name. You'll learn how to do this shortly.

You can compare your code with upload_test_02.php in lesson09/completed and process_upload_02.php in lesson09/completed/scripts.

Removing spaces from filenames

Windows and Mac OS X permit spaces in filenames. While spaces make filenames more user friendly, they cause problems on Linux servers, so it's a wise precaution to filter the names of uploaded files and to replace spaces with underscores. Even if your site is hosted on a Windows server, it's still a good idea to remove spaces, particularly if the uploaded files will be used in a website. Spaces are not permitted in URLs and need to be replaced by %20, which looks ugly and unprofessional.

The following exercise improves process_upload.php by removing spaces from the name of an uploaded file. Continue working with the files from the previous exercise, or use a copy of lesson09/completed/process_upload_02.php as your starting point.

1 Locate the following section of code in process_upload.php (it should be around lines 12–18):

```
$success = $uploader->receive();
if (!$success) {
```

```
    $messages = $uploader->getMessages();
} else {
    $filename = $uploader->getFileName(NULL, FALSE);
    $messages[] = "$filename uploaded successfully";
}
```

This is the code that handles the actual upload and prepares the message(s) informing the user of the result.

2 To remove spaces from the filename, you need to access it before the transfer takes place. Cut the line of code highlighted in the preceding step, and paste it above the first validator like this:

```
$uploader->setDestination($destination);
$filename = $uploader->getFileName(NULL, FALSE);
$uploader->addValidator('Size', FALSE, '50kB');
```

3 You can remove the spaces from a string using str_replace(), which takes up to four arguments, of which the first three are required:

- The character(s) you want to replace

- The replacement character(s)

- The string you want to alter

- A variable to store the number of replacements

Although the most logical place to add the code to replace spaces in the filename with underscores would appear to be on the next line, you'll be making further changes to the script. So, put it just before the call to the receive() method:

```
$uploader->addValidator('NotExists', FALSE, $destination);
$no_spaces = str_replace(' ', '_', $filename, $renamed);
$success = $uploader->receive();
```

The fourth argument, $renamed, stores the number of replacements. If no replacements are made, $renamed is 0, which PHP implicitly treats as FALSE. Anything else is treated as TRUE. You'll use this value later to inform the user if the filename has been changed.

4 The amended filename is now stored in $no_spaces. To rename the file being uploaded, use the addFilter() method like this:

```
$no_spaces = str_replace(' ', '_', $filename, $renamed);
$uploader->addFilter('Rename', array('target' => $no_spaces));
$success = $uploader->receive();
```

The addFilter() method takes at least two arguments: the name of the filter (in this case Rename) and an array of options. The key 'target' assigns the new name. If it's a filename, the uploaded file is stored with the new name. If it's a folder or directory name, the uploaded file is stored with its original name in the indicated folder. In this case, $no_ spaces is a filename, so the uploaded file will be stored in the upload_test folder, but with any spaces replaced by underscores.

> **TIP:** If your upload form is in a password-protected part of your site, you can use addFilter() to change the directory where the uploaded files are stored depending on the identity of the person who has logged in. Store the location of the user's directory with the login details and use it as the value of 'target'.

5 Alert the user to any name change by amending the else block that generates the messages like this:

```
if (!$success) {
  $messages = $uploader->getMessages();
} else {
  $uploaded = "$filename uploaded successfully";
  if ($renamed) {
    $uploaded .= " and renamed $no_spaces";
  }
  $messages[] = $uploaded;
}
```

Instead of assigning the success message to $messages[], it's stored in a new variable, $uploaded. If any spaces have been replaced, $renamed equates to TRUE, and the combined concatenation operator appends the file's new name. Then the complete message is reassigned to $messages[].

6 Save process_upload.php, and use Explorer (Windows) or Finder (Mac OS X) to delete all the files in the upload_test folder.

7 In the Dreamweaver Files panel, rename lasvegas1.jpg in the images folder to **las vegas1.jpg**, inserting a space in the filename.

8 Test upload_test.php in Live View or in a browser by selecting the file you have just renamed and clicking Upload File. You should see confirmation that the file has been uploaded and renamed.

```
• las vegas1.jpg uploaded successfully and renamed las_vegas1.jpg

File to upload: [                    ]    [ Browse... ]
[ Upload File ]
```

9 Select the same file and click Upload File. You get the same result.

What's happening here? The file has overwritten the version you transferred in the previous step. Because the file hasn't changed, it doesn't matter. But it would matter if the file were different.

So, why doesn't the NotExists validation class prevent the transfer? It's because the file in the upload_test folder is called las_vegas1.jpg, not las vegas.jpg. You know it's the same file, but PHP doesn't know the file's name has been changed. You need to prevent files from being overwritten.

Before improving the renaming system, check that the script still works correctly with files that don't have spaces in their names.

10 Click Browse or Choose File and select an image that doesn't have any spaces in its name, for example, lasvegas2.jpg in the images folder. You should see confirmation of the transfer, but there's no mention of renaming, because $renamed is 0 and treated as FALSE.

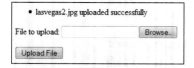

11 Try uploading the same file. This time, the NotExists validation class prevents the transfer. However, a solution that works only part of the time is no use. You'll fix that in the next section.

You can compare your code with process_upload_03.php in lesson09/completed/scripts.

Renaming files with duplicate names

Once the upload has been initiated, there's no way to allow the user to decide what to do if the file has the same name as an existing one. Unless you move the uploaded file into your web server's file system, PHP discards it.

A simple solution is to rename the file automatically, appending a number between the name and the filename extension. You can do this by loading the names of existing files into an array with the scandir() function and then looping through the array until you find the first available number. You build the new filename by using string manipulation functions to break apart the existing name and then joining the parts together again with the concatenation operator. Don't worry if it sounds like voodoo magic. The process should become clearer as you work through the following steps.

Continue working with the files from the preceding section. Alternatively, use a copy of lesson09/completed/scripts/process_upload_03.php as your starting point.

1 As you have seen, the NotExists validation class no longer works satisfactorily after the changes made in the preceding section. So, *delete* the following line of code (it should be around line 12):

```
$uploader->addValidator('NotExists', FALSE, 'C:/upload_test');
```

2 Although the receive() method automatically tests whether a file is valid, it makes more sense to use the isValid() method to test the file yourself before going to the trouble of checking for a duplicate name. If the file doesn't pass validation, it's going to be rejected anyway.

Create a conditional statement to test the file's validity, and wrap the processing script in the else block like this:

```
$uploader->addValidator('ImageSize', FALSE, array('minheight' => 50,
➥ 'minwidth' => 100));
if (!$uploader->isValid()) {
  $messages = $uploader->getMessages();
} else {
  $no_spaces = str_replace(' ', '_', $filename, $renamed);
  $uploader->addFilter('Rename', array('target' => $no_spaces));
  $success = $uploader->receive();
  if (!$success) {
    $messages = $uploader->getMessages();
  } else {
    $uploaded = "$filename uploaded successfully";
    if ($renamed) {
      $uploaded .= " and renamed $no_spaces";
    }
    $messages[] = $uploaded;
  }
}
} catch (Exception $e) {
```

If the file fails validation, the error messages are stored in $messages, and the rest of the script is ignored.

3 The code to rename duplicate files will insert a number between the name and the filename extension, but what if the filename extension is missing? The MimeType validation class doesn't rely on the filename extension. It actually checks the MIME type. To make sure the name ends with a recognizable filename extension—such as .jpg, .png, or .gif—you need to do a further check with the Extension validation class. Add the following code immediately after the line that removes spaces from the filename:

```
$no_spaces = str_replace(' ', '_', $filename, $renamed);
$uploader->addValidator('Extension', FALSE, 'gif, png, jpg');
```

```
$recognized = FALSE;
if ($uploader->isValid()) {
  $recognized = TRUE;
} else {
  $mime = $uploader->getMimeType();
  $acceptable = array('jpg' => 'image/jpeg',
                      'png' => 'image/png',
                      'gif' => 'image/gif');
  $key = array_search($mime, $acceptable);
  if (!$key) {
    $messages[] = 'Unrecognized image type';
  } else {
    $no_spaces = "$no_spaces.$key";
    $recognized = TRUE;
    $renamed = TRUE;
  }
}
$uploader->clearValidators();
$uploader->addFilter('Rename', array('target' => $no_spaces));
```

The third argument passed to addValidator() is a comma-separated list of acceptable filename extensions. To control what happens later, a Boolean variable, $recognized, is set to FALSE. If the file passes validation, $recognized is reset to TRUE. Otherwise, the else clause tries to establish the MIME type and add the appropriate filename extension.

The getMimeType() method returns the official media type format, such as image/jpeg. To convert this format to a filename extension, the $acceptable array lists each extension as the key and the media type as the value. The media type stored in $mime and the $acceptable array are then passed as arguments to array_search(), which searches an array and returns the key of the first matching value. So, if $mime is image/jpeg, it returns jpg.

If the MIME type is not in the $acceptable array, $key is FALSE, and an error message is assigned to $messages[]. Otherwise, a period and $key are appended to $no_spaces. For example, if a file called lasvegas1 is uploaded without a filename extension, and its MIME type is image/jpeg, the filename changes to lasvegas1.jpg, and $recognized and $renamed are reset to TRUE.

▼ **CAUTION!** The period between $no_spaces and $key is treated as a literal character because it's inside a double-quoted string. If you omit the quotation marks, the period is treated as the concatenation operator, producing lasvegas1jpg instead of lasvegas1.jpg.

Although the missing filename extension will be added when the file is renamed, the receive() method automatically runs the validation tests again. So, a file without an extension will still fail at that stage. Calling the clearValidators() method prevents the tests from being rerun.

4 The file should be uploaded only if it has a recognized filename extension. Wrap the remaining code in a conditional statement like this:

```
$uploader->clearValidators();
if ($recognized) {
  $uploader->addFilter('Rename', array('target' => $no_spaces));
  $success = $uploader->receive();
  if (!$success) {
    $messages = $uploader->getMessages();
  } else {
    $uploaded = "$filename uploaded successfully";
    if ($renamed) {
      $uploaded .= " and renamed $no_spaces";
    }
    $messages[] = $uploaded;
  }
}
} catch (Exception $e) {
```

5 Now that you have a filename with no spaces and a valid filename extension, you can check for a duplicate filename and build a new one, if necessary. The code goes at the top of the conditional statement you have just created. It's relatively short, so rather than building it line by line, add it all at once. The code has been commented to help you understand how it works.

```
if ($recognized) {
  // get the names of existing files
  $existing = scandir($destination);
  // check if the name of the uploaded file is in the array
  if (in_array($no_spaces, $existing)) {
    // get the position of the final period
    // use it to get the base name and extension
    $dot = strrpos($no_spaces, '.');
    $base = substr($no_spaces, 0, $dot);
    $extension = substr($no_spaces, $dot);
    // initialize a counter
    $i = 1;
    // use a loop to add the counter after the base name
    // check whether the new name exists in the array
    do {
      $no_spaces = $base . '_' . $i++ . $extension;
    } while (in_array($no_spaces, $existing));
    // set $renamed to TRUE
    $renamed = TRUE;
  }
  $uploader->addFilter('Rename', array('target' => $no_spaces));
```

The scandir() function examines a folder and returns an array of the names of all files and folders it contains. So, the first highlighted line stores an array of the contents of the upload_test folder in $existing.

The conditional statement uses in_array() to find out whether a file of the same name as the uploaded file ($no_spaces) is present in the array of existing files. If the file doesn't already exist, the rest of the highlighted script is ignored and the file is transferred without any further change to its name.

If, on the other hand, a file of the same name already exists, the code inside the if block is executed. It begins by using strrpos() to find the position of the last dot or period in the name of the uploaded file.

> ⚠ **CAUTION!** Notice the double "r" in the middle of strrpos(), which finds the position of the last instance of a character in a string. It's easy to confuse with strpos(), which finds the first instance of a character. The way to remember the difference is that the second "r" stands for "reverse."

The position of the period is then used with substr() to split the filename into two sections: $base and $extension. So, if the value of $no_spaces is las_vegas1.jpg, $base is "las_vegas" and $extension is ".jpg".

The do. . . while loop (see "Using a do. . . while loop" in Lesson 3) increments the $i counter and builds a new name like this:

```
$no_spaces = $base . '_' . $i++ . $extension;
```

This simply joins the filename back together with an underscore and a number. So, the first time the loop runs, $no_spaces becomes las_vegas1_1.jpg. The while condition of the loop uses in_array() again to see if the new name exists in the upload folder. If it does, the loop keeps running. As soon as there's no match, the loop stops, and $renamed is set to TRUE.

6 Save process_upload.php, and test the upload form again, selecting an image that has already been uploaded. This time you are informed the file was uploaded and renamed.

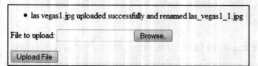

If you try it again, you'll see the number appended to the base name increases by one. Also, try it by deleting the filename extension before uploading. The script renames the file and adds the correct extension.

7 Check the contents of the upload_test folder in Explorer or Finder. You should see that the files have been transferred and renamed correctly.

You can compare your code with process_upload_04.php in lesson09/completed/scripts.

Adding an option to overwrite files

What if you don't want to give files a new name but just want to overwrite them? It's just a question of wrapping the rewrite section of the script in a conditional statement and adding an option in the upload form to indicate which action to take.

Continue working with the same files. Alternatively, use a copy of process_upload_04.php as your starting point.

1 In upload_test.php, click to the right of the Browse button in Design view, and press Enter/Return to insert a new paragraph.

2 In the new paragraph, type **Overwrite existing file?**, and press Enter/Return to insert another paragraph.

3 With the insertion point in the empty paragraph, choose Insert > Form > Radio Group to open the Radio Group dialog box.

4 Type **overwrite** in the Name field, and create two radio buttons for **Yes** and **No**, setting the values to **y** and **n** respectively. Leave the "Lay out using" radio button at the default "Line breaks (
 tags)," and click OK.

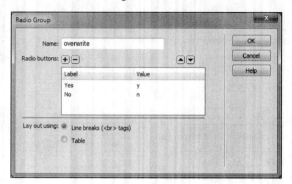

5 In Design view, select the No radio button, and set "Initial state" in the Property inspector to Checked.

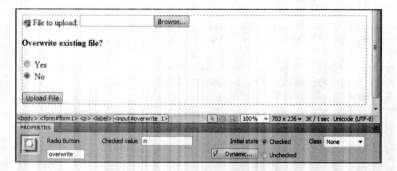

6 Save upload_test.php, and switch to process_upload.php.

7 Add the following conditional statement just before the try block:

```
require_once('library.php');
$overwrite = FALSE;
if (isset($_POST['overwrite']) && $_POST['overwrite'] == 'y') {
  $overwrite = TRUE;
}
try {
```

This assumes the default option is not to overwrite existing files and sets $overwrite to FALSE. However, if the Yes radio button has been selected, the value of $_POST['overwrite'] is "y" and $overwrite is set to TRUE.

▼ **CAUTION!** Don't forget to use two equals signs when comparing values for equality. Also note that string comparisons are case sensitive. If you used an uppercase Y in the Radio Button dialog box, it needs to be uppercase here, too.

8 To prevent the script from assigning a new name to the file, you need to wrap a conditional statement around the whole block of code that you inserted in step 5 of the previous section like this:

```
if ($recognized) {
  if (!$overwrite) {
    // get the names of existing files
    $existing = scandir($destination);
    // check if the name of the uploaded file is in the array
    if (in_array($no_spaces, $existing)) {
      // get the position of the final period
      // use it to get the base name and extension
      $dot = strrpos($no_spaces, '.');
      $base = substr($no_spaces, 0, $dot);
      $extension = substr($no_spaces, $dot);
      // initialize a counter
      $i = 1;
      // use a loop to add the counter after the base name
      // check whether the new name exists in the array
      do {
        $no_spaces = $base . '_' . $i++ . $extension;
      } while (in_array($no_spaces, $existing));
      // set $renamed to TRUE
      $renamed = TRUE;
    }
  }
  $uploader->addFilter('Rename', array('target' => $no_spaces));
```

This section of code will now run only if $overwrite is *not* TRUE.

✱ **NOTE:** Files that don't have a filename extension are always renamed, because they are never stored in the upload folder without the extension.

9 Save process_upload.php, and delete all the files in the upload_test folder.

10 Select an image to upload, and leave the radio buttons at the default No. Click Upload File. You should see confirmation of the transfer.

11 Select the same image, but change the radio button to Yes, and click Upload File. Again, you should see confirmation of the transfer but not that the file has been renamed. The existing file has been overwritten.

12 Select the same image for a third time, leave the radio button at the default No, and click Upload File. This time you get confirmation of the transfer and that the file has been renamed.

13 Check the contents of upload_test folder. There should be two copies of the same file, one with the original name and the other with a number appended to the base name.

You can compare your code with upload_test_03.php in lesson09/completed as well as process_upload_05.php in lesson09/completed/scripts.

Handling multiple file uploads

The great thing about using Zend_File is that it automatically handles multiple files. All that's needed to adapt the processing script is to get a reference to each file and pass it as an argument to each method. Getting the reference to each file is as simple as this:

```
$files = $uploader->getFileInfo();
foreach ($files as $file => $info) {
  // refer to each uploaded file as $file
}
```

⚠ CAUTION! Even if you don't need to access information about individual files, you must use the $array as $subarray => $item structure in the foreach loop. Using foreach ($files as $file) results in the upload failing.

Your upload form needs a file field for each file to be uploaded. This presents the problem of what to do about fields that are left blank. Zend_File deals with that by allowing you to set an option to ignore blank fields and by checking whether a file has been uploaded.

To ignore blank fields, you use the setOptions() method like this:

```
$uploader->setOptions(array('ignoreNoFile' => TRUE));
```

✱ NOTE: There are no other options available, but you still need to use an array as the argument. This allows other options to be added in the future, or if you're a PHP OOP whiz kid, you could extend the class to add your own.

To check whether a file has actually been uploaded, you pass a reference to the file to the isUploaded() method.

The following instructions show you how to adapt process_upload.php to handle multiple file uploads. Continue working with the same script as in the preceding section. Alternatively, use a copy of process_upload_05 in lesson09/completed/scripts as your starting point.

1 Copy upload_test_multi.php from lesson09/completed to your workfiles folder. The page has two extra file fields.

2 Include process_upload.php with `require_once()` above the DOCTYPE declaration.

3 Use the `setOptions()` method to allow file fields to be left blank.

```
$uploader->setDestination($destination);
$uploader->setOptions(array('ignoreNoFile' => TRUE));
$filename = $uploader->getFileName(NULL, FALSE);
```

4 To process the uploaded files individually, you need to get their details. Do this by calling the `getFileInfo()` method on the line after the one you just inserted.

```
$uploader->setOptions(array('ignoreNoFile' => TRUE));
$files = $uploader->getFileInfo();
```

This stores the details of all the files as a multidimensional array in `$files`.

✱ NOTE: When no argument is passed to the `getFileInfo()` method, it retrieves details from every file field in the form, even if the field has been left blank. So, your script needs to check for empty fields.

5 The rest of the script in the `try` block needs to be wrapped in a `foreach` loop that processes each file individually. Add this code on the next line:

```
foreach($files as $file => $info) {
```

Each time the loop runs, the current file can be accessed as `$file`.

6 Scroll down to the end of the `try` block, and add a matching closing curly brace. To keep your code correctly indented, select the code inside the new `foreach` loop, and click the Indent Code icon ⬝⬝ in the Coding toolbar *twice*. The double indent is needed because you'll add a conditional statement inside the loop.

7 The code now inside the `foreach` loop processes each file, but there's no point running it if there's no file to process. Add the following line immediately inside the loop:

```
foreach($files as $file => $info) {
  if ($uploader->isUploaded($file)) {
```

This ensures that the remaining code is executed only if the current instance of `$file` is actually an uploaded file.

8 Scroll down to the end of the `foreach` loop, and add another closing curly brace for the conditional statement you just added. If you indented your code, the location should be easy to spot, but if you're unsure, it's the one highlighted here:

```
        $messages[] = $uploaded;
      }
    }
```

```
    }
   }
 } catch (Exception $e) {
```

9 The first line of code inside the new conditional statement looks like this:

```
$filename = $uploader->getFileName(NULL, FALSE);
```

As it stands, this gets the names of all uploaded files. Replace NULL with the reference to the current file like this:

```
$filename = $uploader->getFileName($file, FALSE);
```

10 Four lines farther down, the first call is made to the isValid() method, which also needs a reference to the current file. Pass $file as an argument to it like this:

```
if (!$uploader->isValid($file)) {
```

Make the same change in the call to isValid() six lines farther down after the Extension validation class is added.

11 Similarly, you need to specify the current file as an argument to getMimeType():

```
$mime = $uploader->getMimeType($file);
```

12 The same change applies to receive() near the bottom of the script:

```
$success = $uploader->receive($file);
```

13 The addFilter() method on the line above receive() takes a slightly different reference to the file. Use the temporary name assigned to it by PHP, which can be accessed from the $info subarray created by the foreach loop. Change the code like this:

```
$uploader->addFilter('Rename', array('target' => $no_spaces,
➥ $info['tmp_name']));
```

14 The final change is to the code that gets the error messages. Change it like this:

```
$messages□ = implode('. ', $uploader->getMessages());
```

Because the foreach loop handles each file separately, $messages needs to become an array. Otherwise, it would be overwritten each time the loop runs. However, the getMessages() method outputs an array. To avoid the need to process a multidimensional array, the output of getMessages() is converted to a string by implode(). Each message generated by getMessages() begins with an uppercase letter, so the first argument to implode() adds a period and a space to separate each message.

This change needs to be made in *two* places: in the conditional statement that immediately follows the call to `receive()` and in the first conditional statement that uses the `isValid()` method (see step 10).

15 Save process_upload.php, upload_test_multi.php, and test the multiple file upload form. It works exactly the same as before except you can now upload one, two, or three files simultaneously.

The fact that it can handle a single file means this script works equally well with the original upload form with just one file field.

You can compare your code with process_upload_06.php in lesson09/completed/scripts.

Customizing error messages

The file upload script is basically complete. All you need to do to adapt it to your own website is to change the destination of the upload folder and use your own selection of validation classes. The only fly in the ointment is the slightly odd phrasing of some error messages generated by the `getMessages()` method. The problem has been partially solved by adding the code to rename files and choosing whether to overwrite existing ones. However, choosing a file of the wrong MIME type still produces a message about a "false" type.

How much effort you want to put into customizing error messages depends on your coding skills and the target audience for your upload form. A simple—but rather crude—way of avoiding using the default error messages is to generate your own message if the file fails validation:

```
if (!$uploader->isValid($file)) {
  $messages[] = "Sorry, $filename doesn't match the requirements";
} else {
```

The problem is this doesn't give any indication of what's wrong with the file.

A better approach is to use the `getErrors()` method to find out what the error is, and then substitute your own message in those cases where you feel customization is necessary. The `getErrors()` method returns an array of error codes.

The code returned for an incorrect MIME type is `fileMimeTypeFalse`. So, to display a customized error message when the wrong type of file is uploaded, amend the same section of code like this:

```
if (!$uploader->isValid($file)) {
  $error_codes = $uploader->getErrors();
  if (in_array('fileMimeTypeFalse', $error_codes)) {
    $messages[] = "$filename is not an image";
  } else {
    $messages[] = implode('. ', $uploader->getMessages());
  }
} else {
```

If the file fails validation, the getErrors() method retrieves the error codes, and a conditional statement uses in_array() to check if fileMimeTypeFalse is in the array. If it is, a customized message is added to $messages reporting that the file is not an image. If fileMimeTypeFalse is not in the $error_codes array, it's a different problem, so the standard messages are used instead.

Selecting a nonimage for upload now presents a more user-friendly message.

- time.php is not an image
- bryce2.jpg uploaded successfully and renamed bryce2_1.jpg
- las vegas1.jpg uploaded successfully and renamed las_vegas1.jpg

Table 9.2 lists common error codes that can be used to create custom messages.

Table 9.2	**Common File Validation Error Codes**
Code	**Meaning**
fileExcludeExtensionFalse	Filename extension is not on permitted list.
fileExcludeMimeTypeFalse	File is of an excluded MIME type.
fileExcludeMimeTypeNotDetected	MIME type cannot be detected.
fileExcludeMimeTypeNotReadable	File cannot be read.
fileExtensionFalse	Filename extension is not on permitted list.
fileIsCompressedFalseType	File is not compressed.
fileIsCompressedNotDetected	MIME type cannot be detected.
fileIsCompressedNotReadable	File cannot be read.
fileMimeTypeFalse	File is of an excluded MIME type.
fileNotExistsDoesExist	File of the same name exists.
fileUploadErrorFormSize	File exceeds limit set by MAX_FILE_SIZE.
fileUploadErrorAttack	Illegal upload.
fileWordCountTooMuch	Number of words exceeds permitted limit.
fileWordCountTooLess	Number of words is lower than minimum required.

The code is in process_upload_07.php in lesson09/completed/scripts. The script has been extensively commented to help you understand how it works.

Sending Email Attachments

Now that you know how to upload files, it's easy to add attachments to an email sent from an online form. To send an attachment with an email, you upload the file to the web server. Then you use the PHP function file_get_contents() to get the contents of the file, and pass it to the Zend_Mail createAttachment() method. Unless you want to make changes to the default encoding (base64) and disposition (inline), that's all there is to it!

A potential problem with attachments—apart from malware—is that uploaded files are discarded if you don't store them in your web server's file system. It's annoying for users to need to upload their files again if there's an error with the form when submitted. On the other hand, you don't want to fill your file system with files that have already been sent as attachments.

The solution chosen here is to store the files temporarily by prefixing the filename(s) with a value stored in a session variable. This allows you to retrieve the correct file(s) when the form is resubmitted. When the mail is sent, you can delete the files, keeping your temporary upload directory clean.

To conclude this lesson, you'll adapt the file upload script from this lesson and merge it with the feedback form from Lesson 8 to allow users to send attachments from your website.

Adapting the file upload script

When uploading files to be sent as attachments, you can simplify the script. For example, you don't need to worry about overwriting existing files, because the attachments will be stored temporarily with a unique prefix and will be deleted from the file system after being sent.

1 Create a new PHP page and save it as **get_attachments.php** in lesson09/workfiles/scripts.

2 Delete the default HTML code, and add an opening PHP tag.

3 The script uses session variables, so begin by adding session_start(), followed by the definition of some basic settings:

```
session_start();
$destination = 'C:/upload_test';
$max_size = '50kB';
$not_allowed = 'exe,vbs,shs,pif,lnk,dll';
```

Defining the basic settings here makes it easier to edit them if you need to change them. As before, $destination is the upload folder; $max_size sets the maximum size for each attachment; and $not_allowed is a comma-separated list of the filename extensions that will be rejected by the ExcludeExtension validation class.

4 You don't want the upload script to run if the attachments are already stored in the file system. So, it should be wrapped in a conditional statement that checks for the existence of a session variable. If the variable doesn't exist, you know that this is the first time the form has been submitted. Add the following code:

```
if (!isset($_SESSION['att_id'])) {
  $_SESSION['att_id'] = 'att' . time() .'-';
  $_SESSION['attachments'] = array();

}
```

If $_SESSION['att_id'] doesn't exist, it's created by building a string based on the current time. The time() function returns a timestamp that represents the current date and time as the number of seconds elapsed since 00:00:00 UTC on January 1, 1970. So, it creates a string similar to att1273166609- that will be prefixed to each filename.

✳ **NOTE:** Expressing the current date and time as the number of seconds elapsed over the past 40 years or so might seem bizarre. Although timestamps look incomprehensible to humans, PHP functions use them to perform date calculations quickly and easily, avoiding all the complexities of different length months and leap years. January 1, 1970 is known as the Unix epoch, and this way of expressing the date and time is normally referred to as a Unix timestamp.

$_SESSION['attachments'] is also initialized as an empty array.

5 Inside the conditional statement you just created, instantiate a file transfer object and set the upload destination and validation classes:

```
$uploader = new Zend_File_Transfer_Adapter_Http();
$uploader->setDestination($destination);
$uploader->setOptions(array('ignoreNoFile' => TRUE));
$uploader->addValidator('Size', FALSE, $max_size);
$uploader->addValidator('ExcludeExtension', FALSE, $not_allowed);
```

This is basically the same as in the main upload script. Instead of using the MimeType validation class, it uses ExcludeExtension.

6 The remaining code also goes inside the conditional statement and looks like this (highlighted lines are explained after this code listing):

```
$files = $uploader->getFileInfo();
foreach($files as $file => $info) {
  if ($uploader->isUploaded($file)) {
    $filename = $uploader->getFileName($file, FALSE);
    if (!$uploader->isValid($file)) {
      $messages[] = "$filename exceeds $max_size or is not an acceptable
      ➥ type";
```

(code continues on next page)

```
  } else {
    $attachment = $_SESSION['att_id'] . str_replace(' ', '_',
    ➥$filename);
    $uploader->addFilter('Rename', array('target' => $attachment),
    ➥$file);
    $success = $uploader->receive($file);
    if (!$success) {
      $messages[] = "$filename could not be attached";
    } else {
      $messages[] = "$filename attached";
      $_SESSION['attachments'][] = $filename;
    }
   }
  }
 }
}
```

This follows a similar pattern to the file upload script you built earlier, although it's shorter and simpler. If the file fails validation, a message is created using `$filename` and `$max_size`.

Inside the main `else` block, spaces are removed from the filename and the prefix is added, resulting in a name that looks like att1273166609-bryce1.jpg. The amended name is stored in `$attachment`, but the original name remains unchanged in `$filename`.

The `Rename` filter uses `$attachment`, which stores the file with a name like att1273166609-bryce1.jpg. On the other hand, `$_SESSION['attachments']` uses `$filename` to preserve the original filename(s) for the email.

You can compare your code with get_attachments.php in lesson09/completed/scripts.

Adapting the mail processing script

Make the following changes to the mail processing script from Lesson 8:

1 Make a copy of lesson09/start/scripts/process_attachments.php, and save it in your workfiles/scripts folder for this lesson. Alternatively, you can work with process_comments.php from the previous lesson.

2 In process_attachments.php, use `require_once()` to include get_attachments.php. The code should go between the last validator and the conditional statement that checks there are no errors (around line 30).

```
if (!$val->isValid($_POST['comments'])) {
   $errors['comments'] = 'Required';
}
require_once('get_attachments.php');
if (!$errors) {
```

This ensures the attachments will be stored, even if the form has errors.

3 The code that attaches the uploaded files goes just before the email is sent (around line 48). The complete block of code looks like this:

```
$mail->setBodyHtml($html, 'UTF-8');
if (isset($_SESSION['attachments']) && !empty($_SESSION['attachments'])) {
  foreach($_SESSION['attachments'] as $attached) {
    $current_file = $destination . '/' . $_SESSION['att_id'] . $attached;
    $contents = file_get_contents($current_file);
    $att = $mail->createAttachment($contents);
    $att->filename = $attached;
    unlink($current_file);
  }
  unset($_SESSION['attachments']);
  unset($_SESSION['att_id']);
}
$success = $mail->send();
```

The code is wrapped in a conditional statement that checks whether `$_SESSION['attachments']` exists, and if it does, that it's not empty. This ensures that the code is executed only if there are attachments to send.

Inside the conditional statement, a `foreach` loop processes the filenames stored in `$_SESSION['attachments']`, assigning each one to the temporary variable `$attached`. Each time the loop runs, `$attached` contains the original name of the current file. However, to get the contents of the file from the upload folder, you need to use the full path, including the prefix that was used to store the file. This is done by the following line:

```
$current_file = $destination . '/' . $_SESSION['att_id'] .
➥ $attached;
```

`$destination` is the upload folder. This is followed by a forward slash. `$_SESSION['att_id']` is the time-based prefix, and `$attached` is the original filename. So, this produces something like this:

```
C:/upload_test/att1273166609-bryce1.jpg
```

The full path of the file is passed to `file_get_contents()`, a core PHP function that does what it says—it gets the contents of a file and is safe to use for both text and binary files.

The contents of the file are stored in `$contents`, which is then passed to the `Zend_Mail` object's `createAttachment()` method. The method takes up to five arguments, but only the first one—the attachment contents—is required. The other four arguments set the attached file's MIME type, disposition, encoding, and filename. If left out, `Zend_Mail` uses the defaults, which are fine in most cases. However, using the default filename results in the recipient getting a file with a name like att1273166609-bryce1.jpg instead of the original filename.

An advantage of the object-oriented approach taken by ZF is that you can set properties independently of the constructor method. Instead of passing all five arguments to `createAttachment()`, the attachment is assigned to a variable, `$att`, and its `filename` property is set like this:

`$att->filename = $attached;`

Since `$attached` contains the original filename of the current file, the recipient receives the attachment with a name like bryce1.jpg.

The final line in the `foreach` loop uses another core PHP function, `unlink()`, to delete the file from the upload folder.

After the loop has attached all the files to the mail object, the two session variables are unset to enable the user to reuse the online form.

You can compare your code with process_attachments.php in lesson09/completed/scripts.

Adapting the feedback form

All that remains to do is to adapt the feedback form, which needs to display the file fields for the attachments when the page first loads but hides them and displays a message about the attachments if the form is submitted with errors.

1 Copy send_attachments.php from lesson09/start to your workfiles folder. This is the same as comments.php from Lesson 8, with the addition of three file fields between the Comments text area and the reCAPTCHA widget.

2 In Design view, click to the right of the PHP shield that indicates the location of the Display Error Message server behavior next to the Comments text area. Open Split view to make sure the insertion point is between the closing `</span>` and `</p>` tags. With the focus still in Design view, press Enter/Return to insert a new paragraph.

3 In the new paragraph, type **Attachments do not need to be uploaded again.** Your page should look like this:

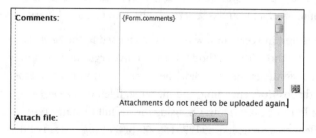

4 If the form has been submitted with errors, you need to show this paragraph together with any messages generated by get_attachments.php. To avoid confusion, it's also a good idea to hide the file fields. Wrap the paragraph and file fields in conditional statements like this:

```php
<?php if (isset($_SESSION['att_id'])) { ?>
<p>Attachments do not need to be uploaded again.</p>
<?php }
if (isset($messages)) {
  echo '<ul>';
  foreach ($messages as $item) {
    echo "<li>$item</li>";
  }
  echo '</ul>';
} else { ?>
<p>
  <label for="attachment1">Attach file:</label>
  <input type="file" name="attachment1" id="attachment1" />
</p>
<p>
  <label for="attachment2">Attach file:</label>
  <input type="file" name="attachment2" id="attachment2" />
</p>
<p>
  <label for="attachment3">Attach file:</label>
  <input type="file" name="attachment3" id="attachment3" />
</p>
<?php } ?>
```

$_SESSION['att_id'] exists only if the form has been submitted with errors. So, the paragraph you added in steps 2 and 3 is displayed together with messages generated by get_attachments.php. If the form hasn't been submitted with errors, the else block displays the file fields.

5 To test the form, include process_attachments.php with require_once() above the DOCTYPE declaration in send_attachments.php, and check the following:

- Make sure $public_key and $private_key in process_attachments.php use your reCAPTCHA keys.

- Make sure process_attachments.php includes the version of mail_connector.php that contains your email connection details.

6 Select some files, but leave at least one of the text fields blank, and submit the form. You should see the form redisplayed with error messages. But the text is preserved in fields that weren't blank, and there's a list of the attached files in place of the file fields.

Get In Touch

Sorry, there was a problem. Please retry.

All fields are required

Your name: Arthur Dent

Email address: hitchhiker@example.com

Comments: | Required

Attachments do not need to be uploaded again.

- bryce1.jpg attached
- joshuatree2.jpg attached
- upload_test_multi.php attached

reCAPTCHA field is required

strafes to

Type the two words:

reCAPTCHA
stop spam.
read books.

Send Comments

7 Fill in the missing fields, and click Send Comments again. This time the form reappears reporting the message has been sent, clearing the text fields, and redisplaying the file fields.

If mail_connector.php has the correct authorization and address details, you should receive an email with the files attached.

You can compare your code with send_attachments.php in lesson09/completed.

Like most projects in this book, the form for sending attachments with an email is designed to teach you how the various tools provided by Dreamweaver CS5 and PHP fit together. It's more a proof of concept than a fully polished application. It could be improved by adding a button that allows the user to cancel sending the message if the attachments are rejected as being too big or of the wrong type. You could also explore the use of Ajax to upload or remove attachments before the form is submitted. This is one of the joys—and challenges—of developing websites with PHP: The possibilities are limited only by your imagination and skill.

What You Have Learned

In this lesson, you have:

- Built a basic form for uploading files (pages 306–308)
- Created a local folder to test upload scripts (pages 308–309)
- Used `Zend_File_Transfer` to copy files to a specified location (pages 309–311)
- Validated files before transferring them to their final location (pages 312–318)
- Automatically replaced spaces in filenames with underscores (pages 318–321)
- Created the option to overwrite or rename files that have the same name (pages 321–333)
- Created and sent email attachments (pages 334–340)

What You Will Learn

In this lesson, you will:

- Plan the content management system for a travel website
- Define the structure for tables related through foreign keys
- Build a server behavior to populate a <select> menu from a SQL query
- Use a <select> menu to insert a foreign key into a database table
- Simultaneously upload images and insert related data into a database

Approximate Time

This lesson takes approximately 3 hours to complete.

Lesson Files

Media Files:

 images/bryce1.jpg
 images/bryce2.jpg
 images/grandcanyon1.jpg
 images/grandcanyon2.jpg
 images/joshuatree1.jpg
 images/joshuatree2.jpg
 images/lasvegas1.jpg
 images/lasvegas2.jpg
 images/longbeach1.jpg
 images/longbeach2.jpg
 images/losangeles1.jpg
 images/losangeles2.jpg
 images/newportbeach1.jpg
 images/newportbeach2.jpg
 images/sanfrancisco1.jpg
 images/sanfrancisco2.jpg
 images/sanjose1.jpg

images/sanjose2.jpg
images/zion1.jpg
images/zion2.jpg
styles/admin.css

Starting Files:

lesson10/start/insert_photos.php
lesson10/start/insert_places.php
lesson10/start/menu.php
lesson10/start/scripts/cms_structure.sql
lesson10/start/scripts/db_insert_photos.php
lesson10/start/scripts/library.php
lesson10/start/scripts/process_upload_06.php

Completed Files:

lesson10/completed/insert_photos_01.php
lesson10/completed/insert_photos_02.php
lesson10/completed/insert_place_01.php
lesson10/completed/insert_place_02.php
lesson10/completed/menu.php
lesson10/completed/scripts/db_definitions_01.php
lesson10/completed/scripts/db_definitions_02.php
lesson10/completed/scripts/db_definitions_03.php
lesson10/completed/scripts/db_insert_photos_01.php
lesson10/completed/scripts/db_insert_photos_02.php
lesson10/completed/scripts/db_insert_place_01.php
lesson10/completed/scripts/db_insert_place_02.php
lesson10/completed/scripts/db_insert_place_03.php
lesson10/completed/scripts/library.php
lesson10/completed/scripts/upload_images.php

Inserting Data into Multiple Tables

In this lesson and the next, you'll build a custom content management system (CMS) to store text and image details for a travel website in four related tables in the **phpcs5** database. This project brings together many techniques from previous lessons: validation, file uploads, and inserting, updating, and deleting data.

The content management system uploads images and related data.

Assessing the Task

To manage the content for a website, you need to be able to upload images to the site's file system and to store all related information in the database. After the information has been stored, you need to be able to update or delete it. Storing all the data in a single table is impractical.

As you learned in Lesson 5, you avoid inconsistency by moving repetitive information into a separate table. The two tables are linked by storing the primary key from one table as a foreign key in the other table. Lesson 5 showed a first attempt at designing the CMS with just tables called places and states.

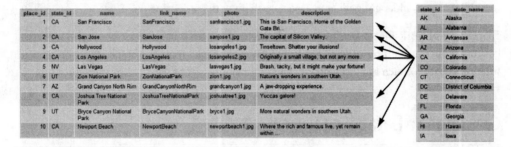

The problem with this structure is that the photo column means you can associate only one image with each place. Some people try to overcome this sort of limitation by creating multiple columns: photo1, photo2, and so on. But this results in forever needing to add new columns, a recipe for disaster.

The solution is to put the photos in a separate table and to use a cross-reference table to associate the primary key of each photo with the primary key of the place to which it belongs. The final structure looks like this:

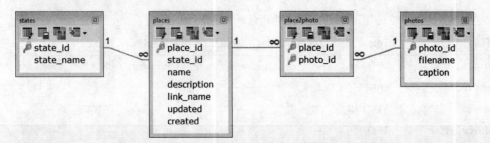

The relationship between the states and places tables remains the same as in the first attempt. Photos are in a dedicated table linked to the places table through a cross-reference table called place2photo, which stores the primary key of each place together with the primary key of each photo associated with it. This structure allows you to associate as many photos as you like with a single place. Not only that, but you can also associate the same photos with other places. For example, you might want to associate a photo of Grauman's Chinese Theater with entries in the places table for both Hollywood and Los Angeles. Another advantage is that you can store a caption with each photo.

Although place_id and photo_id are stored as foreign keys in the cross-reference table, each pair must be unique. So, the place_id and photo_id columns are declared as a joint primary key in place2photo. Generating the values to insert in place2photo is done programmatically by querying the database. The page that inserts a new place also uploads associated images, but updating records in the places and photos tables is handled separately. There's also a page to upload images independently and associate them with an existing place.

There's a lot of work ahead. Don't try to rush. Most of the techniques used in this lesson were covered earlier in this book. Now's the time to bring them all together. You'll learn some useful new skills, too, such as automatically paging through a set of database results.

Creating the Database Structure

The CMS uses four tables—states, places, place2photo, and photos—as shown in the preceding diagram. You imported the states table in Lesson 5. If necessary, return to that lesson before continuing with these instructions.

1 Launch phpMyAdmin, and select the phpcs5 database.

2 In the "Create new table on database phpcs5" section, type **places** in the Name field and set "Number of fields" to **7**. Click Go to open the definition matrix.

3 Use the settings in **Table 10.1** to define the columns for the places table, and click Save.

Table 10.1	Settings for the places Table					
Field	**Type**	**Length/Values**	**Default**	**Attributes**	**Index**	**A_I**
place_id	INT	—	—	UNSIGNED	PRIMARY	Selected
state_id	CHAR	2	—	—	—	—
name	VARCHAR	60	—	—	UNIQUE	—
description	TEXT	—	—	—	—	—
link_name	VARCHAR	60	—	—	UNIQUE	—
updated	TIMESTAMP	—	CURRENT_ TIMESTAMP	on update CURRENT_ TIMESTAMP	—	—
created	TIMESTAMP	—	—	—	—	—

4 Check that the structure of the table looks like this:

Field	Type	Collation	Attributes	Null	Default	Extra
place_id	int(10)		UNSIGNED	No	None	auto_increment
state_id	char(2)	latin1_swedish_ci		No	None	
name	varchar(60)	latin1_swedish_ci		No	None	
description	text	latin1_swedish_ci		No	None	
link_name	varchar(60)	latin1_swedish_ci		No	None	
updated	timestamp		on update CURRENT_TIMESTAMP	No	CURRENT_TIMESTAMP	on update CURRENT_TIMESTAMP
created	timestamp			No	0000-00-00 00:00:00	

The link_name column is intended to store a user-friendly link for web servers that support URL rewriting. The updated column automatically records the date and time a record is first created and subsequently updated. You'll learn more about rewriting URLs and handling dates in Lesson 12.

5 If necessary, click the Details link below the table structure to reveal the Indexes section, which should look like this:

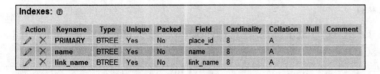

Indexes: ⑦

Action	Keyname	Type	Unique	Packed	Field	Cardinality	Collation	Null	Comment
✏ ✕	PRIMARY	BTREE	Yes	No	place_id	8	A		
✏ ✕	name	BTREE	Yes	No	name	8	A		
✏ ✕	link_name	BTREE	Yes	No	link_name	8	A		

In addition to the primary key, name and link_name have unique indexes to prevent duplicate entries.

6 Click the phpcs5 database link on the left of the screen to access the "Create new table on database phpcs5" section again. Type **photos** in the Name field and set "Number of fields" to **3**. Click Go to open the definition matrix.

7 Use the settings in **Table 10.2** to define the photos table, and click Save.

Table 10.2	Settings for the photos Table					
Field	**Type**	**Length/Values**	**Default**	**Attributes**	**Index**	**AUTO_INCREMENT**
photo_id	INT	—	—	UNSIGNED	PRIMARY	Selected
filename	VARCHAR	30	—	—	—	—
caption	VARCHAR	150	—	—	—	—

8 Check that the table structure looks like this:

Field	Type	Collation	Attributes	Null	Default	Extra
photo_id	int(10)		UNSIGNED	No	None	auto_increment
filename	varchar(30)	latin1_swedish_ci		No	None	
caption	varchar(150)	latin1_swedish_ci		No	None	

The only index on this table is photo_id, which is the primary key.

9 Click the phpcs5 database link on the left of the screen to access the "Create new table on database phpcs5" section again. Type **place2photo** in the Name field and set "Number of fields" to **2**. Click Go to open the definition matrix.

10 Name the fields place_id and photo_id. The remaining settings are the same for both columns:

- **Type.** INT

- **Attributes.** UNSIGNED

- **Index.** PRIMARY

Do *not* select the AUTO_INCREMENT checkbox for either column. The values will be inserted by a SQL query.

11 Click Save, and check that the table structure looks like this:

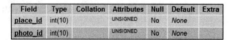

Field	Type	Collation	Attributes	Null	Default	Extra
place_id	int(10)		UNSIGNED	No	None	
photo_id	int(10)		UNSIGNED	No	None	

The Indexes section should look like this:

Action	Keyname	Type	Unique	Packed	Field	Cardinality	Collation	Null	Comment
✎ ✕	PRIMARY	BTREE	Yes	No	place_id	0	A		
					photo_id	0	A		

By using a joint primary key, you ensure that each pair of values is unique. This keeps your cross-reference table efficient by preventing duplicate links.

If you have any difficulty setting up the tables, you can use cms_structure.sql in lesson10/start/ scripts to import the structure (see "Importing data from a .sql file" in Lesson 5). The .sql file doesn't contain any data, but it deletes existing tables of the same name and creates the correct structure for the places, photos, and place2photo tables.

Building the CMS

Because there's a lot of PHP coding involved, the HTML elements of the administration pages have been created for you. Many of the scripts use common routines, such as validating input and querying the database. To avoid repetition, these routines have been turned into functions stored in a single file.

Preparing the administration pages

When complete, the administration section will consist of nine pages: a menu, and two pages each for inserting, listing, updating, and deleting records. In this lesson, you'll concentrate on the pages that insert the records and upload the images. The rest of the CMS will come together in Lesson 11.

1 Because this project spans two lessons, create a folder called **cms** in the phpcs5 site root. Copy the following files from lesson10/start to the new folder: insert_photos.php, insert_place.php, and menu.php.

If Dreamweaver prompts you to update the links, click Don't Update. The relative links in each file relate to the same folder, and the style sheet link should recognize admin.css in the styles folder.

2 Create a folder called **scripts** inside the cms folder, and copy your version of library.php to the scripts folder.

3 Open your copy of insert_photos.php in Design view. It contains a link to menu.php and a form. The PHP shield between the link and the form is a loop that displays error messages. The form contains a file field, a text input field, a `<select>` menu, and a submit button.

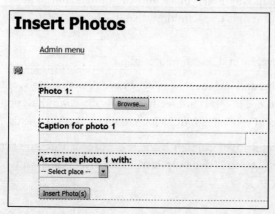

4 Open Code view or Split view to examine the code. The name attributes of the `<input>` and `<select>` elements all end with the number 1. To make the CMS more flexible, you'll create a PHP loop that repeats these three elements. The number of repeats is used several times in other scripts, so it makes sense to define it in a script that centralizes common features.

5 Create a new PHP file, and save it as **db_definitions.php** in the cms/scripts folder.

6 Replace the default HTML with the following PHP code, and save the file.

```php
<?php
$photofields = 3;
```

7 Copy db_insert_photos.php from lesson10/start/scripts to cms/scripts. It contains the skeleton code that should be familiar from previous lessons:

```php
<?php
$errors = array();
require_once('library.php');
try {

} catch (Exception $e) {
   echo $e->getMessage();
}
```

8 Include db_definitions.php using `require_once()` inside the `try` block:

```php
try {
   require_once('db_definitions.php');
} catch (Exception $e) {
```

9 Save db_insert_photos.php, and make four copies of it in the cms/scripts folder, saving them as **db_delete_place.php**, **db_insert_place.php**, **db_update_photo.php**, and **db_update_place.php**. All five scripts use definitions that will be created in db_definitions.php.

10 Close all files except db_definitions.php and insert_photos.php.

11 Select the tab for insert_photos.php, and include scripts/db_insert_photos.php above the DOCTYPE declaration using `require_once()`. This indirectly includes db_definitions.php in the page, allowing you to use $photofields to control a loop to repeat the form fields.

12 In Design view, select the text input field for Caption 1, and apply the Redisplay on Error server behavior that you created in Lesson 7. Type **caption1** in the Field Name field.

13 Switch to Code view, and create a for loop surrounding the file field, text input field, and `<select>` menu like this:

```php
<?php for ($i = 1; $i <= $photofields; $i++) { ?>
<p>
  <label for="photo1">Photo 1:</label>
  <input type="file" name="photo1" id="photo1" />
</p>
<p>
  <label for="caption1">Caption for photo 1</label>
  <input value="<?php if ($_POST && $errors) {
    echo htmlentities($_POST['caption1'], ENT_COMPAT, 'UTF-8');
  }?>" type="text" name="caption1" id="caption1" />
</p>
<p>
  <label for="place_id1">Associate photo 1 with:</label>
  <select name="place_id1" id="place_id1">
    <option value="0">-- Select place --</option>
  </select>
</p>
<?php } ?>
```

▼ **CAUTION!** Each form element is wrapped in `<p>` tags. Make sure you include the first opening tag and the last closing one inside the loop. The submit button should remain outside the loop.

14 Save the page and test it in Live View or a browser. You should now have three sets of input fields. The problem is that they all refer to Photo 1.

15 The reason for using a for loop is to utilize the counter `$i`, which is initialized at 1 instead of 0, so that the photos are numbered 1, 2, 3 onscreen. Incidentally, that's why the second argument in the for loop uses `$i <= $photofields`. If you use `$i < $photofields`, the loop runs only twice.

Rather than typing all the code by hand, choose Edit > Find and Replace or press Ctrl+F/Cmd+F to open the Find and Replace dialog box.

16 Use the following settings:

- **Find in:** Current Document
- **Search:** Source Code
- **Find:** 1"
- **Replace:** `<?php echo $i; ?>"`
- **Use regular expression:** Deselected

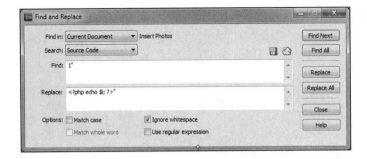

This searches the source code for 1 followed immediately by a double quotation mark and replaces it with <?php echo $i; ?>", changing the number to the value of $i followed by a double quotation mark. Adding the quotation mark makes it easier to find the relevant instances of 1.

17 Click Find Next twice. The first two instances are in the form's opening tag. You don't want to change them.

The next time you click Find Next, Dreamweaver highlights 1" in the following line:

```
<label for="photo1">Photo 1:</label>
```

Click Replace. Dreamweaver changes the code to this:

```
<label for="photo<?php echo $i; ?>">Photo 1:</label>
```

After changing the code, Dreamweaver jumps to the next instance. Click Replace again, and continue doing so until Dreamweaver reaches the end of the form. The Find and Replace dialog box should report that 11 items were found, and that 9 were replaced.

18 Before closing the Find and Replace dialog box, select the PHP code (without the double quotation mark) in the Replace field, and press Ctrl+C/Cmd+C to copy it to your clipboard.

19 In Code view, replace the number 1 in the three <label> tags by pressing Ctrl+V/Cmd+V to paste the code. The first <label> tag should look like this:

```
<label for="photo<?php echo $i; ?>">Photo <?php echo $i; ?>:</label>
```

20 One instance still needs to be fixed. It's in the code created by the Redisplay on Error server behavior. Locate the following code (around line 40):

```
echo htmlentities($_POST['caption1'], ENT_COMPAT, 'UTF-8');
```

The reason the Find and Replace dialog box didn't find it is because the server behavior uses single quotation marks. Also, this line of code is already inside a PHP block, so you can't paste the code you used in all the other instances. Replace the single quotation marks in $_POST['caption1'] with double ones, and embed $i like this:

```
echo htmlentities($_POST["caption{$i}"], ENT_COMPAT, 'UTF-8');
```

By using double quotation marks and wrapping $i in curly braces, this produces $_POST["caption1"], $_POST["caption2"], and so on.

21 Save insert_photos.php and test it in Live View or a browser. You should now have three sets of input fields for photos.

22 Click Live Code in Dreamweaver or check your browser's source code. The for, name, and id attributes should all end in the correct numbers.

The <select> menu doesn't work yet, but you'll come back to that later. You can compare your code with lesson10/completed/insert_photos_01.php.

23 Close insert_photos.php, and open insert_place.php. You need to create a loop for the photo input fields in the same way as you have just done.

Start by including scripts/db_insert_place.php using require_once() above the DOCTYPE declaration.

24 Only two fields are related to photos in this page: the file field and a text input field for the caption. Wrap them in a for loop like this:

```php
<?php for ($i = 1; $i <= $photofields; $i++) { ?>
<p>
  <label for="photo1">Photo 1:</label>
  <input type="file" name="photo1" id="photo1" />
</p>
<p>
  <label for="caption1">Caption for photo 1:</label>
  <input value="<?php if ($_POST && $errors) {
    echo htmlentities($_POST['caption1'], ENT_COMPAT, 'UTF-8');
  }?>" type="text" name="caption1" id="caption1" />
</p>
<?php } ?>
```

25 Repeat steps 14–19 to replace the number 1 with the variable $i. Because there are only two fields related to photos, the Find and Replace dialog box reports finding 8 items, 6 of which should have been replaced.

26 Save insert_place.php, and test it in Live View or a browser. You should see three sets of photo-related fields. You can compare your code with lesson10/completed/insert_place_01.php.

Inserting state_id as a foreign key

When inserting a new record in the places table, you need to store the state_id as a foreign key. This is done by querying the states table to retrieve all records and passing the result to a foreach loop to populate a <select> menu in insert_place.php. The primary key in the states table (state_id) becomes the value of each <option> tag, and the actual name (state_name) is displayed in the menu. So, when the form is submitted, the correct state_id can be inserted in the places table as a foreign key. Populating a <select> menu dynamically like this is a frequently used technique, so it's worth creating a custom server behavior.

This is how it's done:

1 Add the following function definition to db_definitions.php:

```php
function getAllStates($read) {
  $sql = 'SELECT * FROM states ORDER BY state_name';
  return $read->fetchAll($sql);
}
```

This defines a function that takes a single argument, which should be a Zend_Db object. You need to pass the object to the function because variables and objects declared outside a function are outside its scope (see "Understanding Variable Scope" in Lesson 3).

The function creates a SELECT query to retrieve all data from the states table ordered by state_name, passes it to fetchAll(), and returns the result.

2 Save db_definitions.php, and switch to db_insert_place.php. Open it by selecting insert_place.php and clicking db_insert_place.php in the Related Files toolbar. Alternatively, open db_insert_place.php in a separate tab.

3 Insert a new line inside the try block under the line that includes db_definitions.php, and type **$states** = followed by a space.

4 Press Ctrl+spacebar to bring up code hints, and type **geta**. Dreamweaver should present you with a code hint for getAllStates(), the function you created in step 1.

```
try {
  require_once('db_definitions.php');
  $states = geta
} catch (Excepti ■ func_get_arg( int $arg_num )                                          PHP:Core functionality
  echo $e->getMe ■ func_get_args()                                                         PHP:Core functionality
}                   ● getAllStates($read)                                                   db_definitions.php
                    ■ imap_getacl( resource $imap_stream , string $mailbox )                PHP:Miscellaneous functions and classes
                    ■ ini_get_all([ string $extension [, bool $details = true ]] )          PHP:Core functionality
                    ■ ldap_get_attributes( resource $link_identifier , resource $result_entry_identifier )  PHP:Other databases
                    ■ mcrypt_enc_get_algorithms_name( resource $td )                        PHP:Encryption and Compression
                    ■ mcrypt_module_get_algo_block_size( string $algorithm [, string $lib_dir ] )  PHP:Encryption and Compression
                    ■ mcrypt_module_get_algo_key_size( string $algorithm [, string $lib_dir ] )    PHP:Encryption and Compression
                    ■ token_get_all( string $source )                                      PHP:Core functionality
```

Press Enter/Return for Dreamweaver to autocomplete the function name and opening parenthesis. Even though the function is defined in a different page, Dreamweaver recognizes it and creates code hints because the pages are linked. Type **$db** after the opening parenthesis, and select $dbRead from the list of code hints. Type a closing parenthesis and semicolon. The completed line should look like this:

```
$states = getAllStates($dbRead);
```

The getAllStates() function returns the result from the SQL query, which is now stored as a multidimensional array in $states.

5 Click Source Code in the Related Files toolbar to switch to the HTML code in insert_place.php, or select the page's tab if you're working in separate tabs. Locate the <select> menu (around lines 40–41), and insert the following PHP between the opening and closing tags:

```
<select name="state_id" id="state_id">
<?php
foreach ($states as $row) {
  echo "<option value='{$row['state_id']}'";
  if ($errors && $_POST['state_id'] == $row['state_id']) {
    echo 'selected="selected"';
  }
  echo ">{$row['state_name']}</option>";
}
?>
</select>
```

The foreach loop iterates through the $states array, assigning it to the temporary variable $row. Each time the loop runs, $row contains a record from the SQL query in which the column names are used as the array keys. So, $row['state_id'] contains the current value of state_id, and $row['state_name'] contains state_name from the same row.

$row['state_id'] is inserted into the value attribute, and $row['state_name'] is displayed between the opening and closing <option> tags. If the $errors array equates to TRUE, the conditional statement compares $_POST['state_id'] with $row['state_id']. If they are equal, selected="selected" is inserted in the opening <option> tag.

In plain English, this means all the records retrieved from the states table are used to populate the <select> menu. If there are errors when the form is submitted, the menu automatically selects the value chosen by the user.

6 Put it to the test by saving all related files and clicking Live View. You should see Alabama listed in the menu.

Click the menu open, and you should see all 50 states plus the District of Columbia listed. A lot easier than typing them all out by hand!

▶ **TIP:** If it didn't work, compare your code with lesson10/completed/insert_place_02.php, which contains just one minor change that will be made in the next step.

7 Exit Live View, and locate the following line in the PHP code you inserted in step 5 (around line 44):

```
if ($errors && $_POST['state_id'] == $row['state_id']) {
```

Replace the single quotation marks in $_POST['state_id'] with double quotation marks like this:

```
if ($errors && $_POST["state_id"] == $row['state_id']) {
```

This makes no difference to the way the code works, but makes it more adaptable when you convert the entire code block into a server behavior. Using double quotation marks means you can easily embed $i in the value through the server behavior's dialog box without needing to dive into Code view later.

8 Save insert_place.php, and copy the amended PHP block to your clipboard.

9 Click the plus button in the Server Behaviors panel, and choose New Server Behavior. Name the new server behavior **Zend Select Menu**, and click OK.

10 Click the plus button next to "Code blocks to insert," and accept the name suggested by Dreamweaver.

11 Replace the placeholder text in the "Code block" text area by pasting the PHP code from your clipboard.

12 Convert the following variables to server behavior parameters:

- $states: **@@Array Variable@@**

- $row['state_id']: $row['**@@Value@@**']

- $_POST["state_id"]: $_POST["**@@Menu Name@@**"]

- $row['state_name']: $row['**@@Display@@**']

The amended code should look like this:

```php
<?php
foreach (@@Array Variable@@ as $row) {
  echo "<option value='{$row['@@Value@@']}'";
  if ($errors && $_POST["@@Menu Name@@"] == $row['@@Value@@']) {
    echo 'selected="selected"';
  }
  echo ">{$row['@@Display@@']}</option>";
}
?>
```

The parameters will be used as labels in the server behavior's dialog box and allow you to build a dynamic <select> menu quickly and easily.

13 Use the following options at the bottom of the panel:

- **Insert code:** Relative to a Specific Tag

- **Tag:** select

- **Relative position:** Before the Closing Tag

Selecting Before the Closing Tag allows you to add a static <option> tag inside the <select> menu before the loop.

14 Click Next. Dreamweaver offers its suggestions for the new server behavior's dialog box. They're fine, but select Menu Name, and use the up arrow button at the top right to move it above "select tag." Then click OK.

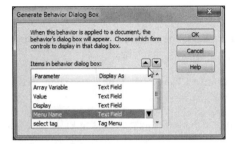

You'll use this server behavior later when completing insert_photos.php.

Inserting details in the places table

The form in insert_place.php is designed to insert the details of a new place and up to three related photos and captions. From the user's viewpoint, the process should appear to be a single, seamless operation. In reality, there are many stages. This is what the script needs to do:

1 When the form is submitted, validate the text fields. If there are any errors, stop processing and redisplay the form with error messages and the text preserved in the input fields.

2 Check the database to see if the name is already registered. If it is, stop processing and redisplay the form.

3 Upload the images. If any image fails validation, abandon the upload process and redisplay the form.

4 If the text and images all validate, insert the data into the places table.

5 If the data is inserted successfully and no images have been detected, redisplay the form with a message indicating that the place has been inserted in the database.

6 If images have been detected, query the database to get the new place's primary key.

7 Loop through the images. Each time the loop runs, the following events take place:

- Insert the filename and caption into the photos table.

- Query the database to get the photo's primary key.

- Insert both primary keys as a pair in the place2photo table.

8 Report the successful upload of the images and insertion of the new place.

This process involves more than 130 lines of code. Most of it is code that you have already used in previous lessons, so you can save some time by editing an existing script, as well as copying and pasting. However, if you need a break, now is a good time to take one. The good news is that the other scripts reuse a large part of this code and are considerably shorter.

If you're ready, let's begin.

1 The first task of the script is to validate the text fields. Because the forms that insert the photos and update existing records also need to validate them, it makes sense to create custom functions that can be reused. Add the following function definition to db_definitions.php:

```
function validatePlaceName($name, &$errors) {
    $val = new Zend_Validate_Regex('/^[a-z]+[-\'a-z ]+$/i');
    if (!$val->isValid($name)) {
        $errors['name'] = 'Place name is required: no special characters';
    }
}
```

You should recognize the code inside the function from Lesson 7. It was used to validate the first and family names in the user registration system. It accepts alphabetic characters, spaces, hyphens, and apostrophes. If you need to accept a wider range of characters, including accented characters and other writing scripts—such as Arabic, Chinese, Cyrillic, Hindi, and Japanese—change the first line inside the function to this:

```
$val = new Zend_Validate_Regex('/^\p{L}+[-\'\p{L} ]+$/u');
```

The code inside the function is very straightforward. However, the function works in a very different way from most functions. Normally, when you pass an argument to a function, it's *passed by value*. Whatever happens inside the function has no effect on the variable outside unless the value is returned by the function and reassigned to the original variable.

However, validatePlaceName() doesn't return a value. Instead, it uses a technique known as *passing by reference*, which *does* change the original value.

Look closely at the two arguments in the parentheses—the *function signature*. The first argument, $name, represents the value in the name text input field. The second argument, $errors, represents the $errors array that stores error messages. What's different is that it's preceded by an ampersand like this: &$errors. This results in a permanent change to the value(s) stored in the variable passed as an argument to the function.

This means that if the $name variable fails validation, a name element will be added to the $errors array passed as the second argument to the function.

✳ NOTE: Although the function definition uses the same name as the array in the rest of the script, it's the ampersand in front of the argument that makes the difference. It would work the same if you passed an array called $messages to the function.

2 The other text fields that you need to validate are the description and photo captions. Add the following function definitions to db_definitions.php:

```
function validateDescription($description, $val, &$errors) {
  if (!$val->isValid($description)) {
    $errors['description'] = 'Description is required';
  }
}

function validateCaption($caption, $num, $val, &$errors) {
  if (!$val->isValid($caption)) {
    $errors["photo{$num}"] = "Caption for photo $num is too long";
  }
}
```

Like validatePlaceName(), these two functions pass the $errors argument by reference. So, they result in elements being added to the original $errors array if the value passed to the validator is rejected. Unlike the previous function, they don't instantiate a Zend_Validator object. Instead, they expect a validator ($val) to be passed to them as an argument.

The validateCaption() function also expects an argument called $num. The function will be used inside a loop, so it's necessary to keep count of how many times the loop has run. $num is used inside double quotation marks to insert the correct photo number in the $errors array.

3 The validator for the description and captions checks the length of the string. To avoid the need to change the minimum and maximum values in multiple places, add the following definitions at the top of db_definitions.php:

```
$captionMin = 0;
$captionMax = 150;
$descriptionMin = 10;
$descriptionMax = NULL;
```

These set the minimum length of a caption to zero and the maximum to 150 characters. The minimum for a description is set to 10 characters. Setting the maximum to NULL means there's no upper limit.

4 After validating the text fields, the script needs to check if the place name already exists in the database. Again, this uses a technique from Lesson 7. You need to run a SELECT query to see if there is a match for the name. Add the following function definition to db_definitions.php:

```
function checkDuplicatePlacename ($read, $name, &$errors) {
  $sql = $read->quoteInto('SELECT place_id FROM places WHERE name = ?',
  ➥ $name);
```

```
    $result = $read->fetchAll($sql);
    if ($result) {
      $errors['name'] = $_POST['name'] . ' is already listed';
    }
  }
}
```

The function signature has three arguments: $read is a Zend_Db object capable of running SELECT queries; $name is the name you want to check; and &$errors is the array of error messages—again it's passed by reference.

The code in the body of the function creates a SQL query to select the primary key of a record that has the same name as $name and then executes the query. If a match is found, $result equates to TRUE, adding a message to the $errors array. If no match is found, the name is not a duplicate.

5 With those definitions in place, you can now start building the processing script. Save db_definitions.php, and switch to db_insert_place.php.

Add a conditional statement to ensure that the code runs only when the submit button has been clicked. The name attribute of the button is insert, so the code looks like this:

```
try {
  require_once('db_definitions.php');
  $states = getAllStates($dbRead);
  if (isset($_POST['insert'])) {
    // processing code goes here
  }
} catch (Exception $e) {
```

6 Inside the conditional statement, call the first of the functions you just defined by pressing Ctrl+spacebar and typing **va**. Code hints display the three validation functions. Select validatePlaceName() and double-click or press Enter/Return. Code hints also remind you of the arguments required. The first one is the name submitted from the form, $_POST['name'], and the second one is the $errors array. The new line of code should look like this:

```
validatePlaceName($_POST['name'], $errors);
```

▼ CAUTION! When you use a function that passes an argument by reference, do not prefix the argument with an ampersand. The ampersand is used only in the function definition.

7 Create an instance of the StringLength validation class, and set the minimum and maximum values for the description using the variables defined in step 3 (they should appear in code hints after you type a dollar sign):

```
$val = new Zend_Validate_StringLength($descriptionMin, $descriptionMax);
```

8 Pass the description submitted from the form, together with the validator and the $errors array to validateDescription(). Don't forget that pressing Ctrl+spacebar will bring it up in code hints for autocompletion.

```
validateDescription($_POST['description'], $val, $errors);
```

9 The captions use different minimum and maximum lengths, so you need to change them using the setMin() and setMax() methods like this:

```
$val->setMin($captionMin);
$val->setMax($captionMax);
```

10 The form contains multiple caption fields, so you need to use a loop to check each one. The $photofields variable controls the number of photo and caption fields, so you can use it to limit the number of times the loop runs. Add the following code to your script:

```
for ($num = 1; $num <= $photofields; $num++) {
  validateCaption($_POST["caption{$num}"], $num, $val, $errors);
}
```

The counter $num is initialized at 1. It's embedded in a double-quoted string in the $_POST variable's key, so the loop validates $_POST["caption1"], $_POST["caption2"], and so on. $num is also passed as an argument to add the correct number to any error messages. The third and fourth arguments are the validator and the $errors array.

11 The next stage is to check whether the place is already listed in the database. This involves querying the database, but there's little point in doing so if the validation tests have failed. Wrap the call to checkDuplicatePlacename() in a conditional statement like this:

```
if (!$errors) {
  checkDuplicatePlacename($dbRead, $_POST['name'], $errors);
}
```

12 Save db_insert_place.php, and test insert_place.php in Live View or a browser. Start by submitting a blank form, remembering to hold down Ctrl/Cmd when clicking Insert Place in Live View. You should see the following error messages at the top of the page:

Insert New Place

Admin menu

- Place name is required: no special characters
- Description is required

Place name:

13 Type in a place name and photo caption, and select a state, but leave the Description text area blank. When you submit the form again, the values should be preserved in the fields you filled in.

You can compare your code with db_definitions_01.php and db_insert_place_01.php in lesson10/completed/scripts.

Validating and uploading the photos

Validating and uploading the photos is the longest part of the processing script. The excellent news is that you have already built most of it in Lesson 9. Instead of completely reinventing the wheel, you can adapt the multiple file upload script to work with this project. The ability to upload images is also required by the form that inserts new photos, so the upload script needs to be in a separate page.

1 Copy process_upload_06.php from lesson10/start/scripts to the cms/scripts folder, and rename it **upload_images.php**.

2 You don't need the try and catch blocks, because this page will be included in the try block of the other processing scripts. Delete the code shown on lines 2–8 and 80–83 of the following screen shot.

```
1    <?php
2    if (isset($_POST['upload'])) {
3        require_once('library.php');
4        $overwrite = FALSE;
5        if (isset($_POST['overwrite']) && $_POST['overwrite'] == 'y') {
6            $overwrite = TRUE;
7        }
8        try {
9            $destination = 'C:/upload_test';
10           $uploader = new Zend_File_Transfer_Adapter_Http();
11           $uploader->setDestination($destination);
12           $uploader->setOptions(array('ignoreNoFile' => TRUE));
13           $files = $uploader->getFileInfo();
14           foreach ($files as        $info) {
                   $upload
```

```
67                    ...cess) {
68                        $messages[] = implode('.   , $uploader->getMessages());
69                    } else {
70                        $uploaded = "$filename uploaded successfully";
71                        if ($renamed) {
72                            $uploaded .= " and renamed $no_spaces";
73                        }
74                        $messages[] = $uploaded;
75                    }
76                }
77            }
78        }
79    }
80    } catch (Exception $e) {
81        echo $e->getMessage();
82    }
83  }
```

3 Select the remaining code after the opening PHP tag, and click the Outdent Code icon ⬚ in the Coding toolbar to correct the indenting.

4 The first line of code now defines the $destination variable. Delete it. The definition should be with the others in db_definitions.php.

5 Before adding the definition, create a new folder called **image_upload** inside the cms folder. Mac users should make the folder writable by everyone, as described in "Creating a local folder for testing uploads" in Lesson 9.

6 At the top of db_definitions.php, add a definition for $destination using the full path to the image_upload folder. The path depends on your setup, but the value used in the files on the accompanying CD looks like this:

```
$destination = 'C:/vhosts/phpcs5/cms/image_upload';
```

7 As it stands, the upload script simply moves images from one location to another. However, the CMS not only uploads images, but also stores details about them in the database. To make sure the right data is associated with each image, you need to keep track of each image's caption. The form in insert_photos.php has a <select> menu that allows you to associate a new image with a place, so you need to keep track of that information, too.

The existing script handles each image separately in a foreach loop. So, the way to keep track of associated data is to capture their values in variables at the start of the foreach loop and use them to build an array at the end of the loop. Add the following code to capture the values:

```
$files = $uploader->getFileInfo();
$filenum = 1;
foreach($files as $file => $info) {
  $file = "photo{$filenum}";
  $caption = $_POST["caption{$filenum}"];
  if (isset($_POST["place_id{$filenum}"])) {
    $place_id = $_POST["place_id{$filenum}"];
  } else {
    $place_id = NULL;
  }
  $filenum++;
  if ($uploader->isUploaded($file)) {
```

In the original upload script, the foreach loop used the temporary variable $file to identify the file. Zend_File also lets you refer to specific files by the name attribute in the upload form. The loops in insert_place.php and insert_photos.php use a counter to name the file fields photo1, photo2, and so on. This loop does the same by initializing $filenum as 1 and using it to ensure photo1 is associated with $_POST["caption1"] and $_POST["place_id1"]. To make the code easier to read, these values are assigned to $file, $caption, and $place_id respectively. The second time the loop runs, these variables store the values of photo2, $_POST["caption2"] and $_POST["place_id2"].

$_POST["place_id{$filenum}"] exists only when the form in insert_photos.php is submitted, so the conditional statement sets the value of $place_id to NULL if it hasn't been submitted by the form.

8 Several lines farther down, after the validators have been added to the $uploader object, the script validates the file and gets the error messages if it fails. The code looks like this:

```
if (!$uploader->isValid($file)) {
  $messages[] = implode('. ', $uploader->getMessages());
} else {
```

Change it to this:

```
if (!$uploader->isValid($file)) {
  $errors[$filename] = "$filename doesn't meet the requirements for an
➥ image";
} else {
```

This creates a generic message instead of getting the messages generated by Zend_File_Validate. Note also that the error message is added to the $errors array, not $messages. The $errors array is used at various stages throughout this script to halt processing when a problem arises. You don't want to insert information in the database if the uploaded file doesn't meet the validation requirements. The filename is used as the array key to identify the problem image.

9 Around line 36, you need to make a similar change to an error message. Locate this code:

```
if (!$key) {
  $messages[] = 'Unrecognized image type';
} else {
```

Change it like this:

```
if (!$key) {
  $errors[$no_spaces] = "$filename is an unrecognized image type";
} else {
```

The variables $no_spaces and $filename refer to the same file: $no_spaces is the internal name used by the upload script after stripping out any spaces. To identify the correct file internally, $no_spaces needs to be used as the array key, but the error message preserves the original filename.

10 Six lines farther down is the section that renames duplicate files. It looks like this:

```
if (!$overwrite) {
  // get the names of existing files
  $existing = scandir($destination);
  // check if the name of the uploaded file is in the array
  if (in_array($no_spaces, $existing)) {
    // get the position of the final period
    // use it to get the base name and extension
    $dot = strrpos($no_spaces, '.');
    $base = substr($no_spaces, 0, $dot);
    $extension = substr($no_spaces, $dot);
    // initialize a counter
    $i = 1;
    // use a loop to add the counter after the base name
    // check whether the new name exists in the array
    do {
      $no_spaces = $base . '_' . $i++ . $extension;
    } while (in_array($no_spaces, $existing));
    // set $renamed to TRUE
    $renamed = TRUE;
  }
}
```

Remove the conditional statement by deleting the `if` clause and the closing curly brace at the bottom of this section of code. Files will be automatically renamed, because the CMS allows the user to view and delete images. Renaming prevents files from being overwritten accidentally. The removal of duplicates is up to the user.

To keep your code tidy, select the code that was in the conditional statement, and click the Outdent Code icon ⬚ in the Coding toolbar once.

11 The final changes are made to the section of code that handles the messages relayed to the user depending on the success or failure of the upload. The existing script looks like this:

```
if (!$success) {
  $messages[] = implode('. ', $uploader->getMessages());
} else {
  $uploaded = "$filename uploaded successfully";
  if ($renamed) {
    $uploaded .= " and renamed $no_spaces";
  }
  $messages[] = $uploaded;
}
```

Change it like this:

```
if (!$success) {
  $errors[$no_spaces] = implode('. ', $uploader->getMessages());
} else {
  $uploaded = "$filename uploaded successfully";
  if ($renamed) {
    $uploaded .= " and renamed $no_spaces";
  }
  $images[] = array('filename' => $no_spaces,
                    'caption' => $caption,
                    'place_id' => $place_id);
  $messages[] = $uploaded;
}
```

If the upload fails, the error messages are added to the `$errors` array instead of the `$messages` array. To prevent the details of a problem file from being inserted into the database, it's identified by using `$no_spaces` as the array key.

The other change is that if the upload succeeds, the file's name, caption, and associated `place_id` are added as an array to a new array called `$images`. Each element of the top-level array contains the details of a single image. For example, the first array element contains the following subarray: `$images[0]['filename']`, `$images[0]['caption']`, and `$images[0]['place_id']`.

12 Save upload_images.php, and include it in db_insert_place.php after the conditional statement for checkDuplicatePlacename(). The include command should similarly be wrapped in a conditional statement like this:

```
if (!$errors) {
  checkDuplicatePlacename($dbRead, $_POST['name'], $errors);
}
if (!$errors) {
  require_once('upload_images.php');
}
```

You can compare your code with upload_images.php, db_definitions_02.php, and db_insert_place_02.php in lesson10/completed/scripts.

Inserting the place and photo data

Once the data has been validated and the photos uploaded successfully, you're ready to insert the data into the places, photos, and place2photo tables. A SQL INSERT query cannot deal with multiple tables, so you need to handle each table separately. You also need to query the database to obtain the primary key for each place and photo so that you can insert them as foreign keys in the place2photo table. This is done with the Zend_Db lastInsertId() method, although you must remember to use it immediately after inserting a record.

The rest of the script is relatively short and easy to understand.

1 In db_insert_place.php, add another conditional statement to make sure there were no errors when the photos were uploaded:

```
if (!$errors) {
  require_once('upload_images.php');
}
if (!$errors) {

}
```

All remaining code goes inside this conditional statement.

2 Create an array of values to be inserted in the places table:

```
$data = array('name'        => $_POST['name'],
              'state_id'    => $_POST['state_id'],
              'description' => $_POST['description'],
              'link_name'   => str_replace(' ', '', $_POST['name']),
              'created'     => new Zend_Db_Expr('NOW()'));
```

The values for the name, state_id, and description columns come directly from the form. The link_name column takes its value from the name field in the form after it has been passed to the str_replace() function. The first argument passed to the function is a pair of quotation marks with a space between them; the second argument is also a pair of quotation marks but without a space. This closes up any spaces—San Francisco becomes SanFrancisco. Spaces should never be used in a URL.

The updated column doesn't need a value, because it's automatically initialized to the current timestamp. However, the timestamp needs to be set explicitly in the created column by using the MySQL NOW() function, which inserts the current date and time. As explained in "Using SQL functions with Zend_Db" in Lesson 8, functions need to be wrapped in a Zend_Db_Expr object.

3 Insert the data with the insert() method like this:

```
$inserted = $dbWrite->insert('places', $data);
```

4 If any photos have been uploaded, you need to get the primary key of the new record and insert the details in the photos and place2photo tables. However, if nothing has been uploaded, there's nothing more to do apart from display a message reporting the result.

The result of the insert() method is captured in $inserted. If the $images array created by upload_images.php contains any values, you know images have been uploaded. Use both values to determine whether to retrieve the new record's primary key. Add the following code on the next line:

```
if ($inserted && isset($images)) {
  $place_id = $dbWrite->lastInsertId();
}
```

This gets the primary key from the places table and stores it in $place_id.

5 You can now loop through the $images array to insert the filename and caption for each image in the photos table. Immediately after inserting the data, capture the primary key using the lastInsertId() method, and insert the primary keys from the places and photos tables in place2photo. The loop that does all that looks like this:

```
if ($inserted && isset($images)) {
  $place_id = $dbWrite->lastInsertId();
  foreach($images as $image) {
    $data = array('filename' => $image['filename'],
                  'caption'  => $image['caption']);
    $dbWrite->insert('photos', $data);
    $photo_id = $dbWrite->lastInsertId();
    $data = array('place_id' => $place_id,
                  'photo_id' => $photo_id);
    $dbWrite->insert('place2photo', $data);
  }
}
```

There's no need to check for errors in the image uploads, because the conditional statement you added in step 1 prevents the script from getting this far if there are any problems.

6 All that remains is to do is to prepare the messages to report what has happened. The next section of code needs to go after the conditional statement that handles the images. It looks like this:

```
        $dbWrite->insert('place2photo', $data);
      }
    }
    if ($inserted) {
      $messages[] = $_POST['name'] . ' is now listed in the database';
    } else {
      $errors[] = $_POST['name'] . ' could not be inserted';
    }
  }
}
} catch (Exception $e) {
```

7 Save db_insert_place.php, and test insert_place.php by typing values in the "Place name" and Description fields, and selecting a state. Browse to the images folder to select a couple of images and add captions. Then click Insert Place. If all your code and the database structure are correct, you should see a series of success messages at the top of the form.

Insert New Place

Admin menu

- sanfrancisco1.jpg uploaded successfully
- sanfrancisco2.jpg uploaded successfully
- San Francisco is now listed in the database

8 Check the image_upload folder in the Files panel. Copies of the photos you selected should have been added to the folder. Also check in phpMyAdmin. The places, photos, and place2photo tables should have the first set of data.

place_id	state_id	name	description	link_name	updated	created
1	CA	San Francisco	The very hilly city that Dreamweaver calls home.	SanFrancisco	2010-05-14 15:23:48	2010-05-14 15:23:48

photo_id	filename	caption
1	sanfrancisco1.jpg	Cable car
2	sanfrancisco2.jpg	Golden Gate Bridge

place_id	photo_id
1	1
1	2

If it didn't work, compare all your files carefully with insert_place_02.php in lesson10/completed and with db_definitions_02.php, db_insert_place_03.php, and upload_images.php in lesson10/completed/scripts. Also check your database structure, and load it from lesson10/start/scripts/cms_structure.sql. This is a complex script, so there are many places where you might have made a mistake.

Before moving on to the next section, add two or three more places to the database. The images folder contains photos of ten locations in Arizona, California, Nevada, and Utah, but you don't need to confine yourself to them. Not every place needs to be accompanied by a photo, and captions are optional. The CMS is designed to allow you to add photos and edit their details later.

Inserting photos separately

All the hard work for this administration page has already been done. The script in upload_images.php validates the images and uploads them. The main task is to create the script that inserts the image details into the database.

1 Open insert_photos.php. The `<select>` menu needs to be populated with a list of the places already registered in the database. This will be used in the same way as the State `<select>` menu in insert_place.php, storing the primary key of each place so it can be inserted as a foreign key in the place2photo table.

2 Create the following function in db_definitions.php to select the place_id and name columns for each record in the places table:

```
function getAllPlaces($read) {
    $sql = 'SELECT place_id, name FROM places ORDER BY name';
    return $read->fetchAll($sql);
}
```

This is similar to the getAllStates() function you created earlier. It takes as its single argument a Zend_Db object with read permission and returns the database result as an array.

3 Save db_definitions.php, and switch to db_insert_photos.php. Inside the try block, call the function you just created and assign the result to $places like this:

```
try {
    require_once('db_definitions.php');
    $places = getAllPlaces($dbRead);
} catch (Exception $e) {
```

Save db_insert_photos.php after making this edit, and switch to insert_photos.php.

4 You can now use $places to populate the <select> menu. Select the menu in Design view, click the plus button in the Server Behaviors panel, and choose Zend Select Menu. Use the following settings in the dialog box:

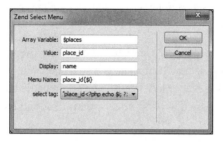

The <select> menu is inside a loop, so the value in the "select tag" menu includes a PHP tag and the $i counter. However, the value in Menu Name should be simply **place_id{$i}**, because it will be used as the key of a $_POST variable.

5 Click OK to close the Zend Select Menu dialog box, and examine the code that has just been inserted (the values entered in the dialog box are highlighted):

```php
<select name="place_id<?php echo $i; ?>" id="place_id<?php echo $i; ?>">
  <option value="0">-- Select place --</option>
<?php
foreach ($places as $row) {
  echo "<option value='{$row['place_id']}'";
  if ($errors && $_POST["place_id{$i}"] == $row['place_id']) {
    echo 'selected="selected"';
  }
  echo ">{$row['name']}</option>";
}
?>
</select>
```

6 Save the page, and click Live View to test it. Click open each of the <select> menus in turn. They should display a list of the place names registered in the places table.

If it doesn't work, compare your code with insert_photos_02.php, scripts/db_definitions_03.php and scripts/db_insert_photos_01.php in lesson10/completed.

7 The form for inserting photos is now complete. Next, you need to build the script that processes the form when the submit button is clicked.

The name attribute of the submit button is insert, so the processing script needs to go inside a conditional statement in db_insert_photos.php. Add the conditional statement after the code you added in step 3:

```
$places = getAllPlaces($dbRead);
if (isset($_POST['insert'])) {
  // processing code goes here
}
} catch (Exception $e) {
```

8 Inside the conditional statement, add a validator to check the length of the captions and loop through them. Then include upload_photos.php if there are no errors. The code looks like this:

```
$val = new Zend_Validate_StringLength($captionMin, $captionMax);
for ($num = 1; $num <= $photofields; $num++) {
  validateCaption($_POST["caption{$num}"], $num, $val, $errors);
}
if (!$errors) {
  require_once('upload_images.php');
}
```

This is the same as in db_insert_place.php, so it needs no further explanation.

9 If photos have been uploaded, the final section of code loops through the $images array created by upload_photos.php to insert the details in the photos and place2photo tables. Add the following code immediately after the code in the previous step:

```
if (isset($images)) {
  foreach($images as $image) {
    if (!array_key_exists($image['filename'], $errors)) {
      $data = array('filename' => $image['filename'],
                    'caption'  => $image['caption']);
      $dbWrite->insert('photos', $data);
      $photo_id = $dbWrite->lastInsertId();
      if ($image['place_id']) {
        $data = array('place_id' => $image['place_id'],
                      'photo_id' => $photo_id);
        $dbWrite->insert('place2photo', $data);
      }
    }
  }
}
```

The code in upload_images.php stores the filename, caption, and primary key of the related place in the $images array. The foreach loop that you just inserted deals with each image in turn.

It first makes sure the image was uploaded successfully by checking the $errors array with array_key_exists(). If the filename hasn't been used as an array key, you know the image is OK, and the code inside the conditional statement inserts the values into the filename and caption columns of the photos table, and uses lastInsertId() to capture the primary key of the new record as $photo_id.

Another conditional statement then checks the place_id associated with the current image. If the <select> menu in the form is left at the default "Select place," the value is 0, so the condition fails, and no data is added to the place2photo table. However, if a place has been selected, its primary key (place_id) is inserted into place2photo with the photo's primary key (photo_id).

10 Save db_insert_photos.php, and test the form in insert_photos.php. If you select a photo that has already been uploaded, you should see a report that it has been renamed.

Insert Photos

Admin menu

- lasvegas1.jpg uploaded successfully and renamed lasvegas1_1.jpg

---

Check the files in cms/image_upload to verify that the original file and the renamed file are both there.

If you have any problems, compare your code with db_insert_photos_02.php in lesson10/completed/scripts.

Reviewing the project so far

This project has been a lot of work, and the CMS is still not complete. In the next lesson, you'll create the pages to list all places and photos, as well as to update and delete individual records. You might be wondering if this could have been created more easily using the dialog boxes of Dreamweaver's built-in server behaviors. The answer is no. It would involve extensive editing of the automatically generated code, resulting in considerably longer scripts. Dreamweaver does not have the built-in capability to upload files or to insert data into multiple tables.

Building a custom CMS requires a lot of planning, but it has the advantage that it does exactly what you want. Even if you eventually decide to adapt an existing CMS, such as Drupal, Joomla!, or WordPress, the experience gained by building a custom management system like this will give you a greater understanding of the underlying principles. In turn, that will make it easier to adapt an existing system to your own needs.

What You Have Learned

In this lesson, you have:

- Planned the CMS for a travel website (pages 345–346)

- Defined the structure for tables related through foreign keys (pages 346–348)

- Created forms and scripts to upload images and simultaneously insert related data into a database (pages 349–374)

- Built a server behavior to populate a `<select>` menu from a SQL query (pages 355–358)

- Used a `<select>` menu to insert a foreign key into a database table (pages 371–374)

What You Will Learn

In this lesson, you will:

- Study the basic syntax of SELECT queries

- Learn how to join tables with INNER JOIN and LEFT JOIN

- Use Zend_Paginator to display database results over several pages

- Create a server behavior for Zend_Paginator

- Update and delete data stored in multiple tables

Approximate Time

This lesson takes approximately 3 hours to complete.

Lesson Files

Media Files:

Same as Lesson 10

Starting Files:

lesson11/start/delete_photo.php
lesson11/start/delete_place.php
lesson11/start/list_photos.php
lesson11/start/list_places.php
lesson11/start/update_photo.php
lesson11/start/update_place.php

Completed Files:

lesson11/completed/delete_photo.php
lesson11/completed/delete_place.php
lesson11/completed/list_photos.php
lesson11/completed/list_places_01.php
lesson11/completed/list_places_02.php
lesson11/completed/update_photo.php
lesson11/completed/update_place_01.php

Dw

lesson11/completed/update_place_02.php
lesson11/completed/scripts/db_definitions_04.php
lesson11/completed/scripts/db_definitions_05.php
lesson11/completed/scripts/db_definitions_06.php
lesson11/completed/scripts/db_definitions_07.php
lesson11/completed/scripts/db_delete_place_01.php
lesson11/completed/scripts/db_delete_place_02.php
lesson11/completed/scripts/db_update_photo_01.php
lesson11/completed/scripts/db_update_photo_02.php
lesson11/completed/scripts/db_update_place_01.php
lesson11/completed/scripts/db_update_place_02.php
lesson11/completed/scripts/library.php

Updating and Deleting Files in Related Tables

In this lesson, you'll complete the multiple-table CMS from Lesson 10. To update records, you need to select the data stored in related tables and display it in a form ready for editing. When the form is submitted, the data must be validated again before the database can be updated. Fortunately, you can reuse many of the functions defined for the insert forms in the previous lesson. You'll also use `Zend_Paginator` to display database results over several pages.

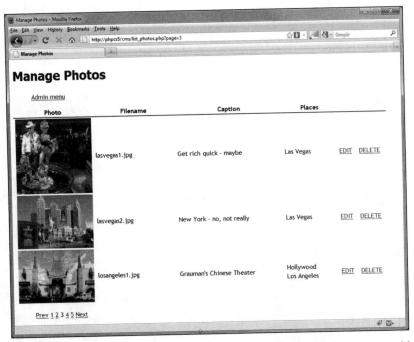

The photo management page draws data from the file system and three separate tables.

Selecting Records with SQL

Now that you have records stored in multiple tables, it's necessary to take a more detailed look at how to select records. The basic syntax of a SELECT query looks like this:

```
SELECT column(s)
FROM table(s)
WHERE condition
ORDER BY column(s)
```

SQL keywords are case insensitive, but the normal convention is to type them in uppercase to make them easier to identify. Splitting the query over several lines is also only a convention, but it enhances readability and maintenance.

The WHERE and ORDER BY clauses are optional. In fact, there are several other options that have been omitted here for the sake of simplicity.

Selecting all records in a table

To retrieve all records in the places table, the SELECT query looks like this:

```
SELECT * FROM places
```

This selects every record in every column of the places table. Unless you really need every column, it's better to specify the columns you want by listing them separated by commas. For example,

```
SELECT place_id, name, description
FROM places
```

This selects the named columns from all records in the places table.

Specifying search criteria with WHERE

Adding a WHERE clause narrows down the results, usually by specifying a value to match or a comparison. For example,

```
SELECT place_id, name, description
FROM places
WHERE name = 'San Francisco'
```

This retrieves the place_id, name, and description fields for the record that has San Francisco as the value in the name column.

> ✱ **NOTE:** Unlike PHP, SQL uses a single equals sign to test for equality.

You can specify multiple conditions in a WHERE clause by separating the conditions with the keywords AND and OR. For example,

```
SELECT place_id, name, description
FROM places
WHERE name = 'San Francisco' OR created >= '2010-01-01'
```

This retrieves San Francisco *and* all records created since January 1, 2010. If you use AND, it finds San Francisco only if the record was created on that date or later.

Specifying the sort order

By default, a SELECT query returns the results in the same order as they are stored in the database. Initially, this is the same order as the data was inserted but is likely to change as records are updated or deleted. To specify the order of results, add an ORDER BY clause, listing the column(s) that determine the order. You can specify a column, even if it's not included in the SELECT part of the query. For several columns to affect the order, add them as a comma-separated list in order of precedence like this:

```
SELECT place_id, name, description
FROM places
ORDER BY created, name
```

This retrieves the three named columns with the results sorted chronologically by their date of creation. Any records that were created at the same time are sorted alphabetically by the name column.

> **✳ NOTE:** In this example, the name column has no effect, because the created column stores both date and time. In Lesson 12 you'll see how to extract date parts from a DATE or TIMESTAMP column.

By default, the sort order is ascending—in other words, alphabetical, smallest to largest, or oldest to most recent. To sort in reverse (descending) order, add the keyword DESC after the column name like this:

```
SELECT place_id, name, description
FROM places
ORDER BY created DESC, name
```

This sorts the results with the newest record first.

You can use ORDER BY without specifying a WHERE clause. However, if you include a WHERE clause, it must come *before* ORDER BY like this:

```
SELECT place_id, name, description
FROM places
WHERE created >= '2010-01-01'
ORDER BY created DESC
```

If you put the WHERE clause *after* ORDER BY, the database rejects the query.

Joining tables

When data is stored in separate tables, you retrieve related data by joining the tables on the fly. You list the names of the columns after the SELECT keyword and perform the join(s) in the FROM clause. Where columns share a common name, you must prefix the column name with the table name separated by a period. For example, you distinguish between the state_id columns as states.state_id and places.state_id.

The most common type of join is an INNER JOIN. Used on its own, it produces what's known as a *Cartesian join*—every possible combination of rows from both tables. This is rarely practical, so you normally qualify the join by adding a condition, such as matching the foreign key of one table to the primary key of the other table using an ON clause. This is how you join the places and states tables to get the state name associated with each place:

```
SELECT name, state_name
FROM places
INNER JOIN states ON places.state_id = states.state_id
```

The result looks like this:

The values stored in places.state_id are the USPS abbreviations for the states, but using INNER JOIN to match states.state_id allows you to retrieve the value of state_name for each record in the places table.

An alternative syntax is to use WHERE instead of ON:

```
SELECT name, state_name
FROM places
INNER JOIN states WHERE places.state_id = states.state_id
```

Although a WHERE clause can be used to specify the condition for joining tables, it's recommended to use ON. Use WHERE to restrict which rows you want in the result set.

> ✱ **NOTE:** MySQL also permits you to replace INNER JOIN by a comma when using WHERE to specify the condition. However, this syntax sometimes causes errors and is not recommended in MySQL 5.0 or later.

When the same name is used in both tables, you can use this syntax:

```
SELECT name, state_name
FROM places
INNER JOIN states USING (state_id)
```

Using a LEFT JOIN to find missing values

Let's say that California has been accidentally deleted from the states table. Using INNER JOIN on the same data produces this result:

name	state_name
Bryce Canyon	Utah
Grand Canyon	Arizona
Las Vegas	Nevada

INNER JOIN works only when there are matching rows in both tables. To find all places, even if there isn't a matching value in the states table, use a LEFT JOIN. The syntax is the same:

```
SELECT name, state_name
FROM places
LEFT JOIN states USING (state_id)
```

Changing INNER JOIN to LEFT JOIN produces the following result:

name	state_name
Joshua Tree National Park	NULL
Los Angeles	NULL
Bryce Canyon	Utah
Hollywood	NULL
San Francisco	NULL
Grand Canyon	Arizona
Long Beach	NULL
Las Vegas	Nevada

You might have some records in the database that don't have any photos associated with them. Using INNER JOIN would omit places without photos. Using LEFT JOIN gets all places, even if they don't have photos.

In a LEFT JOIN, all records are found in the table on the left, even if there's no match in the table on the right. Left and right refer to the order in which the tables are listed in the SELECT query. In this example, places comes before the keywords LEFT JOIN, so it's on the left. The states table comes after the keywords, so it's on the right. As a result, the query retrieves all records from the places table and uses NULL as the value in the states table where there's no match.

Using the Zend_Db select() method

You have already used the insert(), update(), and delete() methods, so you would be right to assume there's also a select() method. Most of the time, it's more convenient to create your own SELECT query and pass it to fetchRow() or fetchAll(). One case where it makes sense to use the select() method is with Zend_Paginator, which automatically paginates through a set of database results. Zend_Paginator works in combination with the select() method to retrieve the exact number of rows from the table for the current page, which is more efficient than retrieving all records and discarding those that aren't displayed.

The instructions in this lesson for pages that use Zend_Paginator show the basic use of the select() method. For full details of the many other options, see http://framework.zend.com/manual/en/zend.db.select.html.

Completing the CMS

Before building the remaining pages of the CMS, add about four or five more records to the places table. The images folder contains photos of 10 locations in Arizona, California, Nevada, and Utah. Captions are optional, as are photos, but the description should be at least 10 characters. Don't worry about crafting perfect prose. All you need is dummy data to test the update and delete scripts.

Using Zend_Paginator to page through database results

The Zend_Paginator component is the equivalent of Dreamweaver's Recordset Navigation Bar, which lets you page through a set of database results. It involves a little more work than Dreamweaver's built-in solution, but it's more versatile, and you can convert it into a custom server behavior.

You use the component by passing an array or a Zend_Db_Select object to the static factory() method like this:

```
$paginator = Zend_Paginator::factory($places);
```

To display the appropriate records, the component needs to know the current page. The navigation links pass the selected value through a query string. So, if you use page as the variable in the query string, you set the current page with the setCurrentPageNumber() method like this:

```
if (isset($_GET['page'])) {
    $paginator->setCurrentPageNumber($_GET['page']);
}
```

If page isn't in the $_GET array, the paginator defaults to the first set of results.

By default, the component sets the number of items to display to 10. The number of navigation links also defaults to 10. To change either number, use the setItemCountPerPage() and setPageRange() methods. For example:

```
$paginator->setItemCountPerPage(5);
$paginator->setPageRange(6);
```

This displays five items per page and sets the maximum number of navigation links to six.

To display the items, use a foreach loop. Let's say your database result is in $places. Pass it to Zend_Paginator::factory() and use the paginator in the loop:

```
$paginator = Zend_Paginator::factory($places);
foreach ($paginator as $row) {
  // display $row['column_name']
}
```

Zend_Paginator does all the necessary calculations and displays the appropriate section of the database result.

You build the navigation links by getting an array of pages in the current range with the getPages() method, which optionally takes as an argument a string specifying how the links should be displayed. There are four options:

- **All.** All pages are included.
- **Elastic.** The range expands and contracts as the user moves through the links.
- **Jumping.** The page numbers remain fixed until the user reaches the end of the current range. Then the page numbers start at the beginning of the next range. For example, if the range is set at 5, links for pages 1–5 are displayed until the user clicks Next on page 5, triggering the display of links to pages 6–10.
- **Sliding.** The current page number is always displayed at the center of the range with numbers added or removed at each end, depending on which direction the user selects. This is the default.

Links to specific pages are created by using the paginator's properties, which are listed in **Table 11.1**.

Property	Description
Table 11.1	Zend_Paginator Properties
first	First page number (i.e., 1)
last	Last page number
next	Next page number
current	Current page number
previous	Previous page number
firstItemNumber	Number within the whole series of the first item on the current page
lastItemNumber	Number within the whole series of the last item on the current page
pagesInRange	Array of page numbers in the current range
firstPageInRange	Number of first page in the current range
lastPageInRange	Number of last page in the current range
currentItemCount	Number of items on the current page
itemCountPerPage	Number of items on each page
pageCount	Total number of pages
totalItemCount	Total number of items

You'll learn how to build the navigation links in the next section.

Creating a management page for the places table

Updating and deleting records first involves displaying them as a list and then creating links to the update and delete pages. These instructions explain how to create a page to list all records in the places table. Although you have only a handful of records at the moment, you'll add an instance of Zend_Paginator to navigate through them.

1 To make sure you have the appropriate pages to link to, copy the following files from lesson11/start to the cms folder you created in Lesson 10:

- delete_photo.php
- delete_place.php
- list_photos.php

- list_places.php

- update_photo.php

- update_place.php

If Dreamweaver prompts you to update the links, click Don't Update.

2 Open your copy of list_places.php. It contains a two-row table with EDIT and DELETE in the last two cells of the second row. These will be used to create links to the edit and delete scripts.

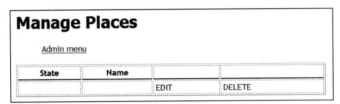

3 The only external file you need for this page is scripts/library.php. Use require_once to include it above the DOCTYPE declaration.

4 To build the page, you need to select the place's primary key, its name, and the state's name from the database. This involves joining the places and states tables like this:

```
SELECT place_id, name, state_name
FROM places
INNER JOIN states USING (state_id)
ORDER BY state_name, name
```

Although you could use this SQL with fetchAll() and pass the resulting array to Zend_Paginator, it's a waste of resources to retrieve all records every time. For a small number of records it might not matter, but as your database grows it becomes increasingly inefficient. Instead, you need to use the select() method to build the same query. Add the following code in the PHP block above the DOCTYPE declaration:

```
<?php
require_once('scripts/library.php');
try {
  $places = $dbRead->select()
                  ->from('places', array('place_id', 'name'))
                  ->joinUsing('states', 'state_id', array('state_name'))
                  ->order(array('state_name', 'name'));
?>
```

You'll add the closing brace of the try block at the foot of the page in a moment. First, just concentrate on the way the select() method builds the same query by chaining three other methods:

- The from() method takes two arguments: the name of the table and an array of column names that you want from the table.

- The joinUsing() method takes three arguments: the table you want to join, the name of the column that acts as the join condition, and an array of columns you want from the table.

- The order() method takes one argument: an array of the columns that determine the sort order.

This is more complex than the equivalent SQL, but it's worth using here to avoid fetching a full database result each time a page link is clicked.

5 Scroll to the bottom of the page, and add a PHP block below the closing </html> tag to end the try block and add a catch block:

```
</html>
<?php
} catch (Exception $e) {
   echo $e->getMessage();
}
?>
```

6 Scroll back to the top of the page, and add the code for the paginator inside the first PHP block:

```
$paginator = Zend_Paginator::factory($places);
if (isset($_GET['page'])) {
   $paginator->setCurrentPageNumber($_GET['page']);
}
$paginator->setItemCountPerPage(2);
$paginator->setPageRange(3);
```

This passes $places to the Zend_Paginator static factory() method and sets the paginator's basic settings. The number of items per page is deliberately low to show how the paginator works. As long as you have at least three records in the places table, it will display the results across multiple pages.

7 Wrap the second table row in a foreach loop, assigning $paginator to the temporary variable $row, and use echo to display the values of the state_name and name columns in the first two table cells like this:

```
<?php foreach ($paginator as $row) { // paginator repeat region ?>
<tr>
  <td><?php echo $row['state_name']; ?></td>
  <td><?php echo $row['name']; ?></td>
  <td>EDIT</td>
  <td>DELETE</td>
</tr>
<?php } // end of paginator repeat region ?>
```

▶ **TIP:** When using echo to insert a brief snippet of code in HTML, use the echo icon [echo] in the PHP category of the Insert panel/bar.

Although $paginator is an object that contains a database result, you can loop through it with foreach as if it were an ordinary array.

When adding this foreach loop, use the same comments as shown here. They're designed to help Dreamweaver recognize the code when you later convert it into a server behavior.

8 Save list_places.php, and click Live View to test your code so far. Depending on what's in your database, your page should look similar to this:

State	Name		
Arizona	Grand Canyon	EDIT	DELETE
California	Hollywood	EDIT	DELETE

You can compare your code with list_places_01.php in lesson11/completed.

9 Exit Live View, and select the EDIT text in the third cell. Create a link to update_place.php. Select the DELETE text, and create a link to delete_place.php.

10 You need to add a query string to each link. Click in Code view to position the insertion point before the closing quotation mark of the href attribute, and type **?place_id=**. Then use the echo icon to add **$row['place_id']**. The EDIT link should look like this:

```
<a href="update_place.php?place_id=<?php echo $row['place_id']; ?>">
➥ EDIT</a>
```

Do the same for the DELETE link.

11 Add a paragraph between the closing </table> and </body> tags, and create the navigation links for the paginator like this:

```
<p>
<?php
$pages = $paginator->getPages('Elastic');
if (isset($pages->previous)) {
  echo '<a href="' . $_SERVER['PHP_SELF'] . '?page=' . $pages->previous .
  ➥ '">Prev</a>';
```

```
}
foreach ($pages->pagesInRange as $page) {
  if ($page != $pages->current) {
    echo " <a href='" . $_SERVER['PHP_SELF'] . "?page={$page}'>$page</a>";
  } else {
    echo ' ' . $page;
  }
}
if (isset($pages->next)) {
  echo ' <a href="' . $_SERVER['PHP_SELF'] . '?page=' . $pages->next .
  ➥ '">Next</a>';
}
?>
</p>
```

The first line of code inside the PHP block uses the getPages() method to get an array of the pages needed to display the other database results and selects the Elastic scrolling method. The array is stored as $pages.

The next line checks whether $pages has a previous property (see Table 11.1). If it does, a link to the previous page is created. The link is built from $_SERVER['PHP_SELF'], which contains the URL of the current page, followed by a query string that uses the previous property to insert the correct page number. For example, if the current page is the third in the navigation sequence, it creates a link to page 2. If the current page is the first in the sequence, no link is created.

The center section of links is created by a foreach loop that uses the array stored in the pagesInRange property and assigns each element temporarily to $page. Inside the loop, a link is created for each page in the range except the current one. The current page number is displayed as plain text.

The final section of the code checks the next property and creates a text link to it if necessary.

▼ **CAUTION!** When copying this code, pay careful attention to the mixture of single and double quotation marks. Also, note that the strings include a space before each link except the first one.

12 Save the page, and click Live View to test it. You should see a set of navigation links below the table. The number of links depends on how many records you inserted in the places table.

State	Name		
Arizona	Grand Canyon	EDIT	DELETE
California	Hollywood	EDIT	DELETE
1 2 3 Next			

13 Hold down Ctrl/Cmd and click the Next link. You should be taken to the second set of results, and a Prev link should appear at the start of the row.

State	Name		
California	Joshua Tree National Park	EDIT	DELETE
California	San Francisco	EDIT	DELETE
Prev 1 2 3 Next			

You can compare your code with list_places_02.php in lesson11/completed.

Converting the paginator into a server behavior

Zend_Paginator involves code in different parts of the page, but that's not a barrier to converting it to a server behavior. This is how you do it:

1 Exit Live View, if necessary, and copy the PHP code from step 11 in the previous section to a plain text editor. You need to paste two sections of code into the Server Behavior Builder dialog box, so it's more convenient to have the second section saved temporarily outside Dreamweaver.

2 Copy to your clipboard the code from step 6 in the previous section, click the plus button in the Server Behaviors panel, and choose New Server Behavior.

3 In the New Server Behavior dialog box, type **Zend Paginator** in the Name field, and click OK.

4 Click the plus button next to "Code blocks to insert," and click OK to accept the suggested name.

5 Paste the code from step 6 of the previous section into the "Code block" text area, and amend it to convert some of the original values to server behavior parameters. The edited code should look like this:

```php
<?php
$paginator = Zend_Paginator::factory(@@Result@@);
if (isset($_GET['page'])) {
    $paginator->setCurrentPageNumber($_GET['page']);
}
$paginator->setItemCountPerPage(@@Items Per Page@@);
$paginator->setPageRange(@@Pages in Range@@);
?>
```

6 Leave the "Insert code" and "Relative position" menus at their default settings.

7 Click the plus button next to "Code blocks to insert," and click OK to accept the suggested name.

8 Replace the placeholder text in the "Code block" text area with the following:

```php
<?php foreach($paginator as $row) { // paginator repeat region ?>
```

9 Set the "Insert code" menu to Relative to the Selection and the "Relative position" menu to Before the Selection.

10 Click the plus button to insert another code block.

11 Replace the placeholder text in the "Code block" text area with a closing curly brace and inline comment:

```php
<?php } // end of paginator repeat region ?>
```

✱ **NOTE:** The comments after the curly braces in steps 8 and 11 are essential to prevent Dreamweaver from mistaking other loops as part of this server behavior. If you omit them, Dreamweaver incorrectly lists Zend Paginator in the Server Behaviors panel on any page that uses a closing curly brace on its own.

12 Set the "Insert code" menu to Relative to the Selection and the "Relative position" menu to After the Selection.

13 Click the plus button to create a fourth code block, and paste the code from step 11 of the previous section into the "Code block" text area. Edit the value in the getPages() method to convert it into a server behavior parameter:

```php
$pages = $paginator->getPages('@@Scroll Type@@');
```

The rest of the code is fine as it is. Make sure the placeholder text has been deleted and that the code block has opening and closing PHP tags.

14 Use the following settings for the options at the bottom of the Server Behavior Builder dialog box:

- **Insert code.** Relative to a Specific Tag
- **Tag.** p
- **Relative position.** After the Opening Tag

15 Click Next, and use the up and down arrows to reorder the parameters like this:

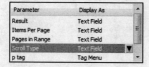

16 Click OK to save the new server behavior.

Creating a management page for the photos table

The page to list photos and links to the update and delete pages utilizes the new Zend Paginator server behavior and is very similar to list_places.php.

1 Open your copy of list_photos.php and include scripts/library.php above the DOCTYPE declaration with require_once().

2 This page needs to select all columns from the photos table and order the results by the filename column. This makes using the select() method much simpler than in list_places.php. Add the following code to the PHP block:

```
try {
    $photos = $dbRead->select()->from('photos')->order('filename');
```

Not specifying any columns in the from() method retrieves all columns.

3 Scroll to the bottom of the page, and add the closing brace of the try block and the catch block below the closing </html> tag:

```
</html>
<?php
} catch (Exception $e) {
    echo $e->getMessage();
}
?>
```

4 In Design view, put the insertion point in the second table row, and click <tr> in the Tag selector at the bottom of the Document window to select the whole row.

5 Click the plus button in the Server Behaviors panel, and choose Zend Paginator. Use the following settings in the Zend Paginator dialog box:

The page contains a paragraph that has an id attribute of paginator below the table. This makes it easy to select the correct <p> tag in the Zend Paginator dialog box. You could also use the ID to create a special style rule for the paginator links.

6 Click OK to close the Zend Paginator dialog box, and switch to Code view. You'll see that Dreamweaver has put the first block of code for the paginator right at the top of the page. Move the original block of PHP code above the paginator code:

```php
<?php
require_once('scripts/library.php');
try {
  $photos = $dbRead->select()->from('photos')->order('filename');
?>
<?php
$paginator = Zend_Paginator::factory($photos);
if (isset($_GET['page'])) {
  $paginator->setCurrentPageNumber($_GET['page']);
}
$paginator->setItemCountPerPage(3);
$paginator->setPageRange(5);
?>
```

7 In Design view, click in the first cell of the second table row, and choose Insert > Image to open the Select Image Source dialog box. Navigate to the image_upload folder, and select any image. Click OK (Choose on a Mac).

8 In the Image Tag Accessibility Attributes dialog box, set the "Alternate text" menu to <empty>, and click OK to insert the image in the table cell.

9 With the image still selected in Design view, change the value in the W field in the Property inspector to **200**, and press Tab to switch the focus to the H field. Press Delete to remove the value, and press Enter/Return to confirm.

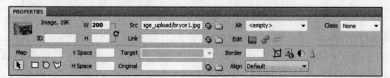

This sets the width attribute of the <img> tag to 200 pixels and removes the height attribute.

10 Switch to Code view, and delete the filename in the <img> tag. Replace it with a PHP block that uses echo to display the value of the filename column from the database result:

```php
<img src="image_upload/<?php echo $row['filename']; ?>" width="200" alt=""
➥ />
```

11 Use a PHP block with `echo` to display the values of the filename and caption columns in the next two table cells:

```
<td><?php echo $row['filename']; ?></td>
<td><?php echo $row['caption']; ?></td>
```

12 At the moment, a photo can be related with only one place, but update_photos.php lets you associate photos with multiple places. So, the next cell needs a `SELECT` query of its own to retrieve all the places a photo is related to.

Scroll to the top of the page and include scripts/db_definitions.php using `require_once()` inside the try block:

```
try {
    $photos = $dbRead->select()->from('photos')->order('filename');
    require_once('scripts/db_definitions.php');
```

13 Switch to db_definitions.php, and add the following function definition:

```
function getRelatedPlaceNames($read, $photo_id) {
    $sql = "SELECT name
            FROM places
            INNER JOIN place2photo USING (place_id)
            WHERE photo_id = $photo_id
            ORDER BY name";
    $result = $read->fetchAll($sql);
    $places = array();
    foreach ($result as $row) {
        $places[] = $row['name'];
    }
    return $places;
}
```

This function takes two arguments: a `Zend_Db` object with read permission and the primary key of a photo.

The `SELECT` query inside the function selects the `name` column from the `places` table using an `INNER JOIN` with the `place2photo` cross-reference table, matching records on `place_id`. This matches all photos to their related places. However, you want to show the related places only for the current photo, so the `WHERE` clause limits the search to a single photo.

The `foreach` loop creates an array of place names, which is returned by the function.

14 Switch back to list_photos.php in Code view, and add the following code to the fourth table cell in the second row:

```
<td><?php $places = getRelatedPlaceNames($dbRead, $row['photo_id']);
    echo implode('<br />', $places); ?></td>
```

This uses the function you just created and stores the result in $places, which is then passed to implode(). $places is an array, so implode() joins the array parts (if any) with <br />, effectively displaying each place on a separate line.

15 Select the EDIT and DELETE text in the last two cells, and create links to update_photo. php and delete_photo.php respectively. Use the same technique as in steps 9 and 10 of "Creating a management page for the places table" to add a query string to each link, using **photo_id** as the variable and setting its value to **$row['photo_id']**. The EDIT link should look like this:

```
<a href="update_photo.php?photo_id=<?php echo $row['photo_id'];?>">
➥ EDIT</a>
```

16 Save the page, and test it. You should see three photos per page, resized to 200-pixel width, but remaining proportional because the height attribute has been removed. Each photo is accompanied by its filename, caption (if any), associated place(s), and links to the update and delete scripts. There are also navigation links to display other photos in the series.

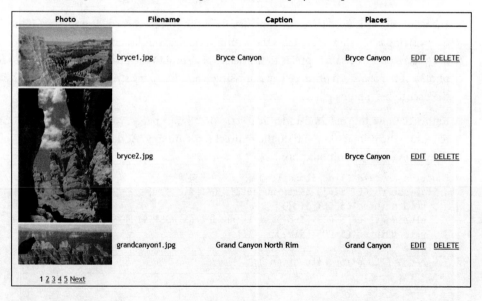

Photo	Filename	Caption	Places		
	bryce1.jpg	Bryce Canyon	Bryce Canyon	EDIT	DELETE
	bryce2.jpg		Bryce Canyon	EDIT	DELETE
	grandcanyon1.jpg	Grand Canyon North Rim	Grand Canyon	EDIT	DELETE

1 2 3 4 5 Next

You can compare your code with lesson11/completed/list_photos.php and lesson11/completed/scripts/db_definitions_04.php.

Updating records in the places table

Now that you can list the places and photos stored in the database, you can create the scripts to update and delete them.

The update form for the places table contains fields to edit the name, state_id, description, and link_name columns. Unlike the insert form, it does not allow you to add new photos. Instead, it displays details of related photos, and links directly to the update and delete pages for each photo.

1 In update_place.php, include scripts/db_update_place.php above the DOCTYPE declaration using require_once(). You should have created a copy of this file in the cms/scripts folder in the previous lesson.

2 When the EDIT link is clicked in list_places.php, the query string passes the primary key of the record you want to update like this:

http://phpcs5/cms/update_place.php?place_id=2

The primary key is used to retrieve the details of the correct record for updating. If the query string is missing or contains the wrong variable, you should redirect the user to list_places.php. The same applies to the delete page and to the update and delete pages for photos; if the photo_id primary key is missing from the query string, you should redirect the user to list_photos.php.

Rather than writing an almost identical script in all four pages, you can create a function to extract the primary key and do the redirect if it's missing. Add the following function definition to db_definitions.php:

```
function checkId ($id, $location) {
  if (isset($_GET[$id]) && is_numeric($_GET[$id])) {
    return intval($_GET[$id]);
  } elseif (isset($_POST[$id]) && is_numeric($_POST[$id])) {
    return intval($_POST[$id]);
  } else {
    header("Location: $location");
    exit;
  }
}
```

The checkId() function takes two arguments: the primary key that you want to extract from the query string (place_id or photo_id) and the page to which the user should be redirected if there's a problem.

When the update page is first loaded, the primary key should be in the query string. So, the first conditional statement checks the $_GET array for $_GET['place_id'] or

$_GET['photo_id']. If it exists, is_numeric() tests that it represents a number. If it passes both tests, the value is passed to intval() to convert it to an integer, and the result is returned by the function.

✱ NOTE: Using both is_numeric() and intval() ensures that only a whole number is passed to the script. PHP has a function called is_int() that tests whether a value is an integer. However, values passed through the $_GET and $_POST arrays are always strings. The is_int() function tests not only the value, but also the data type, so it won't work here.

If the first conditional statement fails, the elseif clause performs the same tests on the $_POST array and returns the value as an integer. If that fails, the header() function redirects the user, and exit brings the script to an end.

3 Save db_definitions.php, and use the new checkId() function to assign the place_id primary key to a variable in db_update_place.php like this:

```
try {
  require_once('db_definitions.php');
  $place_id = checkId('place_id', 'list_places.php');
} catch (Exception $e) {
```

This passes the name of the primary key as the first argument and the redirect page as the second argument.

4 Save db_update_place.php, and try to load it into a browser. You should be redirected to list_places.php.

Manage Places

Admin menu

State	Name		
Arizona	Grand Canyon	EDIT	DELETE
California	Hollywood	EDIT	DELETE

1 2 3 Next

5 The update page needs to display the details of the record in the places table that you want to update. Create a function in db_definitions.php to execute a SELECT query and return the result as an array. The code looks like this:

```
function getPlace($read, $place_id) {
  $sql = "SELECT name, places.state_id, state_name, description, link_name
          FROM places
          INNER JOIN states USING (state_id)
          WHERE place_id = $place_id";
  return $read->fetchRow($sql);
}
```

The function takes two arguments: a Zend_Db object with read permission and the primary key of the record you want to fetch.

In the SELECT query, you need to qualify state_id in the list of columns as places.state_id to avoid a conflict with states.state_id, because the same column name is used in both tables. It's safe to inject $place_id directly into the query without using quoteInto(), because the checkId() function that you created in step 3 ensures that it's an integer. You don't need state_name for the update form, but it will be used by the delete form.

Only a single record will be selected, so the final line uses fetchRow(), which returns an associative array using the column names as the array keys.

6 To display photos related with the place, you need a SELECT query that joins the photos table with the cross-reference table, place2photo. Add this function to db_definitions.php:

```
function getRelatedPhotos($read, $place_id) {
  $sql = "SELECT photos.photo_id, filename, caption
          FROM photos
          INNER JOIN place2photo USING (photo_id)
          WHERE place_id = $place_id";
  return $read->fetchAll($sql);
}
```

7 Save db_definitions.php, and switch to db_update_place.php. To populate the update page, you need the details of the selected record, a complete list of all states (for the <select> menu), and the related photos. Add the following three lines inside the try block:

```
try {
  require_once('db_definitions.php');
  $place_id = checkId('place_id', 'list_places.php');
  $place = getPlace($dbRead, $place_id);
  $states = getAllStates($dbRead);
  $photos = getRelatedPhotos($dbRead, $place_id);
} catch (Exception $e) {
```

This uses the two functions you just created, plus getAllStates(), which was created in Lesson 10 for insert_place.php.

8 After updating the record, you should send users back to the page from which they started. Returning them to list_places.php puts them back at page 1, which is annoying for someone who started from deep in the list.

The superglobal variable $_SERVER['HTTP_REFERER'] stores the URL of the referring page. Unfortunately, it's not supported by all servers, so you need to check for its existence and set a default value as well. Add this code within the try block immediately after the code you just inserted:

```php
if (isset($_SERVER['HTTP_REFERER'])) {
    $returnto = $_SERVER['HTTP_REFERER'];
} else {
    $returnto = 'list_places.php';
}
```

✳ NOTE: HTTP_REFERER is correct. Don't add an extra R.

9 Save db_update_place.php, and switch to update_place.php.

Set the action attribute in the opening `<form>` tag to use `$_SERVER['PHP_SELF']`. As you learned in Lesson 8, this strips from the URL the query string, which is not needed when the form is submitted:

```php
<form action="<?php echo $_SERVER['PHP_SELF']; ?>" method="post"
➥ name="form1" id="form1">
```

10 Start adding the code to populate the form with the details of the record, which are stored in the $place and $photos arrays.

The text fields and text area in the form can be populated by using echo to display $place['name'], $place['description'], and $place['link_field']. However, if the updates fail validation, you need to preserve any changes the user has made. Edit the name text input field like this:

```php
<input type="text" name="name" id="name" value="<?php if (!$errors) {
    echo $place['name'];
} else {
    echo $_POST['name'];
}?>" />
```

When the page first loads, the $errors array is empty, so the conditional statement uses the database result, $place['name']. If the user makes a mistake when submitting the form, $errors equates to TRUE, and $_POST['name'] is displayed instead, preserving any edits.

11 Edit the value attribute of the link_name text input field in the same way, using link_name as the array key.

12 There is no value attribute in a `<textarea>` tag, so add the same PHP block between the opening and closing tags using description as the array key.

13 It's a good idea to check that your code is working so far. Save update_place.php, and load list_places.php in Live View. Hold down Ctrl/Cmd and click one of the EDIT links. The "Place name," Description, and "Link name" fields should be populated with values from the database.

```
Update Place

    Admin menu
    Place name
    Grand Canyon

    State:
    [  ÷ ]

    Description:
    A jaw-dropping experience.



    Link name:
    GrandCanyon

    [ Update Place ]
```

If you encounter problems, compare your code with update_place_01.php, scripts/db_update_place_01.php, and scripts/db_definitions_05.php in lesson11/completed.

14 Exit Live View, and select the State <select> menu in Design view. Click the plus button in the Server Behaviors panel, and choose Zend Select Menu. Use the following settings in the Zend Select Menu dialog box, and click OK:

- **Array Variable.** $states
- **Value.** state_id
- **Display.** state_name
- **Menu Name.** state_id
- **select tag.** "state_id" in "form1"

15 The code inserted by the server behavior redisplays the selected value if a mistake is made when the form is submitted, but it doesn't select the value already stored in the database. So, edit the code like this:

```php
<?php
foreach ($states as $row) {
  echo "<option value='{$row['state_id']}'";
  if ($errors && $row['state_id'] == $_POST['state_id']) {
    echo 'selected="selected"';
  } elseif (!$errors && $row['state_id'] == $place['state_id']) {
    echo 'selected="selected"';
  }
  echo ">{$row['state_name']}</option>";
}
?>
```

> **TIP:** This change results in Dreamweaver removing Zend Select Menu from the list of server behaviors applied to the page. You could adapt this code to create a new server behavior if you want the ability to control it through a dialog box. You should have sufficient practice in creating server behaviors by now to know how to do it.

16 In Design view, click to the right of the submit button, and choose Insert > Form > Hidden Field. In the Property inspector, change the name to **returnto**, and type **<?php echo $returnto; ?>** in the Value field.

This stores the URL of the page to which the user should be redirected.

17 Insert a second hidden field, set its name to **place_id**, and type **<?php echo $place_id; ?>** in the Value field. This stores the primary key of the record to be updated.

18 At the bottom of the page is a table that will display the photos related to this record. Details of the photos were retrieved by getRelatedPhotos() and stored in $photos. Wrap the <tr> tags of the table row in a foreach loop, assigning $photos to $photo as the temporary variable. Check the finished code in step 21 if you're unsure how the code should look.

19 In Design view, position your insertion point in the first cell, and insert an image from the image_upload folder. Use the same technique as in steps 7–10 of "Creating a management page for the photos table" to turn this into a dynamic image using $photo['filename'] as the variable.

20 In the second cell, use echo to display $photo['caption'].

21 Convert the EDIT and DELETE text into links pointing to update_photo.php and delete_photo.php respectively, and add a query string that assigns $photo['photo_id'] to the variable photo_id. This is the same technique used in both list_places.php and list_photos.php.

After you have finished steps 18–21, the table row should look like this:

```
</colgroup>
<?php foreach ($photos as $photo) { ?>
  <tr>
    <td><img src="image_upload/<?php echo $photo['filename']; ?>"
    ➥ width="200" alt="" /></td>
    <td><?php echo $photo['caption']; ?></td>
    <td><a href="update_photo.php?photo_id=<?php echo $photo['photo_id'];
    ➥ ?>">EDIT</a></td>
    <td><a href="delete_photo.php?photo_id=<?php echo $photo['photo_id'];
    ➥ ?>">DELETE</a></td>
  </tr>
<?php } ?>
</table>
```

22 Save update_place.php, and test it again by clicking an EDIT link from list_places.php. All fields should be populated by values drawn from the database, and all related photos should be displayed at the bottom of the page with their captions and links to update_ photo.php and delete_photo.php, as shown in the following screen shot.

This completes the coding of the update form. If necessary, compare your code with update_place_02.php in lesson11/completed.

23 Displaying the existing record in the update form is only half the story. You now need to add the code to validate and insert changes into the database. Switch to db_update_place. php, and insert the following code between the calls to checkId() and getAllStates():

```
$place_id = checkId('place_id', 'list_places.php');
if (isset($_POST['update_place'])) {
  validatePlaceName($_POST['name'], $errors);
  $val = new Zend_Validate_StringLength($descriptionMin, $descriptionMax);
  validateDescription($_POST['description'], $val, $errors);
  $val = new Zend_Validate_Alnum();
  if (!$val->isValid($_POST['link_name'])) {
    $errors['link_name'] = 'Link name must be alphanumeric characters
    ➥ only; no spaces';
  }
}
$states = getAllStates($dbRead);
```

This conditional statement precedes the code that populates the form because it will eventually redirect the user to another page if the update is successful, so there's no point in querying the database unnecessarily to get the old information again.

Inside the conditional statement, the three text fields are validated. This code should be familiar.

24 Before updating the record, you need to check that changes to the name and link_name fields don't clash with existing values in the database. You already have a function called checkPlacename() in db_definitions.php, but it won't work for the update form—at least not until you have amended it.

This is what the function definition looks like at the moment:

```
function checkDuplicatePlacename ($read, $name, &$errors) {
  $sql = $read->quoteInto('SELECT place_id FROM places WHERE name = ?',
  ➥ $name);
  $result = $read->fetchAll($sql);
  if ($result) {
    $errors['name'] = $_POST['name'] . ' is already listed';
  }
}
```

This function does the job perfectly when a record is first inserted into the places table. However, assuming the name isn't changed, the query always finds a match during the update process, *because the name is already listed*. The solution is to exclude the current place_id from the search.

Rather than creating a separate function, you can amend this one by adding a fourth argument and making it optional by assigning a default value in the function signature. Revise the function like this:

```
function checkDuplicatePlacename ($read, $name, &$errors, $place_id =
➥ NULL) {
  $sql = $read->quoteInto('SELECT place_id FROM places WHERE name = ?',
  ➥ $name);
  if ($place_id) {
    $sql .= " AND place_id <> $place_id";
  }
  $result = $read->fetchAll($sql);
  if ($result) {
    $errors['name'] = $_POST['name'] . ' is already listed';
  }
}
```

If the fourth argument is not supplied, $place_id is automatically set to NULL. A NULL value is treated as FALSE, so the function works exactly the same as before. However, if you pass a fourth argument to the function, $place_id takes the new value, and the conditional statement inside the function uses the combined concatenation operator to add a second condition to the WHERE clause. In SQL, the <> operator means "not equal to."

25 The function to check the link_name field uses a similar SELECT statement, but the fourth argument is not optional. Add this to db_definitions.php:

```
function checkLinkname($read, $link_name, &$errors, $place_id) {
  $sql = $read->quoteInto("SELECT place_id FROM places WHERE link_name =
  ➥ ? AND place_id <> $place_id", $link_name);
  $result = $read->fetchAll($sql);
  if ($result) {
    $errors['link_name'] = "$link_name is already listed";
  }
}
```

26 Add calls to both functions in db_update_place.php like this:

```
      $errors['link_name'] = 'Link name must be alphanumeric characters only;
      ➥ no spaces';
    }
    if (!$errors) {
      checkDuplicatePlacename($dbRead, $_POST['name'], $errors, $place_id);
      checkLinkname($dbRead, $_POST['link_name'], $errors, $place_id);
      if (!$errors) {
        // update the record and redirect
      }
    }
  }
$states = getAllStates($dbRead);
```

27 Add the code to update the record and redirect the page:

```
if (!$errors) {
  //update the record and redirect
  $data = array('name' => $_POST['name'],
                'state_id' => $_POST['state_id'],
                'description' => $_POST['description'],
                'link_name' => $_POST['link_name']);
  $dbWrite->update('places', $data, "place_id = $place_id");
  header('Location: ' . $_POST['returnto']);
  exit;
}
```

The update code is straightforward, so it needs little explanation. The created field is not updated, but MySQL updates the updated field automatically to the current date and time as long as at least one of the other fields is changed. If you submit the form without making any changes, the date and time in the updated field is not affected.

Finally, header() redirects the user to the URL stored in the hidden field.

28 Save db_update_place.php, and test the update form by selecting an EDIT link from list_places.php. Make some changes to the record, and click Update Place. You should be taken back to your original page. Click the same EDIT link to verify that the changes were registered in the database.

You can compare your code with db_definitions_06.php and db_update_place_02.php in lesson11/completed/scripts.

Deleting records from the places table

Deleting records is considerably simpler than updating them. Once you have confirmed the correct record has been selected, all that's necessary is to delete it from the table. A complicating factor with this CMS is that photos are related to places, and you might not always want to delete a photo when you delete a place. So, the delete form needs to make the deletion of related photos optional. The following instructions show how this is done:

1 Open your copy of delete_place.php, and use require_once() to include scripts/db_delete_place.php above the DOCTYPE declaration.

2 In db_delete_place.php, add the following code:

```
try {
  require_once('db_definitions.php');
  $place_id = checkId('place_id', 'list_places.php');
  if (isset($_POST['delete_place'])) {
    // delete and redirect
```

(code continues on next page)

```
  }  elseif (isset($_POST['cancel'])) {
    header('Location: ' . $_POST['returnto']);
    exit;
  }
  $place = getPlace($dbRead, $place_id);
  $photos = getRelatedPhotos($dbRead, $place_id);
  if (isset($_SERVER['HTTP_REFERER'])) {
    $returnto = $_SERVER['HTTP_REFERER'];
  } else {
    $returnto = 'list_places.php';
  }
} catch (Exception $e) {
```

This is very similar to the basic structure in db_update_place.php. The first line after db_definitions.php is included uses checkId() to get the primary key from the $_GET or $_POST array and redirects the user to list_places.php if the primary key is missing.

The first conditional statement sets the logic for which code to execute depending on whether the Delete Place or Cancel button was clicked. The remaining code gets the details of the place and related photos, as well as the referring page's URL.

3 Save db_delete_place.php, and switch to delete_place.php. Set the form's action attribute to **<?php echo $_SERVER['PHP_SELF']; ?>**.

4 Create two hidden fields in the form to store $place_id and $returnto (see steps 16 and 17 in the previous section).

5 Display the names of the place and state next to the labels in the text:

```
<p><strong>Place name:</strong> <?php echo $place['name']; ?></p>
<p><strong>State:</strong> <?php echo $place['state_name']; ?></p>
```

Both values come from the $place array created by getPlace().

6 The next section of the delete form needs to be displayed only if any related photos are found by getRelatedPhotos(). Add the start of a conditional statement on the next line:

```
<p><strong>State:</strong> <?php echo $place['state_name']; ?></p>
<?php if ($photos) { ?>
<p>The following photos are linked with this place.
```

7 Add the conditional statement's closing brace after the closing </table> tag.

```
</table>
<?php } ?>
```

8 The table row at the bottom of the page should be wrapped in a loop and display each related photo and caption, assigning its filename to the checkbox value. This doesn't involve any new techniques, so here is the code:

```
<table width="600">
<?php
$num = 0;
foreach ($photos as $photo) { ?>
  <tr>
    <td><input type="checkbox" name="photo[]" id="photo<?php echo $num;
    ➥ ?>" value="<?php echo $photo['filename']; ?>" />
      <label for="photo<?php echo $num++; ?>" class="checkbox_label">
      ➥ Delete photo</label></td>
    <td><img src="image_upload/<?php echo $photo['filename']; ?>"
    ➥ width="200" alt="" /><br /><?php echo $photo['caption']; ?></td>
  </tr>
<?php } ?>
</table>
<?php } ?>
```

9 Save delete_place.php, and test the code so far by clicking a DELETE link in list_places.php. You should see the names of the place and state displayed, together with related photos.

10 Click Cancel to return to the same page of list_places.php as you started from. If necessary, compare your code with delete_place.php and scripts/db_delete_place_01.php in lesson11/completed.

11 Now, add the script to delete the record and photos that have been selected:

```
if (isset($_POST['delete_place'])) {
  // delete and redirect
  $dbWrite->delete('places', "place_id = $place_id");
  $dbWrite->delete('place2photo', "place_id = $place_id");
  if (isset($_POST['photo'])) {
    foreach ($_POST['photo'] as $filename) {
      $dbWrite->delete('photos', "filename = '$filename'");
      unlink($destination . '/' . $filename);
    }
  }
  header('Location: ' . $_POST['returnto']);
  exit;
} elseif (isset($_POST['cancel'])) {
```

When you delete a record from the places table, you also need to remove all references to its primary key from the place2photo cross-reference table, even if you decide not to delete the photos. Failure to do so results in the cross-reference table trying to link to a place that no longer exists. Of course, you could be left with photos that are no longer related to records in the places table, but the page that updates photos allows you to associate a photo with more than one place. For example, Hollywood is in Los Angeles, so it makes sense to associate photos of Hollywood with both places. You might also want to use some generic photos associated with several places.

The form in delete_place.php has a checkbox for each photo. The name attribute, photo[], ends with an empty pair of square brackets, so it's treated as an array. As explained in Lesson 8, if no checkboxes are selected, the name isn't included in the $_POST array. However, if $_POST['photo'] exists, the foreach loop removes the record for each file from the photos table and then uses unlink() to delete the file from the image_upload folder.

Finally, header() redirects the user to the original referring page.

12 Save db_delete_place.php, and test the page's functionality by selecting a DELETE link from list_places.php. If necessary, compare your code with db_delete_place_02.php in lesson11/completed/scripts.

Updating records in the photos table

The options for updating the photos table are relatively simple. Each record consists of a primary key, the filename, and a caption. The primary key is also stored in the place2photo table to indicate which places (if any) the photo is associated with. There's no point allowing a user to change the filename. That should be done by deleting the record and uploading a different photo. So, the only options that remain are changing the caption and the places with which a photo is associated. To allow a photo to be associated with more than one place, the form uses a multiple-choice <select> list rather than a single-choice menu.

This is how the form handles the update process:

1 Open update_photo.php, and include scripts/db_update_photo.php using require_once() above the DOCTYPE declaration.

The page is designed to display the selected photo. Below it, the update form contains a text input field for the caption, a multiple-choice <select> list, a submit button, and two hidden fields: one for the primary key of the selected photo and the other to store the name of the referring page.

The code to display the selected photo and for all fields, except the multiple-choice <select> list, has been covered in previous sections and has already been added to the page. The only part you need to edit is the <select> list.

2 To populate the form with the details of the selected photo, you need to query the photos table. Add the following function to db_definitions.php:

```
function getPhotoDetails($read, $photo_id) {
  $sql = "SELECT filename, caption FROM photos WHERE photo_id =
  ➥ $photo_id";
  return $read->fetchRow($sql);
}
```

This is a simple SELECT query that gets the filename and caption fields for the selected photo. It takes two arguments: a Zend_Db object with read permission and the primary key of the selected photo.

3 The <select> list needs to display the names of all places associated with the selected photo. The getAllPlaces() function in db_definitions.php retrieves an array of all places. To match the places associated with the current photo, you also need to query the place2photo cross-reference table. Add the following function definition to db_definitions.php:

```
function getRelatedPlaces($read, $photo_id) {
  $sql = "SELECT place_id FROM place2photo WHERE photo_id = $photo_id";
  $result = $read->fetchAll($sql);
  $places = array();
  foreach ($result as $row) {
    $places[] = $row['place_id'];
  }
  return $places;
}
```

This takes the same arguments as the previous function and returns an array of the primary keys of places related to the selected photo by searching for matches in place2photo. The fetchAll() method returns a multidimensional array, so the foreach loop reduces the result to a simple array.

4 Save db_definitions.php, and switch to db_update_photo.php. Add the following code to gather the data for the update form:

```
try {
  require_once('db_definitions.php');
  $photo_id = checkId('photo_id', 'list_photos.php');
  if (isset($_POST['update_photo'])) {
    // update and redirect
  }
  $photo = getPhotoDetails($dbRead, $photo_id);
  $places = getAllPlaces($dbRead);
  $related = getRelatedPlaces($dbRead, $photo_id);
  if (isset($_SERVER['HTTP_REFERER'])) {
```

```
    $returnto = $_SERVER['HTTP_REFERER'];
  } else {
    $returnto = 'list_photos.php';
  }
} catch (Exception $e) {
```

This gets the primary key with the checkId() function. The details of the selected photo are retrieved by getPhotoDetails(), whereas getAllPlaces() and getRelatedPlaces() retrieve the information needed for the multiple-choice <select> list. As in the other update and delete scripts, the URL of the referring page is stored as $returnto.

5 Now, you can add the code for the multiple-choice <select> list in update_photo.php. It looks like this:

```
<select name="places[]" size="6" multiple="multiple" id="places">
<?php
foreach ($places as $row) {
  echo "<option value='{$row['place_id']}'";
  if (!$errors && in_array($row['place_id'], $related)) {
    echo ' selected="selected"';
  } elseif ($errors && isset($_POST['places']) &&
    ➥ in_array($row['place_id'], $_POST['places'])) {
    echo ' selected="selected"';
  }
  echo ">{$row['name']}</option>";
}
?>
</select>
```

$places contains an array of all records in the places table. The foreach loop traverses the array using $row as a temporary variable. The first condition checks that no errors have been detected, as is the case when the page first loads. It then uses in_array() to check whether place_id in the current record is in the $related array. If it is, it means the selected photo is related to that place, and the current <option> is selected in the <select> list.

The elseif condition performs a similar test if the $errors array contains any elements, this time checking whether $_POST['places'] exists, and if it does, that it contains place_id. It's necessary to test for the existence of $_POST['places'] because it won't be included in the $_POST array if no places are selected in the <select> list.

6 Save all related files, and test the code so far by clicking an EDIT link in list_photos.php. The selected photo should be displayed with its caption ready for editing and the related place selected in the <select> list.

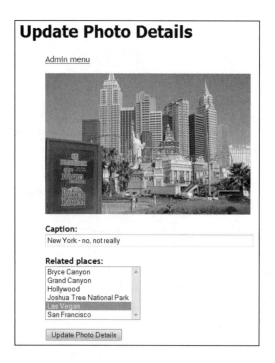

If necessary, compare your code with update_photo.php, scripts/db_update_photo_01.
php, and scripts/db_definitions_07.php in lesson11/completed.

7 You can now complete the script in db_update_photo.php by adding the validation and
update code, which looks like this:

```
if (isset($_POST['update_photo'])) {
  // update and redirect
  $val = new Zend_Validate_StringLength($captionMin, $captionMax);
  if (!$val->isValid($_POST['caption'])) {
    $errors['caption'] = "Caption exceeds $captionMax characters";
  }
  if (!$errors) {
    $data = array('caption' => $_POST['caption']);
    $dbWrite->update('photos', $data, "photo_id = $photo_id");
    $dbWrite->delete('place2photo', "photo_id = $photo_id");
    if (isset($_POST['places'])) {
      foreach ($_POST['places'] as $place) {
        $data = array('place_id' => $place,
                      'photo_id' => $photo_id);
        $dbWrite->insert('place2photo', $data);
      }
```

```
    header('Location: ' . $_POST['returnto']);
    exit;
    }
  }
}
```

The StringLength validation class checks that the caption doesn't exceed the maximum length. If it's OK, the caption is updated in the photos table.

Updating the place2photo table involves several steps. The table stores place_id and photo_id as a joint primary key, so each pair must be unique. To avoid problems with trying to insert a pair that already exists, all records that contain the selected photo's primary key are deleted from place2photo.

The conditional statement verifies the existence of $_POST['places'], which contains an array of the primary keys of related places. You need to test for its existence, because it won't be in the $_POST array if no places are selected. If it exists, the foreach loop inserts the primary key of each selected place paired with the primary key of the photo. Because references to the photo were deleted earlier, the loop uses the insert() method, not update().

Finally, the header() function redirects the user to the original referring page.

8 Save db_update_photo.php, and try updating a photo to change its caption. Also, try selecting multiple places to associate with the photo. It doesn't matter if they aren't really related. You can edit any changes once you have verified that the script is working correctly. All places linked to a photo are displayed in list_photos.php. As the following screen shot shows, Grauman's Chinese Theater has been associated with Hollywood and Los Angeles.

Photo	Filename	Caption	Places		
	losangeles1.jpg	Grauman's Chinese Theater	Hollywood Los Angeles	EDIT	DELETE

You can compare your code with db_update_photo_02.php in lesson11/completed/scripts.

Deleting photos

The script for delete_photo.php assumes that you want to remove the photo from the file system and remove its details from the photos and place2photo tables. Since the photo is displayed next to the DELETE link, there's no need to create a confirmation page. The script is very short, and it contains nothing new, so the version of delete_photo.php that you copied from lesson11/start contains the complete script, which looks like this:

```php
<?php
require_once('scripts/library.php');
try {
  require_once('scripts/db_definitions.php');
  $photo_id = checkId('photo_id', 'list_photos.php');
  $photo = getPhotoDetails($dbRead, $photo_id);
  unlink($destination . '/' . $photo['filename']);
  $dbWrite->delete('photos', "photo_id = $photo_id");
  $dbWrite->delete('place2photo', "photo_id = $photo_id");
  if (isset($_SERVER['HTTP_REFERER'])) {
    $returnto = $_SERVER['HTTP_REFERER'];
  } else {
    $returnto = 'list_photos.php';
  }
  header("Location: $returnto");
  exit;
} catch (Exception $e) {
  echo $e->getMessage();
}
```

The checkId() function gets the photo's primary key, which is fed to getPhotoDetails(). The file is removed by unlink(), and the records are deleted from the photos and place2photo tables. Finally, the user is redirected to the referring page.

If you test the DELETE link in list_photos.php, you'll be returned to the same page, but the photo will no longer be listed. The photo will also have been removed from the image_upload folder.

There's a full working version of the CMS in cms_complete in the sample files for this book. For it to work, you need to adjust the paths in db_definitions.php and library.php in the cms_complete/scripts folder to match your local setup.

What You Have Learned

In this lesson, you have:

- Studied the basic syntax of SELECT queries (pages 379–381)

- Learned how to join tables with INNER JOIN and LEFT JOIN (pages 381–383)

- Used Zend_Paginator to display database results over several pages (pages 383–390)

- Created a server behavior for Zend_Paginator (pages 390–392)

- Updated and deleted data stored in multiple tables (pages 396–414)

What You Will Learn

In this lesson, you will:

- Install the Adobe Widget Browser
- Download and configure the LightBox Gallery Widget
- Populate the gallery widget dynamically from the database
- Create a master/detail set
- Format a MySQL date
- Use jQuery to send a request to the web server and refresh content without reloading the page
- Understand how to rewrite URLs to eliminate a query string

Approximate Time

This lesson takes approximately 3 hours to complete.

Lesson Files

Media Files:

Same as Lessons 10 & 11 plus
images/destinations.jpg
styles/destinations.css

Starting Files:

lesson12/start/details.php
lesson12/start/gallery.php
lesson12/start/scripts/db_definitions.php
lesson12/start/scripts/jquery-1.4.2.min.js
lesson12/start/scripts/library.php
lesson12/start/scripts/phpcs5-lesson12.sql

Completed Files:

lesson12/completed/details.php
lesson12/completed/details_clean.php
lesson12/completed/gallery_01.php
lesson12/completed/gallery_02.php
lesson12/completed/gallery_03.php
lesson12/completed/gallery_04.php
lesson12/completed/gallery_clean.php
lesson12/completed/scripts/.htaccess
lesson12/completed/scripts/db_definitions_08.php
lesson12/completed/scripts/db_definitions_09.php
lesson12/completed/scripts/db_definitions_10.php
lesson12/completed/scripts/gallery_01.js
lesson12/completed/scripts/gallery_02.js
lesson12/completed/scripts/gallery_03.js
lesson12/completed/scripts/gallery_clean.js
lesson12/completed/scripts/jquery-1.4.2.min.js
lesson12/completed/scripts/library.php
lesson12/completed/scripts/load_gallery.php
lesson12/completed/scripts/load_gallery_clean.php
lesson12/completed/scripts/load_places.php
lesson12/completed/scripts/load_places_clean.php

Using Ajax to Refresh Content

Displaying content stored in a database simply involves querying the database and using **echo** to embed the result in a web page. The principle is identical to the technique you used in the previous lesson: a query string appended to the URL tells the script what information to display. Conditional statements control what happens if certain data doesn't exist or if multiple values need to be handled.

This lesson introduces JavaScript into the equation, allowing you to refresh the information without reloading the whole page. But it's important to ensure the page still works if JavaScript is disabled.

The page uses Ajax to refresh the photo gallery and text, but it still works when JavaScript is turned off.

Enhancing Pages with Ajax

Ajax isn't a particularly new technology. Nor is it clearly defined. The term was coined by Jesse James Garrett in 2005 for a technique that used JavaScript and XML to refresh content without needing to reload the web page. Since then, Ajax has taken on the broader meaning of exchanging data with the server to refresh part of a page without reloading it. XML frequently plays no part in the exchange, and JavaScript's role is sometimes replaced by VBScript. Some people use Ajax in an even looser manner to describe using JavaScript to manipulate page content. From a technical point of view, though, Ajax normally involves communication with the web server.

In this lesson, you'll use Ajax to display a photo gallery and refresh page content by sending requests to the web server in the background. In the example that you'll build, all the content is replaced. This has been done deliberately to keep the code simple and allow you to concentrate on the Ajax techniques. However, replacing the entire content prevents users from bookmarking the information they want. When you apply these techniques in a real website, you should replace only part of a page. For example, you might create a panel that displays details of forthcoming events and use Ajax to change the content according to the type of events selected by the user.

It's also important to remember that some people turn off JavaScript. Even if your pages don't look as good, they should still work with JavaScript turned off. Enhance the experience for the majority without relying exclusively on Ajax to deliver your content.

Preparing for the exercises

To ensure that you have sufficient content in the database from the previous two lessons, the files for this lesson contain a .sql file to populate the tables. Use the following instructions to get ready for the exercises in this lesson:

1 The .sql file deletes all existing content in the photos, place2photo, places, and states tables in the phpcs5 database. If you're happy to wipe the slate clean, continue with step 2.

   On the other hand, if you have entered data you want to preserve, back it up by creating a .sql file using the instructions in "Using phpMyAdmin" in Lesson 13 before continuing with the remaining instructions.

2 Open phpMyAdmin, and log in as the root user, if necessary.

3 Select the phpcs5 database, and click the Import tab at the top of the screen.

4 Click Browse in the "File to import" section, select phpcs5-lesson12.sql in lesson12/start/ scripts, and click Go. phpMyAdmin should report that the import was successful.

5 Click the places link in the list of tables on the left of the screen. There are 11 places listed. Some have been edited to shorten their link_name. You'll also notice that places aren't sorted alphabetically or grouped by state.

place_id	state_id	name	description	link_name	updated	created
1	CA	San Francisco	The hilly city that Dreamweaver calls home. There ...	SF	2010-06-10 11:05:19	2010-05-25 10:04:57
2	AZ	Grand Canyon	Nothing can really prepare you for that moment whe...	GrandCanyon	2010-06-06 17:22:24	2010-06-06 17:12:47
3	NV	Las Vegas	Las Vegas is a city you either love or hateâ€ther...	LasVegas	2010-06-10 11:19:26	2010-06-06 17:21:19

✱ **NOTE:** Don't worry about the apparently garbled characters in the description column for Las Vegas. This is an em dash that phpMyAdmin fails to handle correctly. It should display correctly in the finished pages.

6 Copy all 20 images from cms_complete/image_upload to the cms/image_upload folder. It doesn't matter if you have other images in the folder, just make sure that you have all the images that are recorded in the updated database tables.

7 Copy gallery.php and details.php from lesson12/start to lesson12/workfiles. If Dreamweaver prompts you to update the links, click Don't Update.

8 Copy db_definitions.php from lesson12/start/scripts to the scripts folder in lesson12/workfiles. You also need a copy of your library.php file in the lesson12/workfiles/scripts folder.

Introducing Adobe Widget Browser

Many excellent JavaScript widgets are freely available on the Internet. However, a major stumbling block for many designers is customizing the widgets to fit in with their web pages. It often requires a solid knowledge of both JavaScript and CSS. Adobe Widget Browser attempts to overcome the problem by providing a visual interface changing the way selected widgets look and behave.

Adobe Widget Browser isn't installed by default, but it's closely integrated with Dreamweaver CS5. Once you have installed the Widget Browser, you can use it to preview widgets on the Adobe Exchange. When you find one you like, you can download and customize it, saving your changes for automatic insertion in a Dreamweaver site. The widgets are free. All you need is an Adobe ID to log into the Adobe Exchange to download them.

The Widget Browser uses a specification laid down by the OpenAjax Alliance (www.openajax.org), an organization of software companies, open-source initiatives, and individuals dedicated to the adoption of open and interoperable Ajax technologies. Consequently, the widgets on the Adobe Exchange are not limited to using the Spry framework, Adobe's implementation of Ajax. Many, including the one selected for this lesson, use jQuery (http://jquery.com/), the most popular JavaScript library, which is designed to take a lot of the hard work out of developing cross-browser scripts.

Launching the Widget Browser

Although the Widget Browser is a separate application, the easiest way to access it is through Dreamweaver.

1 Make sure you are connected to the Internet, click the Extend Dreamweaver icon in the Application Bar, and choose Widget Browser.

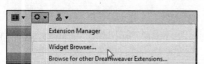

On a Mac, if you can't see the Extend Dreamweaver icon, choose Window > Application Bar. (The Application Bar can't be hidden on Windows.)

2 If the Widget Browser is already installed, it should launch. Skip ahead to the next section, "Choosing widgets from the Adobe Exchange."

If you see the following alert, continue with the remaining steps.

3 Click OK. This launches your default browser and takes you to the Widget Browser's page on the Adobe website.

4 Click the link to download the Widget Browser. At this stage, you might be prompted to log in with your Adobe ID. This is normally your email address.

If you don't have an Adobe ID, click Create an Adobe Account. The registration process should take only a couple of minutes.

On the download page, click Install Now if you have the Flash Player installed. Otherwise, click the download link.

5 When prompted to open or save the file, click Open.

6 When asked to confirm if you want to install the application, click Install, and enter your computer's administrator password if necessary.

7 You will be prompted to choose the installation location. Click Continue after making your choice (or accepting the default).

8 When the installation has completed, the Widget Browser should launch automatically. Click Accept to accept the license agreement.

Choosing widgets from the Adobe Exchange

The Widget Browser lets you inspect widgets in action before deciding whether to download them. In this section, you'll log into the Adobe Exchange, and select a widget for use in gallery.php.

1 You need to be signed into the Adobe Exchange to preview and download widgets. Click Sign In at the top right of the Widget Browser.

2 Type in your Adobe ID and password. If you want to avoid signing in every time, select the "Stay signed in" checkbox before clicking the Sign In button.

3 The Widget Browser displays thumbnail images of the widgets, together with brief details, including the author's name and user ratings.

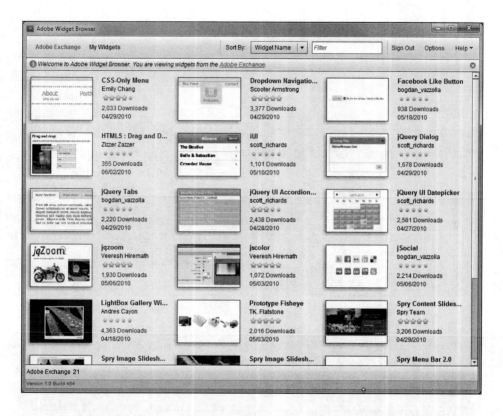

You can sort the thumbnails with the Sort By menu in the title bar. You can also narrow down the display by typing in the Filter field.

4 The widget you'll use is the LightBox Gallery Widget by Andres Cayon. It's at the bottom left in the preceding screen shot, but you can find it quickly by typing Andres's name in the Filter field. Click the thumbnail to see details of the framework used, browser compatibility, and license.

5 To inspect the widget more closely, click the Preview button at the top right. This opens the widget in Live View, where you can test it by hovering your pointer over the gallery thumbnails and clicking one of them.

The Preview screen also lets you inspect the code that the widget inserts into the web page by clicking the Code tab. Many widgets also come with several presets. This one has an orange color scheme and a vertical version in white.

6 Click Add to My Widgets at the bottom right of the Widget Browser.

7 When the widget finishes downloading, click Go to My Widgets.

If you click Close by mistake, you are returned to the widget's description. Click Adobe Exchange at the top left of the Widget Browser. From there, you can click My Widgets at the top left.

My Widgets looks the same as the main screen except it contains only the widgets you have downloaded.

8 Leave the Widget Browser open to continue in the next section.

Configuring a Widget

A major advantage of the Widget Browser is that it provides a visual context for you to change a widget's default settings and save your own presets. The degree of configuration possible within the Widget Browser depends on how the author has set it up, but Andres Cayon's LightBox Gallery Widget has many options.

Creating your own widget preset

The following instructions show how to change the color scheme and adjust the layout ready for insertion into gallery.php.

1 Open the Adobe Widget Browser, if necessary, select My Widgets, and click the LightBox Gallery Widget thumbnail.

2 Make sure the Preview button at the top right of the Widget Browser is selected, and select "Vertical white" in the Developer Presets.

3 Click Configure at the bottom left to display the available options.

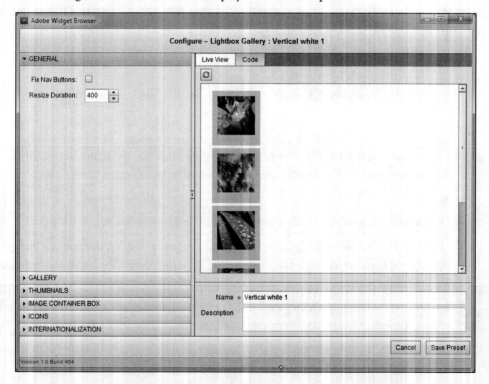

The sliding panels on the left provide access to the widget's editable features. Hover your pointer over a setting to display a tooltip describing its purpose. Changes are reflected immediately in the Live View tab on the right.

4 Type **Vertical phpcs5** in the Name field at the bottom right. Adding a description is optional.

5 Click GALLERY to reveal the next options. Change Width from 120 to **240**, and leave the other settings unchanged. Live View displays the thumbnails in rows of two.

6 Click THUMBNAILS to reveal the options for styling the thumbnails.

7 Click the Background color box, and select white from the color palette.

8 Click the Hover Background color box. When the pointer is over the thumbnails, they will have a sky blue border. Type **79B4D9** into the text box at the top of the color palette, and press Enter/Return to apply the value.

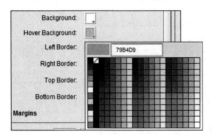

✳ **NOTE:** The color palette in the Widget Browser doesn't use a hash sign at the beginning of the color value. At the time of this writing, moving the pointer over any of the color swatches changes the color displayed next to the hexadecimal value. However, the correct color is registered when you press Enter/Return.

9 Change Bottom Border from 20 to **10**, and set all Margin values to **0**.

10 Click IMAGE CONTAINER BOX to display the options for the full size image. Change Opacity to **0.6**, and select light gray (CCCCCC) for Background. These two settings control the color and transparency of the page when the full size image is displayed.

You can test the effect by clicking one of the thumbnails in the Live View tab. Resize the Widget Browser, if necessary, to see the full effect.

11 The ICONS section lets you choose your own images for a loading indicator (such as an animated .gif file), as well as next, previous, and close buttons. The defaults are fine.

12 The INTERNATIONALIZATION section controls the text used to display the image count (for example, "Image 3 of 10"). The defaults are fine for a website in English. JavaScript is Unicode-compliant, so you can use accented characters or nonalphabetic scripts for other languages.

13 Save the changes by clicking Save Preset at the bottom right of the Widget Browser. *This is very important.* If you forget to do so, your settings won't be reflected in the widget when you insert it in the page in Dreamweaver.

The Widget Browser returns you to the normal Preview screen with "Vertical phpcs5" listed under MY PRESETS.

14 Close the Widget Browser. You'll be working in Dreamweaver for the rest of this lesson.

Inserting a widget in a page

The integration of the Widget Browser with Dreamweaver CS5 makes it very easy to insert a preconfigured widget into a page. Here's how you do it.

1 Open your copy of gallery.php in the lesson12/workfiles folder, and click anywhere inside the <h2> text that reads "Places to visit in."

2 In the Tag selector at the bottom of the Document window, click <div#places> to select the <div> that contains the heading. Dreamweaver's visual aids display the margins on both sides as hatched areas. (Choose View > Visual Aids > CSS Layout Box Model if you can't see the hatched areas.)

The gallery widget is designed to fit in the 240-pixel margin on the left of the <div>. To position the insertion point correctly, press the left keyboard arrow once. Open Split view to confirm that the insertion point is immediately to the left of the opening <div> tag, as shown at the beginning of line 12 in the following screen shot.

```
10    <div id="wrapper">
11        <img src="../../images/destinations.jpg" width="960" height="232" alt="Destinations West" />
12       |<div id="places">
13          <h2>Places to visit in </h2>
14        </div>
15    </div>
```

3 Choose Insert > Widget, and select LightBox Gallery Widget and the "Vertical phpcs5" preset in the Widget dialog box.

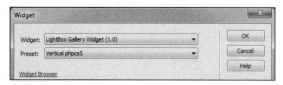

4 Click OK to insert the widget. It should be inserted in the margin to the left of the text. While selected, it's surrounded by a turquoise border with a tab at the top left indicating the widget type and its ID. The thumbnails are represented by broken image icons.

NOTE: If you can't see the widget's turquoise border and tab, choose View > Visual Aids, and click Invisible Elements.

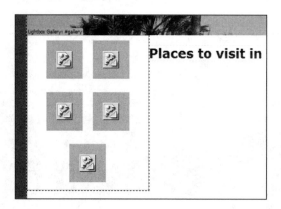

5 Save gallery.php. Dreamweaver displays Copy Dependent Files, which lists 17 files that will be inserted into various folders when you click OK. The number of files and their ultimate location depends on the widget you have chosen. See the sidebar "Keeping Track of a Widget's Files."

If your phpcs5 site is in a virtual host, the broken image icons will be replaced by thumbnail images as soon as you click OK. If you're working in a subfolder of localhost, there's no change. However, it doesn't matter, because you're not going to use the default images anyway.

6 Look at the Dependent Files toolbar at the top of the Document window. In addition to Source Code and destinations.css, four new files have been added: jquery.js, lightbox.js, lightbox.css, and sample_lightbox_layout.css.

Keeping Track of a Widget's Files

Most widgets insert a mixture of images, style sheets, and JavaScript files. Spry widgets accessed through the Widget Browser keep all related files together in a folder called Spry-UI-1.7. Other widgets follow their own conventions.

The LightBox Gallery Widget uses three separate folders in your site root: css, images, and scripts. If the folders already exist, the widget's files are mixed in with yours. It also creates a subfolder called lightbox in the images folder. This is what the folders contain:

- **css.** Two style sheets, lightbox.css and sample_lightbox_layout.css

- **images.** Ten images with names beginning with lightboxdemo

- **images/lightbox.** Five navigation images

- **scripts.** Two JavaScript files, jquery.js and lightbox.js

Deleting a widget removes the code and links from the page but not the files that have been added to your site, because they might be required by other pages. So, it's important to read the Copy Dependent Files alert to know where all the files will be stored. If you're not sure whether to use a widget, set up a separate test site in Dreamweaver to avoid cluttering your file structure with unwanted files.

7 Open gallery.php in Code view, and make sure that Source Code is selected in the Related Files toolbar. In the <head> of the page, you'll see that the external JavaScript and CSS files have been attached (around lines 7–10). Immediately following is a large block of embedded CSS (around lines 11–65). The <style> block begins with the following comment:

```
/* BeginOAWidget_Instance_2127022: #gallery */
```

At the end of the block is a similar comment:

```
/* EndOAWidget_Instance_2127022 */
```

Instead of editing the external style sheets, the Widget Browser exploits the CSS cascade by embedding all your changes in the <head> of the page. The comments enable Dreamweaver to identify the relevant code if you decide to delete the widget.

8 Immediately following the `<style>` block is the following code:

```
<script type="text/xml">
<!--
<oa:widgets>
  <oa:widget wid="2127022" binding="#gallery" />
</oa:widgets>
-->
</script>
```

Again, the purpose is to identify the widget and its related code.

9 Inside the `<body>` of the page, locate the section of code that begins like this (around lines 78–86):

```
<div id="gallery" class="lbGallery">
```

This is the HTML code that contains the thumbnails. It's an unordered list restyled by the widget's CSS.

10 Immediately after the gallery `<div>` is a `<script>` block (around lines 87–107) that initializes the Ajax gallery. Again, it contains comments that identify the widget number and its ID.

Even if you don't understand the JavaScript code, it's easy to see that it contains the paths to the widget's loading, previous, next, and close buttons. You should also be able to recognize the values set for opacity (`0.6`) and background color (`#cccccc`) in the IMAGE CONTAINER BOX section of the Widget Browser.

All the changes you made in the Widget Browser have been added to the page where the widget is used but not to any of the external files.

If you mouse over the widget in Design view and select the turquoise tab at the top left of the widget, you can remove the widget and its associated files from the page by pressing Delete. For this exercise, you don't want to delete the widget unless you inserted it in the wrong part of the page.

Populating the gallery widget dynamically

The gallery widget uses hard-coded links to the full size images and thumbnails, but since the details of the images are stored in a database, it makes more sense to query the database and use a PHP loop to generate the links dynamically. By adding a `<select>` menu, visitors can select a state and control which images are displayed. The following steps explain how:

1 Include db_definitions.php and library.php above the DOCTYPE declaration in gallery.php using `require_once()`, and open a `try` block like this:

```php
<?php
require_once('scripts/library.php');
require_once('scripts/db_definitions.php');
try {
?>
<!DOCTYPE html PUBLIC "-//W3C//DTD XHTML 1.0 Transitional//EN"
```

2 Scroll down to the bottom of the page. Close the `try` block and add a `catch` block after the closing `</html>` tag:

```php
</html>
<?php
} catch (Exception $e) {
  echo $e->getMessage();
}
?>
```

3 In Design view, move your pointer over the gallery widget, and click the turquoise tab at the top left to select it. You'll insert a form and `<select>` menu above the widget, so the insertion point needs to be immediately before the widget's opening `<div>` tag.

Press the left keyboard arrow once. This is the same technique you used in step 2 of the preceding section.

In Design view, the cursor looks as though it's still inside the widget, but you can confirm the insertion point's location in Split view. Don't move the focus into Code view, because inserting form elements is easier in Design view.

4 Choose Insert > Form > Form. The red outline of the form appears above the widget and the `<h2>` heading in Design view.

5 The `<select>` menu will pass the selected state name through a query string, so the form needs to use the GET method. With the form still selected, change the value of Method in the Property inspector to **GET**.

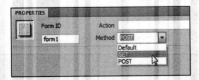

6 Make sure the insertion point is inside the form, and choose Insert > Form > Select (List/Menu).

In the Input Tag Accessibility Attributes dialog box, type **state** in the ID field and **Select a state:** in the Label field. Click OK.

7 Click to the right of the <select> menu you just inserted and choose Insert > Form > Button.

In the Input Tag Accessibility Attributes dialog box, type **selectState** in the ID field, and leave the Label field blank. Click OK.

8 With the button still selected, change the Value field in the Property inspector from Submit to **Go**. The form should look like this in Design view (don't worry if the thumbnails still show broken image icons):

If you need to check your code so far, compare it with gallery_01.php in lesson12/completed.

9 In Lesson 10, you created a function in db_definitions.php to populate a <select> menu with the names of all states. However, not all states have places and photos associated with them in the database, so you need to create a different function to select only those states that do.

Select db_definitions.php in the Related Files toolbar, and add the following function definition:

```
function getRegisteredStates($read) {
  $sql = 'SELECT DISTINCT state_name FROM states
          INNER JOIN places USING (state_id)
          ORDER BY state_name';
  return $read->fetchCol($sql);
}
```

The SELECT query uses an INNER JOIN between the states and places tables. An INNER JOIN selects only records that have matches in both tables, so this query excludes states that don't have photos or places associated with them. However, there are 11 records in the places table, so using SELECT on its own would produce duplicate results. The DISTINCT keyword ensures only one instance of each state_name is retrieved.

The final line of the function uses fetchCol(), a Zend_Db method you've not encountered before. It returns an indexed array of results from the first column in the SELECT query. Since the query selects only the state_name column, this makes it a lot simpler to loop through the results.

10 You also need a function to retrieve the image filenames, captions, and associated place names to populate the gallery widget. Add the following code to db_definitions.php:

```
function getGalleryByState($read, $state_name) {
    $sql = $read->quoteInto('SELECT name, filename, caption
            FROM places
            INNER JOIN states USING (state_id)
            INNER JOIN place2photo USING (place_id)
            INNER JOIN photos USING (photo_id)
            WHERE state_name = ?
            ORDER BY name', $state_name);
    return $read->fetchAll($sql);
}
```

This function takes two arguments: the Zend_Db object with read permission and the state name. Because the state name is passed through the query string, the SQL query needs to use the quoteInto() method to sanitize the value (see "Using a variable in a SELECT query" in Lesson 7).

The query joins all four tables in the CMS with INNER JOIN, using the foreign keys to identify related records.

11 Save db_definitions.php, and click Source Code in the Related Files toolbar to return to the code in gallery.php.

Add the following code in the try block above the DOCTYPE declaration:

```
try {
    $states = getRegisteredStates($dbRead);
    if (isset($_GET['state']) && in_array($_GET['state'], $states)) {
        $selected = $_GET['state'];
    } else {
        $selected = 'California';
    }
    $pix = getGalleryByState($dbRead, $selected);
?>
```

The first line uses the function you created in step 9, and it assigns the result to $states, which will be used to populate the <select> menu.

The conditional statement checks for the existence of $_GET['state'] and uses in_array() to make sure the value is in the $states array. This ensures that only a state name with records in the database can be assigned to $selected. If the condition fails, California is assigned as the default value.

The final line passes $selected to the function created in step 10, and it stores the result in $pix, which will be used to populate the gallery widget.

12 Amend the page's `<title>` by displaying the name of the selected state:

```
<title>Destinations West: <?php echo $selected; ?></title>
```

13 Scroll down to around line 92 to locate the `<select>` menu, and add the following code to populate it:

```
<select name="state" id="state">
  <?php
  foreach ($states as $state) {
    echo "<option value='$state'";
    if ($state == $selected) {
      echo 'selected="selected"';
    }
    echo ">$state</option>";
  }
  ?>
</select>
```

Because `getRegisteredStates()` uses `fetchCol()`, the value stored in `$states` is a simple array of state names, so you can access each one by assigning it to the temporary variable `$state` in a `foreach` loop. If the current value of `$state` is the same as `$selected`, `selected="selected"` is inserted in the opening `<option>` tag to display the value in the menu.

14 Save gallery.php, and click Live View to test the menu. It should automatically select California. When you open the menu, just four states should be listed.

15 Exit Live View, and return to the code in gallery.php. Locate the unordered list that houses the gallery widget's thumbnails (around lines 106–112).

Delete four of the `<li>` elements. The unordered list should look like this:

```
<ul>
  <li> <a href="/images/lightboxdemo1.jpg" title=""><img
  ➥ src="/images/lightboxdemo_thumb1.jpg" width="72" height="72"
  ➥ alt="Flower" /></a> </li>
</ul>
```

16 In Design view, select the remaining image (or broken image icon) in the gallery widget so that its properties are displayed in the Property inspector.

17 Use the Point to File tool or click the folder icon next to the Src field to select an image in cms/image_upload.

Do the same with the Link field. It doesn't matter which image you select, because the image is a placeholder for changes you'll make in step 19.

▼ **CAUTION!** The LightBox Gallery Widget uses links relative to the site root. As a result, Dreamweaver assumes the replacement links should be the same. This poses no problems if you're developing in a virtual host. If you're using a subfolder of localhost, use the folder icon in the Property inspector to open the Select Image Source dialog box, and set the "Relative to" menu to Document.

18 Change the value in the W field to **120**, and delete the value in the H field. Press Enter/ Return after deleting the value to confirm the change. The selected image should spring back to the correct proportions.

19 To populate the gallery widget with the results from the database, you need to wrap the `<li>` element in a `foreach` loop, and replace the static image references with PHP variables. The place name and image caption also need to be added to the `title` attribute, and the caption is used again as the alternative text. When you have made all the changes, the widget's unordered list looks like this:

```
<ul>
<?php foreach ($pix as $pic) { ?>
  <li> <a href="../../cms/image_upload/<?php echo $pic['filename']; ?>"
 ➥ title="<?php echo $pic['name'] . ': ' . $pic['caption']; ?>">
 ➥ <img src="../../cms/image_upload/<?php echo $pic['filename']; ?>"
 ➥ width="120" alt="<?php echo $pic['caption']; ?>" /></a> </li>
<?php } ?>
</ul>
```

The links in the href and src attributes in this listing have been made relative to the document. The leading ../.. is not required if your phpcs5 site is in a virtual host—although the widget still works if you include it.

20 If your phpcs5 site is in a subfolder of localhost, you need to convert the links to the navigation images to be relative to the document. They're in the JavaScript block that follows the widget's HTML code. Locate the following code (around lines 117–121):

```
imageLoading:  '/images/lightbox/lightbox-ico-loading.gif',
➥ // (string) Path and the name of the loading icon
imageBtnPrev:  '/images/lightbox/lightbox-btn-prev.gif',
➥ // (string) Path and the name of the prev button image
imageBtnNext:  '/images/lightbox/lightbox-btn-next.gif',
➥ // (string) Path and the name of the next button image
imageBtnClose:  '/images/lightbox/lightbox-btn-close.gif',
➥ // (string) Path and the name of the close btn
imageBlank:     '/images/lightbox/lightbox-blank.gif',
```

Make each path relative to the document by adding ../../ to the beginning in place of the leading slash. The first one should look like this:

```
imageLoading:  '../../images/lightbox/lightbox-ico-loading.gif',
➥ // (string) Path and the name of the loading icon
```

You don't need to make these changes if your site is in a virtual host.

21 Save gallery.php, and click Live View to test it. A series of thumbnail images of California appears down the left side of the page. Click one of them to launch the lightbox, which dims the page and displays the full size image in the center. Navigate through the images with the Next and Prev buttons that appear when your pointer is over the right or left of the lightbox.

22 Close the lightbox by clicking the CLOSE button, and then select a different state from the `<select>` menu. Hold down Ctrl/Cmd and click the Go button to load thumbnails related to that state. You now have a dynamic lightbox gallery. Later, you'll improve it so that you can display images from different states without reloading the page. Before that, you need to display the text that goes in the main part of the page.

You can compare your code with gallery_02.php in lesson12/completed and db_definitions_08.php in lesson12/completed/scripts.

You've probably realized that the thumbnails in this exercise use the same files as the full size image. Their size is simply constrained by setting the `width` attribute in the `<img>` tag to 120. Generally speaking, this is a bad practice, because it means loading all the full size images even if the visitor never views them. For a live website, you should create thumbnails of uniform dimensions and optimize them to reduce the file size as much as possible.

Creating a Master/Detail Set

A master/detail set is one of the most common design patterns in web development. The master page presents a list of related items, often with a brief description of each one, and links to a separate page that describes the item in detail. The technique used to create a master/detail set is the same as for the update pages that you built in Lesson 11. The master page uses a loop to display the results of a database search, and the link to the detail page uses a unique identifier— normally the record's primary key— that is passed through a query string. However, any unique value associated with the record is fine.

Displaying the master list of places

As well as the gallery widget, gallery.php will display the names of places associated with the selected state, together with the first sentence of the description and a link to the detail page.

Continue working in the same page as the previous exercise.

1 Exit Live View, if necessary, and select db_definitions.php in the Related Files toolbar. Add the following function definition:

```
function getPlacesByState($read, $state_name) {
    $sql = $read->quoteInto('SELECT name, description, link_name
            FROM places
            INNER JOIN states USING (state_id)
            WHERE state_name = ?
            ORDER BY name', $state_name);
    return $read->fetchAll($sql);
}
```

This is very similar to the `getGalleryByState()` function created in the previous section. It uses `quoteInto()` to prepare the value in `$state_name` for insertion into the query, and it returns a multidimensional array of results.

2 Save db_definitions.php, and select Source Code in the Related Files toolbar to return to the code in gallery.php. Add the following code to the PHP block above the `DOCTYPE` declaration:

```
$pix = getGalleryByState($dbRead, $selected);
$places = getPlacesByState($dbRead, $selected);
```

This passes the name of the selected state to the function you just created, and it stores the result in `$places`.

3 In Design view, click to the right of the `<h2>` headline that reads "Places to visit in," and press Enter/Return once to create a new paragraph.

The underlying HTML now looks like this:

```
<div id="places">
  <h2>Places to visit in </h2>
  <p> </p>
</div>
```

4 To display the master page list, use `echo` to display the name of the selected state in the heading, and wrap the paragraph in a `foreach` loop to display the place name in bold followed by a colon and a space between the paragraph tags. The amended code looks like this:

```
<div id="places">
  <h2>Places to visit in <?php echo $selected; ?></h2>
  <?php foreach ($places as $place) { ?>
  <p><strong><?php echo $place['name']; ?>: </strong></p>
  <?php } ?>
</div>
```

5 Save gallery.php, and click Live View to test it. The heading now reads "Places to visit in California," and it's followed by a list of related place names. Select a different state, hold down Ctrl/Cmd, and click Go to see the places related to that state.

Exit Live View when you have verified that the code is working.

6 The descriptions are too long for the master page. A simple way to extract the first sentence is to look for the first period followed by a space, and cut the text at that point. Some sentences might end in a question mark, or the period might be followed by a quotation mark, but this technique should extract a short section at the beginning of the text.

The PHP function `strpos()` finds the first instance of a character sequence and returns its position in the string. You can combine this with `substr()` to extract the first section of text. The arguments passed to `substr()` are the target string, the position of the first character, and the length you want to extract. Amend the code between the paragraph tags like this:

```
<p><strong><?php echo $place['name']; ?>: </strong><?php echo
➡ substr($place['description'], 0, strpos($place['description'], '. ')+1);
➡ ?></p>
```

This code might be difficult to understand, so let's break it into sections.

The first argument passed to `substr()` is `$place['description']`, which contains the whole description stored in the database record.

The second argument is `0`. PHP, in common with other computing languages, counts from 0, so this indicates the beginning of the string.

The third argument is `strpos($place['description'], '. ')+1`. This calculates the position of the first period followed by a space, and adds 1 to the result. You could rewrite the code like this:

```
$first_period = strpos($place['description'], '. ')+1;
echo substr($place['description'], 0, $first_period);
```

However, you don't need the value of `$first_period` again, so it's more efficient to pass an expression as the third argument. As long as the expression produces the correct data type, PHP doesn't object.

⊳ **TIP:** If you find this style too cryptic, there's nothing wrong with using the more verbose style. As you gain more PHP experience, you'll discover many shortcuts like this.

7 To complete the master page, you need to add a link to details.php, and add a query string that contains the value of the `link_name` column. The finished code inside the paragraph tags looks like this:

```
<p><strong><?php echo $place['name']; ?>: </strong><?php echo
➡ substr($place['description'], 0, strpos($place['description'], '. ')+1);
➡ ?> <a href="details.php?place=<?php echo $place['link_name']; ?>">Learn
➡ more</a></p>
```

8 Save gallery.php, and test it in a browser. As you hover over the "Learn more" links, you should see URLs similar to this:

```
http://phpcs5/lesson12/workfiles/details.php?place=Hollywood
```

The link_name column in the places table has a unique index, ensuring that there are no duplicate values. Using a human-readable value like this is far more user friendly than a query string that looks something like ?place_id=4.

You can compare your code with gallery_03.php in lesson12/completed and db_definitions_09.php in lesson12/completed/scripts.

Creating the detail page

The detail page needs to query the database to retrieve the details of the selected place and then display them. When building a static web page, you can insert images manually and position them to the best aesthetic effect. That's more difficult with dynamically generated pages. One solution is to embed the image details directly in the text, which a CMS like WordPress does. The following exercise uses a different approach. In every other paragraph, the PHP detects whether an image is available. If there is, it inserts it and uses CSS to float it in the opposite direction from the previous one, producing the following result.

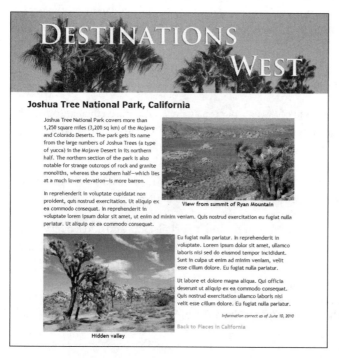

The following exercise doesn't involve a lot of code, but some of it might be hard to understand if you're relatively inexperienced with PHP. Don't rush. Read the explanations carefully, and all should become clear.

1 Open lesson12/workfiles/details.php, and include db_definitions.php and library.php above the DOCTYPE declaration using require_once(). Also, create try and catch blocks in the same way you did with gallery.php (see steps 1 and 2 of "Populating the gallery widget dynamically").

2 Select db_definitions.php in the Related Files toolbar, and add the following function definition:

```
function getPlaceByLinkname($read, $link_name) {
  $sql = $read->quoteInto('SELECT place_id, name, state_name, description,
  ➥ DATE_FORMAT(updated, "%M %e, %Y") AS updated
                          FROM places
                          INNER JOIN states USING (state_id)
                          WHERE link_name = ?', $link_name);
  return $read->fetchRow($sql);
}
```

As in other functions that receive input from a query string, the SELECT query is built using the quoteInto() method. The query selects the place_id, name, state_name, description, and updated fields from the record where the link_name field matches the value passed through the query string.

The updated field is wrapped in the MySQL DATE_FORMAT() function and assigned an alias using the AS keyword like this:

```
DATE_FORMAT(updated, "%M %e, %Y") AS updated
```

An *alias* specifies how you want a column name to be represented in the result. In this case, the original column name has been used, but you could use a different name, such as formatted. Without an alias, the field would be represented in the result as DATE_FORMAT(updated, "%M %e, %Y").

The DATE_FORMAT() function takes two arguments: the column you want to format and a string specifying how to format it. The format string uses specifiers that begin with a percentage sign—those most commonly used are listed in **Table 12.1**. The string can also include literal text. This listing includes a comma after %e, producing a date such as June 12, 2010.

▼ **CAUTION!** There must be no space between a MySQL function name and the opening paren-thesis. Also, pay attention to the combination of single and double quotation marks. The format string can be enclosed in either. Double quotes are used here to avoid conflict with the SQL query, which is in single quotes.

Table 12.1   Commonly Used MySQL Date Format Specifiers

Period	Specifier	Description
Year	%Y	Four digits
	%y	Two digits
Month	%M	Full name (January, February, etc.)
	%b	Abbreviated (Jan, Feb, etc.)
	%m	Number with leading zero
	%c	Number, no leading zero
Day of month	%d	Number with leading zero
	%e	Number, no leading zero
	%D	With English suffix (1st, 2nd, 3rd, 4th)
Weekday name	%W	Full name
	%a	Abbreviated name (Mon, Tue, etc.)

3 Save db_definitions.php, and select Source Code in the Related Files toolbar to access the code in details.php. Add the following code in the try block at the top of the page:

```
try {
  if (isset($_GET['place'])) {
    $place = getPlaceByLinkname($dbRead, $_GET['place']);
  } else {
    $place = NULL;
  }
?>
```

This checks whether a variable called place has been passed through a query string. If it has, the value is passed to the function you created in step 2, and the result is assigned to $place. Otherwise, $place is set to NULL.

4 Display the place name in the `<title>` tag:

```
<title>Destinations West: <?php if ($place) { echo $place['name']; }
➥ ?></title>
```

The conditional statement is needed in case `$place` is `NULL`.

5 Scroll down to the maincontent `<div>` (around line 21), and wrap the `<h2>` heading in a conditional statement to display "No result found" if `$place` equates to `FALSE`. In the `else` clause, display the place's name and state name in another `<h2>` heading like this:

```
<div id="maincontent">
  <?php if (!$place) { ?>
    <h2>No record found</h2>
  <?php } else { ?>
    <h2><?php echo $place['name'] . ', ' . $place['state_name']; ?></h2>
  <?php } ?>
</div>
```

6 Save details.php, and click Live View to test it. You should see "No record found." Exit Live View, and switch to gallery.php.

Click Live View in gallery.php, and select one of the "Learn more" links, remembering to hold down Ctrl/Cmd as you click. You should see the name and state of the place you selected.

Exit Live View, and return to details.php.

7 The text in the description field has been broken up into paragraphs by pressing Enter/Return twice in the insert form, but that doesn't insert `<p>` tags. Without them, the text will be displayed as one continuous block, because HTML ignores newlines in the underlying code. A common solution is to pass text to the `nl2br()` function, which converts newline characters into HTML `<br />` tags. But it doesn't solve the problem of injecting images into every other paragraph. You need to build the HTML structure dynamically. The first task is to break up the text into an array of paragraphs.

In details.php, select db_definitions.php in the Related Files toolbar, and add the following function definition:

```
function splitParas($string) {
  return preg_split('/[\r\n]+/', $string);
}
```

This uses the preg_split() function, which splits a string into an array of elements using a regex (see "Building the validation script (1)" in Lesson 7 for an explanation of regexes). The regex used here matches one or more newline characters and/or carriage returns.

8 Save db_definitions.php, and select Source Code in the Related Files toolbar to return to the code in details.php. Use the function you just created to convert the content of the description field into paragraphs, and use a for loop to build the HTML like this (the new code goes inside the final PHP code block that previously contained only a closing curly brace):

```
<h2><?php echo $place['name'] . ', ' . $place['state_name']; ?></h2>
<?php
  $paras = splitParas($place['description']);
  for ($i = 0, $num_paras = count($paras); $i < $num_paras; $i++) {
    echo '<p>';
    echo $paras[$i];
    echo '</p>';
  }
} ?>
```

A for loop allows you to initialize multiple values separated by commas. In addition to setting the counter variable $i, this loop initializes $num_paras using the count() function to get the number of elements in the $paras array. The loop traverses the $paras array using the counter to display $paras[0], $paras[1], and so on. The opening and closing <p> tags are on separate lines in preparation for adding the logic that inserts the images.

9 If you repeat the test in step 5 now, you'll see the description displayed in paragraphs. Use the Live Code button to see the <p> tags inserted in the underlying HTML.

10 To display the images, you need to create an array of photos that are associated with the selected place. A function that does this was created in Lesson 11, so add the following code to the PHP block at the top of details.php:

```
if (isset($_GET['place'])) {
  $place = getPlaceByLinkname($dbRead, $_GET['place']);
  if ($place) {
    $pix = getRelatedPhotos($dbRead, $place['place_id']);
  }
} else {
  $place = NULL;
}
```

This ensures that $place contains a result from the database and then uses the place's primary key (place_id) to get the filenames and captions of related photos, which are stored in $pix.

11 Inserting an image in every other paragraph involves checking whether an image is associated with the place and keeping count of where you are in the loop. This requires another counter. You also need to get the dimensions of the image. They haven't been stored in the database, but PHP provides the getimagesize() function to detect them. Amend the code like this:

```php
<?php
  $paras = splitParas($place['description']);
  $imagedir = '../../cms/image_upload/';
  for ($i = 0, $j = 0, $num_paras = count($paras); $i < $num_paras; $i++){
    echo '<p>';
    if (isset($pix[$j]) && !($i % 2)) {
      $image = $imagedir . $pix[$j]['filename'];
      $imagesize = getimagesize($image);
    }
    echo $paras[$i];
    echo '</p>';
  }
} ?>
```

The first new line of code assigns the path to the image folder to $imagedir to make it easier to refer to the image file later.

A new counter called $j is initialized in the first argument of the for loop to keep track of the images. Unlike $i, $j is not automatically incremented each time the loop runs. So, although they start with the same values, $j remains unchanged until it's incremented inside the loop in code that you'll add later.

A conditional statement inside the loop checks whether $pix[$j] exists. The first time, this looks for $pix[0]. The mysterious looking second condition uses some elementary math to determine whether $i is an odd or even number. The percentage sign is an arithmetic operator that performs modulo division (see "Using Operators for Calculations and Joining Strings" in Lesson 3). Modulo division by 2 always results in 1 or 0. Since PHP treats 0 as FALSE and any other number as TRUE, you can use $i % 2 to alternate between FALSE and TRUE each time the loop runs. The first time it runs, $i is 0, so the result is 0, but the condition is preceded by the logical Not operator, so it's treated as TRUE. The next time, the result is 1, which the logical Not operator converts to FALSE, and so on. As a consequence, the code inside the conditional statement is executed only every other paragraph *and* if the $pix array contains an element with the index $j.

> **TIP:** Understanding this sort of conditional logic can be a challenge, but once you do, it dramatically increases the flexibility of your scripts.

The code inside the conditional statement concatenates the path to the images folder with the filename of the current element of the $pix array and assigns it to $image, resulting in a value like this:

```
../../cms/image_upload/bryce1.jpg
```

This value is then passed to getimagesize(), which returns an array of the image's dimensions that are stored in $imagesize.

> **⚹ NOTE:** In a virtual host, you can use a site-root-relative path most of the time. However, getimagesize() doesn't understand site-root-relative path. If you use a site-root-relative path to the images folder, use getimagesize($_SERVER['DOCUMENT_ROOT'] . $image) instead of getimagesize($image).

12 The next section of code inserts the image, if one is available. It's a mixture of HTML and PHP that looks complicated at first glance, but it's simply a <span> tag wrapped around an <img> tag and the image's caption. All the attributes are generated dynamically by echo.

```
   $imagesize = getimagesize($image);
?>
<span class="<?php echo ($j % 2) ? 'floatleft' : 'floatright'; ?>"
➥ style="width:<?php echo $imagesize[0]; ?>px"><img src="<?php echo
➥ $image; ?>" alt="<?php echo $pix[$j]['caption']; ?> <?php echo
➥ $imagesize[3]; ?> /> <?php echo $pix[$j++]['caption']; ?></span>
<?php
   }
echo $paras[$i];
```

The <span> tag has two attributes: class and style. The code that generates the value of the class attribute looks like this:

```
<?php echo ($j % 2) ? 'floatleft' : 'floatright'; ?>
```

This uses modulo division again, but this time with the $j counter. It also uses the *conditional operator* (also known as the *ternary operator*), a shorthand way of writing a simple conditional statement. Instead of using the if and else keywords, it uses ? and : as operators. The condition precedes the question mark. If it equates to TRUE, the value to the right of the question mark is used. If it's FALSE, the value to the right of the colon is used. You could rewrite the same line of code like this:

```php
<?php
if ($j % 2) {
  echo 'floatleft';
} else {
  echo 'floatright';
}
?>
```

When the loop encounters the first image, $j is 0, so the condition equates to FALSE, and floatright is set as the class. The next time, floatleft is used. If there's a third image, floatright is used again, and so on.

The inline style sets the width of the <span> using the first element in the $imagesize array returned by getimagesize(). Setting a width forces long captions to wrap to the same width as the image.

In the <img> tag, the src attribute is set to $image, which contains the full path to the image, and the alt attribute uses the caption. $imagesize[3] inserts a string in the <img> tag with the correct width and height attributes.

Finally, $pix[$j++]['caption'] is used to display the caption inside the <span>. This is the last reference to $j, so the increment operator (++) increases its value by 1 *after* it has been used (see "Using Operators for Calculations and Joining Strings" in Lesson 3 if you don't understand why).

13 The final touches are to add a paragraph to display when the page was last updated and add a link back to the master page. The code looks like this:

```
    echo $paras[$i];
    echo '</p>';
  }
} ?>
  <p id="updated">Information correct as of <?php echo $place['updated'];
  ➥ ?></p>
  <p><a href="gallery.php?state=<?php echo $place['state_name']; ?>">Back
  ➥ to places in <?php echo $place['state_name']; ?></a></p>
</div>
```

The value of the formatted date is displayed using echo, and the link back to gallery.php uses state_name in both the query string and the link text.

14 Save details.php, and test it by clicking various links in gallery.php. The detail page should look like the screen shot at the beginning of this section. There's only one image associated with Hollywood, but all other places have two. The PHP code handles the different numbers without difficulty. If you switch to a different state in gallery.php, the link at the bottom of details.php returns you to the same view of the master page.

You can compare your code with lesson12/completed/details.php and db_definitions_10.php in lesson12/completed/scripts.

If you're wondering how the captions are positioned under the images, it's because of the following style rule in destinations.css:

```
.floatleft img, .floatright img {
   display:block;
}
```

Instead of floating the image, the CSS floats the `<span>` that's wrapped around the image and the caption. This style rule uses a descendant selector to display an image inside a floated element as a block, forcing the caption onto a separate line. The inline style added in step 11 constrains the width of the span, ensuring that the caption doesn't protrude beyond the image.

Refreshing a Page Without Reloading

As noted earlier, the LightBox gallery widget uses the jQuery framework. With a little help from the jQuery `$.get()` utility function, you can send a request to a PHP script and refresh the page when it receives the response. Teaching you to write jQuery is beyond the scope of this book, but the next section gives you sufficient knowledge to follow the explanations in the remaining exercises.

A short jQuery primer

To manipulate elements in a web page, you first need to select them. Unfortunately, the native JavaScript ways of doing so are cumbersome, and the situation is complicated by Internet Explorer's nonstandard implementation of some features. jQuery simplifies access to elements in a cross-browser way by using CSS selectors like this:

```
$('#gallery a')
```

Don't confuse the use of the dollar sign with PHP syntax. In PHP, $ identifies a variable, but in jQuery, $() is a function that accepts a CSS selector as an argument and uses it to select page elements.

NOTE: Technically speaking, $() is an alias (or shorthand) for the jQuery() function, which selects page elements. The only time you need to spell out jQuery() in full is if you're using jQuery in combination with another JavaScript library, such as Prototype, that also has a $() function.

The preceding example selects all `<a>` tags inside an element with the ID gallery. You manipulate selected elements with jQuery methods or custom functions, such as lightBox(). Methods and functions are applied using dot notation like this:

```
$('#gallery a').lightBox(options);
```

If you need to access a set of elements more than once, it's more efficient to assign them to a variable using the var keyword like this:

```
var gallery = $('#gallery > ul');
```

Variable scope in JavaScript—and therefore jQuery—is different from PHP. A variable declared outside a function has global scope. There's no need to pass it as an argument to a function to access its value inside the function. But variables declared with the var keyword *inside* a function cannot be accessed elsewhere.

Most built-in jQuery methods have intuitive names, such as hide(), fadeIn(), and fadeOut(). One that's useful for refreshing page content is html(), which replaces all the HTML code inside the selected element(s). Most methods can be chained, allowing you to perform multiple operations. For example, the following line of code replaces the HTML in gallery and immediately hides it:

```
gallery.html(data).hide();
```

To send a request to the web server by the GET method, use the $.get() utility function, which takes three arguments: the path to the script to execute, a JavaScript object containing values to pass to the script, and a function to handle the response. A JavaScript object is enclosed in curly braces and looks like this:

```
{ state : selectedState, place : "Los Angeles" }
```

In this example, the object has two properties: state and place. The value of a property follows the colon, so the value of state is selectedState, a variable that has been declared elsewhere, and the value of place is the string "Los Angeles." Property/value pairs are separated by commas.

jQuery makes considerable use of anonymous functions. In practice, this means you define the response function between the parentheses of $.get() like this:

```
$.get('scripts/load_gallery.php', {state: selectedState}, function(data) {
  // function definition goes here
});
```

> **TIP:** There are numerous jQuery tutorials online. A good place to start is http://docs.jquery.com/Tutorials. Among the many books available, jQuery in Action, 2nd Edition by Bear Bibeault and Yehuda Katz (Manning, 2010, ISBN: 9781935182320) has detailed coverage of using jQuery to interact with a web server.

Adapting the LightBox gallery

To refresh the gallery without reloading the page, you need to add an onchange event handler to the <select> menu to send the selected value to a PHP script that queries the database and outputs the gallery's HTML. When the event handler receives the response from the server, it replaces the existing HTML with the output from the PHP script, refreshing the page. Here's how it's done:

1 Use your existing version of gallery.php. Alternatively, use gallery_03.php from lesson12/completed as your starting point, but you must have done the earlier exercises, because gallery_03.php relies on files that won't exist otherwise.

Open gallery.php, and select jquery.js in the Related Files toolbar. Check the jQuery version number at the top of the file. At the time of this writing, the version included in the LightBox gallery widget is jQuery 1.2.3. You need to replace this with a more up-to-date version.

2 Copy jquery-1.4.2.min.js from lesson12/start/scripts to lesson12/workfiles/scripts.

3 Select Source Code in the Related Files toolbar to return to the code in gallery.php, and locate the following <script> tag (around line 20):

```
<script src="../../scripts/jquery.js" type="text/javascript"></script>
```

Change the src attribute to point to the new version of jQuery:

```
<script src="scripts/jquery-1.4.2.min.js" type="text/javascript"></script>
```

Save gallery.php, and select jquery-1.4.2.min.js in the Related Files toolbar to verify that the file has been correctly linked to the page. Then select Source Code to return to gallery.php.

4 Scroll down to the `<script>` block that follows the gallery widget's HTML. It begins like this (around lines 113–114):

```
<script type="text/javascript">
// BeginOAWidget_Instance_2127022: #gallery
```

The block ends like this (around lines 132–133):

```
// EndOAWidget_Instance_2127022
</script>
```

Select the entire block, including the opening and closing tags, and cut it to your clipboard.

5 Choose New > Blank Page, select JavaScript as Page Type, and click Create to open a new JavaScript file. Paste the code from your clipboard into the new file, and then delete the opening and closing tags and comments. You should be left with the following code (to make the code easier to read on the printed page, the inline comments have been removed):

```
$(function(){
    $('#gallery a').lightBox({
        imageLoading: '../../images/lightbox/lightbox-ico-loading.gif',
        imageBtnPrev: '../../images/lightbox/lightbox-btn-prev.gif',
        imageBtnNext: '../../images/lightbox/lightbox-btn-next.gif',
        imageBtnClose: '../../images/lightbox/lightbox-btn-close.gif',
        imageBlank: '../../images/lightbox/lightbox-blank.gif',
        fixedNavigation: false,
        containerResizeSpeed: 400,
        overlayBgColor: "#cccccc",
        overlayOpacity: 0.6,
        txtImage: 'Image',
        txtOf: 'of'
    });
});
```

✳ NOTE: The image paths have been converted to be relative to the document. This is not necessary if your phpcs5 site is in a virtual host.

6 The code highlighted in the preceding step is a JavaScript object that defines the settings for the thumbnail links, which need to be reapplied when the gallery widget is refreshed. Cut the highlighted code, assign it to a variable called `options`, and pass the variable as the argument to `lightBox()`. The reorganized code looks like this:

```
$(function(){
  var options = {
    imageLoading: '../../images/lightbox/lightbox-ico-loading.gif',
    imageBtnPrev: '../../images/lightbox/lightbox-btn-prev.gif',
    imageBtnNext: '../../images/lightbox/lightbox-btn-next.gif',
    imageBtnClose: '../../images/lightbox/lightbox-btn-close.gif',
    imageBlank: '../../images/lightbox/lightbox-blank.gif',
    fixedNavigation: false,
    containerResizeSpeed: 400,
    overlayBgColor: "#cccccc",
    overlayOpacity: 0.6,
    txtImage: 'Image',
    txtOf: 'of'
  }
  $('#gallery a').lightBox(options);
});
```

The meaning of this code is exactly the same as before, but assigning the settings to the options variable makes it easy to reuse them later.

7 Save the JavaScript file as **gallery.js** in lesson12/workfiles/scripts.

8 Switch to gallery.php, and insert a new line immediately above the closing </body> tag. With the insertion point in the new line, click the Script icon [icon] ▾ in the Insert panel/ bar or choose Insert > HTML > Script Objects > Script to open the Script dialog box.

Leave the Type menu at the default "text/javascript," and click the folder icon next to the Source field. Navigate to gallery.js, select it, and click OK to close the Script dialog box and insert a link to the JavaScript file like this:

```
</div>
<script type="text/javascript" src="scripts/gallery.js"></script>
</body>
```

9 Save gallery.php, and test the gallery widget to make sure it's still working. If necessary, compare your files with gallery_04.php in lesson12/completed and gallery_01.js in lesson12/completed/scripts.

10 In gallery.js, create a variable to identify the <select> menu, which has the ID state:

```
$(function(){
  var stateSelector = $('#state');
  var options = {
```

11 The purpose of this script is to refresh the gallery without needing to reload the page, so you need to hide the Go button, which has the ID selectState, and create an onchange event handler for the menu. Add the following code after the line that initializes the widget (around line 19):

```
$('#gallery a').lightBox(options);
$('#selectState').hide();
stateSelector.change(function() {
   var selectedState = stateSelector.val();
   var gallery = $('#gallery > ul');
   gallery.fadeOut();
   $.get('scripts/load_gallery.php', {state: selectedState},
   ➥ function(data) {
     gallery.html(data).hide();
     gallery.fadeIn();
     $('#gallery a').lightBox(options);
   });
});
```

The event handler gets the name of the selected state from the <select> menu and fades out the gallery thumbnails.

The jQuery $.get() utility function then submits a GET request to load_gallery.php in the scripts folder (you'll create this file in the next step).

The second argument to $.get() is a JavaScript object containing the name/value pairs to be submitted. In this case, state is the name of the variable, and selectedState is the value from the <select> menu. So, if Utah is selected, this is the equivalent of a query string like this: ?state=Utah.

The final argument to $.get() is an anonymous function that takes as its argument the response from the PHP script. When the response is received, the html() method replaces the widget with the HTML output from the PHP script and immediately hides it so that it can be faded in gently. Finally, the lightbox options are applied to the refreshed widget. Save gallery.js.

❋ **NOTE:** Although it's more efficient to use a variable to refer to elements that are accessed more than once, the function that handles the response from the server needs to use $('#gallery a') explicitly, because the original links no longer exist.

12 Create a new PHP page and save it as **load_gallery.php** in lesson12/workfiles/scripts. Strip out the HTML code, and insert the following PHP code:

```php
<?php
require_once('library.php');
require_once('db_definitions.php');
if (isset($_GET['state'])) {
  try {
    $pix = getGalleryByState($dbRead, $_GET['state']);
    if ($pix) {
      // generate the new widget
    }
  } catch (Exception $e) {
    echo $e->getMessage();
  }
}
```

13 In gallery.php, locate the `foreach` loop that populates the gallery widget (it should be around lines 108–110). Copy it to your clipboard, and paste it in load_gallery.php under the "generate the new widget" comment. Remove the opening and closing PHP tags from the code you just pasted. The finished code in load_gallery.php looks like this:

```php
<?php
require_once('library.php');
require_once('db_definitions.php');
if (isset($_GET['state'])) {
  try {
    $pix = getGalleryByState($dbRead, $_GET['state']);
    if ($pix) {
      // generate the new widget
      foreach ($pix as $pic) { ?>
      <li> <a href="../../cms/image_upload/<?php echo $pic['filename'];
      ➥ ?>" title="<?php echo $pic['name'] . ': ' . $pic['caption']; ?>">
      ➥ <img src="../../cms/image_upload/<?php echo $pic['filename']; ?>"
      ➥ width="120" alt="<?php echo $pic['caption']; ?>" /></a> </li> <?php }
    }
  } catch (Exception $e) {
    echo $e->getMessage();
  }
}
```

This script takes the value of `state` passed to it by the `GET` method and uses it to generate the `<li>` elements for the gallery widget. This listing uses links relative to the document, but if your phpcs5 site is in a virtual host, the `../..` at the beginning of the file paths is not needed.

14 To test this script in Live View, you need to pass a value to it using the GET method. Choose View > Live View Options > HTTP Request Settings.

In the dialog box that opens, click the plus button next to "URL request," and type **state** in the Name field and **California** in the Value field. Set the Method menu to **GET**, and click OK.

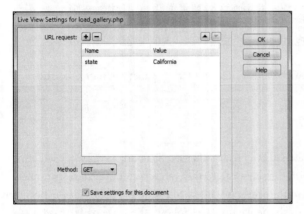

If your testing environment is in a virtual host and the image paths are relative to the site root (in other words, they begin with a leading slash), you can test the page immediately.

If you're using a subfolder of localhost, you need to add ../ to the beginning of the image paths so they begin ../../../cms. This is a temporary measure, because the script is lower in the site hierarchy than gallery.php.

Save load_gallery.php, select Split or Design if you're still in Code view, and click Live View. You should see the thumbnail images related to California with a bullet point to the left of each one. The bullet points are suppressed by CSS when the widget is displayed in gallery.php.

Exit Live View. If you added the extra ../ at the beginning of the image paths, delete it, and save the script again. *This is very important.* The image paths need to be relative to gallery.php, not to this script.

15 Now test gallery.php in a browser. The Go button is hidden by jQuery, but when you select a different state from the <select> menu, the California thumbnails fade out and those related to the selected state fade in—without reloading the page. Proof that the page hasn't been reloaded lies in the fact that the master details for California haven't been replaced by the selected state.

You can compare your code with gallery_02.js and load_gallery.php in lesson12/
completed/scripts.

Refreshing the list of places

Refreshing the images without the matching list of places looks odd. In theory, you could
refresh the gallery and the text with the same call to the web server, but text loads more
quickly than images, so two calls to the server are likely to result in a better user experience.
The code for the PHP script to refresh the list of places follows the same pattern as for the gallery widget. Here it is in full (it's in lesson12/completed/scripts/load_places.php):

```php
<?php
require_once('library.php');
require_once('db_definitions.php');
if (isset($_GET['state'])) {
  try {
    $places = getPlacesByState($dbRead, $_GET['state']);
    if ($places) { ?>
      <h2>Places to visit in <?php echo $_GET['state']; ?></h2>
      <?php
      foreach ($places as $place) { ?>
        <p><strong><?php echo $place['name']; ?>: </strong><?php echo
        ➥ substr($place['description'], 0, strpos($place['description'],
        ➥ '. ')+1); ?> <a href="details.php?place=<?php echo
        ➥ $place['link_name']; ?>">Learn more</a></p>
<?php }
    }
  } catch (Exception $e) {
    echo $e->getMessage();
  }
}
```

This outputs the contents of the <div> with the ID places. The jQuery onchange event handler needs to fade out the existing content of the <div>, display a message that it's fetching
new content, and then refresh the page when the response is received from the server. The

amended function looks like this (the complete JavaScript file is in gallery_03.js in lesson12/completed/scripts):

```
stateSelector.change(function() {
  var selectedState = stateSelector.val();
  var gallery = $('#gallery > ul');
  var places = $('#places');
  places.fadeOut();
  places.html('<h2>Getting places to visit in ' + selectedState +
  ➥ '</h2>');
  $.get('scripts/load_places.php', {state: selectedState},
  ➥ function(data) {
    places.html(data).hide();
    places.fadeIn();
    document.title = 'Destinations West: ' + selectedState;
    gallery.fadeOut();
    $.get('scripts/load_gallery.php', {state: selectedState},
    ➥ function(data) {
      gallery.html(data).hide();
      gallery.fadeIn();
      $('#gallery a').lightBox(options);
    });
  });
});
```

Notice that the second call to `$.get()` is nested inside the anonymous function that handles the response to the first call to the server. This ensures that the gallery is refreshed only after the list of places has been updated.

Amend gallery.js and copy load_places.php from lesson12/completed/scripts to the scripts folder in lesson12/workfiles, and then reload gallery.php in your browser. Selecting a new state from the <select> menu now refreshes the whole page. As noted earlier, Ajax shouldn't be used to replace the entire content of a page. This is simply a demonstration of how to combine jQuery and PHP to refresh multiple page elements.

Creating Clean URLs

Search engines and browsers are quite happy dealing with query strings, but many people dislike them, because they look ugly and are hard to remember. One reason for using the state_name and link_name values in the query strings was to make the URLs more user friendly. If your web server supports URL rewriting, you can go one step further, and use those values in the URL without a query string. Not all web servers support URL rewriting, so you need to check with your hosting company or server administrator for advice and instructions.

If your web server runs on Apache, a quick way to find out is to run `phpinfo()` and search for `mod_rewrite`. If it's listed and your server allows you to create an .htaccess file, you should be able to use clean URLs. The rules for using `mod_rewrite` can be confusing, but it's relatively simple to replace a single value in a query string. For example, the following URL:

```
http://phpcs5/lesson12/workfiles/details.php?place=Hollywood
```

can be rewritten like this:

```
http://phpcs5/destinations/Hollywood
```

This is done by placing an .htaccess file with the following commands in the phpcs5 site root:

```
<IfModule mod_rewrite.c>
  RewriteEngine on
  RewriteCond %{REQUEST_FILENAME} !-f
  RewriteCond %{REQUEST_FILENAME} !-d
  RewriteRule ^places/(.*)$ /lesson12/completed/details_clean.php?place=$1
  RewriteRule ^states/(.*)$ /lesson12/completed/gallery_clean.php?state=$1
</IfModule>
```

The two lines beginning with `RewriteCond` exclude file and directory names from the rewriting rules, which are defined in the lines beginning with `RewriteRule`.

The rewriting rules are constructed like this:

```
RewriteRule Pattern Substitution
```

The pattern is a regex. The first matches places/ followed by anything. The second one matches states/ followed by anything. The parentheses capture the value after the slash and use it in place of $1. So, places/Hollywood actually looks for /lesson12/completed/details_clean. php?place=Hollywood.

If you're using a virtual host in Apache as your testing environment, copy .htaccess from lesson12/completed/scripts to the phpcs5 site root, type **http://phpcs5/states/** into your browser address bar, and press Enter/Return. This loads a modified version of gallery.php into the browser, which works in exactly the same way. Instead of query strings, the links use places/ followed by a `link_name` value or states/ followed by a `state_name` value. (You might need to amend the path to the Zend Framework library.php.)

You can study the code in the files that contain _clean at the end of the filename in lesson12/ completed and lesson12/completed/scripts. All links have been made relative to the site root, so it won't work if you're using a subfolder of localhost for testing. This has been only a brief introduction to rewriting URLs. Hopefully, it will encourage you to search online for more detailed tutorials.

What You Have Learned

In this lesson, you have:

- Installed the Adobe Widget Browser (pages 420–422)

- Downloaded and configured the LightBox Gallery Widget (pages 422–430)

- Populated the gallery widget dynamically from the database (pages 430–437)

- Created a master/detail set (pages 437–448)

- Formatted a MySQL date (pages 441–442)

- Used jQuery to send a request to the web server and refresh content without reloading the page (pages 448–457)

- Learned how to rewrite URLs to eliminate a query string (pages 457–458)

What You Will Learn

In this lesson, you will:

- Learn how to create a `.sql` file to transfer data to your remote database
- Consider alternative methods of transferring data to your remote server
- Remove error messages from scripts and write them to a log file
- Adjust file paths, user accounts, and passwords
- Check whether the Zend Framework needs to be uploaded
- Create and set the permissions on a folder for file uploads
- Define the FTP connection settings for a remote server
- Explore the Files panel in expanded mode
- Devise a strategy for transferring files outside the site root

Approximate Time

This lesson takes approximately 1 hour to complete.

Lesson Files

Media Files:

None

Starting Files:

None

Completed Files:

None

LESSON 13

Deploying Your Site Online

In most respects, deploying a PHP website online is no different from a static site built entirely in HTML. However, there are some differences. In this lesson, you'll learn how to transfer a database from your local environment to a remote server. There's also a rundown of changes you might need to make to ensure a smooth transition to the Internet.

Exporting data as a `.sql` *file in phpMyAdmin is a common way of transferring a database.*

Transferring a Database

MySQL doesn't store data in a single file that you can upload to your website. How the data is stored on disk depends on the engine you selected when creating each table, but the method of storage is irrelevant. You don't transfer the database files to your remote server. Instead, you transfer only the data stored in them. There are several ways of doing so.

Using phpMyAdmin

If phpMyAdmin is installed on your remote server, you can create a .sql file to upload the data from your local computer.

1 Open your local version of phpMyAdmin, select the database that you want to transfer, and click the Export tab. This opens a screen with a large number of options, as shown in the screen shot on the preceding page. Most of the default settings are fine.

2 In the Export section at the top left, check that the tables you want to export are selected. Ctrl-click/Cmd-click to deselect any tables you want to exclude.

3 The radio button in the Export section determines the format. The default is SQL, which is what you want.

4 In the Options section, the "SQL compatibility mode" menu adjusts the syntax for compatibility with different servers:

- **MySQL 4.1, 5.0, and 5.1.** Select NONE (default).
- **MySQL 4.0.** Select MYSQL40.
- **MySQL 3.23.** Select MYSQL323.
- **Microsoft SQL Server.** Select MSSQL.

5 The Structure checkbox is selected by default. Deselect this only if you have already created the table structure on the remote server.

The only option that you might need to change in the Structure section is Add DROP TABLE / VIEW / PROCEDURE / FUNCTION / EVENT, which is deselected by default. Select this checkbox to replace any tables on your remote server that have the same name as those you are exporting. This option is useful if you have redesigned the database structure but want to use the same table names.

▼ CAUTION! The DROP TABLE option irretrievably deletes all data on the remote server in elements with identical names to those you're exporting.

6 The Data checkbox must remain selected to transfer the data.

The Export Type menu in the Data section should normally be set to INSERT. This is intended for populating new tables with data. There are two other options:

- **UPDATE.** Existing data is updated with values from the `.sql` file. Only existing records are affected. New records are *not* inserted.

- **REPLACE.** New records are inserted, and existing data is updated with values from the `.sql` file.

7 The "Save as file" section sets various options for the `.sql` file.

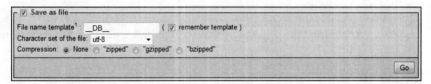

If you deselect the checkbox at the top left of the section, phpMyAdmin lets you preview the contents of the file that it will generate. Click the browser's back button to return to the main screen.

"File name template" automatically names the `.sql` file. The default value depends on whether you clicked the Export tab from the page showing the structure of the database or an individual table. __DB__ gives the `.sql` file the same name as the database. __TBL__ uses the table's name. The template recognizes `strftime()` formatting characters (see www.php.net/strftime) and plain text, so you can add the date to the file name like this:

`__DB__-%Y-%m-%d`

This produces a file name like phpcs5-2010-06-09.sql. By default, phpMyAdmin remembers your custom template for future use.

"Character set of the file" should normally be left at the default utf-8.

The `.sql` file is output as plain text, but the Compression radio button offers the option to compress it as a `.zip`, `.gzip`, or `.bzip2` file. This is useful if you have a large amount of data. When importing, phpMyAdmin automatically recognizes the file type and decompresses it.

8 When you have made your selections, check that "Save as file" is selected, click Go, and save the `.sql` file to your local computer.

9 Log into phpMyAdmin on your remote server. If you have more than one database, select the one you want to use, and click the Import tab to upload the data from the `.sql` file you just created. There is no need to create the table structure on your remote server. The `.sql` file does it for you. The process is exactly the same as described in "Importing Existing Data" in Lesson 5.

Using phpMyAdmin to create a `.sql` file usually takes only a few seconds. It's not only useful for transferring your data to another server, it's a vital way of backing up your database. You should make a habit of exporting the data from your remote server on a regular basis, so you can restore your database if it's accidentally deleted or corrupted.

A serious limitation of using phpMyAdmin for transferring data to a remote server is that it relies on uploading the data from the `.sql` file by the POST method. By default, the maximum size of a file that can be uploaded by PHP is 2 MB. This represents a lot of data, but an active database can rapidly grow in size. Using compression is one solution. You can also transfer single tables by creating separate `.sql` files for each one, but this is cumbersome.

Using a commercial administration tool

If the 2 MB limitation poses a problem for you, or if you don't have access to phpMyAdmin on your remote server, you should consider using a commercial tool. Among the best known administration tools for MySQL are Navicat for Windows, Mac OS X, and Linux (www.navicat.com) and SQLyog for Windows only (www.webyog.com/en/). Both programs offer an impressive range of features and are available in free and paid-for versions. An important advantage of the paid-for versions is that they simplify the process of data transfer to a remote server. They can also automate scheduled backups.

Most hosting companies disable remote connections to MySQL for security reasons. However, the paid-for versions of Navicat and SQLyog allow you to connect to a remote MySQL database using a technique known as tunneling, which connects to the web server and then creates a local connection to MySQL.

The most efficient method of tunneling is through an SSH (Secure Shell) account. If your remote server permits access through SSH, the program logs into the web server with the SSH account and then makes a local connection to the database with your MySQL user account. Once you have stored both sets of credentials in the program, connection is swift and secure.

If your remote server doesn't permit SSH access, you can use HTTP tunneling instead. This involves uploading to your website a PHP file, which the program uses to communicate locally with MySQL. For extra security, the file can be located in a password protected directory. HTTP tunneling is much slower than SSH, but it's useful when no alternative is available.

Navicat and SQLyog also support connection to MySQL through SSL (Secure Sockets Layer). However, this requires SSL to be supported by the remote MySQL server. This is not always the case.

Using your remote server's control panel

If your website's control panel has an option for backing up and restoring databases, try exporting a .sql file from phpMyAdmin and using the control panel's restore option. In cPanel, for example, the Backup Wizard in the Files section has an option to back up MySQL databases. It creates a gzipped .sql file for you to download to your local computer. The restore option simply uploads the .sql file in the same way as phpMyAdmin but without the 2 MB size limitation.

Preparing Your PHP Files

The purpose of creating a local testing environment is to replicate your live website. In theory, you just upload to your remote site, and everything should work. The following sections cover what you need to check or change.

Removing error messages

When executing a database query, Dreamweaver's built-in server behaviors include the following code, which displays error messages onscreen:

```
$Result1 = mysql_query($insertSQL, $cs5write) or die(mysql_error());
```

This stops the script in its tracks, and presents the user with the MySQL error message and no way of getting back to other pages (apart from clicking the browser's back button). It looks very unprofessional.

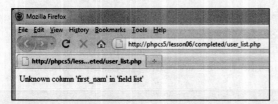

The catch block used in Lessons 7–12 also displays error messages that you probably don't want your visitors to see, although it does have the advantage in many cases of displaying the rest of the page.

The error code in the Dreamweaver server behaviors and the catch block is intended for development purposes and should never be used in a live website.

Before deploying pages containing built-in server behaviors on the Internet, you should delete or die(mysql_error()) and implement a more user-friendly strategy. One solution is to redirect the user to an error page by testing the value returned by mysql_query() like this:

```
$Result1 = mysql_query($insertSQL, $cs5write);
if (!$Result1) {
  header('Location: http://www.example.com/error.php');
  exit;
}
```

This redirects the user to an error page. The name of the variable you need to test differs according to the server behavior. For a recordset, it's the recordset name prefixed by a dollar sign.

You can use the same code without the conditional statement to replace echo $e->getMessage(); in a catch block:

```
} catch(Exception $e) {
  header('Location: http://www.example.com/error.php');
  exit;
}
```

Although this technique prevents the user from seeing the error message, you also need to be alerted to the problem. A simple way to do so is to write the error message to a log file like this:

```
$log_message = date('M j, Y H:i:s') . ' -- ' . mysql_error() . "\r\n";
error_log($log_message, 3, '/path/to/log/error.log');
header('Location: http://www.example.com/error.php');
exit;
```

The first highlighted line uses the date() function to format the current date and time in a human-readable format, such as Jun 9, 2010 15:05:12, and concatenates it with a double-dash followed by the MySQL error message, a carriage return, and a newline character. For a catch block, use $e->getMessage() instead of mysql_error(). This string is then written to a text file called error.log by the error_log() function, which requires at least two arguments: the message and an integer indicating how to handle it. The second argument must be one of the following:

- **0.** The error message is written to the default PHP log file.

- **1.** The message is sent to the email address specified in the third argument. A fourth argument can also specify additional email headers (see "Using the core mail() function" in Lesson 8).

- **3.** The message is written to the file specified in the third argument. The file must be in a folder that the web server can write to. Replace /path/to/log with a fully qualified path to the file.

Of course, writing errors to a log file is meaningless if you don't check it from time to time. Using the option to send error messages by email is not the brilliant idea you might first think. It sends an email every time the error is generated, which could result in a flood of emails if an error is triggered repeatedly.

Adjusting file paths, user accounts, and passwords

Before uploading your files to the remote server, check that your scripts point to the correct location for the Zend Framework (if you're using it) and that you have the correct login details for MySQL user accounts. Also, some hosting companies locate their database servers on a different IP address, so you might need to change the host name for MySQL from localhost to the correct value.

✳ **NOTE:** In many cases, localhost is the correct host name for MySQL, but it's becoming increasingly common for databases to be hosted on a separate server. Check with your hosting company for the name you should use.

Usually, these changes need to be made only in one or two files. In the case of Dreamweaver's built-in server behaviors, the changes should be made in the Connections folder. If you're using the Zend Framework, all the changes are made in library.php.

After you have uploaded the amended file(s), you need to restore the local values in your local version(s) to be able to continue testing new or amended pages. When you have restored the local values, right-click the files in the Files panel, and choose Cloaking > Cloak to prevent the files from being uploaded again and overwriting your remote versions when you choose Site > Synchronize Sitewide, and select the option to upload newer files to the remote server.

▼ **CAUTION!** Cloaking has no effect when you select the option to upload dependent files. PHP includes are considered to be dependent. If you find the files in your Connection folder or library.php being overwritten, choose Edit > Preferences (Windows) or Dreamweaver > Preferences (Mac), select Site, and then select the "Dependent files: Prompt on put/check in" checkbox. The next time you're prompted about dependent files, select "Don't show me this message again" and click No.

A useful technique that works on most servers is to wrap the local and remote values in a conditional statement, and use $_SERVER['HTTP_HOST'] to determine which to use. If your server supports $_SERVER['HTTP_HOST'], it contains the site's domain name. For example, on my website at http://foundationphp.com, it contains foundationphp.com. To set different values for local and remote use, the conditional statement looks like this:

```
if ($_SERVER['HTTP_HOST'] == 'foundationphp.com') {
  // set remote values
} else {
  // set local values
}
```

> **TIP:** When developing a site intended for deployment on the Internet, use the same username(s) and password(s) in your local development environment as on the remote server.

Uploading the Zend Framework

There's no denying it. The Zend Framework is huge. The minimal version is approximately 25 MB. Before uploading the framework, find out whether your remote server has it already installed. Some hosting companies use Zend Server, which automatically includes the framework.

If you need to install ZF yourself, make sure you choose the minimal version, which contains all the class files but isn't bloated by documentation, demonstrations, and test files. Since you're not using every available component, you might wonder if you can upload just those components that you need. In theory, ZF's loosely coupled architecture means that you can. In practice, it's not so easy and is definitely not recommended. Using Zend_Mail not only requires Mail.php in the main Zend folder and all the files and folders in the Mail folder, but also all the files and folders for Zend_Mime, which in turn requires Zend_Exception.

You should treat ZF as a single entity and upload it to a folder outside your site root. Most hosting companies provide a private folder outside the site root where you can store scripts that don't need to be viewed in a browser. If you don't have a private folder, create a separate library folder inside the site root.

> **TIP:** The next major version, Zend Framework 2.0, is being designed to make it easy to install only those components that you want to use.

If you don't have control over php.ini on your remote server, just change the value of $library in scripts/library.php to point to the new library folder.

If you have control over php.ini on your remote server, add the ZF library folder to your include_path directive. The format of the directive depends on the server's operating system.

On Linux, add a colon at the end of the existing value, followed by the fully qualified path to the library folder like this:

```
include_path = ".:/php/includes:/home/mysite/private/library"
```

On Windows, the fully qualified path to the library folder needs to be preceded by a semicolon like this:

```
include_path = ".;C:\php;C:\sites\mysite\private\library"
```

After changing php.ini, remove the following lines from the beginning of scripts/library.php:

```
$library = 'C:/php_library/ZendFramework/library';
set_include_path(get_include_path() . PATH_SEPARATOR . $library);
```

It goes without saying that the actual paths depend on your server.

Creating a folder for file uploads

Where you locate a folder for file uploads depends on who will have the right to upload files and what the files will be used for. Unless only registered and trusted users will have the right to upload files, it's advisable to locate the folder outside the site root. Doing so gives you the opportunity to examine the files before allowing them to be displayed or accessed by others. If you give everyone the freedom to upload images for immediate display, don't be surprised when you get complaints about pornographic material on your site.

The web server needs permission to write to the upload folder. It also needs execute permission if you plan to use subfolders. How you set this up depends entirely on the operating system and the security policies used on your remote server. Some server administrators set up PHP so that it runs in your name. If that's the case, you probably don't need to change any permissions. Other server administrators designate a special folder that you can write to, but in many cases, it's left up to you to set the correct permissions. The best way to find out is to ask the hosting company or server administrator.

On Windows servers, permissions need to be changed by the server administrator. On Linux servers, permissions are allocated to three groups: the owner of the file or folder, other members of the owner's group, and everyone else. Permissions are usually set by adding the following values together:

- **Read.** 4
- **Write.** 2
- **Execute.** 1

The execute permission has a dual role. When applied to a file, it makes it executable, like a program or a batch file. When applied to a directory (folder), it gives users permission to see files and subfolders inside. The owner needs all three permissions for a folder—in other words 7. Members of the group and everyone else are often given read and execute permissions for folders—in other words 5. This set of permissions is expressed as 755. Permissions for files normally exclude execute, so are set at 644.

If you need to set your own permissions for an upload folder on a Linux server, begin by setting them at 755. If that doesn't work, try 775. As a last resort, try the least secure setting 777. Using 777 is far from ideal. If you have no alternative, make sure you check your site regularly and employ strong security measures in all your scripts.

Setting Up Your Remote Server in Dreamweaver

Dreamweaver has a built-in FTP program to upload your files to the remote server. Unfortunately, you can't use it to access folders outside the site root—at least, not if your site definition is based on the site root folder.

This is how you set up FTP access to your remote server in Dreamweaver CS5:

1 Choose Site > Manage Sites, select the site you want to upload in the Manage Sites dialog box, and click Edit to open the Site Setup dialog box.

2 Select Servers from the list on the left of the Site Setup dialog box, and click the "Add new Server" icon ☑ at the bottom of the main panel. This opens a panel where you enter the details of your FTP connection.

3 With the Basic button selected at the top of the panel, fill in the details:

- **Server Name.** This is used internally by Dreamweaver to distinguish it from other server definitions. Choose a name like **Live Site** to differentiate it from your local testing server.

- **Connect using.** If your remote site supports Secure FTP, select SFTP. Otherwise, select FTP.

- **FTP Address.** Get this from your hosting company or server administrator. It is usually your domain name preceded by www. or ftp.

- **Port.** Leave this at the default 22 for SFTP or 21 for FTP unless instructed otherwise by your hosting company or server administrator.

- **Username.** Get this from your hosting company or server administrator.

- **Password.** Use the password associated with your username. Dreamweaver automatically selects the Save checkbox. Deselect it only if you want to be prompted for your password each time you connect to the remote server.

After typing in your username and password, click the Test button to see if you can connect to the server. If connection fails, make sure your login details are correct. If you still cannot connect, try setting some of the options described later in this list.

- **Root Directory.** This value depends on how your remote server account has been set up. In some cases, you can leave this blank. In other cases, you need to enter the name or path to the site root folder, which is often called public_html, www, or wwwroot. Follow any instructions from your hosting company or server administrator.

- **Web URL.** This should be the URL you enter in the browser address bar to access the top level of your site. Unfortunately, Dreamweaver sometimes tries to guess the correct value and gets it wrong. Check this carefully. Don't just accept the default value.

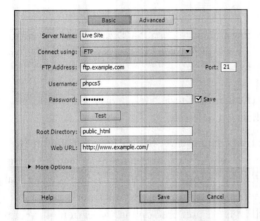

4 If your connection failed when clicking Test, click the right-facing triangle next to More Options to reveal the following options:

- **Use Passive FTP.** Select this if your security software or a firewall is preventing access to the remote server.

- **Use IPV6 Transfer Mode.** Select this *only* if your remote server uses the newer IPv6 protocol.

- **Use Proxy.** Select this and click the Preferences link to specify a proxy port or server.

- **Use FTP performance optimization.** This is selected by default. Deselect it if you still cannot connect after selecting Use Passive FTP.

- **Use alternative FTP move method.** Select this if you experience problems when moving files on your remote server.

5 If you still can't connect, try FTP instead of SFTP. Also, try turning off your security software temporarily. If turning off the firewall allows you to connect, you need to adjust the settings in your security software.

6 Assuming you're able to connect, click the Advanced button at the top of the panel. The Remote Server section has the following options:

- **Maintain synchronization information.** This is selected by default. It creates hidden _notes folders in each folder of the local version of your site. These are used to keep track of when files were most recently updated so you can automatically synchronize your remote and local files. Unfortunately, the twice yearly switch to and from daylight saving time tends to render this information unreliable until you manually synchronize the files.

✱ NOTE: Even if you deselect "Maintain synchronization information," Dreamweaver still creates _notes folders to store information about other features, such as Design-Time Style Sheets and Photoshop Smart Objects.

- **Automatically upload files to server on Save.** This is rarely, if ever, a good idea. If you make a mistake, it's there for the whole world to see.

- **Enable file check-out.** This feature is in Dreamweaver mainly for compatibility with previous versions and is intended for developers working in teams. When this option is enabled and a file is checked out from the remote server, no one else can update it until it is checked back in by the same developer. Dreamweaver now supports integration with Subversion version control, which is the preferred option. To learn more about using Subversion, open Dreamweaver Help and choose Creating and Managing Files > Checking in and checking out files > Use Subversion (SVN) to get and check in files.

7 When you have made your selections, click Save. The new server is listed in the Site Setup dialog box with the Remote checkbox selected.

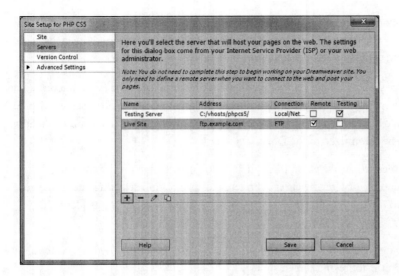

You can list as many servers as you like in the Site Setup dialog box, but only one Remote and one Testing checkbox can be selected at the same time. Dreamweaver's FTP program is not capable of simultaneous communication with multiple servers.

8 Click Save to exit the Site Setup dialog box, and then click Done to close the Manage Sites dialog box.

Transferring files to and from your remote server

To upload files to your remote server, select the files in the Files panel, and click the Put icon ⬆ at the top of the panel.

To download files from your remote server, select Remote server from the menu at the top right of the Files panel.

Dreamweaver connects to your remote server and displays the file structure. As a visual clue that you're no longer looking at your local files, the folder icons are displayed in yellow on Windows and light blue on Mac OS X. Select the file(s) you want to download, and click the Get icon ⬇ at the top of the Files panel. You can also click the Get icon in Local view if the selected file(s) exist on the remote server.

✳ **NOTE:** Repository view displays folders in the same colors as Remote server. Repository view is available only when you have created a connection to a Subversion repository in the Version Control section of the Site Setup dialog box. Testing server displays folder icons in deep pink.

If you prefer to see your local and remote files at the same time, click the Expand icon ⬚ at the top of the Files panel. On Windows, this fills the program window with a screen displaying both views side by side. On Mac OS X, it converts the Files panel into a resizable floating window that can be minimized to the Dock.

By default, local files are displayed on the right, but you can change this by choosing Edit > Preferences (Windows) or Dreamweaver > Preferences (Mac), and selecting Site from the Category list. Two menus give you the option to always show local or remote files on the left or right.

When the Files panel is expanded, the display is controlled by a series of icons next to the site name, as shown in the following screen shot.

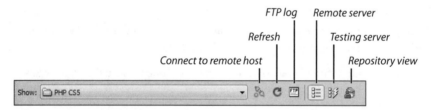

When using the Files panel in expanded mode, it's important to check that the correct icon is selected. Otherwise, you might transfer files to and from your testing server rather than the live website. Although the color of the folder icons provides an important visual clue, you need to be careful if you have defined a Subversion repository, because the color is the same as for a remote server.

To transfer files in expanded mode, either use the Put and Get icons or drag and drop selected files and folders to their target destination.

▼ **CAUTION!** When dragging and dropping, you must drop files and folders exactly where you want them. Just dragging from one side of the Files panel to the other and dropping puts the selected items in the site root. Only the Put and Get buttons automatically select the correct destination.

To restore the Files panel to its normal size and position, click the Expand icon ⬚ again.

Transferring files outside the site root

Dreamweaver's site management system is based on the site root. If you need to upload files to locations outside the site root, you need to use a separate FTP program or create a second site definition in Dreamweaver. The second site definition needs to be based on the same folder hierarchy as your remote server with the public files nested inside.

Let's say your website's root folder is called public_html, and you have a folder called private outside the site root like this:

Set up your public files in the public_html folder and designate that as the site root in the Dreamweaver site setup. Then define a new site in Dreamweaver and designate the mysite folder as the site root. Dreamweaver warns you that a site is already nested inside the site root and that some functions, such as site synchronization, won't work. Just ignore the warning and create the site. Then create a definition for the remote server using mysite as the value for Root Directory. You don't need to enter a value in the Web URL field.

Do most of your work in the site based on public_html and use the outer site definition for transferring files to the private folder. It's not an ideal method of working, but it solves the problem of uploading files outside the site root.

What You Have Learned

In this lesson, you have:

- Learned how to create a `.sql` file to transfer data to your remote database (pages 462–464)
- Considered alternative methods of transferring data to your remote server (pages 464–465)
- Amended scripts to write error messages to a log file (pages 465–467)
- Reviewed necessary adjustments to file paths and user accounts (pages 467–468)
- Created and set the permissions on a folder for file uploads (pages 469–470)
- Defined the FTP connection settings for a remote server (pages 470–473)
- Explored the Files panel in expanded mode (pages 473–474)
- Considered ways of transferring files outside the site root (page 475)

Index

Symbols

! operator, 76, 78–79
!= operator, 75
!== operator, 75
""(double quotation marks), 67–68
(hash sign), 62
% (percent) operator, 91
$ (dollar sign), 63
   identifying PHP variables with, 448
   using as variable, 20
   using in passwords, 163
$() in jQuery, 448–449
& (ampersand), 361
&& operator, 76
- operator, 91
-> operator, 225
— operator, 91
' (apostrophe)
   enclosing string in double quotations when using, 236
   unwanted backslash with, 237–238
''(single quotation marks), 67
( ) (parentheses), 79–80
)) (extra closing parentheses), 283
/ operator, 91
* operator, 91
/* and */, 62
+ operator, 91
++ operator, 91
. (period), 323
: (colon), 125
; (semicolon)
   comments beginning with, 37
   ending PHP statements with, 63
   removing to enable PHP extensions, 39
?> (closing tag), 61, 224
<? (opening tag), 61
< operator, 75
<= operator, 75
= operator, 379
=> operator, 225
== operator, 75, 328
=== operator, 75
> operator, 75
>= operator, 75
/ (backslash), 237–238
[ ] (square brackets), 225
[(opening square bracket), 225
| (vertical pipe), 38
|| operator, 76, 283

_ (underscore), 16, 63, 225
' (backticks), 150
∞ (infinity symbol), 145

A

activating child themes, 122–127
Active Server Pages (ASP), 29
Add Web Site dialog box, 44
addValidator() method, 312
Adobe Dreamweaver. *See* Dreamweaver
Adobe Dreamweaver Developer Toolbox (ADDT), 208
Adobe Widget Browser, 420–437
   about, 420
   choosing widgets from Adobe Exchange, 422–424
   configuring widgets, 424–427
   illustrated, 423, 424
   installing and launching, 421–422
Ajax
   about, 7
   refreshing content with, 418, 419
aliases, column, 441
anonymous functions, 450, 453
Apache web servers
   integrating PHP into, 29
   location for document root on, 30
   permissions for file uploading on, 309
   registering virtual hosts in Windows OS, 42–44
   verifying support for URL rewriting, 457–458
   virtual host setup on, 41
arguments
   finding function, 82–84
   passing, 80, 359, 361
arithmetic operators, 91
arrays, 70–73. *See also specific arrays*
   associative, 71, 287
   basic, 70
   defined, 61, 70
   $_FILES, 305
   names of functions and, 359
   opening square bracket added to, 225
   superglobal, 71–73
   using with quotation marks, 68–69
associative arrays
   defined, 71
   updating records using, 287
attached files, 334–340
authentication
   types of Zend_Mail, 261
   unsupported by mail() function, 260